STRUCTURE, CONSCIOUSNESS, AND HISTORY

STRUCTURE, CONSCIOUSNESS, AND HISTORY

EDITED BY

RICHARD HARVEY BROWN
The University of Maryland

STANFORD M. LYMAN
The New School for Social Research

CAMBRIDGE UNIVERSITY PRESS

CAMBRIDGE

LONDON · NEW YORK · MELBOURNE

Published by the Syndics of the Cambridge University Press
The Pitt Building, Trumpington Street, Cambridge CB2 1RP
Bentley House, 200 Euston Road, London NW1 2DB
32 East 57th Street, New York, NY 10022, USA
296 Beaconsfield Parade, Middle Park, Melbourne 3206, Australia

First Published 1978

Printed in the United States of America
Typeset by Freedmen's Organization, Los Angeles, California 90004
Printed and bound by
Hamilton Printing Company, Rensselaer, New York 12144

Library of Congress Cataloging in Publication Data
Main entry under title:
Structure, consciousness, and history.
1. Social sciences - Addresses, essays, lectures.
2. Social sciences - Methodology - Addresses, essays, lectures.
I. Brown, Richard, Harvey. II. Lyman, Stanford M.
H61.S883   300   77-90212
ISBN 0 521 22047 5 hard covers
ISBN 0 521 29340 5 paperback

Parts of Robert Darnton's essay, "The history of *mentalités*: Recent writings on revolution, criminality, and death in France," are reprinted with the permission of the *New York Review of Books*.

Dedicated to the memory of
Robert Zane Levine (1947–1974) and Donald Katsumi Sakuma (1936–1975)

CONTENTS

PREFACE

The modern era is characterized not only by advances in the sciences, but also by the rationalization of their application to society. With the application of scientific methods to "societal guidance," positive science has become a dominant political and ethical factor. Science has emerged as a kind of religion, an ultimate frame of reference for determining what is real and true. As such it serves as a vocabulary for public discourse in virtually all areas of social praxis. Scientific management, scientific marketing, scientific warfare, scientific welfare – the application of science in these fields, both substantively and as a legitimating rhetoric – all seem to prefigure a totally rationalized, efficiently administered social order.

Yet in such a world, what is the place for ethics and human values, for moral agency and personal dignity? Indeed, is there not a fundamental conflict between scientism and humanism, between rational calculation and humane values? Such a conflict is expressed in many forms – utilitarian, scientific, or empirical modes of thinking versus intuitive, metaphysical, evaluative ways of feeling; increasing demands for elite technical knowledge to manage complex institutions versus increasing demands for participation, for nonalienating modes of work and governance. In social science itself, this conflict appears in the dispute between value-neutral explanations, as against praxis-oriented interpretations, between deterministic theories of structure as against voluntaristic theories of consciousness.

Descartes hinted at these dystopian potentials when he juxtaposed the *res cogitans* and the *res extensa*. But only when we begin to apply science to society, which Descartes with his "provisional morality" postponed as a distant possibility, do we confront the full seriousness of the problem. Descartes never imagined that man in his being could become wholly the object of other people's expertise, that there would exist an expert other than the person himself, an expert who manipulated and reconstructed the person in all his social relations, an expert who was himself being managed by yet another expert. These images have such notorious implications as to render the idea of scientific or technical expertise an ironic caricature, a destroyer of freedom even while being proclaimed its savior.

Where can we look for a way out of this dilemma? On one hand the manipulativeness of our means for affecting social change tends to negate our humanistic ends. On the other hand in accepting the criticisms of positivist techniques we appear to consign ourselves either to mindless activism or to contemplative passivity. In such a context the debate between positivism and its romantic critics grows more and more sterile. It thus becomes vital to question the basic terms of discourse about the relations between these different forms of theory, as well as between theory and practice. What is needed is a postpositivist, postromantic method for conceptualizing alternative social orders, describing our present conditions, and deriving methods of social change that do not of their nature violate humanistic intentions.

The ten essays of this volume are part of that quest. All the essays are concerned with relations between explanatory and interpretive approaches to understanding conduct, and all of them are sensitive to relations between such theory and an emancipatory practice. All the essays can be placed within the symbolic realist perspective described in the Introduction by Brown and Lyman; all of them address philosophic and theoretical questions in relation to humanistic concerns. Yet each essay is unique in its problem focus and disciplinary moorings.

The book is divided into three parts. Part I addresses relationships between structure and consciousness. One key to that relationship is historicity, in that social structures are historically constructed in consciousnesses and consciousness is structured historically. Part II focuses on values, freedom, and identity. Identity, an active construction of self and personae, is not a fact so much as an exercise of human freedom. Conflict over values and the problem of evil set the scenes in which freedom and dignity perish or survive. Part III concerns the foundations and forms of political discourse. The Hobbesian problem, how is society possible?, devolves into two related questions: How is political discourse possible? And how is it possible to transform a polity?

In the first essay Richard Harvey Brown discusses some of the implications of a symbolic realist ontology for current issues in sociological theory. Then, in a second paper, Brown explores further the logic of method of an aesthetic interpretation of conduct, from the hermeneutics of Wilhelm

Dilthey to the dialectics of contemporary critical theory. These papers are followed by that of Stanford M. Lyman, who explores evolutionary, functionalist, and causal theories of social change, and suggests how they might be reformulated phenomenologically. The next essay, by Robert Darnton, shows how structure, consciousness, and history might be concretely conjoined through an examination of recent works on the history of *mentalités* in France.

Part II is opened by Rom Harré, who demonstrates how two central but usually discrete domains of sociological inquiry might be linked: the phenomenological study of meaning and the structural analysis of order. Then Paul G. Creelan turns from a philosophical analysis of social structuring to a structural analysis of sociological theory. Examining Talcott Parsons's theories as myths, Creelan unveils connections between Parsons's formal theories, his personal background, and his social and civilizational setting. In the final essay of this section Manfred Stanley examines the social and conceptual preconditions for a polity in which human dignity would be fundamental.

The final two essays are concerned with the relation of different forms of discourse to political action and social change. Tracy B. Strong explores this problem by using the rules of drama as a metaphor for the rules by which humanistic political discourse would be governed. Louis Marin discusses differences between the utopian or fictional discourse of moral political criticism, and the descriptive-theoretical discourse of political analysis and action. Marin concludes his essay by recommending a dialectical form of discourse by which social theory could be a self-reflective instrument of social change.

Thus the essays set up reverberations between structure, consciousness, and history and, taken together, open avenues toward the still developing symbolic realist paradigm in the human studies. The introductory essay is an invitation to that highroad; this book, perhaps, provides a guide.

Richard Harvey Brown
College Park, Maryland

Stanford M. Lyman
New York, New York

Symbolic realism and cognitive aesthetics:
An invitation

RICHARD HARVEY BROWN AND STANFORD M. LYMAN

The terms of our title – structure, consciousness, and history – are three
loci of debate in what is conventionally referred to as the crisis in sociology.
That there is a crisis is a matter of little doubt to many concerned scholars.[1]
Yet such a claim is by no means new. Indeed, an historical understanding
of science would have to recognize that crises, rebellions, and revolutions
are irregular but necessary features of the development of any discipline.
One such instance is the revolt against positivism in the 1890s. As H. Stuart
Hughes notes, "In this decade and the one immediately succeeding it, the
basic assumptions of eighteenth- and nineteenth-century social thought
underwent a critical review from which there emerged the new assumptions characteristic of our own time."[2] Despite Hughes's implication that
there has been continuity in social thought since the turn of the century,
other scholars have noted upheavals of equal magnitude in the intervening
decades. For example, in his essay of 1925 introducing *The Social Theory
of Georg Simmel*, Nicholas Spykman writes,

Western civilization has reached a crisis . . . Our knowledge and control of social
life has never kept pace with its growing complexity, and we are farther behind
than ever before . . . Our problem is the problem of the adequacy of our knowledge
about social life and the means of obtaining it. It concerns the methodology of the
social sciences.[3]

Almost a half century later Alvin Gouldner again raised the specter of
crisis haunting sociological theory: "Functional theory, and Academic
Sociology more generally, are now in . . . a continuing crisis . . . When
a system undergoes crisis, it is possible that it will soon no longer be the
thing it was; it may change radically or may even fail to survive."[4]

In general, it might be said that the current awareness of a crisis in
sociology focuses on three main issues. First, no available paradigm has

achieved dominion in the discipline. Instead a plurality of approaches, rooted in different and even opposed epistemologies, compete for regnancy. Second, none of these paradigms appears to have attained internal consistency with respect to its own epistemological, ontological, and praxiological assumptions. Finally, despite sociology's lack of preparedness, a host of moral and political issues demand from it both explication and resolution. As in earlier crises, the task confronting sociology is complex. On the one hand it must resolve its own internal problems as a form of discourse; on the other it must respond with authority to practical questions of social order and change. And, to make things more difficult, it must do both at once.

For most critics of conventional sociology the paradigm that has reached marginal utility is structural functionalism, especially that variant associated with the work of Talcott Parsons. The system that apprehends reality in terms of societal consensus, equilibrium, and slow, orderly, and progressive change has been called retrogressive, conservative, and utopian.[5] Still other critics have asserted that structural functionalism begs the very questions that it originally set out to answer[6] and that it fails in its analyses of the important issues of our time.[7] Finally, irruptions, dangers, and injustices in world politics have accelerated the demand for a social science that is both scientifically sound and socially relevant.[8]

A theory that integrates both sociology of consciousness and sociology of structure, and that also lends itself to a humanizing practice, would have to go beyond the functionalist or positivist models and draw on elements currently represented by divergent paradigms. Yet efforts to integrate such paradigms immediately confront a fundamental obstacle: Each paradigm is founded on different, and often mutually exclusive, criteria of adequacy. Thus theorists are forced to choose between epistemological consistency and partial theory, or general theory and epistemological self-contradiction. An epistemologically consistent general theory would have to meet the following criteria:

1 The theory must be phenomenologically grounded in the actors' own experience and understanding.
2 It must be self-reflective, that is, conscious of its own interests, logic, method, and historical embeddedness.
3 It must be predictive at least at the level of probability.
4 It must be comprehensive, that is, appropriate to social realities at any level of abstraction and scope.
5 It must lend itself to a humanizing practice.

One difficulty with these criteria arises from the fact that each criterion suggests a different paradigm. Seeking to remain faithful to its assumptions, each current paradigm resists encroachment by others. Yet often the basic idea of one paradigm, refused entrance at the front door of another, is smuggled in at the back. For any single paradigm, adequacy at the levels of both logic and substance seems unlikely; achieving the one is purchased by sacrificing the other.

Another problem in creating adequate general theory is the relationship of theory and practice. It is at least imaginable that the causes of social phenomena have nothing whatever to do with the cures of social ills – that is, that there is a radical disjunction between the explanatory devices by which we understand how things have come to be and the praxiological methods we employ to cure the social ills we face. From its very beginning – and with only a few outstanding exceptions – sociology in America held fast to the melioristic assumption that causational knowledge would lead to curative action. But there still remains an immense gap between the sure knowledge of causes and the efficacious practice of societal improvement. Moreover, the achievement of self-reflective and phenomenologically grounded knowledge would appear to preclude the establishment of predictive and comprehensive theory. To be true to itself and to the nature of its subject matter, theory in the social sciences may have to remain dialectical and retrospective. Conversely, to yield an objective and predictive theory, the social sciences may have to dehumanize their subject matter and eliminate human agency.

Sociology's praxiological dilemma also includes the unresolved relationship of social theory to the problems of identity, value, and social policy. The positivist paradigm leaves both the investigator and the objects of his investigation in a state of fatalistic determinism, proposes a sterile neutrality toward values, and conceives of policies either as rationally facilitating a given ethical system or as ideological and hence scientifically unsound. Yet, despite the arguments of positivists, commitment to values and to the possibility of moral agency and personal authenticity seems necessary if sociology is to be made a humanizing resource for societal change. But how can this be achieved without violating the canons of established sociological methods and theory?

In the face of these problems a number of thinkers have sought to invent fundamentally new paradigms for a human-centered science of conduct – ones that are at once objective and subjective, at once scientifically valid and significantly humane. These efforts at paradigm innovation can be seen in relation to three fundamental issues facing the social sciences: the methodological debate among philosophers as to the proper epistemic foundations for sociology; the dispute between various sociological schools as to what type of theory offers the most fitting description of social reality; and the controversies among philosophers as well as sociologists on the proper relationship between theory and practice. Put slightly differently, the focal attention of paradigm innovators has been on the philosopher's concern with reason, the scientist's interest in explanation, and the humanist's struggles for emancipation.

Contributions to this great enterprise have proceeded along somewhat independent lines in the social sciences and philosophy. Whereas social scientists usually have been uncritical about the metaphysical problems involved in using such concepts as truth, self, or action, philosophers by and large have not attempted to integrate their work into the substantive agenda of social science theory. Moreover, within the social sciences different schools have different notions about value neutrality and about their relationships to existing structures of power. The present collection of essays attempts to build several bridges: from philosophy to the social sciences, from positivistic to humanistic approaches within sociology itself, and from philosophical sociology to practical political action. Figure 1, which sketches the main themes of this volume, highlights these relations:

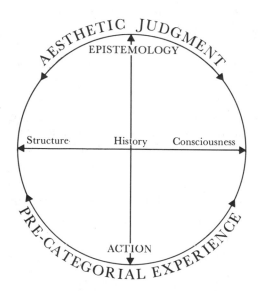

Figure 1

On the horizontal line are the three modes of inquiry referred to by our three key terms. This line is intercepted by a vertical one representing not different modes of analysis, but different levels of thought and action. At the top of this line we place epistemology; in the middle, substantive theories in the human studies; and at the bottom, political praxis, social planning, or citizen action. In addition, at the top of this axis we have drawn an arch – the arch of aesthetics – which covers and provides a vocabulary for these other forms of inquiry and experience. Underneath the axis, we have drawn an arc – the embracing arc of precategorial experience. Together these two – arch and arc – define the circumference of our discourse.

Much of the writing in this volume is informed by what might be called a "symbolic realist" or "cognitive aesthetic" perspective. The two terms are not quite synonymous. Symbolic realism stresses ontology; cognitive aesthetics stresses epistemology. The first focuses on the possibility of our having symbolic worlds; the second provides criteria of adequacy for judging whether such worlds constitute knowledge. Cognitive aesthetics is not the romantic aesthetic of the nineteenth century, but instead a critical theory of interpretation and judgment that has much in common with dialectical hermeneutics and semiotics.

Thinkers from Giambattista Vico to Wilhelm Dilthey to George Herbert Mead have told us that man is the symbol-making animal. Unlike animals that merely live, we have lived experience. The world is apprehended and organized through the mediation of our concepts, categories, and structures of thought. To say this is to say that all knowledge is perspectival: Anything we know is known *as* something; it is construed from some point of view. A library, for example, becomes a different object of experience for the accountant, the scholar, and the custodian. Likewise the rules of baseball define what will be seen as a ball or a strike, much as the rules of psychopathology or of sociology respectively define what is to be apprehended as schizophrenia or role conflict. In this view we cannot know what reality is in any absolute or objectivist fashion; instead, all we can know is our symbolic constructions, the symbolic realities that are defined by our particular paradigms or frames of vision.

Symbolic realism is the view that the only realities accessible to us as knowledge are symbolically constructed. Symbolic realism transvalues and transcends both scientific realism and romantic idealism. The first, scientific realism, reduces knowledge to a copy of the thing known, thereby failing to explain the very creativity of science. The second, romantic idealism, vaporizes knowledge into intuition, mystical insight, or hunch. Faced with these two versions of knowledge, sociology has been forced to choose between becoming either a science or an art. Yet in the symbolic realist view both science and art are formal means for construing worlds through symbols. Both frame or create their own domains of meaning and use.

The symbolic realist position also makes possible a critical aesthetic reinterpretation of both correspondence and cogency theories of truth. In this view there are neither pure correspondence nor pure cogency theories. Instead, a scientific formulation is judged to be successful when its formal internal cogency and its external objects or correspondences both become elements of a single cognitive structure. Just as science affects perceptual and cognitive transformations by changing our models of the world as natural order, so also art affects paradigm induced expectations. Rather than taking science as the measure of all things – as in scientific realism – symbolic realism argues that there is no fundamental difference in the way in which either science or art empowers us to articulate our worlds.[9]

The perspective of cognitive aesthetics has several advantages for social scientific discourse. First, it permits us to go beyond the debate between the positivists' copy theory of truth and the intuitive approach favored by idealists. Second, a cognitive aesthetic framework draws attention to the central role of paradigm innovation in the development of science. Both the artist and the scientist, as well as the politician or citizen who is seeking to create a new mode of public discourse, are seen as having a basic affinity: They are creating paradigms through which experience becomes intelligible. Third, by stressing the world creating aspects of scientific innovation, a cognitive aesthetic approach provides a bridge between what experts do and what all of us do in our everyday lives. We all create worlds.

From such a perspective not only is it possible to draw upon previously discrete paradigms in sociology for more general and adequate theory, it also is possible to link theoretical and political praxes. True, the hermetic dimensions of theory building (and often of theorists' life worlds) may encourage a closer attendance to the formal, rather than to the praxiological, aspects of theory construction. But this is not to say that the cognitive constructs of ordinary people are entirely without formal properties, or that theories are created in a political vacuum. The notion of paradigm innovation as the creation of a world raises the question of power. Which worlds might be more or less useful to the powers that be or to aspiring nonelites? How is the power or capacity to create such worlds differentially distributed socially? What is the proper role of intellectuals?

The aesthetic approach makes social theory one means of reconciling scientific and ethical concerns. As we have seen, however, one rub is that the dominant notion of what constitutes a scientific explanation tends to exclude the type of phenomenological analysis of reality construction we suggest. Analysis of meaning construction involves a hermeneutic interpretation of action, rules and reasons, whereas explanation in positive science has spoken of causes and facts and has viewed behavior as determined by impersonal social forces. But by stressing the function of paradigm creation, an aesthetic perspective dissolves the traditional dichotomies between subjectivist and objectivist ways of theorizing. Such a stress also serves as the beginning of the reformulation of the social sciences themselves. The aesthetic approach to paradigm construction draws the social scientist into a consciousness of the paradigmatic limits imposed by his own outlook. In this process he becomes critical of the modes by which his discourse proceeds and opens himself up to the possibility of a multiplicity of discourses by which he might proceed better and farther. In this sense, the aesthetic model offers to humanistic social theory a special mode of reflection. This mode of reflection is not solipsistic; rather, it creates space for integrating various theoretical streams and for discovering their historical sources – a space in which the archaeology of the human studies and the architecture of the self and society may be held in fruitful tension.[10]

The concerns of this book go beyond pure theory; they also include identity, politics, and action. In this sense, the essays convened here are devoted to the human studies in a humanistic sense. When in the fifteenth century Marsilio Ficino defined man as a "rational soul participating in the intellect of God, but operating in a body," he saw the person as at once subject and object, finite as well as free.[11] That to be human is to be both subject and object also is recognized in Pico della Mirandola's essay "On the Dignity of Man." Pico does not say that man is the center of the world, but only that God placed man in the center of the universe so that he might be conscious of where he stands and so free to decide "where to turn."[12] As Erwin Panofsky tells us:

It is from this ambivalent conception of *humanitas* that humanism was born. It is not so much a movement as an attitude which can be defined as the conviction of the dignity of man, based on both the insistence on human values (rationality and freedom) and the acceptance of human limitations (fallibility and frailty); from these two postulates result responsibility and tolerance.[13]

Whatever luggage the term "humanistic" may have acquired over the centuries, its core referent remains the person as a genuinely conscious and intentional actor, capable of exercising choice for his conduct and responsibility for its consequences. In sociology a counterpart of this concern for moral agency would emerge as a theoretical approach that conceives actors as organizers of meaningful acts and social events as patterned according to reasons, intentions, and imagined consequences. With moral agency for its starting point, a humanist sociology would investigate the person in his social and moral settings, his construction of such settings, the role of power in the negotiation, imposition, and resistance to such constructions, and the ways in which cultures, societies, and political economies serve as resources and constraints. Such a sociology not only recognizes moral man in immoral society, but also uncovers immoral man in moral society.

Critical aesthetics provides a vocabulary useful for linking a general theory of society with a humanizing practice. One term in such a vocabulary is "metaphor." In the broadest sense, metaphor is seeing something from the viewpoint of something else, which means, by modest extension, that all knowledge is metaphoric. In normal science, as in normal political times, the governing paradigms or root metaphors are not brought into question. But in times of crisis such rules of discourse or action are subjected to critical examination. Armed with the view of paradigms as metaphoric, the sociologist immerses himself in just such moments. It is then that the rich tradition of cognitive aesthetics becomes available as an epistemic resource, a means of criticizing the regnant modes of theory and conduct. For example, today the spokesmen for cybernetic systems theory argue that society is (or is like) a great computer, with its input and output, its feedback loops, and its programs; this machine - society - is in turn guided by a servo-mechanism - the techno-administrative elite. To see this imagery as a metaphor, however, is to reject it as a literal description, to unmask it as a legitimating ideology, and to provide a basis for criticizing its rhetorics. By doing a close textual analysis, it becomes clear that in the rhetoric of social cybernetics, there is an atrophy of the very vocabularies of citizenship, moral responsibility, and political community. In place of these, the machinery of governance, initially conceived as serving human values, becomes a closed system generating its own self-maintaining ends. The polity - the arena for the institutional enactment of moral choices - dissolves upward into the cybernetic state, or downward into the alienated individual, whose intentionality is now wholly privatized and whose actions, uprooted from their institutional context, are bereft of social consequence and deprived of moral meaning.

To see paradigms for discourse metaphorically, then, is to recognize that they provide the frameworks for structuring appearance, for creating those realities that become accessible to our understanding. To understand that formal thought has this power – the power to name the real – is to understand that intellection is a highly political act. An aesthetic view sees formal thought as a war game with toy soldiers; but it also sees that soldiers have real guns.

To the extent that sociology assumes scientific realism, present values and social structure are taken as given, out-there-to-be-discovered facts. With such a view social theory lacks the cognitive space within which it might construct alternative social orders. Without such utopias the advice of sociologists on social policy is limited to social reform.[14] In contrast, by adopting an aesthetic perspective, realities that once were obdurate become fragile. Our recognition of the fragility of institutions counterbalances our prior recognition of the frailty of man. Our recognition that social order is a construction invites us to actively reconstruct our worlds.

NOTES

1 Important discussions of contemporary crises in sociological theory, capitalist society, and Western civilization in general include Alvin W. Gouldner, *The Coming Crisis of Western Sociology* (New York: Basic Books, 1970); Norman Birnbaum, "The Crisis in Marxist Sociology," in *Recent Sociology*, no. 2, *On the Social Basis of Politics*, ed. Hans-Peter Dreitzel (London: Collier-Macmillan, 1969), pp. 11–44; Russell Jacoby, "The Politics of the Crisis Theory: Toward the Critique of Automatic Marxism II," *Telos* 23 (1975): 3–52; Jürgen Habermas, *Legitimation Crisis*, trans. Thomas McCarthy (Boston: Beacon Press, 1975); and Richard Barnet, "The Twilight of the Nation State: A Crisis of Legitimacy," in *The Rule of Law*, ed. Robert Paul Wolff (New York: Simon & Schuster, 1971), pp. 221–42.

2 H. Stuart Hughes, *Consciousness and Society: The Reorientation of European Social Thought, 1890–1930* (New York: Vintage Books, 1958), p. 33.

3 Nicholas J. Spykman, *The Social Theory of Georg Simmel* (New York: Russell and Russell, 1925), pp. v, vii.

4 Gouldner, *The Coming Crisis of Western Sociology*, p. 341.

5 See Ralf Dahrendorf, "Out of Utopia: Toward a Reorientation of Sociological Analysis," *American Journal of Sociology* 64 (1959): 115–127. Also see Tom Bottomore, "Out of this World," *New York Review of Books* 13 (November 6, 1969): 34–9.

6 See Kenneth E. Bock, "Evolution, Function, and Change," *American Sociological Review* 28, 2 (1963): 229–37. Also see Robert A. Nisbet, *Social Change*

   and History: Aspects of the Western Theory of Development (New York:
   Oxford University Press, 1969).

 7 See Stanford M. Lyman, *The Black American in Sociological Thought: A
   Failure of Perspective* (New York: G. P. Putnam's Sons, 1972), pp. 145-70.
   Also see Richard H. Brown, "Economic Development as an Anti-Poverty
   Strategy: Notes on the Political Economy of Race," *Urban Affairs Quarterly* 9,
   2 (1973): 165-210, esp. 181-5.

 8 See Saul H. Mendlovitz, ed., *On the Creation of a Just World Order: Preferred
   Worlds for the 1990s* (New York: The Free Press, 1975).

 9 For a fuller development of the concepts symbolic realism and cognitive aes-
   thetics, and their relevance to the human studies, see Richard Harvey Brown,
   A Poetic for Sociology: Toward a Logic of Discovery for the Human Sciences
   (New York and London: Cambridge University Press, 1977).

10 On the archaeology of the human studies, see Michel Foucault, *The Order of
   Things: An Archaeology of the Human Sciences* (New York: Pantheon, 1970),
   and *The Archaeology of Language, and the Discourse on Language*, trans.
   A. M. Sheridan Smith (New York: Pantheon, 1972). On the architecture of
   mind, see Claude Lévi-Strauss, *Structural Anthropology*, trans. Claire Jacobson
   and Brooke Grundfest Schoepf (Harmondsworth: Penguin, 1963).

11 Marsilio Ficino, *Opera omnia* (Torino: Bettega de'Erasmo, 1962).

12 Giovanni Pico della Mirandola, *Oration on the Dignity of Man*, trans. A.
   Robert Caponigri (Chicago: Henry Regnery, 1956).

13 Erwin Panofsky, *Meaning in the Visual Arts* (Garden City, N.Y.: Doubleday,
   1955), p. 2.

14 We use the term "utopia" in the critical and reflective sense discussed by Louis
   Marin in his essay in this volume. Such a usage excludes the alternative futures
   invented by many American policy researchers. These are extrapolations of
   the current social order and essentially functionalist in their formulation.

Part I
Structure, consciousness, and history

1

Symbolic realism and sociological thought: Beyond the positivist–romantic debate

RICHARD HARVEY BROWN

Editors' introduction

Much of contemporary disputes in the social sciences – over hard versus soft paradigms and methods, over politics and values – can be seen as part of an older and larger conflict, that between positivism and romanticism. Each of these basic approaches has a rich history both in social theories as well as in their accompanying philosophic justifications. Yet today this debate appears to have passed the point of diminishing returns: Further heat yields less and less light. Adequate social theory must be both interpretive and explanatory. Likewise, an adequate epistemology for the human studies must account for both discovery and justification, for both reflection and prediction.

A parallel situation occurs on the level of practice. Both positivism and romanticism claim to be acting in the name of humanism. The first camp says that knowledge must be used instrumentally to solve human problems; the second insists that the very hegemony of instrumental reason has dehumanized culture. Positivists tend to be methodologically unequipped to deal with moral and philosophical problems involved in applying knowledge; romantics tend to force a choice between either contemplative passivity or participatory ecstasy. None of these is an adequate response to the genuine crises confronting sociology and society.

In the present essay Richard Harvey Brown explores the background of this dualism in sociological theory. After briefly examining the larger conflict as one between positive science and romantic art, he reviews the efforts of Marx, Weber, Durkheim and their heirs to heal this fissure. This analysis suggests that sociology remains a house divided and that this division goes to the foundations of the discipline. That is, differences between positivism and romanticism rest on their divergent notions of the nature of social reality and how it can be known. In a final section Brown attempts to describe the bases for a reconstituted epistemology and ontology for the human studies, bases that together might be called symbolic realism.

Tell me where is fancy bred,
Or in the heart or in the head?
How begot, how nourished?
Reply, reply?
William Shakespeare,
Merchant of Venice, III:2

Introduction

Symbolic realism holds that all social reality is symbolic, including sociology itself. In the symbolic realist view there are multiple realities, including those of social scientists, and none has absolute priority over others. The task of the sociologist becomes that of describing these various realities, their structures, their processes of change, and their coming to be. Such analyses are not copies or blueprints of "reality," however. Instead they represent a kind of decoding or translation by which the realities constituted by peoples are reconstituted into the reality that is social science.

Such a formulation also reformulates issues in the positivist–romantic debate. Symbolic realism does not require a sacrifice of cognitive rationality in either the romantic or the positivist approach, but it does insist that both are symbolic constructs, the understanding and use of which must grow out of preobjective apprehensions. Existential reality may give itself up to us through any number of symbolic forms. Each of these vocabularies may be rearticulated by using any one of them as the code for representing the others. Interpretive sociology can be reexpressed in the form of, say, statistical sociology, just as statistical sociology can be reinterpreted as a form of belief. Symbolic realism, however, offers a meta-perspective in which both these approaches are seen to have common grounds and criteria of adequacy, and in which each can preserve its unique efficacy while both are transcended and integrated.

Positive science against romantic art

Positivism draws sustenance from the practical experiments of Bacon and the mathematical deductions of Descartes. It takes physical science as its model and assumes a natural standpoint in which reality is strictly distinguished from the symbols that represent it. From this position the meaning of a word or expression is the thing or behavior to which it refers. Statements that are true are those that correspond to objectively verified events or conditions out there. Metaphor and personal meaning – which are explicitly symbolic and subjective – are thus consigned to poetry, which in the positivist view is nothing more than "a kind of ingenious nonsense"[1] "to be accounted rather as a pleasure or play of wit than a science."[2]

In contrast to this view, romanticism crystalized as an opposition ideology in the nineteenth century. Inspired by Vico and Hegel, philosophers and poets defended art as representing various higher truths: the subjective response of the artist to the thing represented; the inner feelings of the artist upon the act of creation; and the artist's vision, philosophy, or personality in general. "We have Beauty," as Nietzsche put it, "in order to preserve us from Truth."

This romantic view was a radical turning point in aesthetic theory. Traditionally art was assumed to represent reality either in its phenomenal or its ideal manifestations – the Platonic and neo-Platonic theories. But in the early modern period this representational function was thought more and more to be the privileged area of science, in the form either of Bacon's phenomenal empiricism or of Descartes's mathematical idealism. In reaction to this view, but at the same time accepting its assumptions about the nature of the scientific enterprise, defenders of art turned inward for the "that which" that art represents. There thus developed a strict dichotomy between reality and symbols, between truth and beauty. Positivists tried to eliminate the use of symbols in science, whereas critics and aestheticians tried to find a home for art outside of nature.

These paired views may be summarized as follows:

Science	*Art*
truth	beauty
reality	symbols
things and events	feelings and meanings
"out-there"	"in-here"
objective	subjective
explanation	interpretation
proof	insight
determinism	freedom

As this thinking found its way into the human studies, there arose a methodological dualism, "two orders . . . separate but unequal."[3] Seeking to be true to what they conceived as science, many sociologists strictly distinguished their subjective sensations from the objective properties of that which they studied. It was thought that the personal feelings, interpretations, and viewpoints of the analyst must not enter into his account of the "out-there" structure of social action. Other sociologists took the opposite view, asserting that personal empathy was required to enter the actors' consciousness and, hence, to discover sociological truth. Thus in the positivist view sociology was to imitate physics, whereas in the romantic view sociology was to emulate art.

Subjective interpretation and objective science in Marx, Weber, Durkheim, and their heirs

The founders of modern sociology were astride two horses at once, each galloping off in its own direction. The efforts of Marx, Weber, and Durkheim to reign their mounts are instructive for us today.

One major attempt to create a middle ground between romantic subjectivism and reductive positivism is the work of Karl Marx. Marx's contributions include not only his sociology of consciousness and his theory of society, but also his dialectical methods for linking the two. For example, in his "Theses on Feuerbach," written when he was twenty-seven years old, Marx could say:

The chief defect of all materialism up to now . . . is that the object, reality, what we apprehend through our senses, is understood only in the form of the *object* or *contemplation*; but not as *sensuous human,* as *praxis* . . . The materialist doctrine that men are products of circumstances and upbringing . . . forgets that it is men that change circumstances . . . The coincidence of the changing circumstances and of human activity can be conceived and rationally understood only as *revolutionizing praxis.*[4]

Yet Marx's later social and economic works are largely deductive and deterministic. Moreover, the dialectic within Marx's formal theories is not so much between personal freedom and social forces as between opposing social forces. Invoking the model of physics, Marx claims to represent "the economic law of motion of modern society" as a "natural law." In the Preface to the second edition of *Capital* he quotes with approval the methodological assessment of a Russian reviewer:

Marx seeks to demonstrate through precise scientific investigation the necessity of definite orders of social relations and to register as irreproachably as possible the facts that serve him as points of departure and confirmation . . . Marx considers the movement of society . . . as governed by laws that are not only independent of the will, consciousness, and intention of men but instead, and conversely, determine their will, consciousness, and intentions.[5]

Marx was aware of contradictions between a theory of revolutionizing praxis and a sociology of structural causation, and his concepts of alienation, reification, and false consciousness provide powerful tools for linking these two realms. But in the end the synthesis is incomplete. In theory and method, as in the world itself, the resolution of the humanistic and deterministic aspects of Marx's work remains a project for Marxist scholars today.[6]

Max Weber also engaged these issues. In his methodological writings Weber, like Kant, Dilthey, and Marx before him, waged a two-front war against reductionist empiricism and subjectivist idealism. Against the first he argued that social conduct – to be social – had to be "meaningfully oriented toward others." Conversely, against romantic idealists he insisted that freedom logically implied, and could be expressed only in terms of, rules:

> The error in the assumption that any freedom of the will – however it is understood – is identical with the "irrationality" of action, or that the latter is conditioned by the former, is quite obvious . . . On the other hand, we associate the highest measure of an empirical "feeling of freedom" with those actions which we are conscious of performing rationally – i.e., . . . in accordance with empirical rules.[7]

For Weber, however, these rules could be understood not only as the social actors' sense of what was possible or proper, but also as causal laws. The problem, then, was to somehow find a way of analyzing the subject matter – which he had defined as meaningfully intended action – in terms of objective causal relations. Heinrich Rickert, Weber's mentor, had opposed sociology to history, saying that the former was concerned with laws whereas the latter dealt with particulars. At the same time, Dilthey insisted that the human studies dealt with meaningfully intended action, whereas science dealt with mere motions and events.[8] Weber's great effort was to unify these perspectives; for him sociology had to take intentional action as its subject matter, but to explain it in terms of nomothetic causal relations. This new definition of the discipline is shown in Figure 1.

Romantic sociology sees its subject matter as meaningfully intended action and strives to interpret its unique properties. Applied sociology defines its subject matter as objects to be worked on, and like romantic sociology it focuses on particular cases. Positivist sociology seeks general laws and, like applied sociology, it defines its subject matter as things and events. In contrast to all these approaches is *Verstehende* sociology, which both defines its subject matter as meaningfully intended action and which also seeks general, nomothetic explanations.

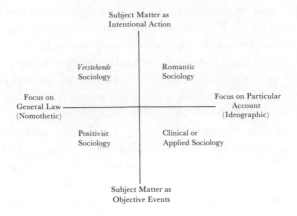

Figure 1

Yet the problem remained as to what method could yield causal laws about meaningfully intended conduct. In grappling with this question Weber's principal tools were hypothetical and comparative analysis. By this method one begins by imaginatively removing various factors in a proposed causal sequence, finally identifying those which, if removed, would render one incapable of conceiving of the occurrence in question. In this frankly fictive approach the crucial device in translating a unit of lived meaning into a hypothesized causal factor was the procedure called *Verstehen* and the elaboration of ideal types.[9] For Weber this notion of *Verstehen* refers to a mode of consciousness in which one suspends one's personal and cultural biases and enters into the perspective of the actor(s) under study. Such intuitive understanding, however, "must be controlled so far as possible by the . . . usual methods of causal imputation, before even the most evident interpretation· can become a valid 'intelligible explanation.' "[10]

It is at this point, when we seek to empirically control for the bias in our intuitive insights, that the concept of ideal types becomes crucial. For it was one of Weber's great contributions to see that the factors and variables of causal analysis were themselves constructions. Unlike social descriptions in terms of categories borrowed from natural science, ideal types are selective organizations of observations of *human* behavior, including expressions of its motivational component. Ideal types make no claim to be absolute copies of social reality; rather they are justified by their analytic utility. In these senses Weber's notion of ideal types adumbrates the concept of model so much in use by sociologists today.[11]

Weber himself distinguishes two forms of ideal types: particular and universal. The first refers to some unique historical phenomenon – Jainism, Puritanism, and so on; the second abstracts from individual ideal types certain elements that are trans-situational or transhistorical – for example, inner worldly asceticism is to be found in both Jainism and Puritanism. Thus, though his method initially focused on the imaginative reconstruction of motives and of individual causal sequences, there seemed no reason why this technique could not be applied in comparative historical analysis, using control groups to hold constant the variables in question. Indeed, Weber's own comparative study of religion is a magnificent effort of just this sort.

Weber's importance can be judged not only by the work of his followers, but also by the range of his critics. One difficulty with his formulation is that he does not provide an ontological grounding for his concept of *Verstehen*. Indeed, as Weber uses the term, *Verstehen* connotes an objectivist notion of history and historical knowledge, in that it assumes one can look at another historical (or social) situation without being historically located oneself. An exploration of the problems involved in phenomenologically bracketing one's own viewpoint, or of dialectically establishing resonances between one's own position and that of one's subjects, might have illuminated these points. Such ideas were available to Weber – dialectical thought from the Hegelian tradition, or phenomenological epoché from Weber's contemporary Edmund Husserl. But Weber appears to have made little use of them.

The lack of an adequate theory of the construction of objects in consciousness weakens any sociology built on the understanding of meaningfully intended action. It also fails to explain how we as social scientists are to construct our ideal types and how these types differ from those of ordinary discourse. Weber uses the term "ideal type" in at least four distinct, but not differentiated, ways: He refers in places to virtually any historical abstractions; elsewhere to assumptions we make about people's motivations; to a model of relationships between factors; or to a scenario. But with each of these uses we know as little about how sociologists construct ideal types as we do about how actors construct their typifications.

Another difficulty in Weber's thinking is his failure to adequately justify his transition from the assumption of freedom in terms of rules to explanation of behavior in terms of causal relations. The notions of rules and of understanding presuppose a teleological account of conduct according to contextual values and projected ends. This is the romantic side. Yet how

can this be reconciled with the positivistic determinism implied by causality? Weber himself seems to acknowledge these difficulties by giving
epistemic priority to causal explanation. *Verstehen* tends to be reduced to
a heuristic starting point, a source of insights that could help us form
hypotheses but that themselves do not constitute knowledge.[12]

It could be argued, of course, that many of the lacunae in Weber's
methodological writings are filled in practically, if not epistemologically,
in his substantive work. One such problem is how to link rule-governed
freedom with a causal sociology. For Weber, it would seem, the rule-
governed conduct *is* the cause. That is, once Weber had a working grasp
of the historical phenomenology of the Puritans' consciousness, he understood how, in their freedom to act on their own moral commitments, their
conduct formed a definite pattern, with both intended and ironic outcomes.

In his methodological statements, however, Weber stresses the rigor by
which theories must be tested and demonstrated, while at the same time
respecting the intuitive ways in which theories get invented. These views
are complementary even though logically incompatible. In positivist theories of science, rigor, testing, and other such concepts are related to proof
(or falsifiability), whereas discovery is either not addressed or is reduced to
psychology. This invites romantics to assert that such discoveries are mysterious insights, a gift of the gods, with the implication that we preserve
our unique humanness because some part of us cannot be explained away.
Both views, however – the positivist and the romantic – reify science as
something external to humans, rather than seeing it as a symbolic human
creation through and through. An adequate epistemology would take as
its domain of application both verification and discovery. It would do for
sociology what sociology seeks to do for conduct: account both for laws
as determined by tests and for creativity as governed by rules.

The Durkheimian tradition reveals another set of proposed resolutions
to these conflicts. With one hand Durkheim inherited the speculative,
moral philosophical discourse of the Enlightenment; with the other he
received the statistical social physics represented by LePlay and Quételet.
In his study of suicide, for example, Durkheim uses the research strategy
of the statisticians – that is, the analytic comparison of various social rates.
"The first and most fundamental rule . . ." he says elsewhere, is to "*consider facts as things.*"[13] Yet even in his definition of suicide, which Durkheim attempts to make strictly objective, the concept of intentionality is
assumed: "We may then say conclusively: The term suicide is applied to

all cases of death resulting . . . from a[n] . . . *act of the victim himself, which he knows will produce this result* (italics added).[14]

A further compromise of Durkheim's objectivist purism comes when he sets about explaining the statistical correlations he has discovered. In the natural sciences a correlation of rates of two types of occurrences – given proper experimental controls – can itself be the basis for attributing causality. In the human studies, however, we usually do not accept such accounts as an explanation unless they are accompanied by some recon-struction of the motivational processes by which certain causes were inter-preted by individuals in such a way that they acted so as to yield certain effects. Positivists would say this insistence on a motivational reconstruction is redundant, a residue of prescientific thinking; nonetheless, they them-selves generally hide such reconstructions beneath the scientism of their theories.[15] Thus, in Durkheim's *Suicide,* the co-variances of religion, mari-tal status, income, and other social rates on the one hand, and the taking of one's life on the other, are not simply assumed to be causal relations. Instead, they are grouped into four "types of suicide" – anomic, egoistic, altruistic, and fatalistic – each type being defined in terms of a different (implicit) model of intentionality. But because these motivational concepts are not granted epistemic status, Durkheim does not ground them empir-ically or even exercise care in defining them in advance. Having eschewed historical or psychological forms of discourse as subjectivistic, Durkheim undercuts his own methodological foundations in that the formal analysis of his statistical data depend for their very meanings on historical contexts and forms of consciousness. For example, altruism as a cause of suicide among widows in Bengal presupposes some notion of that state's history and its peoples' psychology.[16]

Much of Durkheim's genius lies in his having transcended the contra-dictions inherent in his own assumptions. As with Weber and Marx (who even experimented with statistical surveys), Durkheim's insights and prac-tical investigations often exceed the limits of his espoused epistemology. Even his work on *Suicide* drew on many nonstatistical sources – letters, diaries, literary accounts. Equally divergent from social factist canons are *Primitive Classification* and other essays Durkheim wrote with Marcel Mauss.[17] But all this theoretical richness bankrupts Durkheim's methodo-logical account. Individual intentionality, though an embarrassing neces-sity for his explanations, is nevertheless methodologically irrelevant to his espoused notion of a scientific theory of society. Reacting against the radical individualism and atomism of the nineteenth century, Durkheim

insists that human conduct emanates from society. He invents and bril-
liantly applies such concepts as collective and individual representations,
anomie, and categories of consciousness to explain conduct in relation to
the larger social whole. But the person, rather than being seen as a moral
agent, tends to become the carrier or media of collective categories or
forces. Instead of being subjected to an explicitly hermeneutical interpretation, consciousness tends to be absorbed into a societal bondedness – the
conscience collectif – which is then seen as the very fundament of social
reality.[18]

In the Anglo-American tradition, the relationships between positivism
and romanticism can be seen as a co-mingling and reinterpretation of
various solutions proposed by the Germans and the French. In very rough
terms, the admixture that has emerged from this may be characterized as
a macrotheory of social structure and change, uncomfortably coupled
with microtheories of consciousness. For example, Durkheim's work has
given rise to two radically different schools of American sociological theory: a theory of collective action as determined by objective social facts,
and a theory that sees action as the ritual objectification of forms of mind.
As currently practiced, the first might be called a moral calculus; the
second, a calculated morality. The moral calculus (especially that arising
from the American interpretation of *Suicide*) continues as the collection
of statistics and the derivation of explanations to cover the deviancies that
prevail in modern society. The second school, stemming more from *The
Elementary Forms of Religious Life,* finds an apotheosis in such writers
as Erving Goffman or Mary Douglas, for whom morality, itself a collective
representation, becomes embodied in individuals' presentation and development of their own selves in relation to others.[19] Yet in Goffman's writings
the forms and formation of consciousness are seen not only as a research
problem for the sociologist, but also as a practical problem for the actors.
In such a double tiered approach the job of the sociologist becomes that
of uncovering the methods by which people themselves construct meanings; and in this, the sociologist's methods are more akin to those of
literature than to those of science.

Marx's estate also was broken up among legitimate heirs and illegitimate
claimants. In the Soviet Union Marx's legacy of dialectical materialism
was reduced in theory to material determinism and used in practice as a
legitimizing rhetoric of totalitarianism. In the capitalist democracies a
principal representative of Marx has been the Frankfurt School, which
flourished in the 1920s in Germany, largely migrated to the United States
in the 1930s, and returned to Germany in the postwar decades.

While based in America, however, critical theorists discovered themselves to be in a kind of double isolation. Revolutionary praxis was betrayed by the authoritarian bureaucracies of the East and preempted by economic success in the West. The relative satisfaction of workers under capitalism seemed contrary to the Marxist thesis of their progressive impoverishment, while the alienation of workers under Soviet socialism violated the thesis of their progressive liberation. In response to these conundrums critical theorists left the economic arena and began to attack industrial society and instrumental reason in general. Their focus became the cultural or ideational superstructure rather than the base. An extreme example of this is Adorno's musical and literary essays: They reflect critical theory's alienation not only from praxis, East and West, but also from science itself.[20]

Much as the legacies of Durkheim and of Marx seemed to bifurcate after their deaths, so Weber's inheritance – the joining of interpretive and causal, human and nonhuman models of explanation – also has come unstuck. Thus, we find sociologists such as Parsons, Merton, Lipset, and Lazarsfeld who claim descent from Weber but whose explanations assume a social structural determinism. Meanings are still part of their analyses, but they either are added on to "humanize" statistical explanations or are treated as factors that have been internalized by the actors through socialization and hence are no longer subject to the actors' redefinition or volition. Human agency in these approaches is either stillborn or aborted.

In contrast to such thinkers, other American scholars have largely ignored causal explanation in the mechanistic sense and instead have concentrated on decoding meaningful action in specific sociohistorical settings. Such concepts as W. I. Thomas's "definition of the situation," Cooley's "sympathetic introspection," Znaniecki's "humanistic coefficient," MacIver's "dynamic assessment," Sorokin's "logico meaningful analysis," and Mead's concepts of mind, self, and society, though not directly derived from Weber, are all in the *Verstehende* tradition. In stating the central assumptions of this interpretive approach, Howard Becker seeks to expand the definition of rational inquiry itself:

The term "action" is to be used to designate that kind of conduct to which those involved in it assign meanings communicable to others by means of symbols . . . The kind of action which we choose to call "social" conforms to these requirements, but in addition is . . . directed toward the conduct of others . . . If the investigator's constructs are to have any degree of analytic utility, they must be constructs imputing a certain "state of mind" to the actor which is meaningful in the light of the actor's own traits, the elements of the situation and the overall value-system (or systems) within which they derive their ulterior significance.[21]

Central to this symbolic interactionist approach is the belief that action is defined, and can be understood, only in terms of the intentionality of the actor – the way in which he defines his own situation and interprets the rules relevant to it. In this perspective, however, there has been a tendency to impute a differing ontological status to "definitions of situations," that may be unreal, as against the "real consequences" that flow from such definitions. Moreover, having posited the importance of meaning and interpretation, symbolic interactionists have tended to take these processes for granted or to treat them as variables. Meaning and action at times have been hypostatized into two discrete categories, with the implication that the first somehow causes the second, an unjustified assumption for which Weber himself was criticized.[22]

In response to such limitations there has grown up in recent decades a more radical school of interpretive sociology, one that focuses on meaning – not as a presupposition but as a problem. The question theorists of this school ask is not, What are the consequences of certain definitions? but How are the definitions themselves built up? Not, What is the structure of meaningful action? but rather, How is meaning constructed?

This new wave in sociological thought has many factions and goes under various labels. It has been called humanistic sociology, phenomenological sociology, ethnomethodology, the sociology of the absurd, the social construction of reality, existential sociology, cognitive sociology, and reflexive sociology.[23] In "Becoming a Reality-Constructionist," Heeren and Ross argue that this radical humanistic style of theory has almost become an orthodoxy among young American sociologists today.[24]

In this way of thinking there is no outer world and inner world; there is only world – my world, her world, someone's world. There are no real consequences versus defined situations; all situations are consequences. Situations are historic in the Heideggerian sense of being constructed in consciousness; moreover, consequences are merely further situations. Distinctions between subjective experience and objective behavior dissolve into the concept of intersubjectivity, though the extent to which a world is intersubjectively confirmed may range from the world of common sense to that of the insane. There is not a single reality in contrast to our personal interpretations; there rather are multiple realities, each governed by different rules, but none having ontological priority over the others.

The pursuit of studies into the social construction of reality, however, has revealed that the very radicalism of such an inquiry brings problems of its own. As long as sociological analysis confines itself to the study of the process of typification or reality construction, it remains consistent with the assumptions of the phenomenological approach. Yet, as Garfinkel and Cicourel have admitted, the operation of interpretive procedures in everyday life presupposes some background expectancies about what everyone knows; that is, the process of culture construction itself depends on the preexistence of some shared cultural meanings – for example, Garfinkel's "documentary interpretation" or Cicourel's six "properties of interpretive procedures." Thus the new writings, in addition to providing an ethnography of appearances emergent in situated interactions, also suggest a yet-to-be-discovered world of meanings, a transsituational, historical social structure in terms of which the taken-for-granted features of everyday life are built.

Earlier symbolic interactionists took meaning as pure product; they could use it as a resource for explanation, but they could not explain its coming to be. In contrast, ethnomethodologists take meaning as pure process. Yet this process is then understood in terms of certain situationally invariant properties, thereby avoiding the initial question of how understanding emerges historically. Thus, while implying a social structure the new interpretive sociology has not yet accounted for it nor provided a method for decoding its constituent parts. Though we now have an avenue to discovering the methods by which peoples construct their social worlds, we have not yet discovered those worlds themselves. Moreover, the very effort to get at invariant procedures beneath the content of language smacks of just that positivism against which interactionists initially fought. Language is purified of the actors' meanings to get at underlying laws. The old debate is being argued by new performers; the romantic idea of unique meanings again battles the positivist concept of universal laws.

Philosophic bases for a symbolic realist approach to social theory

As it is reenacted today, the debate between positivists and romantics is increasingly sterile. Adequate social theory must be both objective and subjectively meaningful; it must yield understanding of peoples' consciousness and agency as well as explanations of social forces beyond their control. Yet in terms of the positivist–romantic debate such theory would appear to be methodologically impossible, in that each side cherishes different assumptions concerning the nature of social reality and how we can know it. It is thus necessary that both positivism and romanticism be reformulated and that an ontology and epistemology be developed that encompass sociology's scientific and artistic modes. As

Randall Collins says, "Positivism needs to be purged. Romanticism needs to be borrowed from . . . It is the combination of determinism and freedom, after all, that constitutes the greatest art; advances in scientific sociology can move its aesthetics beyond a tired romanticism, hopefully into something greater.[25]

Some clues to just such a postromantic, cognitive aesthetic for sociology are to be found in principal schools of modern philosophy: pragmatism, analytic and ordinary language theories, existential phenomenology, and even neopositivism itself. The perspective that emerges from an examination of these schools might be called symbolic realism, which transvalues and transcends both scientific realism and romantic idealism.

The most striking resemblance of modern philosophic schools is a negative one: their revolt against Bacon and Descartes. In his articles of 1868, for example, Charles Sanders Peirce launches a systematic attack on the basic tenets of positivism: the ontological duality of mind and body; the subjectivism implicit in the ultimate appeal to direct personal verification; the belief that language is a mere vehicle or ornament of thought; the doctrine of clear and distinct ideas and the unreality of that which is vague; the belief that language can be side-stepped in favor of direct intuition of objects; and the method of doubt and the elimination of bias as a path to an absolute foundation of knowledge.[26]

An attack on intuitionism, subjectivism, and the givenness of facts also is found in Wittgenstein's *Philosophic Investigations.* Wittgenstein's very idea of language games presupposes that meaning and truth are relational to rules, intentional action, and intersubjectivity; by contrast, in the Cartesian framework knowledge is wholly contemplative, grounded in logical absolutes, and knowable only through personal intuition.[27]

A critique of positivism is likewise a main theme in existential phenomenology. The primacy of either ideas or perception is challenged by Kant's notion of knowledge as mediated by the categories of the mind. Fichte and Hegel made inquiry dialectical, showing how truth and reality, subject and object, are two moments in the same process. Then Marx, Dilthey, Kierkegaard, Heidegger, Merleau-Ponty, and Sartre grounded knowledge and understanding in the praxis of lived experience.

Neopositivism also lends its voice to critics of naïve positivism, while at the same time reformulating itself so as to avoid weaknesses of its genitors. Indeed, positivism can best be seen to have two components: the naïve, materialist "objectivist" side, and a highly critical component deriving from Berkeley and Hume that actually issues into a new basis for science.[28] In examining and reformulating the premises of earlier positivist thought, neopositivists such as Austin, Polanyi, and Kuhn have drawn on this critical component to open the way to a social conventionalism and a sociology of science (following Hume and Peirce), to a language analytic philosophic sociology (following Winch and Harré), and to the close examination of the empirical workings of intersubjective worlds (following Garfinkel, Cicourel, and Sacks).[29]

Beyond this shared critical bent, there are overlaps in the ideas advanced by neopositivists, pragmatists, existential phenomenologists, and ordinary language philosophers to replace the earlier positivist and romantic models. For example, pragmatists speak of conduct; analytic philosophers have recently shown great interest in action; existential phenomenologists use the term "praxis"; neopositivists allow that objectivity is relative to rules of observation and verification and that these conventions are essentially social and experiential in nature. Though such terms as conduct, action, or praxis have different histories and nuances, each presupposes the person to be a conscious and intentional actor. Moreover, each major school sees the world or worlds as constituted of, or knowable only through, symbolic constructs. Finally, each school conceives formal knowledge – whether in the sciences or the arts – as presupposing consciousness and understanding in everyday social life.

In philosophers as diverse as James, Dewey, Dilthey, Husserl, and Wittgenstein we find agreement that the common sense understanding of experience is the framework within which all inquiry must begin. Dewey speaks of this framework as the social matrix within which emerge unclarified situations that may then be transformed by science into justifiable assertions. Wittgenstein refers to ways of knowledge as "forms of life." Husserl speaks of the "life-world" within which all scientific and even logical concepts originate. Alfred Schutz, in "The Basic Subject Matter of Sociology," says:

Any knowledge of the world, in common-sense thinking as well as in science [or in art], involves mental constructs, syntheses, generalizations, formalizations, idealizations specific to the respective level of thought organization. The concept of Nature, for instance, with which the natural sciences have to deal is, as Husserl has shown, an idealizing abstraction from the *Lebenswelt,* an abstraction which, on principle and of course legitimately, excludes persons.[30]

Major contributions to this general argument also are found in the writings of Charles Peirce. "The very origin of the conception of reality," says Peirce, "shows that this conception essentially involves the notion of a COMMUNITY."[31] This community, or collective world of life and action, is constituted of symbolic interaction. Peirce makes this clear by linking sign processes with processes between persons. One example of such a relationship is giving, which does not occur unless the event of transfer of an object from one hand to another is mediated by the intentions of both parties.[32] Peirce then develops this formulation to show that reality, mind, and, indeed, persons themselves are symbolic.[33] Instead of the sign being for a person, "the word or sign which man uses *is* the man himself." Man *is* no more than he intends.[34]

This idea that all knowledge – whether formal or commonsensical – is symbolic construction brings with it the possibility of multiple realities, each with its own mode of articulation. Alfred Schutz, in his article "On Multiple Realities," provides a phenomenological framework for the philosophic examination of such worlds.[35] Likewise William James in his psychological works speaks of the "sub-universe of sense, of physical 'things' as we instinctively apprehend them"; James also notes "the world of science"; of "ideal relations, or abstract truths"; "the world of 'idols of the tribe,' illusions or prejudices common to the race"; "the various supernatural worlds, the Christian heaven and hell, the world of Hindoo mythology"; "the various worlds of individual opinion"; and "the worlds of sheer madness and vagary."[36]

Ordinary language philosophers, working from a very different direction than Schutz or James, have arrived at similar conclusions. Like Schutz, these thinkers also focus on the clash between the positivist image of the person and the image that is manifested in everyday life.[37] Some ordinary language philosophers argue that the very subject matter of sociology – human conduct – far from being objectlike can be understood only in terms of such concepts as rules, meanings, and intentionality and, hence, that a social science on the model of the physical sciences may be impossible.[38] Richard Bernstein and Charles Taylor carry this line of analysis still further, up to its dialectical turning point.[39] For, even granting that the person conceived as agent cannot be reduced to the positivist model, this does not prove that the model of the intentional person is the only appropriate one. To illustrate: Let us allow a massive conceptual structure to everyday life in which the category of the person as agent is fundamental. Let us also suppose that concepts such as intention, action, and so on cannot be adequately translated to some more basic nonteleological framework. Granting all this, what have we demonstrated? For, even if we have shown an irreducible structure of ordinary language and understanding, we still have not demonstrated that this is the only legitimate or correct view of man. That is to say, as Bernstein has noted, the entire manifest view of conduct, though perhaps not reducible, can instead be side-stepped and simply replaced. The model of intentionality may be the only model suitable for explaining the person conceived as agent; but this in itself is no justification that that is the only legitimate or possible conception of man or the only model of explanation.

By a similar reasoning, Charles Taylor argues against absolutisms of both the positivistic or the romantic approach. Taylor first attacks the bias that scientific explanation must take a causal form. He also argues that teleological explanations are not necessarily mentalistic or exclusive to individual actions; instead, they are empirical and can refer to any actions or movements that occur for the sake of something else. The question for Taylor then is not the possibility of developing a single, all-inclusive theory of behavior, but which models and forms of explanation will be most fruitful for various definitions or ranges of experience. Thus, although he is critical of behaviorism and feels that teleological explanations offer a more hopeful approach, Taylor does not exclude the possibility that some form of mechanistic theory may replace the teleological model.

The concept of multiple realities thus can be critically directed toward the realities of theories themselves. For if no single approach can claim ultimate validity, then all theories in a fundamental sense must be metaphoric. Just because they are instruments of perspective and organization, they must treat their subject matter *as* something; but in so doing they forego any claim to describing their subject matter as it "really is." Instead, all representations of human nature are symbolically mediated; none of them can claim to give us ultimate truths. Thus implicit in ordinary language analyses is the (logical) possibility of dualistic or even multiple systems for accounting for what we are, what we think, and what we do.

Conclusion

In sum, then, on the one side are old-fashioned positivists who want not only explanatory laws to which everyone must agree, but laws that assume a purely material world and deny all subjective reality, including even that of the theorist. Opposing them are romantic subjectivists who want not laws, but experience and intuitions that, they claim, are a higher kind of science. Transcending the views of both these groups is that which seeks generalized explanations of the natural as well as the human world, including subjectivity, without a materialist bias. This view finds its justification in a postpositivist, postromantic, dialectical, symbolic realist theory

of knowledge. In such a view all knowledge is symbolic construction: Causal, lawlike explanation is itself an interpretive procedure, and interpretation itself can be a rigorous way of knowing.

Ironically, the earlier positivists' program, to reduce our vague language
to instant-by-instant experience, is precisely the problem of setting sociological abstractions on an experiential basis. Only now, however, this empiricism need not be either objectivistic or subjective, but intersubjective
and mediated. Informed by Continental and pragmatic thought, contemporary empirical research may abandon the idea of a self-subsisting
world-out-there, a world the data of which could speak for themselves
before any theorizing is done about them. Instead, it can now be recognized that scientific reality is itself symbolic, that validity always depends
on the coherence of our ideas and perceptions, and that what makes a
theory powerful is its capacity to make things coherent most strikingly
and economically. Moreover, this being the case, what methods one uses
to get agreement about the phenomenon depend not on absolutist definitions of knowledge, but on the kind of explanation one chooses to seek.

The subject–object dichotomy of the early positivist–antipositivist debate
also may be transformed. For in the symbolic realists' view one's own subjective states can be an analogic instrument for observing the subjective
states of others. Such observations differ only in degree, not in kind, from
so-called objective observations; both types of observations are mediated
by the instrument of observation, and both are subject in principle to
validation by their coherence with a larger body of data and theory.

From such a perspective the subject matters of both positivists and
romantics are understood to be construed from given points of view.
Neither provides some directly knowable reality. Both explanation and
interpretation, if properly conducted, need not be reductions, but rather
transcodings from one form of reality into another. The scientific realist
would strip off the symbols to expose the underlying scientific reality,
whereas the romantic would dismiss scientific reality to intuit the true
meaning of the symbols. But transcoding is instead an interpretation that
becomes part of the subject matter under study, just as an interpretation
of a poem becomes, on the next reading, a part of what the poem says.
Both subject matter and explanation are symbolic. The interpretation –
the study – becomes a metaphor for the symbolic expressions studied.
Each is deepened. Ways of doing sociology, then, may be judged by
whether they build a wall between us and their objects, or whether they
make them newly accessible to us.[40]

Symbolic realism emerges from the schools we have discussed. It has
roots in the skeptical, conventionalist component of pragmatism and

neopositivism, it borrows from recent German and French philosophic thought, and it is enriched by British linguistic philosophy.[41] Joined under the canopy of symbolic realism, all these schools resist the absolutisms of both naïve positivism and romantic idealism; rather, they seek to borrow from yet transcend the limits of both sides of the old debate. The schools do not deny a distinction between appearance and reality; yet rather than seeking to eliminate appearance in favor of objective representations, they offer remarkable methodological tools for probing the duality itself. All these schools posit the lived world as the framework out of which formal cognition must emerge, and all of them understand knowledge to be relational to an intersubjective community of discourse. Thus each school, with its own particular voice, urges us to attend to the tensions between the given and the constructed and, in so doing, to remain true to the dialectical mediations through which structure, consciousness, and history achieve expression.[42]

Symbolic realism does not solve the dilemmas that inhere in the positivist-romantic debate, but it can be an instrument of greater self-reflection on the terms of the debate by which these dilemmas are created. By raising thought to a higher power, so to speak, symbolic realism may provide the means to dissolve the dualisms of both positivist and romantic approaches in the realization that the methods of any form of thought are the source of its objectivity. What are contradictions on the level at which the debate normally is conducted may become the subject matter of analysis and reformulation from another, dialectically higher level. If this is true of all thought, it must be truer still of the sciences of man, who both creates his world and is yet created by it. That all our world is symbolic – at once an expression and an alienation of reality – is the tragedy of culture. To accept the necessity of such disguises will not make us at home in our worlds. But it is a way to more fully understand them.

NOTES

1 Sir Isaac Newton, quoted in Douglas Bush, *Science and English Poetry* (New York: Oxford University Press, 1950), p. 40.

2 Francis Bacon, "De augmentis scientiarum," in *The Works of Francis Bacon,* ed. Spedding, Ellis, and Heath (New York, 1864): 9:62.

3 Alvin W. Gouldner, "Anti-Minotaur: The Myth of a Value Free Sociology," *Social Problems* 9, 3 (1962):199–213. For quote, see p. 210.

4 Karl Marx, "Theses on Feuerbach," in *Marx and Engels: Basic Writings on Politics and Philosophy,* ed. Lewis Feuer (Garden City, N.Y.: Doubleday, 1959), pp. 243–4.

5 Karl Marx, *Capital* (New York: Everyman's Library, 1946), 1:16–17.
6 Such an integration of the humanistic and deterministic strains in Marx is, of course, a project central to the work of neo-Marxists. One direction for such an effort is to interpret Marx's category of labor as a world-constituting life activity (*Lebenspraxis*) in general. See the journals *Praxis* and *Telos*, as well as Erich Fromm, *Marx's Concept of Man* (New York: Frederick Unger, 1961); Nicholas Lobkowicz, *Marx and the Western World* (Notre Dame, Ind.: University of Notre Dame Press, 1967); and Jean-Paul Sartre, *Critique de la raison dialectique* (Paris: Gallimard, 1960). For arguments that Marx did in fact fuse humanism and determinism in his dialectical method and in such categories as alienation and reification, see Shlomo Avineri, *The Social and Political Thought of Karl Marx* (Cambridge: Cambridge University Press, 1968) and Joachim Israel, "Alienation and Reification," in *Theories of Alienation*, ed. R. Felix Geyer and David R. Schweitzer (The Hague: Martinus Nihhoff, 1975).
7 Max Weber, *The Methodology of the Social Sciences*, trans. and ed. Edward A. Shils and Henry A. Finch (Glencoe, Ill.: The Free Press, 1949), pp. 124–5.
8 See Heinrich Rickert, *Science and History: A Critique of Positivist Epistemology*, trans. Georg Reisman (Princeton, N.J.: Van Nostrand, 1962). Also see Wilhelm Dilthey, *Gesammelte Schriften* (Stuttgart: B. G. Teubner, 1957–60), and *Pattern and Meaning in History: Thoughts on History and Society*, ed. H. P. Rickman (New York: Harper & Row, Harper Torchbooks, 1962).
9 See Talcott Parsons, *The Structure of Social Action* (Glencoe, Ill.: The Free Press, 1949), p. 593; and H. Vaihinger, *The Philosophy of "As If"* (London: Routledge & Kegan Paul, 1924). It could be argued that Weber's positivism was largely a rhetorical or ideological device, and that his actual writings are through and through historicist and interpretive. Such a view is given support by the recent translation by Guy Oakes of Max Weber, *Critique of Stammler* (New York: The Free Press, 1977).
10 Max Weber, "Kategorien der Verstehenden Soziologie," in *Gessamelte Aufsatze zur Wissenschaftslehre* (Tübingen, 1913), p. 428.
11 Otto Stammer, *Max Weber and Sociology Today* (New York: Harper & Row, 1971), pp. 209–20.
12 See Theodore Abel, "The Operation Called Verstehen," *American Journal of Sociology* 14 (1948). Reprinted in Herbert Feigl and May Brodbeck, eds., *Readings in the Philosophy of Science* (New York: Appleton-Century-Crofts, 1953). Also see Arnold Green, *Protestantism and Capitalism: The Weber Thesis and Its Critics* (Boston, 1959).
13 Emile Durkheim, *The Rules of Sociological Method* (New York: The Free Press, 1964), p. 14.
14 Durkheim, *Suicide* (New York: The Free Press, 1951), p. 45.
15 See Peter Park, *Sociology Tomorrow* (New York: Pegasus, 1969).
16 Durkheim, *Suicide*, p. 219.
17 See Jack D. Douglas, *The Social Meanings of Suicide* (Princeton, N.J.: Princeton University Press, 1967; also see Emile Durkheim and Marcel Mauss,

Primitive Classification, trans. Rodney Needham (Chicago: The University of Chicago Press, 1967).

18 In France, Durkheim's influence and struggles with these issues reappear in historical studies by other French scholars, such as Lucien Febvre and Marc Bloch and their students, especially in the burgeoning work being done on the *histoire des mentalités.* In sociology and anthropology Durkheim's (and Mauss's) focus on the analysis of the categories and structures of consciousness (with influences also from Saussure's structural linguistics), has yielded the structuralism of Claude Lévi-Strauss and other cognitive anthropologists. Yet this fusion of neo-Durkheimian and Saussurian approaches has tended, at the epistemological level, toward a kind of Platonism with which few social scientists are comfortable. What seems to have happened, then, is that to provide a more acceptable underpinning for such an approach, existential phenomenological thought has been imported from Germany; i.e., Hegelian, Nietzscheian, Diltheyian, Husserlian, and Heideggerian ideas have appeared in the writings of such French thinkers as Sartre, Merleau-Ponty, Ricoeur, and others. Moreover, as Marx was a philosopher as well as a social scientist and historian, the adoption of the tradition that bears his name also has been all but inevitable. Thus, in France an effort is being made to join these streams in a kind of phenomenological Marxist structuralism - a new admixture the portents of which are as yet unknown.

19 Emile Durkheim, *The Elementary Forms of the Religious Life* (New York: The Free Press, 1965); and with Marcel Mauss, *Primitive Classification* (Chicago: The University of Chicago Press, 1963); Mary Douglas, *Natural Symbols* (New York: Random House, 1973); and Erving Goffman, *Interaction Ritual. Essays on Face-to-Face Behavior* (Garden City, N.Y.: Doubleday, 1967), *Behavior in Public Places. Notes on the Social Organization of Gatherings* (New York: The Free Press, 1963), and *Asylums. Essays on the Social Situation of Mental Patients and Other Inmates* (Garden City, N.Y.: Doubleday, 1961).

20 Curiously, the one positivistic study conducted by Theodor Adorno *et al., The Authoritarian Personality* (New York: Harper & Row, 1950), was later rejected by the school as a whole. See The Frankfort School for Social Research, *Aspects of Sociology* (New York: Herder & Herder, 1972).

21 Howard Becker, "Interpretive Sociology and Constructive Sociology," in *Twentieth Century Sociology,* ed. Georges Gurvitch and Wilbert E. Moore (New York: Philosophical Library, 1945), pp. 75, 78.

22 For example, symbolic interactionists insist that "symbolic interaction is the fundamental datum in the approach of sociology to human conduct. As the process from which all sociocultural patterns emerge, therefore, it is the benchmark or - at least implicit - point of departure for all sociological analysis." But this, characteristically, is ambiguous, for it implies an ontological distinction between the fundamental data - which are "symbolic" - and emergent sociocultural patterns, which are "real." Likewise, W. I. Thomas's dictum that "situations that men define as real are real in their consequences,"

suggests a distinction between "real consequences" and "unreal definitions."
Erving Goffman's distinction between masks and selves is equally ambiguous
but in an opposite sense: For Goffman the emergent selves seem to be less real
than the symbolic masks. See John C. McKinney, "Sociological Theory and
the Process of Typification," in *Theoretical Sociology, Perspectives and Developments,* ed. John C. McKinney and Edward A. Tiryakian (New York:
Appleton-Century-Crofts, 1970), pp. 236–7, for quotations.

23 On humanistic sociology, see Peter Berger, *Invitation to Sociology* (Garden
City, N.Y.: Doubleday, 1963); and John R. Staude, "The Theoretical Foundations of Humanistic Sociology," in *Humanistic Society: Today's Challenge
to Sociology,* ed. John F. Glass and John R. Staude (Pacific Palisades, Calif.:
Goodyear Publishers, 1972).

On phenomenological sociology, see Max Scheler, *Ressentiment,* trans.
William W. Holdheim (New York: The Free Press, 1961), and *The Nature
of Sympathy,* trans. Peter Heath (London: Routledge & Kegan Paul, 1958).
Also see Alfred Schutz, *Collected Papers,* ed. Maurice Natanson (The Hague:
Martinus Nijhoff, 1967–71), as well as George Psathas, *Phenomenological
Sociology* (New York: John Wiley & Sons, 1973).

On ethnomethodology, see Harold Garfinkel, *Studies in Ethnomethodology*
(Englewood Cliffs, N.J.: Prentice-Hall, 1967); also see Roy Turner, ed. *Ethno-
methodology* (Baltimore: Penguin, 1974); and Hugh Mehan and Houston
Wood, *The Reality of Ethnomethodology* (New York: John Wiley & Sons, 1975).

On the sociology of the absurd see Stanford M. Lyman and Marvin B. Scott,
A Sociology of the Absurd (New York: Appleton-Century-Crofts, 1970).

On the social construction of reality, see Peter Berger and Thomas Luckmann, *The Social Construction of Reality* (Garden City, N.Y.: Doubleday,
1966); and Burkart Holzner, *Reality Construction in Society* (Cambridge,
Mass.: Schenkman Publishing Co., 1968).

On existential sociology see Jack D. Douglas and John Johnson, eds.,
Existential Sociology (New York: Cambridge University Press, 1977).

On cognitive sociology, see Emile Durkheim and Marcel Mauss, *Primitive
Classification,* trans. Rodney Needham (Chicago: University of Chicago Press,
1967); Mary Douglas, ed., *Rules and Meanings: The Anthropology of Every-
day Knowledge* (Baltimore: Penguin, 1973); and Aaron V. Cicourel, *Cognitive
Sociology: Language and Meaning in Social Interaction* (New York: The Free
Press, 1974).

On reflexive sociology, see Alvin W. Gouldner, *The Coming Crisis in Western
Sociology* (New York: Basic Books, 1970).

24 John Heeren and Barry Ross, "Becoming a Reality-Constructionist: An Unex-
plored Area of the Sociology of Sociology," *The American Sociologist,* 6, 2
(1971).

25 Randall Collins, *Conflict Sociology: Toward an Explanatory Science* (New
York: Academic Press, 1975).

26 "Questions Concerning Certain Faculties Claimed for Man," "Some Conse-
quences of Four Incapacities," and "Grounds for Validity of the Laws of
Logic: Further Consequences of Four Incapacities," reprinted in the *Collected
Papers of Charles Sanders Peirce,* ed. Charles Hartshorne and Paul Weiss
(Cambridge, Mass.: Harvard University Press, 1931-5). Compare these essays
with Heidegger's insistence that Descartes never accounted for the *sum* that
was presupposed by the *cognito,* in Martin Heidegger, *Being and Time* (New
York: Harper, 1962), p. 24.

It also is interesting to compare Peirce's phenomenology, or what he called
"phaneroscopy," with that of Husserl. Peirce wrote:

It will be plain from what has been said that phaneroscopy has nothing to do with the
question of how far the phanerons it studies correspond to any realities. It religiously
abstains from all speculation as to any relations between its categories and physiological
facts, cerebral or other. It does not undertake, but sedulously avoids, hypothetical
explanations of any sort. It simply scrutinizes the direct appearances, and endeavors
to combine minute accuracy with the broadest possible generalization. The student's
great effort is not to be influenced by any tradition, any authority, any reasons for
supposing that such and such ought to be the facts or any fancies of any kind, and to
confine himself to honest, singleminded observation of the appearances. The reader,
upon his side, must repeat the author's observation for himself, and decide from his
own observation whether the author's account of the appearance is correct or not.
(Herbert Hensel, "Phenomenon and Model," in *Aisthetis and Aesthetics,* ed. Erwin
W. Strauss and Richard M. Griffith [Pittsburgh: Duquesne University Press, 1970],
pp. 40-1).

27 Ludwig Wittgenstein, *Philosophic Investigation,* trans. G. E. M. Anscombe
(Oxford: Basil Blackwell & Mott, 1953).

28 Berkeley and Hume were virtually ignored by British positivist philosophers
in the eighteenth and nineteenth centuries. The actual line of development
in the eighteenth century was from Locke to Stewart and Hartley to Mill and
the Scottish associationists. For example, Laplace's universal determinism —
a *locus classicus* of naïve positivist thought – is exactly the opposite of Berkeley's
antimaterialism and Hume's skepticism. Likewise, John Stuart Mill had read
neither Berkeley or Hume. Their main influence was on Kant, and hence on
German idealism and its relativistic successors. Only in the twentieth century
have Berkeley and Hume been revived in their homeland and honored retro-
spectively for their usefulness in creating a sophisticated pragmatic version
of positivism to replace the older naïve form. (This was first pointed out to
me by Randall Collins.)

29 See Peter Winch, *The Idea of a Social Science and Its Relation to Philosophy*
(New York: Humanities Press, 1958); and Harvey Sacks, "Sociological Description," *Berkeley Journal of Sociology* 8 (1963): 1-16.

30 Alfred Schutz, *On Phenomenology and Social Relations* (Chicago: University
of Chicago Press, 1970), p. 271. The insistence by Schutz and others that
experience is the context of inquiry may be fruitfully compared to Kierkegaard's

notion that concrete individual existence can never be *aufgehoben*. Peirce's statement that "the idea of the other, of *not*, becomes a very pivot of thought" could be taken from Sartre's *Critique of Dialectical Reason*. See Richard Bernstein, *Praxis and Action* (Philadelphia: University of Pennsylvania Press, 1971), p. 182.

31 Peirce, *Collected Papers*, 5: 311.

32 Ibid., p. 484.

33 See Charles Morris, *Six Theories of Mind* (Chicago: University of Chicago Press, 1932), p. 284.

34 Peirce says that

> Man makes the word, and the word means nothing which the man has not made it mean, and that only to some man. But since man can think only by means of words or other external symbols, these might turn around and say: "You mean nothing which we have not taught you, and then only so far as you address some words as the interpretant of your thought." In fact, therefore, men and words reciprocally educate each other; each increase in man's information involves and is involved by, a corresponding increase of a word's information (*Collected Papers*, 5:313) . . . That every thought is an external sign, proves that *man* is an external sign (2:156; italics added).

35 Alfred Schutz, "On Multiple Realities," *Philosophy and Phenomenological Research* 5 (1945):533–76.

36 William James, *Principles of Psychology* (New York, 1893), 2, Chapter 11.

37 For examples, see R. S. Peters, *The Concept of Motivation* (London: Routledge & Kegan Paul, 1960); Charles Taylor, *The Explanation of Behavior* (New York: Humanities Press, 1956); and J. O. Urmson, *Philosophical Analysis* (London: Oxford University Press, 1956).

38 See Winch, *The Idea of a Social Science and Its Relation to Philosophy* (New York: Humanities Press, 1958); A. R. Louch, *Explanation and Human Action* (Berkeley: University of California Press, 1966); and B. F. Skinner, *Science and Human Behavior* (New York: Macmillan, 1953), pp. 14–32.

39 Bernstein, *Praxis*; Taylor, *Explanation of Behavior*.

40 See Paul Ricoeur, *The Symbolism of Evil* (Boston: Beacon Press, 1967). I am indebted to Randall Collins for many ideas in this concluding section.

41 Peirce's pragmatism, for example, gave birth to a sophisticated neopositivism based on a consensual model of truth. Likewise, post-Wittgensteinian philosophers are now finding that their emphasis on (verbal) rules and intentions need not go together with their antibehaviorist program, thus opening a way back to an empirical, transverbal yet nonmechanical sociology. Also defying neat categorization, and illustrating the borrowing and convergence between schools, is Husserl – the phenomenologist as crisis positivist – whose "followers" in fact repudiated his positivistic search for presuppositionless, absolute knowledge in favor of a coherence model of truth tied to an action image of man (with implicit criticism of the purely linguistic model of the analytic approach). Also illustrating this convergence is Willard Quine, a student of Carnap, who

argues that "entification" – the process by which objects are formed in consciousness – begins "at arm's length . . . under conspicuously intersubjective
circumstances" (W. V. O. Quine, *Word and Object* [Cambridge, Mass.:
M.I.T. Press, 1960], p. 1). Likewise, Karl Popper, distinguishes his position
from that of "naive empiricists." Popper allows that

> The empirical basis of objective science has thus nothing "absolute" about it. Science
> does not rest upon rock-bottom. The bold structure of its theories arise, as it were, above
> a swamp. It is like a building erected on piles. The piles are driven down from above
> into the swamp, but not down to any natural or "given" base; and when we cease our
> attempts to drive our piles into a deeper layer, it is not because we have reached firm
> ground. We simply stop when we are satisfied that they are firm enough to carry the
> structure, at least for the time being. (*The Logic of Scientific Discovery* [New York:
> Basic Books, 1959], p. 11).

However, such statements do not constitute agreement with the conceptual
catholicism implicit in a strong symbolic realist approach. For the neopositivist,
science – though now admittedly a symbol system – is still thought of as the
most privileged one. Sellars, for example, says that it is reasonable to accept
the conceptual structure of science as standing behind the manifest images
of the phenomenal world, thereby replacing Kant's *Dinge an sich*. Also see
articles by Morris Zelditch and by Sidney Verba in *Comparative Methods in
Sociology*, ed. Ivan Vallier (Berkeley: University of California Press, 1971).
Also see Thomas S. Kuhn, who writes:

> Karl Popper and I both insist that scientists may properly aim to invent theories that
> *explain* observed phenomena and that do so in terms of *real* objects. . . . On the other
> hand, Sir Karl and I are united in opposition to a number of classical positivism's most
> characteristic theses. We both emphasize, for example, the intimate and inevitable
> intanglement of scientific observation with scientific theory; we are correspondingly
> skeptical of efforts to produce any neutral language of observation. ("Logic of Discovery
> or Psychology of Research?" in *Criticism and the Growth of Knowledge*, ed. Imre
> Lakatos and Alan Musgrave [Cambridge: Cambridge University Press, 1970], p. 2).

42 Maurice Natanson, "Causation as a Structure of the Lebenswelt," in Natanson's
Literature, Philosophy and the Social Sciences (The Hague: Martinus Nijhoff,
1962), p. 211.

2

History and hermeneutics:
Wilhelm Dilthey and the dialectics
of interpretive method

RICHARD HARVEY BROWN

Editors' introduction

If humanist social thought is a meadow in the forest of positivism, much of this space was cleared by Wilhelm Dilthey. Not only did Dilthey attack the fundamental assumptions of positivism, he also formulated a critical method by which the works of free human consciousness could be understood.

First Dilthey undercut the positivist tenet that the world is made up of out-there objectively knowable facts. Instead he asserted that the subject matter of the human studies was not mere facts of nature, but rather objectified expressions of the human mind. The second central assumption of positivism is that facts are explainable or determined by general causal laws. In contrast, Dilthey asserted that, whereas we can explain the natural world, human action must be understood through an interpretive rather than a causal logic. In demonstrating and specifically describing such an interpretive procedure, Dilthey provided an epistemological and methodological grounding for a humanistic science of the person and of the social world.

The problems that Dilthey treated have continued to reappear whenever scholars question the assumptions of their disciplines - whenever they ask, "What is our subject matter?" and "How can we know it?" Thus, Dilthey's seminal insights remain relevant for contemporary methodological debates in psychoanalysis, history, sociology, and hermeneutic theory itself. His ideas illuminate and inform even the works of his critics. An understanding of Dilthey provides a privileged framework for the substantive and methodological discussions of the other essays in this volume. Moreover, reflection on Dilthey's philosophy of historicist construction leads directly to Stanford Lyman's essay on history as a structure of consciousness.

Antecedents

Recognition of Dilthey's importance, and indeed his own period of greatest productivity, began late in his life. Though his *Life of Schleiermacher* was published in 1870 and the *Introduction to the Human Studies* in 1883, the bulk of Dilthey's works appeared only when he was in his sixties and seventies, from 1893 to his death in 1911. It was also in this period that Dilthey's speculation crystalized into a unified vision. His last years were a rush to define a new logic for the humanities, a "Critique of Historical Reason," following Kant's critiques of pure and practical reason, that would be objective and rigorous, yet independent of either natural science or positivism. He spent almost no time propagating his work or even defending it from critics. But despite the incompleteness and disorder of his writings, Dilthey laid out a program and method the depth and influence of which are still unfolding today.

Unlike Descartes, Leibnitz, and Kant, who took their philosophic inspiration from mathematics and the natural sciences, Dilthey was a life philosopher in the tradition of Rousseau, Fichte, and Schelling in the eighteenth century, Neitzsche in the nineteenth, and Sartre or Jaspers today. His central question was not how we can know the world of nature, but how we understand our fellow men; not how we can explain the cause and motion of objects, but how we can interpret the meaning and significance of human works.

In this task Dilthey was influenced by two broad streams: the empiricism and positivism of the British and French, and the romantic idealism and historicism of the Germans. As Kant had tried to join the main strands of philosophical thought at the end of his century, so Dilthey sought such a fusion at the end of his. Dilthey also was a Kantian in another way: Both he and Kant were critical philosophers; both sought to reestablish a basic grounding for the assumptions of logical method itself. In terms of this fundamental stance, Dilthey was probably closer to the spirit of Kant than those official neo-Kantians who were doctrinally more loyal.

But for a Kantian (as Dilthey considered himself), there were few points of the Kantian epistemology or description of consciousness with which Dilthey could agree. For example, concerning the Kantian distinction between the empirical phenomenal self and the unknowable transcendental self, Dilthey asserts that though many thought processes may be unconscious, our experience of the life of our minds is still a direct experience of that life, not something constructed or mediated by a higher, unknowable consciousness. Nor does Dilthey recognize a priori categories of the mind. Though he suggests a relationship between the structuring of life in the world and the inner structure of mental life, the mind does not originate order and impose it on the world. Rather, its own pre-predicative structure is made explicit and becomes logical through inter-action with and in the world. Finally, it follows, again in conflict with the neo-Kantians, that a theory of knowledge cannot be constructed in a void, but rather requires for its basis the totality of mental life and lived experience. Hence – anethema to neo-Kantians – psychology must play a central role in understanding how we think and know.

Dilthey also must be understood in relation to several other Germans. While criticizing Hegel's spiritualization of history, Dilthey still makes use of Hegel's insight that history – and indeed all the human studies – are inquiries into objective mind or the "objectifications of mind" (a term by which Hegel titles the second division of his *Philosophy of Mind*). Another major antecedent of Dilthey was Friedrich Schleiermacher, often called the father of modern hermeneutics. In preparing Schleiermacher's biog-raphy, Dilthey also imbibed his method of textual and historical inter-pretation. One other German influence was romantic idealism in its poetic expression, particularly by Schiller and Goethe. Their sensitivity to feeling, to the ineffability of the individual, and to the centrality of the human in society and history are values that pervade Dilthey's works.

The other broad intellectual stream in Dilthey's time was Anglo-French empiricism and positivism. We have seen in Dilthey's critique of Kantian-ism the influence of the empirical philosophy of Locke and Hume. In the Preface to his *Treatise of Human Nature,* Hume partially adumbrates Dilthey by setting out a plan to reconstruct the whole edifice of knowledge on the basis of an experimental psychology.[1] John Stuart Mill continues this tradition in his *System of Logic* of 1843, and Comte and Spencer apply it in positivist studies of history and society.

The aspect of this thought that attracted Dilthey was its impatience with inconclusive metaphysical debates, its positing the lived-in world as the source of knowledge, its meliorative bent, and its conviction that the central concern of the philosopher should be the study of persons and society. The two great limits of this approach for Dilthey, however, were its assumption that its subject matter consisted of facts that were positively (i.e., unproblematically) knowable and that the experimental methods of the natural sciences also were appropriate to the study of culture.[2] Thus in his writings Dilthey devotes central consideration to the distinction between natural facts and cultural works and to the ways in which the latter can be apprehended and understood. Moreover, in response to

Hume's experimental explanatory psychology, Dilthey establishes the criteria for a descriptive analytic psychology that would take an integrative rather than an atomistic view of mind, that would approach mental life as a living whole rather than an aggregate of sensations or responses, and that would unite the inner with the outer worlds.

Dilthey contrasts his own work and task to both empiricism and positivism, on the one hand, and to Kantian rationalism and romantic expressionism on the other. "Unlike the particular sciences," he says, philosophy and the other human studies seek "to solve the very riddle of the world and of life; [yet] unlike art and religion," they seek "to present this solution in a universally valid form."[3]

The nature and logic of the human studies

In his essay *The Rise of Hermeneutics*, Dilthey states the problem he hoped to solve:

The human studies have indeed this advantage over the natural sciences: that their object is not sensory appearance as such, no mere reflection of reality in consciousness, but is rather itself first and foremost an inner reality, a coherence experienced from within. Yet the very fashion in which this reality is experienced within us raises the gravest difficulties for its objective apprehension . . . Thus the problem is: how can one individually structured consciousness bring an alien individuality of a completely different type to objective knowledge through such a sympathetic reconstruction? What kind of process is this, in appearance so different from the other modes of objective knowledge?[4]

Dilthey's solution to this problem was not a check list of techniques, but rather a part intuitive, part systematic, interpretive method that he demonstrated in his historical writings and commented upon extensively throughout his later years. At the heart of this interpretive procedure, or hermeneutic, are three concepts: lived experience, objectification, and understanding.[5]

Lived experience
There are two words in German for "experience": the conventional one, *Erfahrung,* and the technical one, *Erlebnis,* used by Dilthey. The verb *erleben* is itself fairly recent, formed by adding the emphatic prefix *er–* to the verb "to live." Hence the term suggests neither merely experience nor life alone, but the involvement in, the lived experience of, some whole unit of meaning – as, for example, a work of art, a love affair, a revolution:

That which in the stream of time forms a unity in the present because it has a unitary meaning is the smallest entity which we can designate as an experience. Going further, one may call each encompassing unity of parts of life bound together through a common meaning for the course of life an "experience" - even when the several parts are separated from each other by interrupting events.[6]

The lived experience is thus a subject-object unity. *Erlebnis* does not appear over against us as an idea or intellectual construct or as a physical act *about* something else. It is rather an experiencing of content as itself meaningful or, conversely, an experiencing of meaning as immanent in content. It is not given to us, but rather exists for us by virtue of the fact that we are aware of it, that we have it as in some sense belonging to us. "In itself, purely as *Erlebt,* it is not given and not thought": instead it is comprehended as something lived in and through.[7]

The consciousness which I have in having it (an *Erlebnis*) is not, strictly speaking, a consciousness *of* it at all, but simply the consciousness which belongs intrinsically to it. It may be described as an "immediate knowing" (*Innewerden Innesein*).[8]

In other words, the experience does not stand like an object over against its experiencer, but rather its very existence for me is undifferentiated from the *whatness* which is present for me in it.[9]

It is in this subsoil of pre-predicative consciousness - a subsoil that Husserl and Heidegger were later to mine - that all predicative thought, including that of the natural sciences, must take root. But for the human studies this lived experience is paramount, for the very interpretive categories of these disciplines must be derived from it. Memory, intention, and meaning cannot be imagined except in terms of the presentness and contextual structure already implicit in *Erlebnis* as we enter into it.

Objectification

Ausdruck is usually translated as "expression." We choose the term "objectification" to distinguish Dilthey's meaning from the more narrow usage of the term "expression" in romantic theories of art, which see the "expression" in subject-object terms as a kind of spontaneous outpouring of feelings by the artist. Dilthey's intention is broader and more subtle. For him an objectification is not merely the overflow or representation of a person's emotions, but a concrete embodiment of meaning.

Such objectifications are divided into three categories: ideas, actions, and objectifications of lived experience. Ideas are mere thought content, abstractions independent of any specific time place, and hence easily and directly communicated. Actions are for (or against) something else; hence their contextual meanings cannot be understood in terms of their given presentness, which does not, perforce, include the something else that they are for. Lastly there are objectifications of lived experience, which range from the spontaneous expression of inner life such as gestures, to conscious articulations embodied in systems of religion, law, or works of art. But, while most fully expressing inner lived experience, this third type of objectification is the most difficult to understand, "for it rises out of the depths which consciousness never lights up."[10]

Understanding

Understanding (*Verstehen*) refers to one mind's engaging another mind. We know that other minds exist by analogy to our own mental life. We understand other minds by immersing ourselves in the interpretive study of their external cultural-historical objectifications. "Exactly because a real transposition can take place, because affinity and universality of thought . . . can imagine forth and form a *social-historical world,* the inner events and processes in man can be distinguished from those of animals."[11]

Dilthey, following Schleiermacher, sees this "real transposition" of minds not as the I–It objectivity of the natural sciences, but as an intersubjective relationship between I and Thou. Knowledge of others (and hence of ourselves) is not gained either through introspection or by some direct metaphysical communication with the mind of the other person. On the contrary, it is achieved through the interpretive study of the expressions of that other mind, expressions that can be found in the sociohistorical world, the world of art, religion, law and politics, of language and gesture, of the shared community of experience in its living (and hence historical) aspect.

Such a process depends upon two important facts: first, that human nature is everywhere the same (i.e., that psychological differences between groups are ones of degree rather than quality); and second, that every expression of the mind is continuously linked to some such mental component.[12] This allows the possibility of understanding; but Dilthey goes on to tell us how understanding may be achieved. A lived experience, we saw earlier, is a basic unit of meaning possessing a web of inner structural connectedness of its own. Thus understanding lies in grasping the essential reciprocal interaction of the parts and the whole. As meaning is contextual, so understanding is a process of clarifying and expanding the contextual relationships of the meaning unit under study.

To illustrate this interpretive procedure, Dilthey speaks of autobiography, biography, and history as expanding circles of meaning context.[13] Similarly, he calls Homer, Shakespeare, and Goethe the three greatest poets: Homer for seeing human action as an expression of consciousness, Shakespeare for showing that human consciousness can change, and Goethe for showing that consciousness changes in the cultural-historical world. "When I read a play," says Dilthey,

it is the same as with life itself. I move onward and the past loses its clarity and distinctness. So the scenes fade. Principle: only by holding on to the plot (*Zusammenhang*) do I obtain a unitary survey of the scenes, but then I have only an outline.[14]

In understanding society and history, the outline becomes still more general, but a sense of the specificness and texture of details is retained by distilling them into a few pregnant incidents that symbolize, typify, or represent many others of their kind.[15]

This process begins with a preliminary overview of the subject matter as a whole, which guides us in determining the denotative meaning of its parts (i.e., the relationship of the symbols to the things symbolized). This, in turn, helps us clarify our idea of the whole, which must, if possible, be conceived so that all the parts can be understood in terms of it. We can thus claim to understand an objectification only when this inner structural meaning can be seen in and illuminated by each of the parts. Thus, says Dilthey, closing the hermeneutic circle, "The significance which the fact acquires, as the determination imparted by a meaningful whole to its parts, is a living connection and not an intellectual relation . . . Significance is extracted from life itself."[16]

In this sense all interpretive knowledge is circular, a kind of discovery of forms by looking in the mirror. Yet though we can only apprehend our own likeness, this very restriction turns the unrelieved historicity of human existence into an opportunity for enriched understanding, providing that the correct interpretive procedures are employed. For Dilthey these procedures are both those of more traditional logical and grammatical, as well as social and psychological, interpretation. The grammatical interpreter approaches the so-called texts – of history, art, or conduct – with the aim of reestablishing the connections between the parts and between them and the whole. The sociopsychological interpreter tends to make of himself an analog of the world of the sociohistorical actors. Each procedure is incomplete without the other, but together they enable an understanding not only of "the unity of the works" themselves, but also as they existed "in the mentality and development of their authors."[17] If we cannot live the lives of others with the original experience of them, we can aim, through interpretation, at a second immediacy. It is through interpretation that we can see and hear again, that we can come to understand our antecedents and ourselves.

Criticisms of Dilthey's formulation

The importance of philosophers may be judged not so much by their answers as by how well they put their questions. Certainly the problems that Dilthey illuminated do not admit of pat solutions; rather, one takes a stance toward them. Likewise, by responding to Dilthey one may define and enrich one's own perspective and, thence, further illuminate the questions originally put forward. Thus positivists have criticized Dilthey for his lingering idealism, in that his category *Leben* ("life") in places seems suspiciously akin to Hegel's objective spirit; yet Dilthey himself attacked absolute idealism and sought to ground his hermeneutics in nonmetaphysical empirical facts. At the other extreme, in light of the findings of modern phenomenology, Dilthey's search for "objectively valid knowledge" has been seen as a clinging to scientific ideals that were antithetical to the openness that he himself said historical understanding involves.

From the perspective of symbolic realism,[18] or even of neopositivism itself,[19] the distinction between causal explanation and contextual understanding, between natural fact and constructed meaning, no longer seems so clear. The natural sciences, we understand today, also seek to clarify particulars in terms of paradigms or frameworks that define their own domains of application. Yet as Rudolf Makkreel has shown,[20] Dilthey, despite his old-fashioned epistemology, is defensible on this point. He was aware that natural scientists also practice a hermeneuticlike inductive process (he cited Kepler's discovery of Mars as an example). But in the human studies, Dilthey argues, this hermeneutic is especially crucial, for it derives from and must reflect back upon the meaning structure of lived experience itself.[21] Further, Dilthey's interpretive procedure was not opposed to science in being pretheoretical and devoid of cultural forms, as critics such as Cassirer and Goldmann suggest.[22] On the contrary, Dilthey's hermeneutic circle brings in natural facts and generalizations wherever appropriate, and in his historical writings he gives numerous examples of how interpretations must be constrained by theoretical knowledge of the natural sciences.[23] For example, historical scholarship may involve knowledge of metallurgy to date weapons or coins; archeology may require a knowledge of structural engineering; art history, a knowledge of optics and chemistry. Such scientific knowledge cannot be central to the human studies per se, however, for these depend on hermeneutic procedures for the very definition of their subject matter in the first place. Unlike the natural sciences, which may interpret various sets of events, the events of the human studies are themselves interpretations or, more precisely, the expressions of the interpretations of other persons. The human studies thus emerge as a form of inquiry only when we accept their subject matter as the objectifications of consciousness and intentionality. While being constrained by the sciences, the human studies go beyond them.

Another line of criticism of Dilthey has been from the Freudian perspective. Like Dilthey's historical hermeneutics, psychoanalytic interpretation also is concerned with the relations between symbol or work and meanings and intentions. Moreover, both Dilthey and Freud take biography as the starting point of understanding; both assume a coherent totality of meaning in each individual existence, a totality that develops itself in the struggle between "the most powerful impulses" such as "hunger, love, and war," and the scarcities inherent in the natural and social environment.[24]

For Dilthey, however, the "text" is interpreted as evidence of the conscious intentions of the actor. In contrast, for Freudians the forces at work lie unconscious in the psyche. It is not the author's consciousness that is revealed through interpretation, but rather the author's self-deceptions. In addition to the manifest content and its evident associations, the psychoanalytic "document" reveals that portion of the author's world that has become inaccessible to him. Though the actor is alienated from this "internal foreign territory,"[25] he nonetheless belongs to it. The true meanings of psychotic texts, for example, are far removed from the surface content of their symbols (i.e., the symptoms). The deeper meanings, rather than being transparently conveyed by the symbols, appear as scars upon them.

Yet perhaps even in this area Freud and Dilthey are not so far apart. In his speech on "Poetical Fantasy and Madness," for example, Dilthey shows that in metaphysics, poetry, and myth the same images always recur in the history of mankind. "In dreams and madness, we find, with striking regularity, specific images which are always bound to sensations and internal states, pictures which interpret, explain, and represent these states. They are a kind of poor, shrunken symbol, and the realm of these symbols can be scrutinized."[26] There is, thus, for Dilthey as for Freud, a continuum rather than an opposition between the unconscious or "poor" symbol as it is expressed in dreams or madness, and its richer, more var-iegated reexpression in the great artistic achievements of many cultures and centuries. Hermeneutical thought thus recognizes that the larger, latent meaning of a symbol as grasped by the analyst is not necessarily identical to the meaning originally intended by its maker. Likewise, the praxiological meanings of actions are not always identical to their gram-matical or textual meanings. Hermeneutics cannot be restricted to the description of subjectively intended conscious meaning; it also justifies and underpins attempts at social structural, ideology-critical, or psychoanaly-tical descriptions of objectively meaningful social relations.[27]

As a counterpoint to psychological views of Dilthey, criticisms also can be launched from a neo-Marxist perspective. Different members of this school (and often the same writer at different moments) have held opposite views of Dilthey, alternately praising or attacking his rigor (or reification) of method, or lauding or assailing his stress on personal understanding and psychology. For example, in 1931 Marcuse notes admiringly that Dilthey freed the human studies from the methodology of the natural sciences and restored their philosophical foundation. Marcuse also praises Dilthey's concept of *Leben* because it stresses meaning rather than causal-ity. In another essay Marcuse shows Dilthey's (and Heidegger's) influence by writing that "Nature *has* a history, but *is* not history. Being-there (*Dasein*) *is* history."[28] Lukács makes the same point in *History and Class Consciousness,* thereby distancing himself from the orthodox Marxism of the Second International. Dilthey's influence here, of course, lies in his joining epistemology and ontology in history, made possible by his revival of Hegel's seminal insight that history is the history of consciousness. But this assessment of Dilthey was later rejected. Lukács repudiated his origins in Dilthey, Simmel, and others, whereas Marcuse became skeptical of men's power to make their histories themselves. In contrast to "the concrete 'historicity' of theory," Marcuse pointed to "the actual unfreedom and powerlessness of the individual in an anarchic production process."[29]

A related and equally ambivalent assessment of Dilthey is made by Max Horkheimer.[30] While Horkheimer praises "the ingenuity of some of Dil-they's methodological investigations," he also criticizes his "bourgeois" features: methodological individualism and its concomitant idealism on the one hand and, on the other, the positivism implicit in his search for a value-free science. Horkheimer's assessment is sometimes ungenerous, yet it reflects an intuitive sense of the boundaries of Dilthey's thought. For example, it is inaccurate to say, as Horkheimer does, that Dilthey was "approaching culture from an exclusively psychological point of view."

Dilthey did wish that understanding be grounded in a descriptive and analytic psychology, but such a psychology was to be supportive, not exclusive, of other points of view.[31]

Horkheimer's difficulty seems to lie in his failure to appreciate that the social forces that limit individuals' autonomy – to the extent that these are social – also are expressions of some persons' consciousness. The rationalization of production or the competition for foreign markets may narrow the freedom of workers; moreover, for analytic utility these forces may be treated as impersonal naturalistic events, much as climatic changes can be eventful for historical action. Yet such a heuristic is in no way inconsistent with Dilthey's insistence that such events, if they are to be understood, must be seen as deriving from actions taken by persons. One group may impose its definitions and intentions on other groups; but this in itself provides no logical justification for reifying the actions of more powerful groups into forces. Horkheimer does this, however, even while accusing Dilthey of reifying individual psychology as a unique approach to cultural understanding.

Concerning Dilthey's supposed search for knowledge free of value bias, it should be remembered that Dilthey considered history as itself a calling with its own moral commitments and imperatives. When he substituted for introspective guesswork the methodological analysis of the productions of the mind, he meant to serve human self-understanding. His value freedom was not a sterile neutrality; rather, he opposed value relativism with a philosophy of history and of conduct that was based on and reaffirmed the self-regenerative powers of humans. Dilthey was, in Schlegel's phrase for Herder, a "retrospective prophet"; through historical scholarship he upholds civilized values as witnesses to the present age. For him, "History itself is the productive power for the creation of values, ideals, and ends, by which the significance of men and events is measured."[32]

Such a defense of Dilthey should not blind us to the distinction in Horkheimer's criticism between what might be called interactional as opposed to social structural levels of analysis. In terms of Rousseau's paradox, "Man is born free and yet he finds himself in chains,"[33] Dilthey advanced a program of universal self-analysis through history with respect to human freedom. In contrast, macro-sociologists such as Marx, Weber, or Durkheim were more interested in the chains that limit individual freedom, and this led them to structural analyses of the social scarcities in which we all inevitably are involved. To the extent that society is the product of conscious human intentions, Dilthey's approach will better encompass what is salient. But to the extent that history is made "behind the backs and against the wills" of even powerful persons, then the causal,

structural, and dialectical modes of sociological analysis are to be preferred. Vico said that we can understand history better than nature because we make it, whereas nature is made by God. But perhaps this should
best be taken as a goal, rather than as a statement of the case. Indeed, it
would be easy to argue that the trend in modern life is toward a confound-
ment of human intention, in which the very heightening of our technical
means for realizing intentions has generated new fragmentations that
dramatically narrow the range in which our rational projects can be enacted. Marx called for the "humanization of nature" and the "naturaliza-
tion of man," a society in which labor would become unalienated praxis.[34]
Until such a society is realized, however, it will not be enough to understand history and society; they also will have to be explained.

These criticisms of Dilthey are instances of the *Methodenstreit* – the
debate on methods – that reoccurs in all the human studies. In psychology
there is opposition between behavioristic and humanistic approaches;
sociology is torn by positivistic and interpretive schools; in philosophy some
practitioners accept the word-thing identity posited by the early Wittgenstein, while others are loyal to Wittgenstein's later theories of languages as
forms of life. Yet even today these conflicts are illuminated by Dilthey's seminal insights; for despite criticisms of his particular formulations, his works
present the first modern articulation of these key methodological issues.

One of Dilthey's principal contributions was to destroy the absolutist
pretensions of the social and historical sciences. By seeing the investigator
and the object of his research as joined through the context of history,
Dilthey made it possible for later scholars to explore the life interests that
inform the action and consciousness of the investigator as he proceeds with
his work. The researcher – despite whatever objectivity he may achieve
in his research – still enacts that research in the context of an imagined
future and a historical past. His interpretations and explanations can
exist only within the boundary of his historical situation. Consequently, as
Wellmer puts it, his findings "remain suggestions, which have to be proven
not only in regard to the material already available, [but also in regard
to] the future historical practice of human beings," a practice that will
create its own historical context.[35]

Just as it destroys the fiction of objectivity, hermeneutic thought also
reveals the factual limits of a purely subjective interpretive sociology. Such
a sociology, as Habermas describes it, "explains social behavior in terms
of motives that are identical with the subject's own assessments of situation,
and therefore with the linguistically articulated meaning, or verbal statement, by which he orientates himself."[36] But even linguistic analysis recognizes that explanation in terms of motives is not the same as explanation in

terms of cause. Motives or intentions do not "cause" actions; rather they provide a teleological account for them. Language interpretive sociology has demonstrated that intentional action, as such, is relatively autonomous of nonintentional natural processes, and that it must be accounted for by rules rather than by laws. Yet the question remains: From whence come these rules? And it is here that hermeneutic thought reveals language analytic sociology to be a kind of myth, in that it posits as its subject matter a monadistic and hermetic world of language games outside of time or space.

Explanatory sociology is thus always interpretive sociology; but at the same time interpretive sociology cannot be merely a subjective sociology of the interpretation of meaning for, as we have seen, the historical context of meaning is larger than the contexts of meanings that may have been subjectively intended by the original actors. Thus, for both positivistic and language interpretive sociology, the empirical validity of social theories – their objectivity if you will – can never exceed the degree of concrete historicity of their concepts. This historicity includes not only the content of the theories' concepts themselves, but also the on-going historical process that forms the hermeneutic field of the sociologist's practice. By bringing to awareness the historical life world that is the context for all thought, hermeneutics becomes the boundary for such theories; in so doing, however, hermeneutics shows that it is itself bounded by praxis. Hermeneutics is encompassed by praxis, yet any theory of praxis is encompassed by hermeneutics.

By setting limits on both objectivistic and subjectivistic ways of knowing, hermeneutic thought gives birth to a new freedom, a freedom suggested by Dilthey and expanded by contemporary critical theorists: Stripped by critical hermeneutics of its absolutist illusions, social thought rediscovers its "in-and-for-itself," its practical and emancipatory will to know. Thrust back upon its own resources, the human studies regain the possibility of grounding themselves in an empirical philosophy of history, and of reaching toward liberation in the world of politics and action.

NOTES

The standard guide to Dilthey's works is Ulrich Hermann's *Bibliographie Wilhelm Dilthey. Pädagogische Bibliographien*. Reihe A. Band I. Ed. Leonhard Froese and Georg Ruckriem (Weinheim: Julius Beltz, 1969). Unfortunately Hermann's work misses important articles after 1966. Rudolf Makkreel's bibliography (in his

Dilthey: Philosopher of the Human Studies [Princeton, N.J.: Princeton University Press, 1975]) is thus an indispensable supplement to Hermann's. The translations of Dilthey in our text are borrowed from standard works on Dilthey in English; in these cases we have cited both the original German edition, as well as the English language source. I wish to thank Professor Makkreel for his critical comments on this essay.

1 David Hume, *A Treatise of Human Nature*, Bks. I and II, 2 vols. (London, 1739), Bk. III (London, 1740). See Wilhelm Dilthey, *Gesammelte Schriften*, 17 vols (Stuttgart: B. G. Teubner and Gottingen: Vandenhoeck and Ruprecht, 1914–74), 5:lxxxiv.
2 Hume, *The Essence of Philosophy*, trans. S. and W. Emery (Chapel Hill: University of North Carolina Press, 1961), p. 24.
3 Ibid., p. 26.
4 Hume, "The Rise of Hermeneutics" in *New Literary History: A Journal of Theory and Interpretation*, trans. Fredric Jameson, 3:2 (Winter, 1972): 229–44.
5 Dilthey, *Gesammelte Schriften*, 1960, 7:86; H. A. Hodges, *The Philosophy of Wilhelm Dilthey* (London: Routledge & Kegan Paul, 1952), p. 249.
6 Dilthey, *Gesammelte Schriften*, 8:194; Richard E. Palmer, *Hermeneutics: Interpretation Theory in Schleiermacher, Dilthey, Heidegger, and Gadamer* (Evanston, Ill.: Northwestern University Press, 1969), p. 107.
7 Dilthey, *Gesammelte Schriften*, 6:314; Hodges, *Wilhelm Dilthey*, p. 40.
8 Hodges, *Wilhelm Dilthey*, p. 39.
9 Dilthey, *Gesammelte Schriften*, 7:139; Palmer, *Hermeneutics*, p. 109.
10 Dilthey, *Gesammelte Schriften*, 7:207; Palmer, *Hermeneutics*, p. 113.
11 Dilthey, *Gesammelte Schriften*, 5:250; Palmer, *Hermeneutics*, p. 104.
12 Dilthey, *Gesammelte Schriften*, 5:239.
13 Dilthey, Ibid., 5:206–25.
14 Dilthey, Ibid., 7:226–7; Hodges, *Wilhelm Dilthey*, p. 123.
15 Dilthey, *Gesammelte Schriften*, 5:241–82.
16 Dilthey, Ibid. 7:240; Hodges, *Wilhelm Dilthey*, p. 151.
17 Dilthey, *Gesammelte Schriften*, 5:331; Arnold Bergstraesser, "Wilhelm Dilthey and Max Weber: An Empirical Approach to Historical Synthesis," *Ethics*, 57 (1947):92–110. Quotation on p. 97.
18 On symbolic realism, see Nelson Goodman, *The Structure of Appearance* (Cambridge, Mass.: Harvard University Press, 1951). Also see Richard Harvey Brown, "Symbolic Realism and Perspectival Knowledge," in *A Poetic for Sociology: Toward a Logic of Discovery for the Human Sciences* (London and New York: Cambridge University Press, 1977).
19 See Thomas S. Kuhn, *The Structure of Scientific Revolutions* (Chicago: University of Chicago Press, 1962). Also see Michael Polanyi, *Personal Knowledge: Toward a Post-Critical Philosophy* (Chicago: University of Chicago Press, 1958).

20 Rudolf A. Makkreel, "Wilhelm Dilthey and the Neo-Kantians: The Distinction of the *Geisteswissenschaften* and the *Kulturwissenschaften,*" *Journal of the History of Philosophy* 7, 7 (1969):435.
21 Dilthey, *Gesammelte Schriften,* 7:220-7.
22 See Ernst Cassirer, *Philosophy of Symbolic Forms* (New Haven, Conn.: Yale University Press, 1953-7, and Lucien Goldmann, *The Human Sciences and Philosophy* (London: Jonathan Cape, 1969).
23 Dilthey, *Gesammelte Schriften,* 5:281.
24 Dilthey, Ibid., 5:209.
25 Sigmund Freud, "New Introductory Lectures on Psychoanalysis," *Complete Works* (London: Hogarth Press, 1967), 22:57.
26 Dilthey, *Gesammelte Schriften,* 6:101; Horkheimer, Max. "The Relation between Psychology and Sociology in the Work of Wilhelm Dilthey," *Studies in Philosophy and Social Science* 8, 3 (1939):430-43. Quotation on p. 441.
27 Albrecht Wellmer, *Critical Theory of Society* (New York: Herder & Herder, 1971), p. 33.
28 Herbert Marcuse, "Beitrage zu einer Phanomenologie des historichen Materialismus," *Philosophiche Hefte,* 1, 1(1928):46. Also see Marcuse's *Hegels Ontologie und die Grundlegung einer Theorie der Geschichtlichkeit* (Frankfurt am Main: V. Klostermann Verlag, 1932), and "The Problem of Historical Reality" ("Das Problem der geschichtlichen Wirklichkeit), *Die Gesellschaft.* 7 (1931):4. Also see Martin Heidegger, *Sein und Zeit* (Halle: Niemeyer, 1927). Translated by John Macquarrie and Edward Robinson as *Being and Time* (London: S.M.C. Press, 1962).
29 See Martin Jay, *The Dialectical Imagination: A History of the Frankfurt School and the Institute of Social Research, 1923-1950* (Boston: Little, Brown, 1973), pp. 73-6. Also see Georg Lukács, *Die Zerstorung der Venunft,* in *Werke,* vol. 9 (Neuwied: 1961), and Lukác's *History and Class Consciousness* (Cambridge, Mass.: M.I.T. Press, 1968).
30 Horkheimer, "Psychology and Sociology."
31 Dilthey, *Gesammelte Schriften,* 5:269.
32 Dilthey, Ibid., 7:290.
33 Jean-Jacques Rousseau, *Du Contrat social* (Paris, 1762), 1:i.
34 Karl Marx, *Karl Marx: Early Writings,* ed. Tom Bottomore (New York: 1963), p. 155.
35 Wellmer, *Critical Theory,* p. 33.
36 Jürgen Habermas, *Zur Logik der Sozialwissenschaften* (Tübingen: 1967), p. 182. Also see Habermas's "Dilthey's Theory of Understanding Expression: Ego Identity and Linguistic Communication," *Knowledge and Human Interests* (Boston: Beacon Press, 1968), pp. 140-60.

3

The acceptance, rejection, and reconstruction of histories: On some controversies in the study of social and cultural change

STANFORD M. LYMAN

Editors' introduction

One of the continuing debates in social science concerns the approach best suited to the study of social and cultural change. Ever since Aristotle applied the principles of organic growth to cultural and political phenomena, social science has approached the problem of change largely by assuming that, since change was always going on, the task was to describe its trajectory and predict its outcome. Guided by teleological considerations, social scientists prepared cyclical and sequential scenarios of past and future. Stages of cultural and social development, for example, were illustrated by reference to the conditions of contemporary primitives arranged as if they were on a temporal continuum. The actual occurrences in a people's history either depicted the preconceived developmental sequence or interfered with it. If the latter, such happenings were dismissed as epiphenomenal. Hypotheses about social change thus took the form of proposed evolutions of social and cultural forms.

Stanford M. Lyman's essay explores the major critique of the Aristotelian perspective in social science. The much neglected works of Frederick J. Teggart - and his principal disciples, Hodgen, Bock, and Nisbet - offer a neopositivist assault on the evolutionist and functionalist approaches to the analysis of social change. Attempting to ground the study of history in empirical science, Teggart rejected both the literary insistence on history as the depiction of unique happenings and the developmentalist thesis of organic growth. In their places, he insisted on formal hypotheses tested against the factual data presented in the historical record. Correlations and causes could be obtained from such procedures, resulting in a science of history that might aid statesmen as well as scholars.

However rich the promise of Teggart's project, it fails to cope with some of its own defects. Lyman not only discusses these deficiencies, but also introduces an array of alternatives to both the evolutionist and neopositivist positions. Of these, a phenomenological approach

suggests that all histories are contemporary structures of consciousness
enjoying varying degrees of legitimation and popular support. Perceived in this light, the evolutionist–neopositivist debate becomes a
struggle between contending structures of consciousness for paradigmatic domination within the discipline. History becomes a congeries
of structures of consciousness. Social change becomes an orientation
extant in the present, focused toward the future, and based on some
conception of the past. The sociology of social change becomes the
study of the origin, development, operation, and consequences of
these conceptions.

For the past century a quiet but important battle has raged among the
students of social change. Essentially two positions have been established:
One, that of the evolutionist functionalists, is familiar, rich in antecedents,
and still holds sway in most of the academies; the other, that of the historical positivists, is recessive, unfamiliar, without as affluent a pedigree, and
hardly established in the institutions of higher learning. Yet the former
is coming under attack more and more; while the epistemological assumptions of the latter have yet to be subjected to critical analysis. It is the
purpose of this essay to explore the positions and prospects of this debate
and to suggest some further problems that have yet to be integrated into
the arguments.

More specifically this essay will focus on the several facets of the position
put forth by the founder of what might be called a historical neopositivist
approach to the study of social and cultural change, Frederick J. Teggart
(1870–1946). Teggart's complete works, although available for many
years, have never been subjected to exposition and critical analysis. Nevertheless, the project proposed by Teggart, although neither completed by
his disciples nor accepted by subsequent generations of scholars, provides
perhaps the single most important challenge to both the original evolutionary and the recently developed neoevolutionary approaches. At once a
critic of literary historicism and anthropological evolutionism, Teggart
hoped to establish a scientifically grounded perspective for the study of
social change. Yet, certain difficulties in his own orientation remain unde-
tected and unresolved, and alternatives to his project are yet to be explored.
Among the alternatives neofunctionalism, formal and mythic approaches,
and most important, a phenomenological orientation offer new answers to
the still prominent debate between the neopositivist position on the one
hand and the evolutionary and functionalist positions on the other.

Evolutionism and functionalism

Basic evolutionism

The dominant school of thought in current sociology is evolutionist functionalism. To those familiar with the discussion, the name Talcott Parsons immediately evokes the quintessential statement on the subject. In Parson's book *The Social System* we may find a most complete presentation of functionalist sociology at the societal level;[1] in his *Societies: Evolutionary and Comparative Perspectives* we discover the linkage to older evolutionary theories of change.[2] At one time the functionalist approach served as a special kind of critique of older developmental theories of change. However, the grounds of both theories are ultimately to be found in the solution proposed by Aristotle to the study of order and change. Since sociology in particular and the social sciences in general were founded to discover the bases for order, the causes and consequences of change, and the nature and possibilities of permanence, the Aristotelian answer and its modern counterpart in evolutionist functionalism stand as one of the most significant proposals ever offered to the original question of the discipline.

Evolutionary approaches to the understanding of social change first of all assert that *change is always going on.* Every unit under study is undergoing a constant shift from one state of being to another. Each state of being, hence, is in a process of becoming. Since the evolutionist never assumes that change is *not* going on, or that it is intermittent, the causes of change are not a matter of investigative concern. Instead, the roots of change are said to reside in the thing changing. Change is immanent. For the evolutionist, the real issue is to discover the direction of change, the rate of change, and the (temporary) impediments to change.

The rate of change is also established through an assumption. Change, according to the evolutionist, is not only continuous, but *slow* and *orderly* as well. The organization of action cannot occur faster than the nature of the thing changing. Most changes occur so slowly that they cannot be noticed except by careful measurement or by the discerning eye of later historians. Closely related to the slowness of change is its *orderliness.* Changes that are sudden, chaotic, and irruptive cannot last; only the orderly processes that resonate with the existing state of being and the quality of immanence in the thing changing can form a part of the social trend. In accordance with Leibniz's famous dictum, *Natura non facit saltum,* social change is regarded as *gradual.* In societies and civilizations, as in nature, argues the evolutionist, there is no discontinuity, gap, leap, or failure of growth; there is only gradual and cumulative development. Thus, every present contains the seeds of its own future while at the same moment it embodies the fruits of its own growth from the past.

The direction of change is contained in the *telos* of the thing changing. Evolutionary theory is deterministic in the sense that it holds that every thing contains its own potential; things become what it is in their nature to become. Entelechy is the vital process governing the path that societies, cultures, and civilizations traverse. Thus societies do not move toward chaotic, directionless, and unknowable outcomes. Their destination is contained in their present, rooted in their past, and realized in their future. For the social scientist to discover the telic force at work in any society he must uncover the tap root of that society. Origin is destiny.

Basic to the evolutionist perspective is the conception of development as organic growth. Societies, cultures, and civilizations are treated as if they were organisms. History thus conceived becomes natural history. Growth is defined as the passage through inevitable phases of development until maturity is achieved. In some conceptions societies, cultures, and civilizations are likened in their natural history to the life cycle of a mortal: They are born, nurtured, and educated in their "early" periods; they then expand, test their musculature and possibilities in an "adolescence"; achieve knowledge, attempt greatness, and then affirm the limits of their condition in a "mature" period; and, finally, weaken and decay in their "old age" until decline and death remove them from the worldly scene. Even when their descriptions of social, cultural, or civilizational development did not approximate the life cycle so boldly, evolutionists nevertheless clung to a general, vague, but powerful sense that growth as measured and conceived by science was organic.

The organic analogy led to the designation of development in stages. Evolutionists depicted the stages of social, cultural, or civilizational growth in terms strikingly close to that of biological organisms. Nonliterate peoples tended to be treated as representatives of "early" stages of development, described as "savages," and, as such, compared to infants with respect to mental capacity.[3] Evolutionary historians identified certain occurrences as either exemplars of the telic force at work or impediments to it. The original argument, developed by Aristotle in *Physics,* was taken over in its entirety, including the doctrine of accidents (or, as we shall see presently, impediments or obstacles) that had accompanied it.

The doctrine of accidents is the single most important element in the evolutionist argument. According to this doctrine not everything that happens is "natural." Mistakes and fortuitous occurrences are not unknown;

"chance" produces unusual happenings. What occurs in the world, then, is either "natural" or it is not. As Aristotle conceived of it, there could be no science of unnatural phenomena. Only natural things could be the subjects of science. Two tests might be applied to distinguish the natural from the accidental: Any "thing" that did not contain within itself the principle of immanent and telic change was not natural; any occurrence in the history or experience of a "thing" that could not be associated with its true potential must be regarded as accidental to it.[4]

Armed with his knowledge of the "natural" and the "accidental," the evolutionist approached the record of history with confidence. Those occurrences that exemplified the inherent potential of the society, culture, or civilization under study were proper data of a social science; those that were incidental, contingent, or unrelated to that elemental immanence were "accidents." The record of history thus offered no mystery.[5] Once the potential of the specific entity under study had been established, the record of occurrences disclosed itself as a dichotomous paradigm of natural or nonnatural phenomena.

However, following a clue in Aristotle's discussions of the subject, the evolutionist employed the doctrine of accidents as an explanatory device. It was not merely the case that accidents sometimes occurred. When they occurred they might stand in the way of natural development. Accidents, thus, could be impediments, obstacles, or interferences. Once he knew the dysfunctional consequences of accidents, the evolutionist could explain how it was that a society, culture, or civilization had failed to become what its potential dictated. A society had not advanced into the next stage of its inevitable developmental sequence because something had interfered. Put another way, the evolutionist could argue his case in the future perfect tense. A society would have taken on the character and institutions associated with the next stage in its natural and inherent development if the designated obstacle had not been encountered. In the hands of a deft evolutionist, the doctrine of accidents could be employed to preserve the developmental hypothesis in the face of overwhelming evidence to the contrary. Rather than disconfirming the hypothesis, the seemingly negative evidence might be regarded as a table of impediments preventing the realization of developments in what otherwise would have been a natural sequence.

It is a commonplace of current anthropological and sociological discussion to assert that the evolutionist position has been abandoned in the face of the criticism leveled against it by Boas and his followers.[6] Yet, whatever the lip service paid to diffusionist and related alternatives to developmental theories, evolutionism has survived in other terms, and a neoevolutionist revival is noticeable in recent sociology and anthropology.[7] Indeed, diffusionist ideas had been absorbed by certain evolutionary theories from the beginning, giving added strength to the latter.[8] More recently, the revival of diffusionist approaches to social change has not occasioned an abandonment of evolutionary orientations but instead evoked a call for a more encompassing theory, recognizing both exogenous happenings as diffusionist elements and endogenous trends as evolutionary facets of an enlarged conception of sociocultural change.[9]

Despite the rejection of the "comparative method," certain anthropologists still employ it without explicit identification as such.[10] A striking example is found in a recent socioanthropological study of Chinese social organization in nineteenth-century Singapore by Maurice Freedman.[11] Taking *contemporary* modes of Chinese social organization in Sarawak as the model for all *early* phases of overseas Chinese community form, Freedman designates *contemporary* modes of Chinese social organization in Singapore as "the model of the most developed form of immigrant Chinese settlement in Southeast Asia." Although there is evidence from Freedman's own investigations of the matter that the actual social organization of the earliest Chinese settlement in Singapore was far more complex than that of contemporary Sarawak, he nevertheless reasons that a simpler and smaller scale organization *must* have preceded that of later Singapore. Thus, in strict conformity to the rules of the "comparative method," Freedman has arranged his depiction of spatially and temporally coexistent Chinese communities in Sarawak and Singapore in the form of a chronological natural history. The belief in a uniform development of social institutions, proceeding from small and simple to large and complex forms, has taken precedence over the facts of history uncovered in the investigation.[12]

Although a common thesis holds that sociological employment of the evolutionist perspective is a product of Darwinism, the fundamental ideas of the perspective predate the latters' work by thousands of years.[13] As Bock has urged, Darwin ought not be charged with the burdens and difficulties of sociological evolutionary functionalism.[14] One form of developmentalism in American sociology derived from a synthesis of German sociological thought. Robert Park's race relations cycle, which seems to have arisen from his original combination of the formal sociology of Georg Simmel with the historicist ideas of Wilhelm Windelband and other German historical thinkers provides, perhaps, the paradigmatic example.[15] Taking several social forms – contact, competition, accommodation, assimilation – Park arranged them in a conjectural chronological sequence.

Race relations, he argued, proceed from contact to assimilation, passing through two intermediate stages – competition and accommodation. In presenting this theory Park combined the idea of the recurring cycle with that of the inevitable sequence, an intellectual feat that had previously proved difficult for other social thinkers. As a *cycle* of recurring forms, the phases of race relations occurred for every racial group that came in contact with another group at a racial frontier. At any moment in history several racial groups might be at different points on the cycle: Some were assimilating; others lived in a state of accommodation; still others were suffering the difficulties of competition; and there were yet some groups just starting on the long road to inevitable assimilation. Furthermore, implicit in the argument was the possibility that a racial group might not have even begun the cycle since it had not yet made sustained contact with another race. A race relations cycle recurs so long as races continue on the move and encounter one another in different places on the earth. As a *sequence,* however, Park argued that the stages in the cycle moved down a road on which it was impossible to turn back. Once contact had been made the subsequent phases of orderly transition became irrepressible. As he expressed it: "The race relations cycle which takes the form, to state it abstractly, of contacts, competition, accommodation and eventual assimilation, is apparently progressive and irreversible."[16] Thus the sequence is a covering law outlining the origin, way stations, and inevitable dissolution of race relations at the universal level. The recurring cycle describes the discrete experiences of different racial groups as they travel down the common road to their own inevitable extinction.

However, Park's cyclical sequence did not conform to the record of happenings in the actual world, either as experienced by the social actors or as reported by the sociological observers. Particularly vexing was the failure of the final stage – assimilation – to emerge for any significant number of America's immigrants during the lifetime of Park or his disciples. Faced with a bitter disappointment with their predictive hypothesis, and – for some – an even more bitter dejection over a failure of the fulfillment of what they believed to be an ameliorating step in the general process moving mankind toward a raceless and cosmopolitan world, some disciples of Park searched for the inordinately tough and as yet impenetrable obstacles that hindered the march of progress in race relations.[17] Others constructed more elaborate cycles to account for a particular group's variation.[18] And the most embittered rejected the cycle altogether and with it any possibility of a science of race relations.[19] Those sociologists concerned with the logic of their own science sometimes sought to rescue the race relations cycle by converting it from a "theory" to a "model." Asked to state just what it was a model of, however, they admitted that it was a model of race relations with many exceptions.[20]

By encouraging research that would uncover exceptions, some evolutionary thinkers sought to legitimate the defects in developmental models, such as Park's race relations cycle, thereby converting their empirical shortcomings into theoretical virtues. Applied to the race relations cycle, this approach would assert that it is not a strictly universal law that admits of no exceptions. Rather it is a quasi-law that ought to be employed as an aid to uncovering the as yet hidden conditions of its own applicability.[21] As these conditions – interferences with natural processes – are disclosed, the lawlike aspect of the race relations cycle is steadily encumbered with an increasing number of qualifications that enrich its own application to the world of race relations. Viewed in this light, Park's own development of a table of impedimenta – skin color, group temperament, racial prejudice, and the absence of interracial primary relations – constitutes an elaboration of the original cycle and an invitation to enlarge and verify even further his enumeration of limiting conditions.[22]

However, the search for exceptions as a clue to the conditions of applicability of a lawlike proposition does little more than patch a gaping hole in the scientific procedure of social evolutionism. In terms familiar to readers of Karl Popper, the principal defect is unfalsifiability.[23] Evolutionary cycles, natural histories, and sequences of inevitable stages are not hypotheses in the narrow and restricted meaning of that term, since no set of procedures can be brought to bear as a reasonable and fair test. Such a test would be possible if the doctrine of accidents could be removed from the argument employed by the evolutionist. Unable to preclassify events as "natural" or "accidental," the social scientist could then search for the evidence that would cause him to reject his original hypothesis. Still another approach, only slightly more elaborate than the one just mentioned, would be the reelaboration of the hypothesis with a fixed and finite set of qualifiers such that a discovery of failure in its predictive capacity could be referred to the limiting factor already enunciated, if that factor could also be shown to be present in the existential world of the object under study. If, however, the doctrine of accidents is attached as a corollary to evolutionist theories, no hypothesis can be tested at all; rather, each datum in what would otherwise be recognized as a body of negative evidence will be classified as an interference, obstacle, or accident to the developmental thesis.[24]

The doctrine of accidents also encourages and legitimates *ad hoc* explanations and procedures. Faced with what appears to be disconfirming evidence of a developmental hypothesis, the researcher might seek about for any kind of element, factor, or occurrence to account for the discrepancy between scientific prediction and recorded performance. The history of the use of the doctrine of accidents by scholars investigating Park's race relations cycle is alarmingly instructive on this point. One researcher, seeking to explain why one Japanese community in California seemed to be living in a state of accommodation rapidly approaching assimilation whereas another only a few hundred miles away was riddled with intracommunity conflict, introduced geographical, civic, and collective psychological factors indiscriminately to account for the differences.[25] Seeking to explain why a Jew who had assimilated rapidly and completely was nevertheless rejected by his gentile peers and business associates, Louis Wirth explained that the man had moved too fast: He had acted as an assimilate in the era of accommodation.[26] And Rose Hum Lee, chagrined to find that the Chinese had not assimilated after more than a century of settlement in the United States, charged them with a vested interest in segregation and a failure of nerve.[27] With the recalcitrance of geography, the rhythms of time, and the rumblings of collective and individual psyches available to the researcher seeking an accident, it is no wonder that chaos prevails in the demonstration of these kinds of scientific propositions. The doctrine of accidents provides an embarrassment of untapped riches for an otherwise impoverished mode of social scientific procedure.

Functionalism

Although functionalists are commonly credited with having provided a major critique of evolutionism and with proposing an alternative to it, in fact their original intent was quite limited and, in the end, their approach to the study of social change has become one basis for a neoevolutionist revival. The functionalists insisted that before the stages of societal change could be delineated, an adequate picture of the nature and workings of a society would have to be established. Thus the functionalists did not address themselves to the central problem of evolutionist science – the construction of laws of social dynamics – but rather urged that the evolutionist project be postponed until an adequate account of the unit undergoing change had been rendered. Indeed, the functionalists also opposed the "historical" criticism of evolutionism presented by the diffusionist school. By insisting on the prior importance of establishing the nature of societies, and by opposing a historical analysis of different societies with similar traits or institutions in the manner proposed by Boas and his followers, the functionalists shifted attention from the comparative analysis of societies in history to the intensive analysis of the structure and coherence of discrete societies independent of one another.

However, it would be incorrect to suppose that the functionalists eschewed the study of change. In fact their analyses of particular societies focused on the manner in which order could persevere in the face of change. Functionalists took over the organic metaphor and insisted that societies, like organisms, were composed of interdependent parts. The basic idea was admirably stated by John Stuart Mill:

The state of every part of the social whole at any time, is intimately connected with the contemporaneous state of all the others. Religious belief, philosophy, science, the fine arts, the industrial arts, commerce, government, are all in close mutual dependence on one another, insomuch that when any considerable change takes place in one, we may know that a parallel change in all the others has preceded or will follow it.[28]

Later functionalists, seeking to open the social system sufficiently to permit voluntaristic action, provided for changes that were spontaneous, disjunctive, and deviant.[29] The functionalists had not abandoned the study of change; they had redirected the effort to study it to the interior of discrete societies conceived as social systems.[30]

Moreover, functionalists did not give up Aristotelian ideas of teleology or determinism. Instead, in the spirit of a more objective and value-free social science, they exorcised the explicit values that inhered in older teleological conceptions. In societies, they argued, there was a strain toward equilibrium. Changes did occur, societies were dynamic, but the direction of change was toward the reestablishment of a balanced interdependence among the parts and a continuous re-creation of consensus and coherence.[31] Some functionalists seized upon the social psychology of George Herbert Mead to elaborate this thesis. Just as the impulsive and creative "I," in Mead's famous formulation, is always being checked, modified, and incorporated into an intersubjective consensus by the "me," so also the larger units of the society might "act" disjunctively but *eventually* be brought into line by the new equilibrium that incorporates innovative activity and by that stroke robs it of its deviant and dysfunctional effect.[32] The functionalists thus introduced a bloodless entelechy that not only resonated with organic imagery but also elevated processes above the happenings of which they are composed.

Finally, the functionalists have also held on to the doctrine of accidents but introduced it in a disguised form. Changes within a system are either immanent or "historical." The former fall into two classes: those that are eufunctional and contribute to system maintenance; and those that are dysfunctional (arising, in the usual explanation, from imperfections in socialization and a less than equal intensity of incorporation of fundamental norms and values among the several strata of the society) and disturb systemic balance. Insofar as the system continues to reconstitute itself in a state of dynamic equilibrium, dysfunctional aspects are only harmful in the short run; in the long run their negative effects are absorbed and a new balance is effected. However, the second class of changes – the "historical" ones – are not deducible from the principles of systemic sociology. Often – but not always – these nonsystemic happenings come from "outside" the particular society in the form of invasions, migrations, changes in the world economy, or cataclysmic disasters. In other cases they are unexpected occurrences within the system, such as the sudden mobility of a hitherto stratum-bound group, innovative ideologies, economic depressions, and the like. And in a few perceptive analyses a combination of exogenous and endogenous elements produce a change not anticipated by analysis of immanent elements alone.[33] The "historical" occurrences that are presented to account for the failure of expected changes to occur or to explain changes that do occur but are unexpected by pure systemic analysis are in effect *accidents*. As such they function in precisely the same way as accidents do in evolutionist theories. And just as the doctrine of accidents may encourage particular explanations for exceptions to developmentalist theories, so also it operates in functionalist theories to encourage the *ad hoc* procedure that renders such theories unfalsifiable.

Evolutionist functionalism

When functionalists seek to explain change at the intersocietal or intercivilizational level, they resort to a modified form of evolutionism, usually called neoevolutionism. The recent revival of modified Spencerian ideas among those who once scoffed at the Victorian scholar's efforts illustrates how wrong it has been to suppose that functionalism could only contribute to the study of social statics. In fact functionalism and evolutionism are two aspects of the same basic idea, one which might properly be called *Aristotelianism*. Essential to this idea are the organic model, the assumption that change is always going on, the assertion of entelechy, the insistence that historical events are unique, and the doctrine of accidents.[34]

When evolutionist functionalists assert that they have surmounted the difficulties of earlier forms of evolutionism by eliminating unilinearity, neutralizing a once value-laden entelechy, and giving up their belief in irreversibility, they are not addressing the central question raised against the Aristotelian conception of science. The central questions have been addressed by those scholars interested in scientific history and in a scientific sociology of social change.

The neopositivist position

For more than fifty years there has been a powerful but subterranean stream of criticism against the several aspects of the Aristotelian position in history, anthropology, and sociology. The principal figures in this neopositivist school are Frederick J. Teggart, Margaret T. Hodgen, Kenneth E. Bock, and Robert A. Nisbet. Their works, although directed to different aspects of the Aristotelian heritage, constitute a thorough-going critique of evolutionary developmentalist theories. In addition they offer an approach to the scientific study of history in general and social change in particular that avoids the pitfalls of the developmentalist school. Their neopositivism rejects the original organic analogy that inspired Aristotle's perspective and that has remained central to the developmental approaches. In lieu of the organic analogy they favor a quite different analytical conception of the study of social change that, in Teggart's words "must be founded upon a comparison of the particular histories of all human groups, and must be actuated by the conscious effort to take cognizance of all the available facts."[35]

Central to the neopositivist position is the attention given to the basic unit of study – the *event*. Neopositivists reject both the evolutionists' disposal of happenings as epiphenomena and the narrative historians' treatment of them as grist for the development of a dramatic narrative. As Teggart once put it:

We have before us, in the form of documents and other memorials, evidences of what has taken place in the past. The historian seizes upon these materials and endeavors to "reconstruct the past." What he does is to create for himself, from the data available, a drama of events, and he does this by selecting what he deems to have been the episodes of cardinal importance, supplementing the record by the imaginative reconstruction of the motives of the participants. It is all human and romantic, and, in the hands of a master, of absorbing interest; but the story will never be the same in any two "histories," and the propositions of the "accidental" will vary with every treatment.[36]

The proper scientific study of man, according to the neopositivists, rejects both romantic reconstructions and the *a priori* division of happenings into the "natural" and the "accidental." Teggart asserts that,

The scientific investigator, approaching the same materials will, on the other hand, begin with the present, and he will utilize the facts available in regard to what has happened in the past as so much evidence from which to isolate the various processes through which the existing situation or condition has come to be as it is.[37]

Thus, as the neopositivists see it, it is from the analysis of specific temporal and geographical social facts that the social processes may be uncovered. As Margaret Hodgen claimed,

Guided by precise statements of the temporal and geographical incidence of cultural phenomena, it is not only possible . . . to reconstruct maps of dated distributions of social facts, to arrange dated distributions in their dated order and compare them for the purpose of obtaining insight into time and space similarities or differences, it is also possible to use other dated information for the study of how things worked in past time to produce the results called "distributions," or to deal with the problem of recovering historical processes.[38]

The neopositivist approach to what Teggart[39] called the "humanistic study of change in time" is founded on a fundamental rejection of the evolutionary and Aristotelian paradigm and a revival of the methods associated with David Hume[40] and Anne Robert Jacques Turgot.[41] A true social science must, according to Kenneth Bock, commit itself unequivocally to a comparative study of actual happenings as they occurred in time and space.[42] On behalf of this postulated necessity, Hodgen investigated the distribution of technological innovations in England from 1000 to 1899 and showed that innovations tended to recur in those villages and parishes where a precedent of accepting changes had been established earlier,[43] and, in his most thorough-going study, Teggart uncovered a hitherto unnoticed relationship between the Barbarian invasions of Europe and the wars that were fought on the eastern frontiers of the Roman Imperium and the western regions of the Chinese Empire.[44] Such investigations require, as Bock has suggested, "as a first step toward the formulation of testable statements of social or cultural processes, abandonment of the assumption that historical events are unique and acceptance of the assumption that there are discernible regularities in *all* historical occurrences."[45] Theories of social change thus might arise from the testing of hypotheses formulated around the relation of one class of occurrences to another.[46]

A second aspect of its rejection of the Aristotelian paradigm is abandonment of the biological model that has been employed by both evolutionists
and functionalists. Bock presents this position most clearly:

Use of the biological analogy in any form and to any extent is unwarranted and
dangerous. Considerations of the possible utility of analogical reasoning for conceptualization notwithstanding, the repeated experiences of Western scholars over
more than twenty-five hundred years demonstrates unequivocally that the analogy
between society and an organism has worked uniformly to stop inquiry and to produce images of social process plainly contradicted by evidence at hand.[47]

Abandonment of the biological analogy also entails a rejection of its
subsidiary concepts and orientations about change. Bock points out that
these include "the notions that change has been always from the simple
to the complex, from the homogeneous to the heterogeneous, or from the
undifferentiated to the differentiated."[48] Ultimately this requires rejection
of the Aristotelian picture of motion:

The belief derived from analogy that society is a process of slow and continuous
change generated and directed by potential present within the thing changing
from the beginning, has served only to divert attention from the evidence that must
be admitted in any candid search for processes- evidence that cannot be dismissed
as "secondary" factors of "unnatural" interventions or "anti-evolutionary" forces.[49]

Studies done in the neopositivist tradition have indicated the weaknesses
that exist in the more traditional Aristotelian approach. Hodgen's study
of technological innovation in England showed, among other things, that
"the oft-spoken dictum that man lives in a world of change emerges as only
half-true; and the purported naturalness, continuity and universality imputed by social evolutionists to the process of change is not confirmed."[50]
Teggart has shown how classifications of discrete historical occurrences in
Rome and China may be correlated to upset long-held theories accounting
for major intercivilizational encounters.[51] More recently, Lyman has shown
how commitment to the Aristotelian paradigm has led three generations
of American sociologists to neglect the historical record of blacks in America, stultified the explanation of Chinese immigration and settlement in
America, and produced an irremediable muddle in the most prominent
paradigm of American political sociology.[52]

Moving from its critique of the Aristotelian paradigm to its own constructive formulation we may note four basic postulates: fixity or persis-
tence; crisis and catastrophe; discontinuity and nonuniformity; and open-
ended or nonteleological change. Nisbet, in the most recent statement of

the neopositivist argument, has presented a discussion of these four basic elements of the approach.[53] With certain emendations and qualifications, we shall follow his line of explication.

To study social change, the neopositivists insist that research begin with at least the heuristic assumption that change is not always going on. The alternative, that of assuming a universal, permanent, and uniform rate of change, begs the very question that the study sets out to investigate – the causes or conditions of social change. Thus Hodgen makes no assumption about the trend of technological innovations in England before beginning her study; rather she lets the sited and dated distribution of the innovative happenings produce a pattern for which an account is then required. Teggart refuses to accept the widely held belief that overpopulation produced the Barbarian invasions; rather he carefully notes the temporal and geographical instances of these irruptions and looks to see if there is an antecedent element common to all cases. Thus, the actual pattern of social change emerges from the collection and array of specific historical findings, and the causal agency from the discovery of a recurrent antecedent event or class of events.

Crisis and catastrophe are held out as likely sources for the breakdown of the cake of custom and the continuity of habit. In calling attention to these two elements the neopositivists evoke the earlier work of W. I. Thomas[54] and anticipate some recent phenomenological ideas of Alfred Schutz.[55] Thomas had developed a nonevolutionary approach to the study of social change, emphasizing the relationship between habit, crisis, and attention. Societies persisted in habitual orientations until some crisis upset familiar modes of thought and encouraged innovative attention to the fore. Social changes occurred in such historical moments. In a more individualistic and psychological vein, Schutz emphasized the crisis in the *Lebenswelt* that occurs when habitual modes of action no longer prove efficacious or when familiar human abilities suddenly become inoperative. Such crises cause man to perceive the hitherto taken-for-granted but fundamental workings of social life, and, possibly, to discover new ways to persevere.

Standing at midpoint between the psychologistic sociology of Thomas and the phenomenological psychology of Schutz is the Jamesian cognitive phenomenology of Teggart. In Teggart's concept of release there is described the fundamental individual and collective force potential to the triggering of social change. "The hypothesis," Teggart observed, "may now be stated in the form that human advancement follows upon the mental release of the members of a group or of a single individual from the authority of an established system of ideas."[56] Release, Teggart supposed, occurred for the most part as a consequence of the first contacts and sub- sequent conflicts among culturally or socially distinctive peoples. Thus, he placed great emphasis upon the sociopsychological effects of forced migra- tion and intergroup collision, processes that, whatever calamities they might cause, accomplished "the release of the individual mind from the set forms in which it has been drilled," and gave the persons so liberated "op- portunity to build up a system for themselves anew."[57] Hodgen employed this concept to help account for the adoption of technological innovations among the English. Pointing to the basic conservatism of English villagers and their reluctance to embrace the new or different, she emphasized the disruptions of habitual modes of production created by the influx of for- eign settlers and the rare but significant willingness of certain villages to take up or initiate new ways.[58] The processes of release are the products of "intrusions," the *event* emphasized by Teggart's approach to the study of social change. However, whereas Teggart laid great emphasis on the function of migrations, invasions, wars, and involuntary movements of masses of peoples in creating such "intrusions," he also pointed to the role of new ideas as intruders on the habitual consciousness and thought pro- cesses of people, liberating them from older habits of mind and giving rise to social and cultural changes.[59] The energies of men, Teggart pointed out – borrowing the phrase from William James – are constrained by con- vention and habit. Excitements, startling ideas, contacts with new peoples constitute the crucial events in history since they disrupt convention, defeat habit, and deliver mankind from its sociocultural prison houses. Human advancement is achieved at the price of whatever social secur- ity resides in the old and settled ways, the customs, folkways, and mores of established social organization.

In attacking the evolutionists on their belief in continuity and uniformity the neopositivists strike a blow against one of the more sacred elements of Occidental thought. Social change is real but rare argue the neopositivists. It occurs where the social milieu will permit it, where habit has broken down, where custom no longer prevails. Hence the orderly development seen in evolutionist descriptions is unlikely. Hodgen shows that the bursts of technological innovation in England occurred only in certain places whereas in the other areas during the same period no change occurred.[60] Teggart's investigations of the Barbarian invasions show that they are intermittent in time and discrete in place.[61] Particular changes have par- ticular causes, argue Teggart and his followers, and, although a pattern of change is deducible from the occurrences in history, that pattern is likely to be one of discontinuities and nonuniformities. Max Weber's position on this question is quite close to that of Teggart. While observing that "a genuinely analytic study comparing the stages of development of the ancient *polis* with those of the medieval city would be welcome and productive," Weber urged that "such a comparative study would not aim at finding 'analogies' and 'parallels,' as is done by those engrossed in the currently fashionable enterprise of constructing general schemes of development. The aim should, rather, be precisely the opposite: to identify and define the individuality of each development, the characteristics which made the one conclude in a manner so different from that of the other." "This done," Weber concludes in a manner strikingly similar to that adopted later by Teggart in his study of *Rome and China,* "one can then determine the causes which led to these differences."[62]

According to the neopositivists there is no definite direction or trajectory of social change. Change is neither necessary nor irreversible. Neopositivist sociologists have cast considerable doubt on the findings of Aristotelian-inspired studies. To refute Park's assertion that the race relations cycle is both progressive and irreversible,[63] the neopositivists point to the actual evidence concerning the modes of adjustment and adaptation of America's various racial and ethnic groups. Furthermore, they expose and criticize the embarrassing explanations that Park's disciples employ to rescue his theory from disconfirmation.[64]

In explaining how an investigation of social change ought to be carried out, the neopositivists place their greatest emphasis on the collection, classification, and comparison of specific happenings. To the historian who insists on the singularity of each occurrence, the neopositivist emphasizes the nonunique elements that make for the possibilities of classes of occurrences.[65] To the sociologist who doubts the reliability and validity of documentary reports of happenings in earlier eras, the neopositivists emphasize the superior truth value of such documents over conjectural histories,[66] and they point to the absurdity of placing more trust in the social scientific instruments handled by hardly trained students than in the shrewd perceptions of such on-the-scene investigators as Hesiod, Machiavelli, or Voltaire.[67]

How historical occurrences are to be investigated requires further specification. Without using these precise terms Teggart distinguishes between "exogenous" and "endogenous" events with respect to any system of experience. The former are intrusions and, as such, more likely to upset habitual modes of activity and promote change:

The identification of "events" as "intrusions" is a matter of some importance. To

reach an understanding of "how things work" in the course of time, we may envisage the facts of experience as arranged in a series of concentric circles. Outer-
most, we would have the stellar universe; within this, the world of organic life;
within this, the world of human activities; within this, the local community; and
finally, within this, the individual.[68]

Each circle represents a realm of experience. But to Teggart, each ring
might produce happenings that have an effect on the next circle within
the concentric set. "In such a series," continues Teggart, "it is obvious
that change in any outer circle will affect all that lies within it." Interest
in establishing the study of social change on a sound scientific basis led
Teggart to define events in terms of his conceptualization of concentric
circles: "We may, then, define an 'event' as an intrusion, from any wider
circle, into any circle or condition which may be the object of present
interest."[69] Events then are defined in terms of their function for subsequent happenings in the next lower circle of experience.

Teggart's major investigation, that accounting for the invasions of the
Roman Empire between 58 B.C. and 107 A.D., gives a good example of
his conceptualization of the event as intrusion. The study focuses on intrusions from the fourth circle, that of human activities, on to the fifth, that
of the larger group or the nation. More specifically it explains the relationships between wars, interruptions in trade, and Barbarian invasions in
Europe. Teggart described his method as:

first, to recognize the existence of a class of events, and hence of a problem for
investigation; second, to examine the theories or explanations heretofore put forward to account for the occurrences; third; when these theories were found to be
at variance with the facts, to assemble all data which might be regarded as perti-
nent to the subject.[70]

Employing his method to provide a scientifically grounded explanation
for the Barbarian invasions of the Roman Empire, Teggart

set down, in chronological order, all known events, wars, disturbances in each
separate kingdom or region of the Eurasian continent for a period of five hundred
years. The next step was to compare occurrences in each of the many areas for
which it was possible to find evidence either in European or Asiatic sources.[71]

As a result of this comparison it was discovered that during one period of
a century and a half (58 B.C. - 107 A.D.)

every uprising on the European borders of the Roman Empire had been preceded
by the outbreak of war either on the eastern frontiers of the empire or in the 'Western Regions' of the Chinese. Moreover, the correspondence in events was discovered

to be so precise that, whereas wars in the Roman East were followed uniformly and always by disturbances on the lower Danube and the Rhine, wars in the eastern T'ien Shan were followed uniformly and always by disturbances on the Danube between Vienna and Budapest.[72]

The paired "uniformities" are credited by Teggart with being a "discovery, for the first time, of correlations in historical events," and furthermore with being a demonstration of "the existence of a type of order of historical facts which has not hitherto received attention." But correlation is not the ultimate aim of Teggart's investigation. He also wishes to find a single cause for this class of events. His causal account takes the form of "an hypothesis, and as such [it] is open to revision." As Teggart puts it, "Without further elaboration, I may say that as the outcome of this long and difficult phase of the investigation I reached the conclusion that the correspondence of wars in the East and invasions in the West had been due to interruptions of trade."[73] Thus, the collection, classification, and comparison of happenings results in the discovery of a *correlation*. The correlation, in turn, evokes interest in the suggestion and elaboration of a *causal* hypothesis. Presumably, although Teggart did not himself carry it out, the hypothesis itself could be tested, refined, and, if necessary, reformulated. It could also be rejected if the evidence did not sustain it.

Central to Teggart's general theory of social change is the claim that a class of occurrences locatable in one circle of human experience has the capacity to act as an intrusive event on another, more specifically, on a settled custom-bound population. In his study of the Barbarian invasions his argument proceeds as follows: The general covering argument is stated directly. "Now, wars at all times break in upon the established routine of orderly existence and interfere with the everyday activities of the peoples in conflict, and more especially they put a stop to usual forms of intercourse between the inhabitants of the opposing countries." This statement is itself unproven and rests upon its own implicit plausibility, its appeal to common sense, and the reader's own experience. Read another way it could be taken as an hypothesis that remains to be demonstrated by appropriate historical investigations. Whatever its scientific status, however, the statement circumscribes the specific train of facts arrayed by Teggart's formulation. "Hence, when China initiated war in Mongolia or against the kingdoms in the Tarim basin, and when Rome invaded Parthia or Armenia, the inception of hostilities automatically interrupted communications, however well established, across the border." The next logical step for Teggart is the application of his theory of intrusion and interruption to the explanation of the Barbarian uprisings.

It follows, therefore, that the problem of the relationship between wars in the Far or Near East and the barbarian uprisings in Europe calls for the identification of some usual activity of men which would be subject to immediate interruption in the event of war, and which also might be resumed promptly on the return of peace. The activity which at once suggests itself as complying with these requirements or conditions is that of trade or commerce.[74]

Why trade or commerce "at once" suggests itself as the kind of activity meeting theoretical requirements is not made clear. The general run of the argument would suggest a materialist theory of history standing behind this discussion, but no admission or elaboration of it is made. Rather, with the interruption of trade designated as a causal agency, it remains but to suggest that in the instant cases, those of China, Parthia, and Rome, wars interrupted commerce and the cessation of trade led in turn to hostilities all along the trade routes.

   Teggart is careful to add that the train of happenings set in motion by the wars was not part of the intentions of the emperors and statesmen who led their people into military affrays. "It is of some importance to note that the statesmen who were responsible for or advocated the resort to war, on each of forty occasions, were entirely unaware of the consequences which this policy entailed."[75] Teggart's study thus corresponds with an idea developed at some length by Robert K. Merton – that of the unanticipated consequences of purposeful action, also known to sociologists as the concept of latent function.[76] However, Teggart's intentions are quite different from those of Merton. Whereas, the latter sought to elaborate and extend the idea of function, Teggart's purposes are threefold: to issue a caveat about the relationship between the intentions of statesmen and their decisions; to suggest a specific role for the informed citizen of the modern *polis*; and, most significantly, to indicate the usefulness of scientific history for public affairs. Teggart neither accuses nor blames the leaders of China or Rome for the outbreaks occasioned by their decisions to go to war. Instead he credits them with judiciousness and wisdom. In the case of the Chinese, he points out that their wars "were initiated only after lengthy discussions at the imperial court by ministers who were well versed in Chinese history, and who reasoned from historical experience no less than from moral principles and from expediency." However, these Chinese statesmen did not know that their decisions would lead to conflicts and devastations in regions of which they had never heard, that is, in Europe. The Romans were equally statesmenlike, and, though not entirely ignorant of the fact that disturbances in the East were followed by irruptions in Europe, they failed to make the causal connection. "So Augustus persisted in his attempts to dominate Armenia, though the actual results on the Danube and the Rhine could have been unerringly predicted."[77]

Precisely because unanticipated consequences of purposive decisions can be predicted by persons informed by a scientific approach to history, Teggart proposes a role in public affairs for the private citizen educated in the method and findings of such a history. The Roman statesmen, according to Teggart, were typical of rulers in every age. Dependent on the state of knowledge available to their own generation, they were also too concerned with the immediate present. In times of crisis they could not take the time necessary for prolonged and painstaking investigation. The private citizen, on the other hand, freed from the cares and demands of immediate problems, is, as Teggart sees it, in a position to give aid to the future statesmen in precisely this neglected area. Although the objective of an applied science of history may appear unattainable at the present time, Teggart argues, hope for the future, for avoiding the misfortunes wreaked by well-intentioned but uninformed leaders, rests on the establishment of new forms of knowledge obtained from the record of human experiences. That record, history, has been manifested thus far in literary narratives and patriotic polemics. However, once liberated from these shibboleths, a truly scientific history could save mankind from repetition of its worst errors.

The possibilities for and benefits from a new type of scientific historical investigation have not yet been recognized.[78] According to Teggart, the nineteenth century produced histories that escalated the tensions among nationalities and peoples.[79] Literary and poetic usages of historical materials, he argues, are either irrelevant or pernicious.[80] But, a return to the original promise and hope elicited by the discovery of the scientific approach could reorganize history not only as a useful science but also as a guide to statecraft.[81] Once statesmen understand the relationships of causes to effects, of intended goals and unintended consequences, they might, Teggart seems to suggest, so arrange their affairs that most harmful effects would be avoided. Scientific history, Teggart offers, could become a boon to mankind.[82]

That neither the scientific nor beneficent possibilities of historical investigation had been realized caused Teggart to continue and indeed to intensify his plea for an end to retrogressive, unscientific, and moribund developmentalist approaches. At the time of his death in 1946 he had just completed a long and mournful essay on the argument of Hesiod's *Works and Days*,[83] In that essay he lamented the fact that the ancient poet's ode to even-handed justice as the basis for human progress had been replaced, first by Thucydides' thesis that cultural advancement would follow a determinate trajectory of growth, if nothing interfered, and later by Plato's argument that the good life would follow from an authoritarian state-enforced division of labor. Neither the scientific history that Teggart had labored for nearly four decades to establish nor the melioristic application of a grounded social science to human affairs had found widespread appreciation or legitimation during his own lifetime.

Teggart's legacy is manifold, but his dream of a scientific history aiding in both the advancement of knowledge and the elimination of "the war-compelling spirit of nationality" has not been realized.[84] The iconoclastic perspective that startled and dismayed his more conventional peers did inspire some daring and innovative approaches by younger scholars. Perhaps the two most important historians who took up aspects of Teggart's approach were Arnold J. Toynbee and Joseph Needham. According to Toynbee, "Professor F. J. Teggart, in his *Theory of History*, Chapter 14, showed me where to find the entry into my subject after I had been groping for it without succeeding in discovering it by my own native lights." Toynbee took three of Teggart's directives "to heart, and . . . followed them from beginning to end" in *A Study of History*. These directives, Toynbee observed, proved to be "a sovereign clue which . . . not only initiated me into my subject but also piloted me through it." The directives were first, that "in the study of Man . . . the first step must be a return to the Present"; second, that "the point of departure must necessarily be observation of the differences which particularize the condition of Humanity in different parts of the world"; and, third, that "the observation of the cultural differences which distinguish human groups leads at once to the recognition of the major problem of the Science of Man," namely "How are these differences to be accounted for?"; "How have the differences which we observe in the cultural activities of men come to be as we find them at the present time?"[85]

Teggart's impact on Toynbee was indeed of the greatest significance, for in *The Theory of History* Teggart had singled out for special notice Toynbee's earlier teleological orientation, criticizing its substitution of analogical reasoning for historical investigation. That Toynbee altered his approach fundamentally after reading Teggart may be instantly recognized if we recall the passage by the former that Teggart selected as typifying a mode of history that instituted "an analogy between the life cycle of the individual and the entire existence of humanity."

The germ of Western society, says Arnold Toynbee, first developed in the body of Greek society, like a child in the womb. The Roman Empire was the period of pregnancy during which the new life was sheltered and nurtured by the old. The "Dark Age" was the crisis of birth, in which the child broke away from its parent and emerged as a separate, though naked and helpless, individual. The Middle Ages were the period of childhood, in which the new creature, though immature, found itself able to live and grow independently. The fourteenth and fifteenth centuries, with their marked characteristics of transition, may stand for puberty, and the centuries since the year 1500 for our prime.[86]

Toynbee's subsequent adoption of a comparative historical approach in *A Study of History,* though not without its theological biases and religio-ethnic prejudices – especially its anti-Semitism[87] – has been hailed by Kenneth Bock because it "accepts the canons of scientific inquiry so disdainfully rejected by Spengler" and because it is "a tremendous effort . . . to bring large masses of empirical data to bear on explicitly formulated hypotheses." As Bock has observed, Toynbee made a breakthrough in historiography – the formulation of testable hypotheses and the raising of specific questions: "Toynbee," Bock points out, "can be refuted, rather than just maligned, by those who would go to the trouble."[88]

Although Joseph Needham's employment of Teggart's work seems to be confined to an examination of the war, migration, and invasion thesis presented in the latter's *Rome and China,* in fact the entire enterprise of his own mammoth research project is within the spirit of Teggart's proposed scientific historical orientation.[89] Needham begins with the statement of a problem and observes that the only way to solve that problem is to engage in a careful comparative history of the relevant cultures and civilizations guided by a specific hypothesis. As Needham states the question:

Why, then, did modern science, as opposed to ancient and medieval science (with all that modern science implied in terms of political dominance), develop only in the Western world? Nothing but a careful analysis, a veritable titration, of the cultures of East and West will eventually answer this question. Doubtless many factors of an intellectual or philosophical character played their part, but there were certainly also important social and economic causes which demand investigation.[90]

That Needham is directing his efforts toward a comparative analysis of sociocultural change, very much like that employed by Hodgen in her study *Change and History,* is indicated in his own use of the term "titration," borrowed from chemistry, to designate his methodological procedure:

We may say that titration is the determination of the quantity of a given chemical compound in a solution by observing that amount of a solution of another compound at known strength required to convert the first completely into a third, the

end-point being ascertained by a change of colour or other means . . . Now in my
work with my collaborators on the history of discovery and invention in Chinese
and other cultures we are always trying to fix dates - the first canal lock in China
in A.D. 984, the first irrigation contour canal in Assyria in 690 B.C., the first
transport contour canal in China in 219 B.C., the first eyeglasses or spectacles in
Italy in A.D. 1286, and so on. In such a way one can "titrate" the great civilizations
against one another, to find out and give credit where credit is due, and so also, it
seems, must one analyse the various constituents, social or intellectual, of the great
civilizations, to see why one combination could far excel in medieval times while
another could catch up later on and bring modern science itself into existence.[91]

Precisely because Needham presents his work in the form of a specific
problem, a formulated hypothesis, and an empirical investigation of all
the known and relevant facts, his thesis is subject to concrete criticism,
factual refutation, and hypothetical reconsideration. Like the work of
Toynbee, then, that of Needham can be treated according to the canons
of scientific evaluation, by either raising questions about the nature and
approach of the governing hypothesis or by reinvestigating the factual
materials.[92]

Hailed as "unquestionably the foremost writer in this country, if not in
the world, on the theoretical basis of the new history as a science of social
change,"[93] Teggart was nevertheless ignored by most of his peers and
colleagues, and except for the notable scholars just mentioned, his influence has been confined to his few students and to those historians and
sociologists who borrow portions of his outlook to serve their own intellectual purposes. Carl Becker supposes that, if persistently applied, Teggart's
approach would explain the "universal processes of historical change."[94]
But as Harry Elmer Barnes observes, "Of all the important writers on the
newer methods and attitudes in history, no other suffered more from the
discrepancy between his merits and his influence than Professor Teggart."
Barnes attributes Teggart's failure to influence large numbers of scholars
to "his preference to play a lone hand - denying the significance of what
most others have done and refusing to associate himself actively with those
who have succeeded in establishing the new history."[95] Leaving aside
whatever personality considerations are suggested in this explanation, it
is important to see the lacunae in Teggart's own use of resources. Most
notable is the neglect of the work of Max Weber, Georg Simmel, Emile
Durkheim, and other sociologists in the classical tradition. As Robert
Nisbet reports, "Under Teggart I studied essentially - Teggart! . . . I
never once heard him refer to Durkheim, Simmel, Weber, Tonnies, Cooley, Thomas, Mead, Tocqueville (Comte, Marx, Spencer, yes, but inevitably critically), or any of the other titans of the sociological tradition."[96]

Only a few efforts directed toward uniting the outlook of Teggart with that of Weber and other classical sociologists have been undertaken. Both Bock and Nisbet see Weber's work as falling within the scope of the general orientation proposed by Teggart and, especially, as standing apart from and opposed to the evolutionary tradition represented by Parsons.[97] The recent translations into English of Weber's *Roscher and Knies* and *The Agrarian Sociology of Ancient Civilizations* should reenforce their observations.[98] However, attempts to specify Teggart's relationship to the classical tradition in sociology have proved difficult. At one time Howard Becker argued that Teggart belonged together with that group of scholars – Shotwell, Robinson, Durkheim, and Tonnies – who identified the trend of social development as moving toward greater measures of accessibility, differentiation, integration, and secularization coupled with coordinate trends toward individuation, compartmentalization, and rationality.[99] Furthermore, Becker continued, Teggart's methodological approach was to be distinguished from that of Weber in that the latter insisted on "the methodological precision of culture case study and the ideal-typical method."[100] More recently Boskoff located Teggart within a rather large and disparate aggregate – Weber, MacIver, Mannheim, Sorokin, Redfield, Becker, Pareto, Gluckman, Merton, Toynbee, and Bateson – who, he claims, share an interest in peculiarly *social* theories of social change, ascribing "a critical role to the operation of normally dynamic aspects of social structure – such as systems of stratification, the power structure, institutional role configurations."[101] If Teggart played too much of "a lone hand," his admirers have submerged his original contribution too deeply in a sea of quite different classical and contemporary thinkers. Praised, preserved, and prescribed, Teggart's thought has become more monument than guide.

Among sociologists and anthropologists Teggart has had a small but selective impact. Perhaps most use has been made of his concept of "release," central to the cognitive sociology and sociocultural phenomenology of his theory of social change.[102] Robert E. Park, to take one prominent example, found much theoretical and conceptual value in Teggart's idea of culture, employed Teggart's perspective on the relationship between civilizational change and migration and conquest in his own analysis of race and culture contacts, and made a most fruitful usage of Teggart's idea of "release" to formulate the character of the marginal man. He did not, however, abandon the cyclical schema of his own perspective on race relations.[103] Becker and Barnes, who admired the "sociological orientation of the ablest historical methodologist in the United States, F. J. Teggart," utilized his theory of "release" to explain the passage from sacred to secular

modes of social organization,[104] and Becker did much to elaborate Teggart's original insight on the effects of migration on mental mobility,
personality development, and social change.[105] However, aside from these
pioneering efforts and the work of Hodgen already mentioned,[106] Teggart's
approach has been so woefully neglected that in 1957 McKinney felt it
necessary to point to the fact that "F. J. Teggart . . . made a major contribution to methodology which has been largely ignored by sociologists,"[107]
while a decade later Goldstein paused in his criticism of the revival of
ahistorical evolutionary and developmental theories in anthropology to
observe how "very much worth reading" Teggart's *Theory of History* remains for understanding "present-day developmentalism" such as that
found in Leslie White's *The Evolution of Culture.*[108]

In the three decades since Teggart's death, the debate over social change
and historical process has continued without any single viewpoint emerging
over all others. A proliferation of only slightly varying evolutionist, neoevolutionist, and functionalist approaches has been predominant,[109] but
there has also been a revival of diffusionist theories[110] and a growth in
awareness of difficulties in developmentalism. Moreover, Teggart's disciples have continued and enlarged his project. Hodgen has explored the
varieties of resistance to a scientific history in medieval and modern anthropological thought.[111] Bock has analyzed the "comparative method," traced
the Attic origins of developmentalism, called attention to those classical
sociologists who did not succumb to Aristotelian orientations, revealed the
connections of functionalism to evolutionism, reiterated the basic objections to the biological analogy, and continued the sociological study and
opposition to war and racism.[112] Nisbet has continued the criticism of neoevolutionism by pointing to its effects on functionalist theories of change
and its revival in the work of Talcott Parsons, insisted on Teggart's idea
that history is plural, showed that sociology as an art form would abhor
development of a systems approach, explored the attitude toward history
in the writings of Emile Durkheim, analyzed both the French and American revolutions as intrusions, and attested to the significance of Frederick
Teggart in the establishment of humane letters and social science at the
University of California.[113] The challenge to social theory presented by
Teggart, Hodgen, and Bock has recently been taken up by an erstwhile
Marxist, Ronald L. Meek. Seeking to rescue Turgot[114] and the Scottish
Moralists from charges of ahistoricism, Meek has revived interest in the
thesis that economic and social development has proceeded through four
stages of subsistence – hunting, pasturage, agriculture, and commerce –
and urged that the developmentalist ideas in the works of Adam Smith and

Lord Kames are not entirely bereft of historical evidence.[115] Two other recent Marxist writers seem to have taken very seriously the climate of opinion opposed to evolutionary theory. Seeking to revitalize the idea that the passage of legal ideology and institutions moved from a *Gemeinschaft* to a *Gesellschaft* form, Eugene Kamenka and Alice Erh-Soon Tay reject a "simple, straightforward evolutionary schema," recognize "that *Gemeinschaft, Gesellschaft* and bureaucratic-administrative strains will coexist in all, or at least most, societies," and suggest that "social relations, even in allegedly 'primitive' societies, are complex" and will display at least incipient representations of all characteristics at each stage of social development.[116] Although still adhering to a stage theory of social change, these writers seem nevertheless to have acknowledged much of the message that Teggart sought to deliver. Yet, Richard Beardsley's remarks presented on the recent death of Leslie A. White – the single most important contemporary advocate of the revival of evolutionism – signify how little of Teggart's thought has affected anthropology and related disciplines: "No scholar today is regarded as rash . . . for asserting that human institutions persist and change for systemic reasons rooted in culture; or for formulating ideas or schemes that assert general evolutionary sequences of institutions."[117]

Dilemmas of the neopositivist approach

Although it would be appropriate recognition of an all-too-neglected perspective in social science to halt functionalist investigations, reign in the neoevolutionist revival, and resuscitate the original project enunciated by Teggart and his followers, certain unresolved difficulties require a more critical stance. Most important is a further critique of the concept of "event." Common to all adherents of the neopositivist school is the argument that a properly conducted scientific study of social change requires the comparative analysis of *happenings* and the discovery of a prior intrusive *event* or *class of events* that may be designated as the causal agency. The principal problem of this position, a problem that none of the adherents of neopositivism has addressed directly, is the unanalyzed assumption that both "happenings" and "events" are unambiguously available and clearly identifiable to the researcher. Once the key terms "happenings" and "events" are scrutinized, we discover problematic elements in their recognition as such and a host of difficulties in their usage for comparative historical inquiry.

Central for identifying an "event" or a "happening" is the task of establishing temporal and spatial boundaries. Teggart, of course, recognizes this issue and insists on the classification of occurrences designated specifically in terms of their location in time and space.[118] But this begs the question. What are the peripheries of space and the termini in time that gird happenings? Who establishes these boundaries? Is the establishment of boundaries uniform over time and space so that comparison of like phenomena is possible? Conventional comparative historians have usually treated "happenings" and "events" as if they were uniform in spatiotemporal type and equally available to anyone who cared to take cognizance of the historical record. The historical record, however, like history itself, is a human activity. Hence, as a record, it is subject to the very queries of temporality and parameter, the modifications of crime and custom, the vicissitudes of idiosyncrasy and persecution that are aspects of history itself.

The problem of establishing the spatiotemporal boundaries of "happenings" has been noticed in one of the criticisms of Teggart's study of the Barbarian invasions. C. Martin Wilbur observed, concerning Teggart's claim to have identified no less than forty-nine major disturbances:

> He presents pertinent facts in great detail but fails to indicate clearly which, among the welter of invasions, uprisings, punitive operations, and defensive measures in Europe, were separate occurrences. It is almost impossible to isolate the thirty-one disturbances there and the eighteen in the Roman East theoretically resulting from previous wars in the Near and Far East respectively.[119]

Pitirim Sorokin, in another review of *Rome and China*, goes even further in this line of criticism, suggesting that the temporal boundaries of these supposedly discrete happenings may have been rendered more distinct by Teggart's method than the facts of the case actually warrant:

> Though Professor Teggart claims again and again that the events on the Rumanian Danube, the Rhine, and in the West regularly (he says even "invariably") followed the disturbances in the Chinese West and the Roman East, such uniformity of a temporal sequence is not proved by him. As the beginning and end of each war or uprising is unknown, for this reason only it is hardly possible to contend that the uprisings on the Danube and the Rhine regularly lagged behind the wars or uprisings in the East. As many of these movements went on sporadically in various parts of the Roman Empire, without any clear-cut caesura between them, no convincing evidence is given to support the claim of the uniform sequence . . . This means that there is no possibility to claim which disturbances, those of the Far East or those of the West, led and which lagged in time.[120]

Space and time are indeed the boundaries of "happenings" and the contexts of "events." But to claim that either space or time have fixed and invariable parameters that are universally known, forever beyond custom and culture, and immutable over time or even within the same time period is to accept assumptions about these basic elements that are grounded neither in experience nor experiment.[121] Once we grant that even the members of a given society might disagree over the onset or terminus of anything and the exact length and breadth over which it occurs, we admit ourselves to the world of frame analysis.[122] In such a world the organization of experience is perceived by the social scientist as a problematic feature for those who are experiencing it. Structures of consciousness become important – indeed fundamental – to the understanding of just what is going on, where, and when.

If "happenings" are rendered problematical by the mysteries and variations of time and space, "events" – in the special sense that Teggart used this term – raise even greater questions. Ironically, Teggart's formal and methodical usage of the term – elements in a set of concentric circles representing realms of experience that intrude from one outer circle on to an inner one – suggests a sociocultural system not entirely dissimilar from that "action system" developed by the "Social Relations" School at Harvard University years later.[123] Boundaries are imposed by such a system or more accurately by the system makers, but they exist at the expense of the meanings and relationships that actually prevail among the members of a given society. The imposition of a system a priori would seem to divorce the subject matter of a historical sociology from its substance, giving it a chimerical, conjectural, and literary quality quite independent from its actual context. Teggart's original aim was to liberate social science from this quality.

There is a further logical problem presented by Teggart's concept of "event" that is best exhibited in the sole attempt (to my knowledge) to give methodological precision to the term. In a recent essay Pachter has defined "an event E as *the juncture between two situations S′ and S″*, separating as well as linking them together, and in the process defining both."[124] More prosaically, Pachter tells us that an event has a function, namely, "that the world was never the same afterward." As examples of events Pachter mentions the Battle of Waterloo, the "Battle of Britain" (the intermittent series of air engagements over Britain for ten months of 1940–1) and, from World War I, Ludendorff's "blind assault all along the Allied lines for over a year." Events are those collections of happenings that, treated as a unit, can be seen to change the course of history. Pachter further allows for "chance" events and for the treatment of the failure of any change to occur when one might be expected.[125]

However, the event, E, is a social or personal construction of the historian, as is the original situation, S′, and the subsequent situation, S″. History, even when it employs the symbols of science [e.g., E, S′, S″, and such formulae, suggested by Pachter, as S_a^n S′ (E) S″] would appear to be a human rendering of raw reality. It is, thus, *interpretive* and must be. But what are the criteria of that interpretation to be? Shall sociologists accept the historian's prior claims on the ordering of what is "out there," or shall we ponder more empathically over the condition of Fabrizio, in Stendhal's *La Chartreuse de Parme* (an example suggested by Pachter!) when he finds himself a witness to a welter of happenings – hussars galloping past, peasants in flight, burning homes, guns firing all around – and only later discovers that what he had experienced as a violent chaos now has a name – the Battle of Waterloo. Pachter's "scientific" approach to history leads us back to a fundamental question – whose history, those who live it, or those who interpret it?

The neopositivist position holds that explanations in history can take the form of causal "laws." One set of happenings is interpreted or accounted for as having occurred because of an event or set of events. Not only does this raise the question of what an event actually is, but also of what the causal relationship is composed. Neopositivists would appear to be content to rest their claim on the argument that a cause is a recurrent juxtaposition of similar events and happenings, thus admitting Hume's well-known objections without abandoning the search for the uniform sequences he described.

However, most sociologists appear unsatisfied to discover and report statistical correlations. They want also to understand and explain them. Teggart not only claimed to discover a historical correlation, but also presented a hypothesized causal explanation. He did not, however, demonstrate that his causal hypothesis had validity beyond the immediate case he had investigated, and, indeed, in that case, it rests on its plausibility alone and the willingness of the readers – not all of whom acquiesced[126] – to suspend disbelief in the assumptions grounding it. It would appear that much of the brilliance of neopositivist social science rests not on its mastery of techniques to render raw reality into statistical arrays and formulated findings, but rather on the ingenious arguments that appear *ad hoc* to give *meaning* to these formulations. Perhaps the classic example is that of Durkheim's *Suicide,* which, as Jack Douglas has shown, smuggles in both a latent phenomenology and a familiar narrative and story line to bolster and indeed provide social substance to its scientific value as explanation.[127]

In general, the connection that sociologists employ to stitch together two sets of happenings, or by which they connect an event, E, to an earlier situation, S', and a later one, S", is said to be both *logical* and *meaningful*. However, there are problems with each of these aspects of the connection. The logic employed by most social scientists is the formal logic associated with the original work of Aristotle. Over against this logic are the numerous logics-in-use employed by the historical actors on the scene. The rules of understanding that apply in the former situation may not apply at all at the actual scene of social action and among the social actors who actually produce the happening that the scientist seeks to explain.

The problem of establishing both causal and intelligible explanations in a science of history was addressed most forcefully by Max Weber. Defining sociology as "a science which attempts the interpretive understanding of social action in order thereby to arrive at a causal explanation of its course and effects,"[128] Weber objected to those social scientific approaches – such as that of Wilhelm Roscher – that sought to establish general laws. "The logical ideal of such a science would be a system of *formulae* of absolutely general validity." Composed of statements constituting "an abstract representation of the features common to all historical events," Weber observed that such a system would never permit historical reality to be deduced from it. "Causal 'explanation,'" Weber concluded, "would simply amount to the formation of increasingly *general* relational concepts which would have the purpose of reducing, insofar as possible, all cultural phenomena to purely quantitative categories of some sort."[129] Whether these categories contribute to the intelligibility of history would be formally irrelevant to this kind of science, thus robbing the social sciences of their cultural and humanistic content.

A sociologist who takes Weber seriously must recognize that his own task has not even begun when he collects sets of happenings and finds correlations among them. The sociologist must also ascertain the subjective state of mind and discover the meanings that can be imputed to the intentional actor. Interpretation (*Deuten*) is aimed at the uncovering of meaning (*Sinn*), and meaning in turn refers to the contents of the subjective state of mind or to the symbol systems in use in the minds of the actors.

When faced with asserting a logico-meaningful linkage, a neopositivist all too easily succumbs to the unstated and uncriticized assumption that a common vocabulary of motives obtains among the social or historical actors under study, the social scientist doing the investigation, and the body of scholars and peers who make up the readership of his monograph. Of course there has been much reflection by critical philosophers of history on the subject of empathic understanding, meaning and its social construction, and interpretive procedures in historical scholarship. (Perhaps most important is the attempt by Wilhelm Dilthey to demonstrate that historical understanding can never exceed the empathic imagination of the historian.)[130] Yet, when neopositivist social scientists employ a logico-meaningful explanation, they rarely account for the apparent contradiction between the causal mode of historical understanding stressing interpretive understanding (*verstehen*) and that causal mode based on the correlated relationship among happenings.

The phrase logico-meaningful thus would appear to arise as a compound of Aristotelian systems of logic and Diltheyan hermeneutics. Seeking to combine these two into a single philosophical perspective, neopositivists have glossed over the contradictions and problematics in each and failed to indicate how such a union can be established. Gadamer has recently argued that Dilthey himself failed to resolve all the difficulties of such a position and believes that it awaits the application of Heidegger's and post-Heideggerian historical thought for a solution.[131]

Alternatives to neopositivism

In current sociological thought there are a number of approaches and perspectives that grapple with one or another of the problems raised by the debate between the evolutionary functionalists and the neopositivists. Although each of these orientations attempts to resolve at least some of the difficulties, to take a tentative position, and to proceed with the business of basic sociological research, none has found a fully satisfying resolution to all of the problems raised. Among the several innovative suggestions in sociology, we shall deal with three: neofunctionalism, the "mythic" approach, and certain "phenomenological" orientations to history. Finally, we shall suggest that a "phenomenological" approach offers an embracement of all the schools we have considered.

Neofunctionalism
Neofunctionalism here refers to a functionalist orientation that proceeds with a reflexive awareness of the problematics of its own methodological foundations. On perhaps less firm ground but yet from a more sophisticated basis, neofunctionalism introduces a number of qualifications and

reservations to theorizing and research. First, the a priori positing of a given nature to any social system is no longer admissible. Instead, neofunctionalism rejects the closed and determinate systemics of Parsons in favor of the open systems approach associated most prominently with von Bertalanffy and his followers.[132] Second, over against the formal and one-sided functionalism of Parsons, neofunctionalism reverts to that of Evans-Pritchard or Radcliffe-Brown, functionalists who attempted to make themselves analogs of the system that they studied.[133] Finally, neofunctionalism proposes what might be called a "soft" interdependence; rather than assuming the interdependence of parts a priori, neofunctionalism seeks to discover the actual interdependencies-in-use among societal members. Thus, the determinacy of the system is, in the spirit of Ernest Gellner's discussion of functionalism, a feature of the actors' own constructions of consensus and order.[134]

In an earlier section of this essay we spoke of the two sides of evolutionary functionalist thought. As an answer to the question of social order the functionalist posits a condition of homeostasis; as an answer to the question of social change, the evolutionist posits dynamic equilibrium within the systems and slow, orderly, continuous, and teleological changes among systems and over long periods of time. Neofunctionalists certainly speak of social change or evolution, but unlike their predecessors, they now must do so with the realization that they are engaged in a conjectural history. Their schema may be presented as a form of classification for data that otherwise would be too complicated to form into a coherent unit. This classification system, although uni- or multi-linear and evolutionary in nature, is neither accurate with respect to the dynamics of open systems nor strictly historical in its depiction of sequences. It is not causal, pre-dictive, or a chronicle of what actually happened. It is a heuristic device for ordering data. The justification for the kind of neofunctionalism is an aesthetic one – that of symmetry.

There remains the question of defining a happening. Neofunctionalists have not proposed an answer to this question directly, but a suggestion for a definition may be extracted from the writings of Erving Goffman. Although Goffman has never addressed himself directly to the problems of history, comparative analysis, or social change, it is nevertheless possible to use portions of his approach as a point of departure for our problem.[135]

In his analysis of games, Goffman raises the question, what is a game? Employing chess as an example, Goffman observes that although a vase of flowers might be placed next to the chess board, it has no place whatsoever in the attempt of the players to gain checkmate. That is, we know the

happenings in chess by resort to the *rules of irrelevance,* those understandings that distinguish among the items in the environment according to
their usage for a particular activity. A happening is known to us, Goffman
seems to be saying, by the process of separating that which does not count
in the particular activity in which the happening is embedded.[136]

However, the activity in which the happening occurs is part of an engagement of happenings, the sum total of which may form an event. If
the rules of irrelevance constitute a jurisdictional boundary around the
activity then it follows that the *rules of relevance,* the "juridical" code-
in-use within the activity, describe its positive composition and web of
relationships. Only by ascertaining both "juridical" and "jurisdictional"
codes does the sociologist complete his embracement of the activity, en-
capsulate the event, and contextually establish the affiliated network of
happenings.

Although Goffman's approach and our own extension and application
of it suggest a possible resolution of the problem of defining happenings
and events, it is self-consciously located in cultural and subcultural specificity. Happenings and events established by this procedure are inextric-
ably connected to the time, place, environment, and belief systems of
which they are an expression. Given their embeddedness, the sociologist
interested in comparative analysis and cross-cultural or intercivilizational
research is confronted with the question of whether he is dealing with
comparable units. The greater the contextual knowledge of happenings
and events, the lesser the items under study appear to be similar.

Of course the question we are raising with regard to Goffman's approach is not unique to it. The same difficulties apply to any contextual
model employed, whether it is organic, mechanical, dramaturgic, or
gamelike. Every model that requires a specification of the nature of that
which it represents establishes a unique configuration and a particularity
of boundaries.

Before we accept the narrative historian's conclusion that the enterprise
proposed by the neopositivists is impossible, however, it might be well to
reconsider what it is we are seeking to compare. Rather than comparing
happenings or events, perhaps the proper comparative historical task is to
look for the *underlying rules* that permit the embeddedness of happenings
and events in contexts. Such an enterprise would seek to understand the
codes that permit, shape, and encourage the social constructions of reality.
Examining the rules of relevance and irrelevance in the several societies,
cultures, and civilizations might lead to generalizations about the fundamental basis of human affiliation.

One recent school of thought that bids fair to accept this challenge is ethnomethodology.[137] Although not addressed to historical sociology and never interesting itself directly in any of the problems posed by that sub-discipline, it nevertheless has something to say about the discovery of the rules lying below contextually embedded conduct. Ethnomethodology burrows behind the accepted facticity of positivist sociology in an attempt to describe precisely how social reality becomes an accomplishment of the actors on the scene. Its developments thus far point toward a full-scale analysis of the common sense understandings that undergird both social reality and social science. Its own emphasis on the reflexivity and indexicality of all social expressions, however, would seem to threaten rather than rethread the social scientific project proposed by the neopositivists.

The "mythic" alternative

To be properly understood within the context of the present discussion, the "mythic" approach to historical sociology must be considered in its relation to the original project of Teggart and his followers, especially as it has been developed in the works of Bock and Nisbet. Both Bock and Nisbet have been interested in establishing a firm grounding for the socio-logical study of *social change*. A presumption of their position – one so basic it was never subjected to critical attention – is that social change has occurred and is still occurring. Although the presumption of social change as an on-going process has rarely been challenged by sociologists, it is a worthy subject for critical philosophical investigation. Implicit in the work of the French structuralist anthropologist, Claude Lévi-Strauss, and dra-matically realized in the writings of Kenneth Burke, is an approach that challenges the presumption of social change and that offers an alternative to the study of society and process.

In their own discussions of a theory of social change Teggart, Hodgen, Bock, and Nisbet object to the evolutionary functionalists' assumption that the forces of social change are *always* at work. In contrast, the neoposi-tivists assert that whether, to what extent, at what rate, and with what effect social change is going on are empirical questions that ought to be investigated without the adumbration of any question-begging assump-tions. However, the neopositivists do not consider the possibility that social change has never occurred, that the subject has no locus or objectification in the sociohistorical world. That there can never be anything new under the sun is an hypothesis not entertained by neopositivist sociologists.

The conception of a static world in which social change only appears to go on may seem strange, but it can be derived from the writings of the

French structuralist Lévi-Strauss's approach to the significance of myth for the study of social structures and from Kenneth Burke's analysis of attitudes toward history.

In the structuralist approach of Lévi-Strauss there is a vision of a formal ahistorical position.[138] According to Lévi-Strauss the properties of mind are everywhere and in every time the same: The mind works through the analysis of forms. Forms, furthermore, are always of the same structure, consisting in the creation of paired and balanced opposites. These opposites are built up in various algebraic ways becoming complex structures, which are, of course, capable of decomposition into their fundamental components through structural analysis. In social life, where interaction between persons is basic, there are three basic structures produced: kinship, which structural analysis reformulates as the exchange of women; economy, the exchange of goods and services; and language, the basis of exchange itself.

Lévi-Strauss seems to suggest a role for myth in the construction and the analysis of social history phenomena. Action – in history and in the present and future – occurs as the working out in many diverse ways of a few fundamental myths. The myths in turn are *forms* that can be exposed in their ultimate composition by the same kind of structural analysis that is employed to uncover mental phenomena. Myths, as the *forms* of reality, are understood to be transcendent and permanent, existing above, beyond, and apart (analytically speaking) from the transitory appearances of entities and transformations experienced in history and everyday life. Moreover, all intellectual efforts to find the absolute or fundamental grounding of ontic reality are themselves products of mythological formulations. In Lévi-Strauss's view, Freud's analysis of the Oedipus myth must be treated precisely in the same manner as that of Sophocles. The myth forms are the ultimate reality. The method and approach are Platonic.[139] Like Husserl's presuppositionless philosophy or Chomsky's deep structures of prelinguistic mentation, Lévi-Strauss's formal anthropology of mind and myth seeks to decode or translate its claimed fundamental entity – mind or myth – by looking "behind" the happenings of history and everyday life.

The mythic approach holds, in effect, that there is no history, or rather no history to which the social scientist need attend. Rather, history gives the appearance of change, whereas the ultimate scientific reality is the severality of forms that are behind, beneath, or beyond that appearance. The mythic approach would seem to hold that there is a finite body of ultimate myths that describe the basis for all possible human activities.

What historians record are the epiphenomena of these myths. The social scientist must burrow beneath these epiphenomena to find the basic form. Thus, although historical data are epiphenomena they are also representative or indexical, referring back to the basic mythic text of which they are a particular expression. The project for Lévi-Strauss's approach to social science, then, is the uncovering of the basic myths. Presumably, once they have all been discovered and decoded, all human activity – past, present, and future – will be available to us as extrapolations and variations on these pristine and primary forms.

The mythic approach, however, does not presume to possess any epistemic superiority to its own subject matter. The truths of science are not arrayed against the myths of history; rather, science is itself an expression of myth. Structuralism thus belongs self-consciously to that perspective known as symbolic realism, that is, the myth structures are not taken to stand for some reality that can be objectively known, but, instead, they are taken to be the only reality that we can know. To analyze or explain history in terms of structural analysis, then, is to restate the expression of one discipline in the vocabulary of another, to translate the "epiphenomena" of happenings into the semiotic of a new comparative literature.

The methodological underpinnings of structuralism suggest that it is both a literary approach (and thus another variant on that approach to history that Teggart had originally opposed) and also that it employs a functionalist orientation. Lévi-Strauss borrows the dialectical idea from Hegel and Marx to insist that every myth is a complex structure of paired opposites poised in a state of dramatic tension. The form thus embodies both the homeostatic principle of dynamic equilibrium and the eufunctional thesis about the role of immanent conflict in systemic social formations. Finally and not coincidentally, it might be suggested that the work of Talcott Parsons, reconceived as a formulated mythic structure, fits more closely into the project of Lévi-Strauss than either scholar realizes.

Yet another formalistic, mythic approach derives from the work of Kenneth Burke.[140] Just as Plato's *Republic* is a philosophico-political utopia presented as a dramatic dialog, so Burke suggests that our understanding of history seems to be a recounting of basic dramatic plots. Some of these dramas tell of the return of the prodigal son, the death of the king, sibling rivalry, and so on, but are applied to groups, societies, and nations that are anthropomorphized as persons. Ironically, the study of history as dramatic mode bids fair to become what Plato opposed – a kind of "cookery." Actual histories are the products of "recipes" – combinations, recombinations, remakes, and warmed over scraps of the same basic plots. The dramatistic approach that derives from Burke holds up "cookery" as a process-in-use by both historical actors, historians, and historiographers. As a form of structuralism, however, it suggests a comparative structure of basic plots and an ultimate reduction of all histories to a repertory of scenarios that are enacted and reenacted throughout the ages. (It is not the case, however, that a dramatistic sociology must necessarily avoid matters of history. In a recent study in which they amplify and urge adoption of a dramatistic perspective for sociology, Lyman and Scott have carried out case studies of resistance to Negro slavery and of nineteenth-century social banditry in the American West.[141] Their effort shows that a serious comparative historical sociology can employ an approach that Teggart feared might be too literary and still pay close attention to all the relevant facts.)

The formal approach – Lyman and Scott excepted – resolves the problem of historiography by rejecting history. There are no histories that we must accept. Instead, the welter of happenings, the profusion of events, and the worlds of life are perceived as representations, metaphors, and variations of basic dramas or myths. Once the fundamental structure of these basic scenarios is decoded, the secret of all histories is revealed and neither past, present, nor future can withhold its mystery from the researcher.

A "phenomenological" alternative

Phenomenology has only recently been rediscovered with respect to its potential contribution to sociology and the historical sciences. Although its definition and scope are imprecise and much controversy ranges around the term, we shall employ it in a special way to refer to an approach that sees histories as structures of consciousness. At any moment in time these histories have varying degrees of popularity, political sway, and public support.

According to this phenomenological approach, there are two kinds of history.[142] The first kind is found in the schools, official archives, regal courts, or tribal councils. It prevails in those societies in which there is a sense of the relevance of the past and some kind of bureaucracy through which the accepted version of the past is transmitted from generation to generation. The agency of transmission may take the form of repeated and memorized folk tales, history courses in schools, sacred archival ceremonials, or some other mode that ensures intergenerational continuity and uniformity. Such history enjoys the support of the authoritative elements, is endowed with the claim of superior truth, and stands above refutation and revocation by dint of its embeddedness within the fundamental values and beliefs of the society. It is *legitimated* history.

There is, however, a second type of history. It is unofficial and exists only in the consciousness of people, although in what number, to what extent, and with what variations we can rarely know. It prevails in both societies that have no officially enforced sense of the past, and in those where the legitimated history is unsatisfactory for the popular purposes for which the unofficial history is employed. Unofficial history finds expression in proverbs, legends and folk tales, hidden and secret stories of the past, uncovered but inauthenticated truths, and popular but unproven hypotheses about the relationship between past and present. In brief, *nonlegitimate* history consists in whatever notions, elements, data, or dimensions of the past ordinary individuals and nonelites bring to bear on their everyday understanding of the present.

No difference between these two types of history resides in them of themselves. In fact one type might become the other as the vicissitudes of power and authority shift the fortunes of those who hold to one or another view of the past. Official history is that brand that has won acceptance and is backed by authoritative force. Unofficial history, although it has not obtained political recognition and the stamp of public approval, nevertheless operates as a form of populist and folk wisdom among unknown numbers of the population. As nostalgia, fables, anecdotes, traditions, apocryphal stories, fairy tales, suppressed genealogies, ethnic legends, and the like, this unofficial history is typically supposed to reside in the imaginations of children, primitives, the uneducated, unacculturated immigrants, and unsocialized persons in general. Indeed, its delegitimation in the face of official history consists precisely in the argument that it is magical, superstitious, childish, naïve, primitive, or not properly documented.

The two types of history are both the same and yet different. They are the same in the sense that both are forms of contemporary consciousness about the past. More clearly stated, this phenomenological approach regards history as constituted neither of event or deeds in the past, nor of happenings as expressions of consciousness in the past. Rather, in this approach history is both *conscious* and *contemporary*. In the phenomenological view both official and unofficial histories are expressions of contemporary consciousness. However, official and unofficial history differ from one another in two principal ways. First, official history characteristically has an inner logic and is articulated with a precise and formal cogency. It also has a greater chance for permanence because it tends to be transmitted via the printed page, conveyed in official media, or carved in stone. In contrast unofficial history is characteristically malleable because its expression has not been rationalized and justified in the terms and canons of formal logic and routinized according to approved methodologies. The formal properties of official history – its logic, permanence, and uniformity – lend to it the potential of becoming a state supported ideology, formally organizing seemingly separate realms of data as a basis for mobilizing collective action. It was precisely this potential for becoming ideology in the several national histories that had alarmed Teggart and led him to search for a scientific basis and a truly objective history.

Official history is buttressed by political and economic power, and in modern societies it is institutionalized in bureaucracies. In contrast, unofficial history finds its domain at the interstices of social life, in the little places, corners, crevices, and private arenas where official history either fears to tread or has no right of entry. Unofficial history is a part of the idiosyncratic domain of private life, sustained by personal as opposed to public relations, emotional as opposed to affectively neutral sustenance, and private and folkish rather than literate and correct language. Thus, despite the power that official history may lend to its own version of the past, unofficial history retains a compelling and potentially subversive potency.

Whether official and unofficial history have a patterned relationship is a worthy topic for speculation. It might be the case that the greater the arenas of discourse that are governed by official history, the lesser and more constricted are the arenas of operation for unofficial history, and vice versa. Furthermore, we might speculate that, insofar as unofficial history satisfies a desire for affective sensibility that is not provided by official history, the greater the spread and development of official history, the greater also will be the sense of emotional loss, of deadening ennui, of overrationalized understanding. In such a situation, individuals and groups may redouble their efforts to find release from the iron cage of rationalized official history by resort to ever more fabulous and exotic versions of unofficial history. In a dialectical fashion, then, it may be hypothesized that the very success of the spread of official history means that it will eventually fail, as the forces of unofficial history rise in revolt against their sense of affective deprivation and emotional loss. And, to turn the dialectical screw once more, should unofficial history achieve public dominion, it too will fail, in that it becomes official and loses its subterranean emotive quality.

Although our discussion would seem to suggest that official and unofficial history form a dyadic pair, self-contained in a dialectical structure, in fact the situation is even more complex. Elites vying with one another will have competing versions of official history and aspiring nonelites will cherish and proclaim their versions of the past as well. Indeed, what Herbert Blumer has suggested as the situation in which race prejudice emerges – competing elites struggling for domination in a context of ambiguous and recent race contact[143] – is in fact the general condition for the formation of an official history. Beyond existing elites and up-and-coming near-elites are individuals, groups, and masses of people who, without political aspirations, nevertheless have conceptions of pasts that they can put into use in their everyday lives. Moreover, precisely because it is unofficial – because it tends to pass from person to person by word of mouth, because it is communicated anecdotally or as a brief but definite commentary on the situations in which people find themselves – unofficial history will be much more multifarious and multiform than official history. There will be more unofficial histories than there are official ones.

Although unofficial history is treated as primitive, childish, and magical, its own statements often take the form of lawlike pronouncements. Proverbs are good examples. As aspects of a folk knowledge employed in everyday life, proverbs rest upon the assumption that their truth value is rooted in the accumulated wisdom of the ages. Unlike statements of cause and correlation that arise from the researches of Teggart and Hodgen, proverbial wisdom is not subjected to careful empirical tests. Moreover, in the proverbs, there would appear to be a folk analog to Adam Brateson's principle concerning contradictory laws about the same phenomena – for example, the wave-particle theories of light. In juxtaposing proverbs such as "look before you leap" and "he who hesitates is lost," there is presented the well-known problem that requires a specification of just which conditions must prevail for one or the other prescription to be correct.

The fact that proverbs are not subject to carefully controlled empirical tests makes them more rather than less like official history. For both official history and proverbs are usually pronounced and proclaimed. In the case of folk history a lack of any formal testing procedure derives from the very nonpositivist conditions of its own development, that is, from a lack of formal cogency from which some indication of a test might be derived. In addition there is the "economic" problem of a paucity of resources for mobilizing the necessaries for experiment. Official history, by contrast, need not be subjected to continued empirical verification when it is supported by powerful elites in governmental and educational circles. Such ruling groups may command the resources to make empirical tests possible, but at the same time, out of consideration for the role that official history plays in legitimating their regime, refuse to allocate these resources for that purpose.

Both official and unofficial histories are sediments within structures of consciousness, differing only in terms of their socially constructed and politically supported legitimacy and their institutionalization. From the perspective of a "pure" phenomenology there is no distinction between the two types of history.

A special word must be said about scientific historiography. The history of historiography makes it clear that the modern version of "scientific" historiography had been considered subversive in other times. It too had to struggle for its current place among the officially recognized modes of historical methods. However, at all times, during its nonlegitimate and its legitimate periods, scientific historiography resided in the consciousness of a number of individuals. An investigation of the nature of scientific historiography must examine the structure, contents, and rules of relevance peculiar to this particular form of historical discourse.

Conclusion

The final discussion of the phenomenological approach offers an embracement of all the schools thus far examined. By recognizing that histories and historiographies can be neither more nor less than structures of consciousness with varying degrees of support and popularity, a "phenomenological" approach vitiates the claims for paradigmatic domination of all contending schools at the same time that it recognizes the likelihood of one or another school to achieve domination. Our position bears close resemblance to that of Simmel.[144] As the German philosopher sociologist saw it, histories were contents of realized experience expressed in selected established forms. As such they could not re-present happenings as they actually occurred; instead they could order achieved experience according to interests. The elaboration of these interests are many and varied and the forms of history select their contents accordingly.

Although offering no version of history or method of historiography as its own, the "phenomenological" approach puts each perspective in its respective place. At the same time it offers a truly sociological approach to the study of social change. The study of social change according to a phenomenological perspective becomes a study of present-day structures of consciousness of the past that are brought to bear upon the present or upon some postulated future. According to this view there is only a succession of "presents" and of prevailing notions of the past in relation to them. The particular schools of sociohistorical thought – such as the neopositivist school of Teggart, Hodgen, Bock, and Nisbet – become themselves topics of sociological investigation rather than resources for that investigation.

And what of social change itself? At this juncture in the argument we are in a position similar to that of Nicklaus in the epilogue of Offenbach's opera *Tales of Hoffman*. Like Nicklaus we now perceive that all our tales (historiographies) are a part of one larger tale. Evolutionary functionalist historiography indeed tells us stories, but these conjectural histories can no longer claim that they are accounts of what actually happened; mythic history takes accounts of what purportedly has happened and renders them as timeless social forms; neopositivist historical sociology provides us with a correlated and causal explanation of social changes, but its selection of "events" is problematical and the boundaries of experience it describes are ambiguous. A phenomenological approach insists that there is no one, single, absolute history, but rather that there are only structures of historical consciousness – structures that compete with or accommodate to one another and whose contents, processes, and struggles are grist for a historical sociology.

ACKNOWLEDGMENT

The publication of this essay affords the author a long overdue opportunity to acknowledge and thank certain persons instrumental in the formation of his ideas. Most significant is Kenneth E. Bock, whose years of patient research and quiet but forceful teaching have carried forward the project originated by F. J. Teggart in the Department of Social Institutions at the University of California at Berkeley. My own reservations about certain aspects of that project are not a rejection but rather a reaffirmation of its significance.

While preparing this paper I incurred debts of gratitude to several scholars and students working in related areas. Richard H. Brown has been a resource, critic, and colleague in this endeavor. Marvin B. Scott read and criticized early drafts of the paper. Arthur J. Vidich gave me the benefit of his always perceptive critical judgment. George V. Zito interpreted technical aspects of Pachter's work. Steven Seidman, Jerry Gittleman, Gary Kriss, Cecil Greek, James Cleland, and Gary Johnson aided in the gathering of materials. For all interpretations and any errors I take complete responsibility.

NOTES

1 Talcott Parsons, *The Social System* (Glencoe, Ill.: The Free Press, 1951).

2 Parsons, *Societies: Evolutionary and Comparative Perspectives* (Englewood Cliffs, N.J.: Prentice-Hall, 1966).

3 See, e.g., Joseph-Marie Degerando, *The Observation of Savage Peoples,* ed.
   F. G. T. Moore (London: Routledge & Kegan Paul, 1969; orig. pub. 1800).

4 Kenneth E. Bock, "The Comparative Method" (Ph.D. diss., University of
   California at Berkeley, 1948); "The Comparative Method of Anthropology,"
   Comparative Studies in Society and History 8 (1966):269–80.

5 See, however, William H. McNeil, *A World History* (New York: Oxford
   University Press, 1967).

6 Franz Boas, *Race, Language and Culture* (New York: The Free Press, 1940),
   pp. 243–311, 344–55, 626–47.

7 See, e.g., Gerhard Lenski, "Social Structure in Evolutionary Perspective," in
   Approaches to the Study of Social Structure, ed. Peter Blau (New York: The
   Free Press, 1975), pp. 135–53; "History and Social Change," *American
   Journal of Sociology* 82 (1976):548–64.

8 See Paul Honigsheim, "The Problem of Diffusion and Parallel Evolution with
   Special Reference to American Indians," *Papers of the Michigan Academy
   of Science, Arts, and Letters* 27 (1941):515–24.

9 See Anthony Smith, "Social Change and Diffusionist Theories," *Philosophy
   of Social Science* 5 (1975):273–87.

10 Kenneth E. Bock, "Evolution and Historical Process," *American Anthropologist* 54 (1952):486–96; "Comparative Method of Anthropology."

11 Maurice Freedman, "Immigrants and Associations: Chinese in Nineteenth-
   Century Singapore," *Comparative Studies in Society and History* 3 (1960):
   25–48.

12 See Stanford M. Lyman, "Chinese Secret Societies in the Occident: Notes
   and Suggestions for Research in the Sociology of Secrecy," *The Canadian
   Review of Sociology and Anthropology* 1 (1964):101–2.

13 See Thomas Cole, *Democritus and the Sources of Greek Anthropology* (Cleve-
   land: Western Reserve University Press, 1967).

14 See Kenneth E. Bock, "Darwin and Social Theory," *Philosophy of Science* 22
   (1955):123–34.

15 Robert E. Park, "Our Racial Frontier on the Pacific," *Survey Graphic* 9
   (1926):192–6.

16 Ibid., p. 196.

17 See W. O. Brown, "Culture Contact and Race Conflict," in *Race and Culture
   Contacts,* ed. E. B. Reuter (New York: McGraw-Hill, 1934), pp. 34–47.

18 Emory S. Bogardus, "A Race Relations Cycle," *American Journal of Sociology*
   35 (1930):612–7; "Current Problems of Japanese Americans," *Sociology and
   Social Research* 25 (1940):63–6. See also Robert H. Ross and Emory S.
   Bogardus, "The Second Generation Race Relations Cycle: A Study in Issei-
   Nisei Relationships," *Sociology and Social Research* 24 (1940):357–63.

19 Brewton Berry, *Race and Ethnic Relations,* 3rd ed. (Boston: Houghton
   Mifflin, 1965), p. 135.

20 Tamotsu Shibutani and Kian Moon Kwan, *Ethnic Stratification: A Comparative Approach* (New York: Macmillan, 1965), pp. 116–35.

21 See Nicholas Rescher, "On the Epistemology of the Inexact Sciences," Appendix II in his *Scientific Explanation* (New York: The Free Press, 1970), pp. 163-208.

22 See the two discussions by Stanford M. Lyman, "The Race Relations Cycle of Robert E. Park," *Pacific Sociological Review* 11 (1968):16-22; *The Black American in Sociological Thought: A Failure of Perspective* (New York: G. P. Putnam's Sons, 1972), pp. 27-70.

23 Karl Popper, *The Logic of Scientific Discovery* (New York: Harper & Row, Harper Torchbooks, 1965), pp. 78-92.

24 See Lyman, *Black American*, pp. 27-35.

25 Winifred Raushenbush, "Their Place in the Sun," *Survey Graphic* 56 (1926): 141-5, 203.

26 Louis Wirth, *The Ghetto* (Chicago: University of Chicago Press, Phoenix Books, 1956; orig. pub. 1928). See also Amitai Etzioni, "The Ghetto - A Re-evaluation," *Social Forces* 37 (1959):255-62.

27 Rose Hum Lee, *The Chinese in the United States of America* (Hong Kong: Hong Kong University Press, 1960). For a critical discussion, see Stanford M. Lyman, "Overseas Chinese in America and Indonesia," *Pacific Affairs* 34 (1961-62):380-9.

28 John Stuart Mill, *Auguste Comte and Positivism* (Ann Arbor: University of Michigan Press, 1965), p. 87.

29 Parsons, *Social System*, pp. 249-325.

30 See Robert A. Nisbet, "Social Structure and Social Change," *Research Studies of Washington State College* 20 (1952):70-6.

31 Talcott Parsons, *The System of Modern Societies* (Englewood Cliffs, N.J.: Prentice-Hall, 1971), pp. 4-28.

32 See S. Kirson Weinberg, "Social-Action Systems and Social Problems," in *Human Nature and Social Process*, ed. Arnold Rose (Boston: Houghton Mifflin, 1962), pp. 401-14.

33 A fine example will be found in Talcott Parsons, "Social Strains in America," (1955) and "Social Strains in America: A Postscript," (1962), both in *The Radical Right*, ed. Daniel Bell (Garden City, N.Y.: Doubleday, 1963), pp. 175-200.

34 See Kenneth E. Bock, "Some Basic Assumptions About Change," *Et Al.* 2 (1970):44-8.

35 Frederick J. Teggart, *Theory and Processes of History* (Berkeley: University of California Press, 1941), p. 244.

36 Teggart, "The Approach to the Study of Man," *Journal of Philosophy* 16 (1919):155.

37 Ibid.

38 Margaret T. Hodgen, *Change and History: A Study of the Dated Distributions of Technological Innovations in England*, Viking Fund Publications in Anthropology, no. 18 (New York: Wenner-Gren Foundation for Anthropological Research, 1952), p. 122.

39 Frederick J. Teggart, "The Humanistic Study of Change in Time," *Journal of Philosophy* 23 (1926):309-15.

40 Teggart, *Theory and Processes,* pp. 180-7.

41 Frederick J. Teggart, "Turgot's Approach to the Study of Man," *University of California Chronicle* 28 (1926):129-42.

42 Kenneth E. Bock, *The Acceptance of Histories: Toward a Perspective for Social Science,* University of California Publications in Sociology and Social Institutions, 3, no. 1 (Berkeley: University of California Press, 1956), pp. 108-22.

43 Hodgen, *Change and History,* pp. 48-72.

44 Frederick J. Teggart, *Rome and China: A Study of Correlations in Historical Events* (Berkeley: University of California Press, 1939).

45 Bock, *Acceptance of Histories,* p. 112.

46 Frederick J. Teggart, "Causation in Historical Events," *Journal of the History of Ideas* 3 (1942):3-11.

47 Bock, *Acceptance of Histories,* pp. 114-5.

48 Ibid., p. 115.

49 Ibid.

50 Hodgen, *Change and History,* p. 66.

51 Teggart, *Rome and China,* pp. 225-45.

52 See Lyman, *Black American,* pp. 171-84; *The Asian in the West,* Social Science and Humanities Publication no. 4, Western Studies Center (Reno: Desert Research Institute, University of Nevada System, 1970); *Chinese Americans* (New York: Random House, 1974), pp. 186-91; "Legitimacy and Consensus in Lipset's America: From Washington to Watergate," *Social Research* 42 (1975):729-59.

53 Robert A. Nisbet, *Social Change and History: Aspects of the Western Theory of Development* (New York: Oxford University Press, 1969), pp. 267-304.

54 W. I. Thomas, "Introductory," *Source Book for Social Origins* (Boston: Richard G. Badger, 1909), pp. 3-28.

55 Alfred Schutz, "Some Structures of the Life-World," *Collected Papers III: Studies in Phenomenological Philosophy,* ed. I. Schutz (The Hague: Martinus Nijhoff, 1966), pp. 116-32.

56 Teggart, *Theory and Processes of History,* p. 308.

57 Ibid., p. 307.

58 Hodgen, *Change and History,* pp. 73-96.

59 Teggart, *Theory and Processes of History,* p. 311.

60 Hodgen, *Change and History,* pp. 48-72.

61 Teggart, *Rome and China.*

62 Max Weber, *The Agrarian Sociology of Ancient Civilizations,* trans. R. I. Frank (London: New Left Books, 1976), p. 385.

63 Park, "Our Racial Frontier," p. 196.

64 Lyman, *Black American,* pp. 27-70.

65 Teggart, *Theory and Processes of History,* pp. 51-66.

66 Frederick J. Teggart, "The Capture of St. Joseph, Michigan, by the Spaniards in 1781," *Missouri Historical Review* 5 (1911):214-28.

67 See Frederick J. Teggart, "The Argument of Hesiod's *Works and Days*," *Journal of the History of Ideas* 8 (1947):45-77; Bock, *Acceptance of Histories*, p. 123.

68 Teggart, *Theory and Processes*, p. 151.

69 Ibid.

70 Teggart, "Causation in Historical Events," p. 8.

71 Ibid.

72 Ibid., pp. 8-9.

73 Ibid., p. 9.

74 Teggart, *Rome and China*, p. 240.

75 Ibid., p. 241.

76 Robert K. Merton, *Social Theory and Social Structure*, rev. and enlarged ed. (Glencoe, Ill.: The Free Press, 1957), pp. 19-84.

77 Teggart, *Rome and China*, pp. 241-2.

78 See the appeals by Frederick J. Teggart, "Human Geography, An Opportunity for the University," *The Journal of Geography* 17 (1918):247-67; "Geography as an Aid to Statecraft: An Appreciation of Mackinder's 'Democratic Ideals and Reality,' " *Geographical Review* 8 (1919):227-42.

79 Familiar as he was with German historians of the period, Teggart may have had in mind the inflammatory writings of Heinrich von Treitschke (1834-96). A passage typical of his style illustrates the kind of argument Teggart found so reprehensible:

Thus manifold have been the conflicting influences of the various living forces of history in national questions. When we examine these complicated conditions more closely we find first of all a great antagonism of races among human kind. . . . [B]ut the historian need only concern himself with the broad divisions of white, black, red, and yellow. The yellow race has never achieved political liberty, for their States have always been despotic and unfree. In the same way the artistic faculty has always been denied to the Mongols, in spite of that sense of comfort which we may admire among the Chinese, if we are soft and effeminate enough to wish to. The black races have always been servants, and looked down upon by all the others, nor has any Negro State ever raised itself to a level of real civilization. Physical strength and endurance are such marked characteristics in the Negro that he is employed inevitably to serve the ends of a will and intelligence higher than his own. The red race of North America, although now fallen into decay, once possessed a remarkable talent for State building . . . The red and yellow races spring from a common stock. Opposed to them stands the white race, which falls into two classes, the Aryan and the Semitic peoples. (*Politics*, trans. Blanche Dugdale and Torben de Bille, ed. Hans Kohn [New York: Harcourt, Brace & World, 1963], p. 125.)

80 Teggart, *Rome and China,* pp. 242-3.

81 Frederick J. Teggart, "The Obligation of Peace," *The Public: A Journal of Democracy* 22 (August 30, 1919):928-9; "Education for Life," *The Public: A Journal of Democracy* 22 (1919):1010-11; "The Responsibilities for Leadership," *The Dial* 67 (1919):237-9.

82 Teggart, "War and Civilization in the Future," *American Journal of Sociology* 46 (1941):582-90.

83 Teggart, "Argument of Hesiod's *Works and Days,*"

84 Teggart, *Prolegomena to History: The Relation of History to Literature, Philosophy, and Science,* University of California Publications in History, no. 4 (Berkeley: University of California Press, 1916), p. 277.

85 Arnold J. Toynbee, *A Study of History* (New York: Oxford University Press, 1954), X:232.

86 Teggart, *Theory and Processes of History,* p. 49.

87 See Oscar K. Rabinowicz, *Arnold Toynbee on Judaism and Zionism: A Critique* (London: W. H. Allen, 1974).

88 Bock, *Acceptance of Histories,* p. 120.

89 Joseph Needham, *Science and Civilization in China* (Cambridge: Cambridge University Press, 1954), I:183-7.

90 Needham, *The Grand Titration: Science and Society in East and West* (London: George Allen & Unwin, 1969), p. 11.

91 Ibid., p. 12.

92 See Benjamin Nelson, "Sciences and Civilizations, 'East' and 'West': Joseph Needham and Max Weber," in *Philosophical Foundations of Science,* ed. R. J. Seeger and R. S. Cohen (Dordrecht: D. Reidel, 1974), pp. 445-93; "Copernicus and the Quest for Certitude: 'East' and 'West,' " in *Copernicus Yesterday and Today,* Proceedings of the Commemorative Conference in Honor of Nicolaus Copernicus, Washington, D.C., 1972, ed. Arthur Beer and K. A. Strand (New York: Pergamon Press, 1975), pp. 39-46; "The Quest for Certitude and the Books of Scripture, Nature, and Science," in *The Nature of Scientific Discovery,* ed. Owen Gingerich (Washington, D.C.: Smithsonian Institution Press, 1975), pp. 355-72.

93 Harry Elmer Barnes, *A History of Historical Writing,* 2nd rev. ed. (New York: Dover Publications, 1962), p. 378.

94 Quoted in Burleigh Taylor Wilkins, *Carl Becker: The Development of an American Historian* (Cambridge: M.I.T. Press, 1967), p. 188.

95 Barnes, *History of Historical Writing,* p. 378.

96 Robert A. Nisbet, "Sociology as an Idea System," in *Sociological Self-Images: A Collective Portrait,* ed. Irving Louis Horowitz (Beverly Hills: Sage Publications, 1969), p. 200.

97 Bock, *Acceptance of Histories,* pp. 120-1; Nisbet, *Social Change and History,* pp. 276-7.

98 Max Weber, *Roscher and Knies: The Logical Problems of Historical Economics,* trans. Guy Oakes (New York: The Free Press, 1975); *Agrarian Sociology of Ancient Civilizations.*

99 Howard Becker, "Culture Case Study and Ideal-Typical Method: With Special Reference to Max Weber," *Social Forces* 12 (1933):399-405.

100 Becker, "The Field and Problems of Historical Sociology," in *The Fields and Methods of Sociology,* ed. L. L. Bernard (New York: Ray Long & Richard L. Smith, 1934), p. 24.

101 Alvin Boskoff, "Social Change: Major Problems in the Emergence of Theoretical and Research Foci," in *Modern Sociological Theory in Continuity and Change,* ed. Howard Becker and Alvin Boskoff (New York: Holt, Rinehart & Winston, 1957), p. 288.

102 Teggart, *Theory and Processes of History,* pp. 149-50, 196-7, 307-12.

103 Robert E. Park, *Race and Culture: The Collected Papers of Robert E. Park,* 1, ed. Everett Cherrington Hughes, Charles S. Johnson, Jitsuichi Masuoka, Robert Redfield, and Louis Wirth (Glencoe, Ill.: The Free Press, 1950), pp. 7, 18, 97n, 345, 350-1.

104 Howard Becker and Harry Elmer Barnes, *Social Thought from Lore to Science,* 3rd ed. (New York: Dover Publications, 1951), I:264-5; III:990.

105 Howard Becker, "Forms of Population Movement: Prolegomena to a Study of Mental Mobility," pt. 1, *Social Forces* 9 (1930):147-60; pt. 2, 9 (1931): 351-61; "Processes of Secularization: An Ideal-Typical Analysis with Special Reference to Personality Change as Affected by Population Movement," pt. 1, *Sociological Review* 24 (1932):138-54; pt. 2, 24 (1932):266-87.

106 In addition to those cited, the following works by Margaret T. Hodgen were published during Teggart's lifetime: "The Fitness of British Labor to Rule," *Forum* 69 (1923):1108-19; *Workers' Education in England and the United States* (London: Kegan Paul, Trench, Trubner & Co., 1925); "The Doctrine of Survivals: The History of an Idea," *American Anthropologist* n.s., 33 (1931):307-24; "Survivals and Social Origins: The Pioneers," *American Journal of Sociology* 38 (1933):583-94; "The Negro in the Anthropology of John Wesley," *Journal of Negro History* 19 (1934):308-23; *The Doctrine of Survivals: A Chapter in the History of Scientific Method in the Study of Man* (London: Allenson, 1936); "Domesday Walter Mills," *Antiquity* 13 (1939): 261-79; "Geographical Diffusion as a Criterion of Age," *American Anthropologist* 44 (1942):340-68; "Fairs of Elizabethan England," *Economic Geography* 18 (1942):389-400; "Sir Matthew Hale and the Method of Invention," *Isis* 34 (1943):313-8; "Glass and Paper: An Historical Study of Acculturation," *Southwestern Journal of Anthropology* 1 (1945):466-97.

107 John C. McKinney, "Methodology, Procedures, and Techniques in Sociology," in *Modern Sociological Theory in Continuity and Change,* ed. Howard Becker and Alvin Boskoff, pp. 230-1.

108 Leon J. Goldstein, "Theory in Anthropology: Developmental or Causal?"
     in *Sociological Theory: Inquiries and Paradigms,* ed. Llewellyn Gross (New
     York: Harper & Row, 1967), p. 172n.

109 See, e.g., Ernest Gellner, "Concepts and Society," in *Rationality,* ed. Bryan
     R. Wilson (New York: Harper & Row, Harper Torchbooks, 1970), pp. 18–49;
     Jack Goody, "Evolution and Communication: The Domestication of the
     Savage Mind," *British Journal of Sociology* 24 (1973):1–12; Keith Dixon,
     Sociological Theory: Pretence and Possibility (London: Routledge & Kegan
     Paul, 1973).

110 See Anthony Smith, *The Concept of Social Change: A Critique of the
     Functionalist Theory of Social Change* (London: Routledge & Kegan Paul,
     1973); "Social Change and Diffusionist Theories."

111 See Margaret T. Hodgen, "Similarities and Dated Distributions," *American
     Anthropologist* 52 (1950):445–65; "Karl Marx and the Social Scientists,"
     Scientific Monthly 72 (1951):252–8; "Anthropology, History and Science,"
     Scientia 87 (1952):282–97; "Johann Boemus (Fl. 1500): An Early Anthro-
     pologist," *American Anthropologist* 55 (1953):284–94; "Sebastian Muenster
     (1489–1552): A Sixteenth-Century Ethnographer," *Osiris* 11 (1954):504–29;
     Early Anthropology in the Sixteenth and Seventeenth Centuries (Philadelphia:
     University of Pennsylvania Press, 1964); "Ethnology in 1500: Polydore Vergil's
     Collection of Customs," *Isis* 57 (1966):315–24; "Frederick John Teggart," in
     International Encyclopedia of the Social Sciences, ed. David Sills (New York:
     Macmillan, 1968):XV, 598–9; *Anthropology, History, and Cultural Change,*
     Viking Fund Publications in Anthropology, no. 52 (Tucson: The University
     of Arizona Press, The Wenner-Gren Foundation for Anthropological Research,
     1974).

112 See Kenneth E. Bock, "History and the Science of Man: An Appreciation of
     George Cornewall Lewis," *Journal of the History of Ideas* 12 (1951):599–608;
     "Discussion," *American Sociological Review* 17 (1952):164–6; "Evolution and
     Historical Process"; "Darwin and Social Theory"; "The Study of War in
     American Sociology," *Sociologus* 5 (1955):104–13; "Cultural Difference and
     Race: The History of a Problem," *Commentary* 24 (1957):86–8; "Evolution,
     Function, and Change," *American Sociological Review* 28 (1963):229–37;
     "Theories of Progress and Evolution," in *Sociology and History: Theory and
     Research,* ed. Werner J. Cahnman and Alvin Boskoff (London: The Free
     Press of Glencoe, Collier-Macmillan, 1964), pp. 21–41; "The Comparative
     Method of Anthropology"; "Some Basic Assumptions About Change"; "Com-
     parison of Histories: The Contribution of Henry Maine," *Comparative Studies
     in Society and History* 16 (1974):232–62.

113 See Robert A. Nisbet, "The French Revolution and the Rise of Sociology in
     France," *American Journal of Sociology* 49 (1943):156–64; "Bonald and the
     Concept of the Social Group," *Journal of the History of Ideas* 5 (1944):315–31;
     "Social Structure and Social Change" in *Research Studies of Washington*

State College 20 (1952):70–6; *The Quest for Community: A Study in the Ethics of Order and Freedom* (New York: Oxford University Press, 1953); "Sociology as an Art Form," *Pacific Sociological Review* 5 (1962):64–74; *The Sociological Tradition* (New York: Basic Books, 1966); *Tradition and Revolt: Historical and Sociological Essays* (New York: Random House, 1968); *Social Change and History*; "Sociology as an Idea System"; "Developmentalism: A Critical Analysis," in *Theoretical Sociology: Perspectives and Developments*, ed. John C. McKinney and Edward A. Tiryakian (New York: Appleton-Century-Crofts, 1970), pp. 167–204; *The Sociology of Emile Durkheim* (New York: Oxford University Press, 1974); *Sociology as an Art Form* (New York: Oxford University Press, 1976); "The Social Impact of the Revolution," *The Wilson Quarterly* 1 (1976):93–107; "An Eruption of Genius: F. J. Teggart at Berkeley," *The California Monthly* 87 (1976):3, 6–7; "Vico and the Idea of Progress," *Social Research* 43 (1976):625–36.

114 Meek seems to be unaware of Teggart's essay praising Turgot for being opposed to the organic analogy in the study of cultural change. See Teggart, "Turgot's Approach to the Study of Man."

115 See Ronald L. Meek, "Smith, Turgot and the 'Four Stages' Theory," *History of Political Economy* 3 (1971):9–27; ed. and trans., *Turgot on Progress, Sociology and Economics* (Cambridge: Cambridge University Press, 1976).

116 Eugene Kamenka and Alice Erh-Soon Tay, "Beyond Bourgeois Individualism: The Contemporary Crisis in Law and Legal Ideology," in *Feudalism, Capitalism and Beyond,* ed. Eugene Kamenka and R. S. Neale (London: Edward Arnold, 1975), pp. 126–44.

117 Richard Beardsley, "An Appraisal of Leslie A. White's Scholarly Influence," *American Anthropologist* 77 (1976):619–20.

118 See Frederick J. Teggart, "The Circumstance or the Substance of History," *American Historical Review* 15 (1910):709–19; "Anthropology and History," *Journal of Philosophy* 16 (1919):691–96; "Clio," *University of California Chronicle* 24 (1922):347–60; "The Humanistic Study of Change in Time"; "Notes on 'Timeless' Sociology: A Discussion," *Social Forces* 7 (1929):362–6; *Two Essays on History* (Berkeley: Privately printed, 1930); "A Problem in the History of Ideas," *Journal of the History of Ideas* 1 (1940):494–503; "World History," *Scientia* 69 (1941):30–5.

119 C. Martin Wilbur, "Review of *Rome and China: A Study of Correlations in Historical Events,*" *American Historical Review* 46 (1940):93.

120 Pitirim A. Sorokin, "Review of *Rome and China: A Study of Correlations in Historical Events,*" *American Journal of Sociology* 46 (1940):388–9.

121 See Stanford M. Lyman and Marvin B. Scott, *A Sociology of the Absurd* (Pacific Palisades, Calif.: Goodyear Publishing, 1970), pp. 189–212.

122 See Erving Goffman, *Frame Analysis: An Essay on the Organization of Experience* (Cambridge, Mass.: Harvard University Press, 1974).

123 See Talcott Parsons, et al., "Some Fundamental Categories of the Theory

of Action: A General Statement," in *Toward a General Theory of Action*, ed. T. Parsons and Edward A. Shils (New York: Harper & Row, Harper Torchbooks, 1951), pp. 3–29.

124 Henry S. Pachter, "Defining an Event: Prolegomena to Any Future Philosophy of History," *Social Research* 41 (1974):443–4.

125 Ibid., pp. 448–50.

126 See Sorokin, "Review of *Rome and China*," pp. 389–90; George H. Hildebrand, Jr., "Review of *Rome and China: A Study of Correlations in Historical Events*," *American Sociological Review* 5 (1940):822–5.

127 Jack D. Douglas, *The Social Meanings of Suicide* (Princeton, N.J.: Princeton University Press, 1967), pp. 3–78; "The Rhetoric of Science and the Origins of Statistical Social Thought: The Case of Durkheim's *Suicide*," in *The Phenomenon of Sociology*, ed. Edward Tiryakian (New York: Appleton-Century-Crofts, 1971), pp. 44–57.

128 Max Weber, *The Theory of Social and Economic Organization*, ed. Talcott Parsons, trans. A. M. Henderson and Talcott Parsons (Glencoe, Ill.: The Free Press, The Falcon's Wing Press, 1947), p. 88.

129 Weber, *Roscher and Knies*, p. 64.

130 Wilhelm Dilthey, *Pattern and Meaning in History: Thoughts on History and Society*, ed. H. P. Rickman (New York: Harper & Row, Harper Torchbooks, 1962), pp. 64–168.

131 Hans-Georg Gadamer, *Truth and Method*, ed. and trans. Garett Barden and John Cumming (New York: The Seabury Press, 1975), pp. 192–344.

132 Ludwig von Bertalanffy, *General Systems Theory: Foundations, Development, Applications*, rev. ed. (New York: George Braziller, 1968), pp. 139–54; Ervin Lazlo, ed., *The Relevance of General Systems Theory: Papers Presented to Ludwig von Bertalanffy on his Seventieth Birthday* (New York: George Braziller, 1972).

133 See E. E. Evans-Pritchard, *Social Anthropology and Other Essays* (New York: The Free Press, 1962), pp. 21–63, 172–91; A. R. Radcliffe-Brown, *Structure and Function in Primitive Society* (Glencoe, Ill.: The Free Press, 1952), pp. 178–204.

134 Gellner, "Concepts and Society," pp. 18–49.

135 See Stanford M. Lyman, "Civilization: Contents, Discontents, Malcontents," *Contemporary Sociology* 2 (1973):360–6.

136 Erving Goffman, *Encounters: Two Studies in the Sociology of Interaction* (Indianapolis: Bobbs-Merrill, 1961), pp. 19–26.

137 Harold Garfinkel, *Studies in Ethnomethodology* (Englewood Cliffs, N.J.: Prentice-Hall, 1967).

138 Claude Lévi-Strauss, *Structural Anthropology*, trans. Claire Jacobson and Brooke Grundfest Schoepf (Harmondsworth: Penguin, 1972).

139 See Mary Douglas, "The Meaning of Myth, with Special Reference to 'La Geste d'Asdiwal,'" in *The Structural Study of Myth and Totemism*, ed. Edmund Leach (London: Tavistock, 1969), pp. 49–70.

140 See Kenneth Burke, *Attitudes Toward History* (Boston: Beacon Press, 1959).

141 Stanford M. Lyman and Marvin B. Scott, *The Drama of Social Reality* (New York: Oxford University Press, 1975), pp. 128-46.

142 See Maurice Natanson, "History as a Finite Province of Meaning," in his *Literature, Philosophy and the Social Sciences: Essays in Existentialism and Phenomenology* (The Hague: Martinus Nijhoff, 1962), pp. 172-8.

143 See Herbert Blumer, "Race Prejudice as a Sense of Group Position," *Pacific Sociological Review* 1 (1958):3-7.

144 See Rudolph H. Weingartner, *Experience and Culture: The Philosophy of Georg Simmel* (Middletown, Conn.: Wesleyan University Press, 1962), pp. 85-139.

4

The history of *mentalités*:
Recent writings on revolution, criminality,
and death in France[1]

ROBERT DARNTON

Editors' introduction

Dominant themes in contemporary phenomenological and existential sociology in America, cognitive sociology in England, and structural anthropology in France are outgrowths and extensions of Emile Durkheim's program for the comparative study of civilizational structures of consciousness. Durkheim's investigations of the categories of consciousness of different peoples – expressed chiefly in *Primitive Classification* and *The Elementary Forms of Religious Life* – have not only inspired sociologists within and outside of France, they also – through the writings of Marc Bloch and Lucien Febvre – have led to the creation of a history of *mentalités* by scholars writing on France itself.

In the present essay Robert Darnton describes this school and its problems and methods. Darnton begins by reporting on recent work of Richard Cobb on crime and violence in revolutionary France. Cobb's anarchically individualistic point of view is then criticized from the perspective of historical criminology. Turning to the ideas and conduct of death, Darnton contrasts the sweeping impressionism of Philip Ariès and the detailed statistical analyses of Michel Vovelle.

The specificity of Darnton's discussion introduces the reader to representative writings of the history of *mentalités,* and his contrastive analyses of different writers' approaches reveal what is at stake in these methodological debates: nothing less than the nature and status of the history of *mentalités* itself. Moreover, by interpreting these writings as histories of structure of consciousness, and by subjecting them to a sociological or structuralist critique, Darnton's paper reveals a unity beyond itself, a unity of the three focal terms of this volume as a whole.

The case of the wandering eye

In *A Second Identity*, Richard Cobb tells the story of Marie Besnard, a crafty peasant who confounded an array of lawyers, laboratory technicians, and criminologists trying to get her convicted for murder in a series of spectacular trials from 1952 to 1961. Marie showed that her accusers had scrambled the evidence so badly in their test tubes and jars that a kidney from one victim's body was cohabiting in Exhibit A with the gall bladder from another's, and an eye, which had disappeared from its home cadaver, had turned up in the middle of a foreign skeleton. The wandering eye did the job, Cobb observes with satisfaction: The scientists lost their case, and Marie won her freedom. Cobb does not come right out and say so, but the story stands as a parable to be pondered by sociological historians.

Sociology is the villain of the last three books written by Richard Cobb, professor of history at Oxford University and one of the most controversial, original, and talented historians writing today. If you want to understand the French Revolution, he argues, strike out for the uncharted wilderness constituting the revolutionary *mentalité*. The historiographical frontier is not to be found in statistical tables, economic models, computer print-outs, or social systems, but in the lost mental world of obscure persons like Marie Besnard.

Cobb is the only person to have explored this territory. For a quarter of a century, he has tracked down revolutionary "wildmen" (*enragés*), counterrevolutionary crackpots, neighborhood militants, primitive anarchists, and all the varieties of eccentric humanity that he could find in the labyrinth of France's archives. Not only do his reports on these neglected elements of French humanity provide a vision of the human condition that transcends the conventional limits of history writing; they also illustrate the possibilities and problems involved in the study of *mentalités*.

Revolution

How conventional historiography could accommodate Cobb is not clear because Cobb's viewpoint is sharp and eccentric, while conventional French revolutionary studies have become increasingly sociological and confused. The confusion comes from an outbreak of the old quarrels over the meaning of 1789 and 1793. Right-wing journals have chosen revolutionary historiography as a means of sniping at the left, and the left has replied with a barrage of articles about the true character of "the Mother of us all," as the Revolution is known among her legitimate offspring.[2] The fighting has some characteristics of a *guerre dans la cimetière*; the protagonists seem perched on tombs, defending heritages: Marx versus Tocqueville, Mathiez versus Aulard, Lefebvre versus Febvre. But there is more to it than ancestor worship and ideological tribalism.

In the attempt to strip off the political superstructure of French society and to probe its anatomy, French historians have tended to use the sharp instruments of Marxism.[3] But English and American historians have turned up data that are becoming harder and harder to fit into Marxist categories. George Taylor has exposed the noncapitalist character of the Old Regime's economy. Robert Forster has shown the inaccuracy of identifying feudalism with the nobility; C. B. A. Behrens has revealed the way privilege cut across the boundaries of class and estate; David Bien and Vivian Gruder have measured social mobility within the army and the intendancies and have found the opposition of bourgeoisie and aristocracy to be of little relevance; J. F. Bosher has demonstrated that the royal administration is better understood as the institutional interplay of complex vested interests than as a class government by the nobility. Class proves to be too narrow a concept for the analysis of the complexities and contradictions of revolutionary society and politics as they are unraveled in the work of Charles Tilly, M. J. Sydenham, Isser Woloch, and Colin Lucas. The fundamental Marxist idea that the Revolution resulted from a contradiction between a rising capitalist bourgeoisie and a feudal nobility has been exploded by Alfred Cobban, who stole most of his ammunition from the camp of his ideological enemies.

To be sure, Cobban's explicitly anti-Marxist history (like that of Crane Brinton and R. R. Palmer) has had little effect in France. Albert Sobol, the best of the French Marxists, ignored it while reworking the old orthodoxies in *Précis d'histoire de la Révolution française* (1962) at the same time that Norman Hampson was producing a remarkable non-Marxist work in English, *A Social History of the French Revolution* (1963). The language barrier may have prevented the outbreak of an Anglo–French Battle of Books. But in 1969, Pierre Goubert published the first volume of *L'Ancien Régime,* an extraordinarily penetrating and sophisticated non-Marxist analysis, which has captured the textbook market throughout much of France. Finally, François Furet made a frontal attack on the Marxist interpretation of the Revolution in a brilliant polemical article, "Le Catéchisme révolutionnaire" (*Annales,* March–April 1971), which provoked the present state of open war.

It would be wrong to view this warfare as an American challenge within the history profession or as a combat between Anglo-Saxon empiricism and Continental dogmatism in which the latter, after years of undermining and erosion, is doomed to come crashing down. Not only do the attackers include a heavy proportion of Frenchmen, who draw on their own rich tradition of non-Marxist social history, but the Marxist model is stronger and better defended than the Bastille ever was. Moreover, it is terribly difficult to abandon the idea that Soboul raises aloft in the very first sentence of his *Précis*: "The French Revolution constitutes, with the English revolutions of the seventeenth century, the culmination of a long economic and social evolution, which has made the bourgeoisie the mistress of the world." Put that grandly, the proposition may seem easy to accept; yet it rests on assumptions that cannot be torn away without producing ruin. And if the revisionists succeed in dismantling the Marxist interpretation of the Revolution, what will they do with the rubble? They have no conceptual structure of their own.

Where in the general confusion does Richard Cobb belong? His early work casts him in the company of two Marxists, Albert Soboul and George Rudé, who reoriented the study of the Revolution by looking at it "from below." That phrase has become hackneyed now, but in the 1950s and early 1960s it represented an inspired attempt to examine events from a new perspective, that of ordinary men and women, the people who provided the muscle for forcing the Revolution to the left in the series of Great Leaps Forward, which were known as *journées* (July 14, 1789, October 5-6, 1789, August 10, 1792, and May 31-June 2, 1793), and who were crushed in the riots of Germinal and Prairial, Year III (1795) and rose again in the July Days of 1830, the June Days of 1848, and the May Days of 1871. These, in turn, served as ancestors for August of 1944, and May-June of 1968.

For Cobb, the concern with ordinary people led to the study of mentality (*mentalité* conveys a broader idea than its English counterpart), that is, the examination of the common man's outlook and perception of events rather than the analysis of the events themselves. Cobb's exploration of the revolutionary mentality complemented the work of Soboul and Rudé, who emphasized the institutional, political, and economic aspects of the *sans-culotte* movement; and it communicated the atmosphere of the Terror in ordinary neighborhoods where the desire for cheap bread and for a primitive equality of *jouissances* was more powerful than Rousseauism, and where the belief in counterrevolutionary conspiracy was more important than the conspiracies themselves. By immersing himself in the archives, by his luminous historical imagination and a superb command of

French and English prose, Cobb managed to bring the obscure people of
the Revolution back to life.

In *The Police and the People* and *Reactions to the French Revolution,*
Cobb shifts ground, moving from below to beyond the fringe of the
Revolution. Here he concentrates on banditry, prostitution, vagabondage,
murder, madness, and other forms of deviance. These themes may
fascinate us, but they will not help to sort out the confusion in current
interpretations of the Revolution, because Cobb makes terrorist and
counter-terrorist, *sans-culotte* and criminal, militant and lunatic look
alike; and he seems less intent on explaining the relation of violence to
revolution than on exalting eccentricity and individualism for their own
sake – a kind of upside-down moralizing that he turns against his former
allies. For he never passes up an opportunity to poke at Soboul and to
lunge at Rudé. He accuses them of dehumanizing the past by walling it
up within a dessicated dogmatism. In fact, he pictures the revolutionary
government as a form of totalitarianism *manque,* suggesting that it fell
short of Stalinism for want of technology, not for lack of trying, and he
compares it unfavorably with "the full flowering of anarchical freedom"
during the Thermidorean Reaction.

Where then, in the current historical battle, does Cobb stand? Against
ideology and against sociology. He has placed himself squarely in no man's
land and is fighting a private war on two fronts, in opposition to both the
Marxist and the empirical versions of scientific history. Cobb has become
every man's heretic. His perspective on history is set at such an odd angle
that it compels us to see the Revolution freshly: That is the fascination of
his work, for it challenges us at every turn with its idiosyncrasy – a rare
quality in a profession that tends toward conformism.

Consider Cobb's reassessment of the popular *sans-culotte* movement in
The Police and the People. Soboul showed that *sans-culottisme* developed
as a dialectic between popular revolution and revolutionary government
during the Year II (1793–4); that is, he explained how the *sans-culottes*
forced the Revolution to the left and why they were ultimately destroyed
by the dictatorial Terror that they had brought into being. By close
analysis and careful documentation, Soboul revealed an underlying logic
of events, which still stands as the best explanation of the climactic phase
of the Revolution.

Nothing could be further from Cobb's sense of history than logic; he
attacks Soboul's analysis for excessive intellectuality (it is, he writes, an
overchoreographed historical ballet) and tries to show that the popular
revolution was less a movement than an outbreak of anarchy. Cobb's view
stresses the temperamental defects of the *sans-culottes* – their bluster, their

naïveté and shortsightedness – but it never really undermines Soboul's argument, and it confuses the issues by reversing the chronology of events. Cobb's account runs backward through the Empire, Directory, and Thermidorean Reaction to the Year III (1794–5), which he treats as the turning point of the entire Revolution. Finding no coherent *sans-culottisme* during those periods, he concludes that the movement must have been ephemeral even before them – a bizarre interpretation that seems to argue that because something died, it had not existed. Since Soboul traced the popular revolution's demise to the end of the Year II and showed how and why it occurred, Cobb's revisionism in reverse seems to miss its target. And when Cobb finally backs into the Terror, his account reads like spiced-up Soboul.

But not when he discusses the provinces. Soboul's thesis does not account for the vagaries of the popular revolution outside Paris, whereas Cobb, who is a master of provincial history, reveals all the contradictions and crosscurrents that prevented *sans-culottisme* from gathering into a national force. Not only does he demonstrate that the extremists of Lyon came out on the opposite side of issues being championed by the wildmen of Paris, but he shows how the fire eaters of Vienne opposed the Lyonnais, and how the multitiered antagonisms of Paris-Lyon-Vienne differed from those of Paris-Rouen-Le Havre. Cobb goes further still: He explores the rivalries among neighborhoods, the feuds between families, the solidarity built up by occupational ties, and the schisms derived from quarrels over cock fighting or bowls or women. Everywhere he sees variety, discord, individualism; general lines of interpretation blur, and the Revolution dissolves into buzzing confusion. Perhaps that is all it amounted to for the man in the street. In any case, Cobb shows the limits of the Parisian model.

He already did so in his earlier work. His last book, *Reactions to the French Revolution*, concerns anarchists, bandits, criminals, recluses, madmen, and a wild variety of individuals who lived outside politics, beyond the reach of the state. As these persons had nothing in common except their refusal to become integrated in society, and as asocial individuals have proliferated throughout French history, their stories do not lead to any general conclusions about their lives or their time.

Thus, it would appear that it is the very timelessness of anomie, or "la vie en marge," that attracts Cobb. For twenty-five years he has wandered in the archives, searching out every eccentric he could uncover. He emerges with a fantastic collection of cases of deviant individualism, strung together through "the selective use of the individual 'case history' as a unit in historical impressionism." This method suits Cobb's sense of the uniqueness of things and of the historian's task, which is to show how phenomena are

distinct, not how they are related. By constantly emphasizing the complexity of the past, his work stands as a warning against attempts to make
history fit into prefabricated social structures. But Cobb's insistence on
uniqueness tends toward nominalism or nihilism. It suggests that generalization is impossible and that history can only be reduced to case histories.

There is madness in that method, and a touch of madness may be
necessary to understand the "cannibals" who ran amuck in September of
1792, traumatizing the Republic at its birth. One could hardly imagine
a happier meeting of subject and author than Cobb's sympathetic evocation of what Terror and Counter-Terror meant to people who experienced
them. But his refusal to analyze and generalize makes him sound like an
intellectual Luddite. Not only does he inveigh against "Annales" historians,
intellectual historians, and sociological historians, but in constructing his
own version of events, he refuses to rise above the level of the *fait divers.*
For Cobb, as for Restif de la Bretonne and Louis Sébastien Mercier, the
revolutionary *rapporteurs* in whom he finds his greatest inspiration, it is
enough to glimpse into the heart of the passer-by. History is soul history,
and methodology is empathy.

The danger of this historical impressionism is not that it will budge
Soboul's rocklike thesis, or any other analytical structure, but rather that
it may misdirect the development of the history of *mentalités,* Cobb's
chosen genre. Although it goes back at least as far as Burckhardt, the study
of *mentalité* is undergoing a strong revival in France and has even crossed
the Channel, if not the Atlantic. It is a sort of intellectual history of non-
intellectuals, an attempt to reconstruct the cosmology of the common man
or, more modestly, to understand the attitudes, assumptions, and implicit
ideologies of specific social groups (their *outillage mental,* according to
Lucien Febvre, the great prophet and practitioner of this kind of history).
Mentality is more a subject than a discipline. The French have discussed
it in various prolegomena and discourses on method,[4] but they have not
arrived at any clear conception of the field. Nor has Cobb. His last two
books treat such a bewildering variety of subjects - criminality, vagrancy,
urban-rural conflict, suicide, insanity, popular culture, the family, the
suppression of women - that it is difficult to find any coherent theme in
the rush of chapters and subchapters.

Criminality
But if Cobb's work has any leitmotiv, it is murder; and since most of his
deviants resorted to murder at one time or other, he concentrates on it
long enough to produce some statistics. He counted 846 "political" murders

in the Rhône Valley and adjoining areas during the last five years of the eighteenth century. The homicidal "score" according to time and place convinced him that the murder rate went up drastically during the years between the Terror and the Empire. Although the murders often reflected merely local motives (family feuds, *règlements de compte*; in practice Cobb concedes the impossibility of distinguishing political from nonpolitical killing), he found that they correlated most closely with the political temperature. So he interprets homicide as a form of political protest, a Counter-Terror, which had the support of communities that had been alienated by the agents of the revolutionary government in Paris – hence its relevance to popular mentality and to the decline of the popular movement.

Cobb scatters his statistics in a manner that makes them difficult to evaluate, and trying to correlate them proves nothing at all, because he uses no consistent unit of measurement. For example, instead of telling the reader how many murders occurred each year in the Department of the Rhône, he presents his information as follows: In the Year III (1794–5) there were fifty murders in the Department of the Rhône and the Department of the Loire; in the Year IV there were twenty in the Rhône and the Haute-Loire; he has no figures for the Year V; in the Year VI there were four in the Rhône alone; and he has no figures for the Year VII. The numerical base is trivial, the geographical unit is never the same; and there are no statistics for two of the five years under study. Yet the Rhône was the area that Cobb investigated most intensively. For other regions his statistics are even scantier: they usually cover only one or two years and refer to inconsistent combinations of departments.

Cobb produces no statistics for any period before the Year III, yet he asserts that the murder rate of the Counter-Terror (Years III and after) was as high as that of the Terror (Year II) and was higher than that of nonrevolutionary years. That conclusion can only be substantiated by statistics covering the periods before and after the Revolution, which Cobb does not provide. He gives no idea of the outside boundaries of his data or of the representativeness of his statistics. What fraction of the whole number of murders has he unearthed? What is their relation to the population of the areas under study? How do they measure against some standard rate of murders per 100,000 people over a long series of years?

Cobb never asks these questions; yet until he answers them, his conclusions should be taken as hypotheses. He disparages the importance of statistics, but he relies heavily on them, and on general remarks about incidence, to make sense of a multitude of subjects: prostitution, desertion, disease, vagrancy, and all forms of crime and violence. In every case, he sees a quantitative jump after Thermidor (July 27, 1794), and he seems to explain that increase by the change in the political climate – an interpretation that seems dubious on its face and is undermined by Cobb's admission that much of his evidence comes from notes that he had jotted down *en passant* two decades ago, when he was looking for information about the revolutionary armies. That search took him through thousands of heterogeneous dossiers and made it impossible for him to produce statistics in a series, that is, from a homogeneous source, capable of being quantified in units of equal value.

Does this statistical *insouciance* invalidate the conclusions of Cobb's last two books? Certainly not, because he really cares less about measuring the rate of violence than about understanding the experience of it. In a section following the homicidal "scorekeeping" in *The Police and the People*, he describes the psychological isolation of former terrorists when the Thermidorean Reaction penetrated the countryside. As an imaginative evocation of the nastiness of village life, it is utterly persuasive; and it would compensate for a book full of faulty statistics. The same is true of some marvelous accounts of popular attitudes toward food and "dearth," of the dignity of the man who can say that he has "bread in the house," and of popular language, which extremists manipulated through the use of black humor and scatological hyperbole ("I'm going to eat the head of a bourgeois, with garlic"). In treating this kind of subject, Cobb lets his historical imagination play; and his remarks carry conviction because of his mastery of the material. The problem is how to move beyond evocation by anecdote and to carry the history of *mentalités* past the point reached by masters like Lucien Febvre, who also combined great historical sensitivity with erudition and literary flair.

Criminality and mentality fit together so naturally as subjects that they suggest a way of resolving the antithesis between sociology and the history of *mentalités* that runs throughout Cobb's work. If, instead of building barriers between history and the social sciences, he had made some forays into alien territory, Cobb would have found a rich literature waiting to be exploited. Some familiarity with criminology, for example, might have provoked him to question his thesis that the Revolution or the Counter-Revolution produced an upsurge in violent crime. Historical criminologists have found the opposite to be true, in the case of 1871 as well as 1789.[5] They also have developed techniques for taking the trickiness out of statistics.

A glance at almost any criminology textbook[6] or even at such untouchable journals as the *Revue française de sociologie* or the *Annales* could have helped Cobb untangle his figures on crime rates and might have put him on the track of the *Comptes généraux de l'administration de la justice criminelle,* which provide criminal statistics dating back to 1825. The *Comptes* have supplied material for social history since the time of A. M. Guerry and Adolphe Quételet, early masters of sociology, who lived through the events Cobb describes and who studied criminality with a statistical sophistication that makes his work look primitive.[7]

Of course modern criminology cannot be applied indiscriminately to the past, because of the irregularity of criminal statistics before the nineteenth century. But criminology can suggest approaches, methods, and questions that might never occur to the asociological historian. It can show him how to measure criminality against demography; how to sort out factors such as age, trade, sex, and geography; and how to be sensitive to the attitudes (or *mentalités*) involved in the relations between those who break the law and those who enforce it. For crime provides a negative image of the sacred and a direct reflection of the taboo; and when studied over long periods, it can reveal shifts in a society's value system. Analyses of sentencing show the sociologically significant moments when judges cease to apply laws that remain on the books but have passed out of the mores.

Robert Mandrou developed this approach successfully in his book on the persecution of witchcraft, *Magistrats et sorciers en France au XVIIe siècle,* and today's newspapers are full of analogous cases: trials concerning abortion, homosexuality, and obscenity. Similarly, studies of the incidence of crimes may uncover changes in attitudes and behavior patterns. Thus Enrico Ferri postulated that as societies move into an urbanized and commercialized stage of development, they pass from a pattern of instinctual criminality to a pattern of calculated criminality, from crime against persons to crime against property.[8] Although Ferri's "law" may have been flogged to death, it has proved useful in comparing traditional and modern or rural and urban societies. The rate of violent crimes (murder and felonious assault, for example) tends to be much higher in archaic, agrarian villages, where communal norms regulate conduct, except in its most explosive, impetuous moments, whereas economic crime (theft and fraud) predominates in modern cities, where uprooted, money-oriented individuals struggle anonymously to strike it rich or simply to survive.

This shift from passionate to commercial criminality seems to have occurred throughout the West during the early modern period (the present wave of muggings represents a change of tide), and so does the rise of the underworld, despite the gangland subculture (mostly mythical) that surrounded Robin Hood and Cartouche. Cobb treats rural, urban, and

organized crime as expressions of the same deviant mentality; but criminology suggests that pitchfork murderers, city shoplifters, and *mafiosi*
belong to different species.

Such differences can only emerge by comparative analysis, another genre
that Cobb dislikes and that could have helped him to put his material in
perspective. Do his four murders in the Department of the Rhône during
the Year VI represent a high level of violence? Assuming the Rhône had a
population of approximately two hundred thousand, it had a murder rate
of two per one hundred thousand, which is about that of France today. So
the area around Lyon, which Cobb describes as a gigantic chamber of
horrors, might have passed into a phase of fairly bloodless criminality by
1789, and Cobb's penchant for the violent anecdote may have made him
misrepresent reality. The obscene, ritualistic killings in the remoter regions
he studies suggest a more primitive pattern, like that of Colombia, Burma,
or Indonesia today.[9]

Cross-cultural comparisons on a global scale may have little practical
value, but Cobb might have compared his findings with those of other
historians studying the criminality of eighteenth-century France. Teams
of them have been plowing through archives in Lille, Caën, Bordeaux,
Toulouse, Aix, and Paris; and they already have produced significant
results, as may be appreciated by the works-in-progress reports published
by the groups working with François Billacois in Paris and with Pierre
Deyon in Lille.[10]

The Parisian group found that theft accounted for 87 percent of reported crimes from 1755 to 1785 – a figure that puts prerevolutionary
Paris in a class with the metropolises of modern Europe (99 percent of the
crimes in Paris in the 1970s are thefts), in contrast to eighteenth-century
French villages, where theft represented only one-third or so of recorded
crimes. The homicide rate was low (about one per one hundred thousand),
and all the evidence suggests that the criminal underworld had not yet
come into existence. Even if one allows for considerable discrepancy between real and reported crime, the capital of the Revolution would look
like a haven of nonviolence to anyone who lives in New York in the final
quarter of the twentieth century.

But it was hell for the criminals, who mostly stole to stay alive. Analysis of their origins, trades, domiciles, and family status shows that they
belonged to France's miserable "floating population," which lived on the
road between temporary jobs and stayed in squalid rooming houses. These
"criminals" were the victims of poverty; their own victims were often semi-
indigent also, and their oppressors showed one dominant attitude: protect
property. The judges in the criminal courts of Paris throughout the age

of Enlightenment had thieves hanged and tortured, but they showed indulgence for crimes that seemed less threatening to them: felonious assault, rape, and adultery.

The same pattern emerges from the research historians have done in Lille. It shows that criminal violence decreased dramatically during the entire revolutionary decade and that the rate of crimes against persons declined throughout the eighteenth century, while crimes against property increased. Judges ceased to enforce punishments for sacrilege, showed more leniency toward private immorality, decreased the use of torture (but continued to use it against thieves, if they were poor and ill-born), and suppressed even petty theft with great severity – greatest in the case of servants, beggars, and laborers. Criminal justice, as practiced in Paris and Lille, had abandoned the defense of traditional values and had become essentially an attempt to protect property against the propertyless.

That bottom category of poverty did not include the Parisian *sans-culottes*. They had regular jobs, fixed addresses, families, and bread in the house – even if there was not always enough of it to keep their stomachs full. The criminal population was densest in the very center of Paris, where the cheapest boarding houses were located, not in the *faubourgs* that supplied the *sans-culottes*. It therefore seems that criminal and revolutionary violence were unrelated, that the Bastille-storming and purse-snatching impulses had little in common, and that even seen from "below" the Revolution took place above the heads of France's bread-and-butter criminals.

Historical criminology therefore has revealed realities of behavior and psychology that could not be reached by Cobb's methods. The point is not that Cobb was wrong (his kind of history is too subjective to be classified as right or wrong), but that his historical impressionism does not lead anywhere. The comparison of his work on criminality and that of the social scientists suggests that the history of *mentalités* ought to ally itself with sociology, not fight it to the death.

Death

The study of death illustrates the same point. Death is a subject that has occupied sociologists, anthropologists, painters, poets, and morticians – but not historians. Although it has inexorably followed life throughout all time, historians have assumed it has no history. They generally prefer dramatic events to the great constants of the human condition – birth, childhood, marriage, old age, and death. Yet those constants have changed, however slowly and imperceptibly. Consider the contrast between the medieval art of dying and the American way of death. In the late Middle Ages, the dying man played the central part in a supernatural drama. He staged and managed his death according to a prescribed rite, conscious of the fact that he had reached the climactic moment of his life, that heaven and hell hung in the balance, and that he could save his soul by making a "good death." *L'art de bien mourir,* the *Ars Moriendi,* became one of the most popular and widely diffused themes of literature and iconography in the fifteenth century.

The *Ars Moriendi* depicted a man on his deathbed surrounded by saints and demons who are struggling for the possession of his soul. The devils reenact his sins and claim him for hell. If he resists the temptations of pride and despair, and if he sincerely repents, he dies well. His hands crossed, his head facing eastward toward Jerusalem, his face lifted toward heaven, he emits his soul with his last breath. It emerges from his mouth, looking like a newborn baby, and an angel carries it off to heaven. The spectacle reveals the medieval sense of reality, a cosmological clutter of the exalted and the base, in which ordinary objects are infused with transcendental significance.

Medieval and early modern man had a horror of sudden death, because it might deprive him of his part in the critical, metaphysical moment. In dangerous cases, a doctor's first duty was to get a priest. He was under a solemn obligation to warn his patients if death seemed to be even a remote possibility, because they needed time to prepare for death, to meet it according to the traditional ceremony, in bed. The deathbed scene took place in public. Priests, doctors, family, friends, even passers-by crowded into the room of the dying man. In a "good death," he took stock of his life, called in his enemies and forgave them, blessed his children, repented his sins, and received the last sacraments. Although it varied according to his status and his era, his will regulated the burial and mourning in elaborate detail, specifying the composition of the cortege, the number of candles to be carried, the character of the burial, and the number of masses to be said for his soul. After a prescribed period of withdrawal from society in prescribed dress, the bereaved members of his family would take up life again, fortified for their own encounters with death.

The "good death" represented what Huizinga has called a "cultural ideal," not actuality, for in the age of the Black Death people died miserably and profligately. In times of famine, corpses were found with grass in their mouths. In times of plague, the dying were often abandoned and their bodies piled up and burned or tossed without ceremony into mass graves. At all times, death was familiar and all-pervasive; it was even an object of jokes and social comment, as in the popular literature on the

Dance of Death. In Europe 300 years ago, 600 years ago, public executions were spectator sports; children found dead vagrants in haylofts – *croquants*; and graveyards served as meeting grounds for playing games, pasturing cattle, peddling wares, drinking, dancing, and wenching.

Instead of presiding over his death, modern man is "robbed" of it, to use the expression of Philippe Ariès. About 80 percent of the deaths in the United States now occur in hospitals and nursing "homes." Most Americans die in isolation, surrounded by strangers and medical technicians instead of their families. The priest has been replaced by the doctor, whose training gives him no way of satisfying the psychological needs of the dying and who hides death from the patient. The patient therefore shuffles into death unknowingly; far from being exposed to any ultimate reality, he dies as if death were merely the last drop in the graph on the temperature chart.

The inhumanity of this painless positivism has generated a considerable debate and a large literature in medicine, psychology, and sociology. Recently, hospitals and medical schools have modified their practices. But the problem concerns more than hospital management. As Herman Feifel, Robert Fulton, W. Lloyd Warner, Avery Weisman, and other social scientists have shown, it touches a taboo embedded deep in American culture.

The art and literature of the High Middle Ages dwelt on the worms, dirt, and decomposition that overcome corpses. Baroque art also emphasized death in a spirit of macabre realism. Nineteenth-century cemeteries proclaimed their function with a lavishness that James S. Curl has characterized as "the Victorian celebration of death." But the art of the American mortician paints death to look like life, sealing it up in watertight caskets and spiriting it away to graveyards camouflaged as gardens. Americans take refuge in euphemisms: "passing away," "terminal case," "malignancy."

They also deritualize death. No longer do their bereaved set themselves apart by wearing black or withdrawing from social functions for a specified time. Wakes are almost extinct; many bereaved families discourage the ritual gesture of sending flowers, requesting instead that friends give donations to charities. Children frequently do not attend funerals of close relatives, and their parents avoid discussing the subject of death (but not sex) with them. The code of behavior at funerals prescribes the suppression of grief. Presidential widows have set a standard of not "cracking" – the antithesis of an earlier ideal, which made weeping obligatory. The extreme in the repressive, unceremonial treatment of death seems to have been attained by the professional classes in England – a case of ritualistic vacuum that Geoffrey Gorer has documented movingly in *Death, Grief, and Mourning in Contemporary Britain.* Gorer laments the disappearance of rites for expressing grief and for comforting the bereaved. The "American way of death" has been condemned just as strongly by Jessica Mitford, who contends that commercial interests have taken over the expression of grief in this country and exploited it for their own profit. In both countries death has been transformed into the opposite of what it was 500 years ago.[11]

How did this transformation come about? Philippe Ariès, the masterful social historian who wrote *Centuries of Childhood,* was one of the first to recognize it and has tried to trace its stages in his latest book, *Western Attitudes toward Death.*[12] He argues that the traditional view of death took hold of men's minds during the millennium after the collapse of the Roman Empire. Early medieval men saw death as a collective destiny, ordinary, inevitable, and not particularly fearsome, because it would engulf all Christians, like a great sleep, until they would awaken in paradise at the Second Coming of Christ. Between 1000 and 1250, this attitude shifted in emphasis from the collectivity to the individual; and from the late Middle Ages until the late eighteenth century, death served primarily to sharpen one's sense of self. It became the supreme moment in the personal journey toward salvation. But if mismanaged, it could lead to damnation, as the *Ars Moriendi* made clear. Death therefore became more dramatic, but it remained essentially the same – a familiar presence, acting openly in the midst of life – and the same rituals sufficed in dealing with it. Men sought to die the "good death," in their beds and in public – resolute, repentant, and fortified by the sacrament for eventual elevation to the Celestial Court.

By the nineteenth century, this ritual became charged with a new sense of affection. Death meant primarily the separation of loved ones. Instead of seeming ordinary, it became a catastrophic rupture with the familiar and the familial, for the family that took charge of it ultimately proved unequal to the burden of grief. Death plunged the bereaved into a terrifying realm of irrationality, an experience evoked by the morbid themes in romantic literature and the Dionysian emotionalism of nineteenth-century tomb sculpture. In the mid-twentieth century, Westerners attempted to avoid the paroxysm of grief by interdicting death. First in the United States, then in Britain, northern Europe, and now in Latin countries, they have abandoned the traditional ritual, hidden death from the dying person, and transferred it from the family to the hospital, where the abandoned "patient" passes imperceptibly out of life by degrees, his terminal moment being a technicality instead of a dramatic act over which he presides.

It is an astounding story, told with the incisiveness and mastery characteristic of Ariès's work; but is it true? The rules of evidence in this kind of history – the study of change in attitudes or *mentalités* – remain vague. Shifts in world view normally occur at a glacial pace, unmarked by events and without visible turning points. The subject matter of this history cannot be treated in the same way as the battles, election victories, and stock market fluctuations that punctuate *l'histoire événémentielle* with such precision. *Mentalités* need to be studied over the long term, and Ariès produces all these phrases in the first sentence of his book, as if he were an ambassador from the Annales School of History presenting his credentials to Johns Hopkins University, which invited him to report on his work in a series of lectures.

According to Ariès there are four phases of Western attitudes toward death: the traditional "tamed" death of the first millennium of Christianity, the more personal death of the next 750 years, the family-oriented obsession with "thy death," which prevailed from the late eighteenth to the early twentieth century, and the "forbidden death" of the last thirty years. Very formal and very French, perhaps, but Ariès has the advantage of showing how cultural mutation can occur at different paces. Western attitudes turned and twisted at an accelerating speed until they spun out of control in the contemporary era, which Ariès characterizes forcefully as a time of "a brutal revolution in traditional ideas and feelings."

In discussing the current century, Ariès argues from a position of strength, because he can draw on the work of social scientists like Gorer, who first exposed the deritualization and denial in contemporary attempts to deal with death. Ariès might even have taken his argument further by drawing more on the growing literature about death psychology, sociology, and "thanatology."[13] In analyzing older attitudes toward death, he has less to stand on but more to contribute, for he has mapped an unknown zone of human consciousness as it evolved through time. The audacity of the undertaking must be admired, even if it bears no more relation to reality than the cartography of Amerigo Vespucci. Gorer could study contemporary British attitudes by scientific sampling, questionnaires, and interviews. Ariès had to piece together whatever fragments he could find, rummaging about in archaeology, semantics, literature, law, and iconography.

Fascinating as the evidence is, its heterogeneity and sparseness inevitably weaken the argument. For example, Ariès asserts that man's vision of the

Last Judgment shifted significantly between the seventh and the fifteenth centuries; and to prove his case he refers to one seventh-century tomb, a half-dozen tympana from twelfth and thirteenth century cathedrals, a thirteenth-century hymn, and a fifteenth-century fresco. The reader is left to imagine the counterexamples from the art of those eight centuries, which flash by in four pages.

As evidence of the way death became individualized between the thirteenth and eighteenth centuries, Ariès stresses the importance of donation plaques in churches and cites one example, from 1703. To document the public character of the medieval deathbed rite, he cites one course from the late eighteenth century. He casually strides across continents and over centuries and carries the reader effortlessly from King Arthur's Round Table to Tolstoy's *mir* and Mark Twain's gold country. This fast play with sources may be less illegitimate than it seems, because vestiges of ancient customs survived well into the modern period everywhere in the West. But without firm evidence that the customs flourished earlier, one cannot know whether their later existence really was vestigial. Long-term history has not earned an exemption from the requirement of rigorous documentation.

The difficulty is greatest in research directed at the masses, who lived and died without leaving any trace of their conception of life and death. Ariès generally skirts this problem by restricting his discussion to high culture and the upper classes. When he expounds early medieval attitudes he turns to the *Chanson de Roland.* When he reaches the nineteenth century he cites Lamartine and the Brontës. He uses art history constantly, but normally limits himself to the art of the elite.

The most important exception to this tendency and the most original part of the book comes in Ariès's discussion of burial customs and cemetery design. He argues that early Christian burial reversed the practice of Roman patricians, who were buried in individual mausoleums outside the cities. The early Christians had a quasi-magical belief in the efficacy of interment near the remains of saints and, therefore, favored burial in churches located in the center of towns. For a millennium this burial remained essentially collective. The rich and well-born were placed under slabs of the church floor, the common people in ditches in the churchyard. As each location filled, the bones were transferred to common ossuaries and charnel houses, where they were stacked and displayed with macabre artistry. At the same time, cattle, children, shopkeepers, and bawds surged through the cemeteries.

The promiscuous interpretation of death and life struck Europeans as natural until the late eighteenth century, when enlightened French administrators considered it unhealthy and unseemly, forbade burial in churches, and moved graveyards outside city limits. By that time even the common people began to be buried in individual plots. The personal grave, surmounted by a stone with a biographical inscription, came to be seen as an inviolable preserve in the nineteenth century. Families visited it to honor their own dead both privately and on ceremonial occasions like All Souls' Day. A veritable new cult of the dead came into existence, especially in Latin Europe, where elaborate museums and statuary transformed the appearance of cemeteries. Then suddenly, during the first half of the twentieth century, this tendency was reversed. In contemporary Britain most people are cremated and therefore leave behind no physical testimony to their existence; their survivors rarely put up plaques or make inscriptions in the "Books of Remembrance" provided by the crematoria.

Burial customs therefore illustrate Ariès's contention that Western man first conceived of death as the familiar, collective fate of all Christians, then looked upon it as the supreme moment of a biography, next infused it with familiar affection, and finally attempted to deny it altogether. The resistance to cremation, the ceremonial funeral "homes," and the elaborate cemeteries of contemporary America do not fit this pattern; and Ariès does not explain why deritualization should be so muted here, where the "revolution" allegedly began, rather than in Britain, where it has assumed its most extreme form. But he uncovers some fascinating and unfamiliar aspects of Western culture.

Throughout his work, however, Ariès tries to understand popular mentality through the analysis of high culture, a dubious method, particularly when applied to relatively recent history. In the Middle Ages, it is true, elite and popular culture had not gone their separate ways. The common man carved his cosmology onto his church, where art historians like Erwin Panofsky have been able to decipher it. Millard Meiss, in *Painting in Florence and Siena after the Black Death,* has related the stylistic trends in Tuscan art to a general crisis in late medieval civilization, a crisis in which the Black Death played a crucial part. Huizinga discussed the same crisis in *The Waning of the Middle Ages,* a masterpiece that was inspired by the painting of the van Eycks. Alberto Teneti has attempted, with less success, to glimpse world view through Renaissance art in *Il senso della morte e l'amore della vita nel Rinascimento* and *La vie et la mort à travers l'art du XVe siècle.* And historians of medieval and Renaissance literature – Jean Rousset and Theodore Spencer, for example – have explored the connections between high culture and general attitudes toward death. This approach has proved to be especially useful in the study of genres like

Elizabethan tragedy and of specific works, like the *Faerie Queene,* which, as Kathrine Doller has shown, contains motifs derived from the popular *Ars Moriendi.*

So Ariès can draw on a rich scholarly tradition, and he does so with imagination and erudition. It seems regrettable that he leans heavily on Tenenti, when he could have used the more thorough studies of the *Ars Moriendi* by Mary Catharine O'Connor and Nancy Lee Beaty. He also makes little use of another popular genre, the Dance of Death, which has been studied by J. M. Clark and others. But he cannot be faulted for failing to incorporate traditional cultural history in his *histoire des mentalités.* The fault lies rather in a failure to question the connections between art and the inarticulate. When and to what extent did high culture become severed from the lower classes? That problem could be crucial to the history of popular attitudes, but Ariès rarely mentions class at all.

Gorer found striking differences in the way different classes respond to death in contemporary Britain. He discovered, for example, that the isolation of the dying becomes much greater as one ascends the social scale (family members were present at one of every three deaths in the working class cases he studied and at one of every eight among the upper middle and professional classes). Working class persons seemed considerably more familiar with death and less frightened of it, and they tended to preserve older customs longer (in four-fifths of working class homes the blinds are drawn after a death in the family; they are drawn in two thirds of middle class homes; and the upper middle and professional classes apparently have abandoned the practice altogether). The cultural significance of death may have varied enormously among different social groups, and it may have evolved among them in very different patterns. Ariès ignores such nuances and concentrates on the general Western pattern, assuming that there was one and that it can be known by studying the elite.

Those assumptions, though unproven, may be valid, and Ariès may well have succeeded in the monumental task of tracing the general outline of the changing Western attitudes toward death. How then does he explain them? His explanation is implicit and derives from his earlier study of childhood and the family. In the millennium of tamed death, he argues, men and women were absorbed almost immediately into the collectivity without passing through any clearly defined stage of childhood and without developing strong ties to their families. By the end of the eighteenth century, the family had taken over the socialization of the child, and childhood itself was perceived for the first time as a crucial phase of an individual's development. In response to a new demographic pattern, which made childhood and marriage less vulnerable to mortality, the family became the dominant institution in society: hence the nineteenth-century cult of the dead. Far from having declined, as some maintain, the family is now the focus of the affections. A death in the family therefore leaves modern man paralyzed by grief, for he has little emotional investment in other institutions, and he has but the empty remains of traditional ritual and religiosity to help him through his bereavement.

The argument might seem convincing if Ariès had proved the thesis of his *Centuries of Childhood,* a brilliant book but one that makes the history of childhood hang on the slender thread of the history of education, especially secondary and higher education. Since few children had any formal education before the modern period, it seems unlikely that educational institutions had much effect on general attitudes toward childhood. But all children had families. Contrary to what Ariès asserts, no evidence indicates that the family did not handle the socialization of children at all times in Western Europe and, for that matter, in all other societies.[14] The cohesion of the family probably varied considerably throughout Western history, and it may be stronger than ever today; but it could have been quite strong in the Middle Ages. In building an unsubstantiated interpretation of the evolution of attitudes toward death on an unsubstantiated interpretation of the evolution of the family, Ariès has stacked his hypotheses so precariously that they may collapse.

Ultimately, Ariès, like Cobb, relies on historical impressionism to hold his argument together and, as in Cobb's case, the weakness of that method may be appreciated by comparing his analysis with that of a sociological study of the same subject: *Piété baroque et déchristianisation en Provence au XVIIIe siècle* by Michel Vovelle.

The comparison may be unfair, because the writing of Ariès and Vovelle belong to different historical genres. Ariès produced an essay, a work in a genre that gives the historian an opportunity to take risks, to confront important subjects, and to ask big questions without feeling compelled to prove a case. As an essayist, Ariès could soar over two millenia in 100 pages. Even if he failed to sketch the topography of his subject correctly, he enriched history with a supply of original hypotheses. Vovelle went to the opposite extreme in historical writing. He burrowed deeply into one small corner of the history of death, sifted through his material with extraordinary care, and came up with a work of pure gold.

Vovelle discovered a way to know how ordinary persons conceived of death in eighteenth-century Provence. The work of Gabriel Le Bras and other sociologists of religion convinced him that the religion actually experienced by the inarticulate could be reconstructed by quantitative analysis of religious behavior. A pattern of action (*geste*) would reveal a pattern of attitudes. But where could one get systematic information about religiosity in the past? Vovelle found it in one of the oldest and most unexploited kinds of documents: wills, almost nineteen thousand of them. Far from being impersonal and legalistic as they are today, eighteenth-century wills provide an inventory of the testator's mental world. Most of them were dictated to notaries and therefore give a distorted reflection of that world, but the notaries proved to be varied and flexible in their writing. Even their stylized expressions are revealing, because they evolved in a significant pattern, and they indicate a pattern of behavior among the testators. By studying enormous numbers of Provençal wills over 100 years – and subjecting his data and methods to criticism at every step – Vovelle found that the concept of death and the ritual surrounding it shifted almost as radically in the eighteenth century as Ariès claims it did in the twentieth.

In the late seventeenth and early eighteenth centuries, testators consistently described themselves as adherents of the holy, apostolic Roman Catholic Church, who were prepared to meet their Maker, God the Creator, and Jesus Christ, His Son, by whose death and passion they hoped to be pardoned for their sins and to join the saints and angels in the Celestial Court of Paradise. Having made the sign of the cross in the name of the Father, the Son, and the Holy Ghost, the testators invoked legions of spiritual intercessors: first and most important, the glorious Virgin Mary; then the testator's guardian angel and patron saints; and finally a host of others, especially Saint Michael, who will hold the scales at the Last Judgment, and Saint Joseph, patron of the "good death." These wills were explicitly drawn up, as they put it, "in the thought of death" – an inevitable, solemn, and Christian occasion. By the 1780s most Provençal wills had reduced the traditional formula to a single clause: "Having recommended his soul to God." The Virgin Mary and saintly intercessors were gone, the Celestial Court emptied of angels. Christ himself had receded into the background, while God the Father sometimes took the form of "Divine Providence." Many wills had become totally secularized, and some even described death as "the indispensable tribute that we owe to Nature."

Of course the change in expressions could be attributed to a change in legal conventions. Perhaps the will had become a lay instrument for the transfer of property rather than an outlet for religious sentiment. But it continued to regulate death rites, and their evolution shows that the religious *geste* followed the same pattern as the legal formulas. Funerals were elaborate ceremonies in the early eighteenth century, especially but not exclusively among the wealthy and the well-born. A long procession escorted the casket from the home of the bereaved to the church, touring the town according to a prescribed circuit. Thirteen paupers carried torches decorated with the dead man's coat of arms or initials in one hand and in the other a ceremonial gift of cloth that they received from him. Priests and nuns in ceremonial robes, rectors of hospitals, contingents of orphans and poor people, and fellow members of religious confraternities filed by, carrying torches and candles, which filled the streets with light. Everywhere bells tolled, and everyone knew for whom, because death involved display, the parading of status by a collectivity, which used ceremony to express its own order and the dead man's place in it. After a religious service, whose elaborateness varied according to the "condition" (i.e., rank) of the deceased, alms were distributed to beggars at the church door, and the body was buried – in a family chapel or a monastery for nobles, under the church floor for other important citizens, in the graveyard for ordinary citizens. The testator regulated all these details in his will, down to the number of candles, and expected to enhance his chances of entering heaven and of lessening his penance in purgatory by gifts to the poor, who were to pray for his soul, and by funding hundreds or thousands of masses to be said for him on specified occasions, often in perpetuity.

The baroque funeral had almost become extinct in Provence by 1789. Requests for processions in Marseilles declined fourfold (from 20 percent to 5 percent of the wills in samples where two-thirds of the testators came from the lower middle and lower classes) and were overtaken by a contrary tendency; requests for "simplicity" and for burial "without pomp" (from 0 to 7 percent). The parading, torch carrying, and bell ringing had nearly disappeared. The poor had ceased to play a special part because their prayers were no longer deemed useful for souls in purgatory; and poverty was treated increasingly as an economic ailment rather than a spiritual condition. Driven away from the church doors and shut up in a poorhouse, wandering beggars now received doles, thanks to legacies given in a spirit of secular humanitarianism rather than Christian charity. References to penitential confraternities declined markedly. The percentage of clergymen mentioned in wills also dwindled; and they were more often older and from the secular rather than the regular clergy. Instead of asking to be buried in the old style, "according to his condition," testators left the burial arrangements up to their heirs. (In Marseilles wills expressing indifference about the place of burial increased from 15 percent to 75 percent until 1776, when the king forbade interment in churches.) Above all, the Provençaux abandoned the belief that masses were required for the repose of their souls. Among upper and middle class notables throughout the province, requests for masses declined from 80 percent to 50 percent, and the average number of masses requested dropped from 400 to

100. The decline was still greater in other groups – from 60 percent to around 20 percent among salaried male workers and seamen in Marseilles, and from 35 percent to 16 percent among peasants in the village of Salon-en-Provence.

Every indicator studied by Vovelle points to a decisive shift away from traditional religiosity and toward secularization in the mid-eighteenth century. In fact, it might make sense to conceive of two eighteenth centuries, a devout century (roughly from 1680 to 1750) in which traditional religious attitudes and ceremonies prevailed, and a century of secularization (from 1750 or 1760 to 1815), in which revolutionary de-Christianization only accelerated a process that had gained great momentum during the last decades of the Old Regime. Vovelle does not go so far as to suggest such a radical revision of conventional periodization, but it would fit data that have accumulated in demographic, economic, and intellectual history.[15] He does, however, analyze his material according to chronology, geography, and social structure; and this analysis lifts his account from the level of description to that of explanation.

First Vovelle establishes the details of the chronological pattern by analyzing 1,800 wills in central registries. These covered the entire province very well (they came from 600 notaries in 198 localities, or almost half the towns and villages in Provence). Although they did not represent much of the population below the upper crust notables, they revealed four phases in the evolution of attitudes: from 1680 to 1710, a period of increased religiosity, which Vovelle attributes to the continuation, at a popular level, of the seventeenth-century religious revival and of the Counter Reformation; from 1710 to 1740, a period of decline, which coincided with the most violent episodes of the Jansenist controversies in Provence; from 1740 to 1760, a period of stabilization; and from 1760 to 1790, a period of brutal de-Christianization.

This scheme suggests that Jansenism and the Enlightenment could have acted as the gravediggers of traditional religiosity. Although Jansenism represented only an aspiration for a more intense and inward devotional life, it looked like crypto-Protestantism to many Frenchmen, and it touched off some fierce quarrels between rival factions of the French church in the early eighteenth century. After a long period of latency, the Enlightenment burst into print in mid-century and became widely diffused during the next fifty years. But how deeply did either of those two intellectual movements penetrate into French society?

Vovelle explores these and other problems of cultural diffusion by taking detailed soundings in twelve carefully chosen sites. With the help of several students, he made exhaustive analyses of wills in the notarial archives of one city (Marseilles), a small town and a village in lower Provence, two towns in upper Provence, and seven other towns and villages chosen for their exposure to Jansenism and Protestantism. Each study is a monograph in itself; each is executed with rigor and sophistication; and each touches an aspect of cultural and spiritual life that has eluded previous research.

Take the case of Roquevaire, a village near Marseilles, which had a population of 2,500 in 1765. About two-thirds of its inhabitants left wills when they died, and almost three-quarters of them were peasants. Vovelle studied 500 wills in five samplings taken from 1650 to 1790. He therefore worked with a remarkably representative index to attitudes among the obscure "little people" in village society, and he found that they changed more radically than among the notables throughout the province. In 1700, 80 percent of the peasant landowners requested that masses be said for their souls; by 1750 the proportion had risen to 100 percent; and by 1789 it had dropped to 30 percent. The decline was less severe among the local notables (75 percent to 60 percent), but it was very strong among artisans and shopkeepers (50 percent to 16 percent). Other statistics confirmed this trend: Requests for funeral corteges declined from 23 percent to 2 percent; legacies to religious confraternities dropped from 55 percent to 1 percent; and the phrasing of the wills, which had been rich and varied in devotional expressions, became totally laicized.

Thus the general trend toward secularization could have extended further among the submerged masses than among the elite – at least in southern Provence, where economic and demographic growth and social and geographical mobility were greatest. Vovelle discovered another world in the isolated regions of northern Provence. Religious customs remained almost unchanged in Barcelonnette, an Alpine village where the Counter Reformation had established itself with unusual power and precocity (92 percent of the wills requested masses at the beginning of the century, 81 percent at the end). There was also little change in Manosque, a backward, back-country town, which never adopted the intense religious practices of the mountainous areas and never gave in to the secularization of the *plat pays* (requests for masses remained constant at a low level, appearing in between 20 and 30 percent of the wills). The geographical comparison suggests a link between changes in attitudes and in socioeconomic forces. Did a "modern" world view result from the increased mobility, economic growth, and life expectancy of the second eighteenth century?

Vovelle seems to favor this interpretation, but he shies away from generalizations and concentrates on the effects of cultural factors: hence his emphasis on Jansenism and the Enlightenment. He found secularization

strongest in towns where Jansenism had taken root most deeply (Pigans
and Cotignac) and also where Protestantism had never been completely
extinguished (Cucuron and Pertuis). But in remote Jansenist sites (Blieux
and Senez), orthodox Catholicism reestablished itself with unusual mili-
tancy, making the graphs of requests for masses – which serve as the crucial
indicator throughout the book – rise instead of fall, until the last decades
of the Old Regime, when they drop sharply. So if Jansenism precipitated
de-Christianization, it did so primarily in the open, mobile population of
the South.

The drop that occurs almost everywhere in Vovelle's graphs after 1760
suggests that secularization correlates with the diffusion of the Enlightenment. But attitudes and ideas represent different mental states: The
decline in the devotional treatment of death need not imply a rise in
Voltairianism; and it cannot be measured against the penetration of the
Enlightenment, because that penetration cannot itself be measured. Faced
with this problem, Vovelle uses literacy as a standard of measurement,
although he concedes that it is a crude and unreliable index to the spread
of enlightened ideas. He produces some important statistics on the incidence of literacy insofar as it can be known by the only available evidence,
signatures of wills. His results confirm the celebrated Maggiolo study,
which showed a low rate of literacy in southern France, and they expose
the mythical character of the common view – one that flourished among
nineteenth-century anticlericals – that instruction undermines religion.
Vovelle discovered villages where both literacy and religiosity were very
high (Barcelonnette) and very low (Salon). And he shows that in some
places secularization was stronger among peasants and laborers, who were
predominantly illiterate, than among the highly literate notables. So even
if the spread of the Enlightenment has a correlation with primitive literacy,
as seems unlikely, literacy has none with the secularization of attitudes
toward death.

Marseilles, however, seems to have been a special case. Vovelle found
that lower middle and lower class Marseillais were far more literate and
secularized than their rural counterparts. Some of his statistics strain credi-
bility (on page 377 he notes that by 1789 literacy among female peasants
had risen to 45 percent and among male peasants had dropped to 0). But
they demonstrate that secularization and literacy developed coincidentally
in this urban setting, though at different rates among different social
groups. Thus the literate elite of notables split, the nobles clinging to traditional religiosity while the bourgeois became de-Christianized. By 1789
three-quarters of all male laborers, artisans, and shopkeepers could sign

their names, and the vast majority of them had given up the practice of requesting masses for the repose of their souls.

Vovelle tends to see a class alignment behind this sorting out of attitudes, and he turns it against the revisionist argument that the Enlightenment took root among a mixed elite of nobles and nonnobles. His thesis will go down well with Marxists who treat the Enlightenment as bourgeois ideology,[16] but his data suggest a change of attitudes that go deeper than ideology, and they call for further analysis. They are strikingly clear, by contrast, in showing a split in the devotional practices of men and women. This "sexual dimorphism" was especially strong among the lower classes, where there was also a widening gap between the literacy of men and women. Thus by the nineteenth century, illiterate women servants frequently had become more devout than their mistresses; and male laborers took to drink and newspapers in the bistro while their illiterate wives attended church. Vovelle has most to say about such questions of custom and outlook. He discovered a sea change in man's conception of the sacred, a process that may have disposed the Provençaux to accept enlightened ideas but that had no direct connection with the Enlightenment.

How this change came about remains in the end a mystery. It was not a matter of the masses following the lead of the elite, nor is it a matter of education or of urbanization. Secularization took hold most strongly in areas where social and economic change was greatest; and exposure to disruptive influences like Jansenism, Protestantism, and the Enlightenment probably had a reinforcing effect. But "socioeconomic change" hardly serves as an explanation. Vovelle shows that the established pattern of attitudes in Marseilles was barely disrupted by the devastating plague of 1720, which killed half the population in the city, and by the subsequent tidal wave of immigration, which replaced the dead with a new population of uprooted peasants. And at some points his explanation sounds redundant: Attitudes changed because of a *mutation de sensibilité collective*, that is, a change in attitudes.

Ultimately, his interpretation depends on the words used in the title: He traces a shift from "baroque piety" to "de-Christianization." Instead of defining these terms, he builds associations around them and uses them descriptively, as a kind of shorthand for a pattern of attitudes and actions. But the "baroque" is a particularly ambiguous concept, which means different things to different historians, many of whom will gag on expressions like *sensibilité baroque, moeurs baroques,* and *baroquisme.*

De-Christianization also poses a problem, because most of Vovelle's material concerns the decrease in traditional ways of dealing with death – a

matter of decline, not extinction (by 1789 half of the notables in the province still requested masses for their souls). The abandonment of "baroque" rites need not have implied the renunciation of Christianity. In
fact, deritualization could have meant purification, as it did among the
English Puritans. Ariès tries to explain Vovelle's data by invoking the rise
of the family instead of the decline of traditional death rituals. He claims
that testators stopped regulating their funerals and burials because for the
first time they could trust their relatives to do justice to such ceremonies.
Perhaps other interpretations could fit Vovelle's data, which he expounds
beautifully but never fully explains.

Yet such criticism applies equally to the great theses that established the
economic and demographic patterns of eighteenth-century French history.
We still do not know why the population broke through the old Malthusian
ceiling of twenty to twenty-five million, why agricultural prices should
have increased by half during the last fifty years of the Old Regime, and
why there was a revolution. Now we can ponder a deeper mystery: Why
did attitudes change toward the basic facts of life and death? All these
changes seem related to the emergence of a world that we may recognize
as "modern," but how can we explain these relationships? By penetrating
a previously inaccessible realm of experience, Vovelle has added a new
dimension to the big questions of history, even if he has failed to answer
them.

The importance of his achievement needs to be stressed because few
readers will find his quantification palatable or digestible. There is a kind
of statistical puritanism to this book. No human beings relieve the un-
relenting flow of maps, charts, and graphs, 112 of them, all done without
computers or correlation coefficients. But history has often floundered
in vague talk about world view, climate of opinion, and *Zeitgeist*. To get
beyond Burckhardt, the study of *mentalités* needed new methods and new
materials. Vovelle's use of quantification and sociology made him succeed
where Ariès failed: He managed to chart a significant shift in world view
among groups whose lives had seemed to be irretrievably lost in the past.

Conclusion

This attempt to make contact with the mental life of history's forgotten
men and women distinguishes the history of *mentalités* from the common
varieties of intellectual history. Such contact as can be made usually concerns the fundamentals of the human condition, the way people conceived

of the facts of life and death. But historians of *mentalités* are also investigating popular culture, folklore, vagrancy, family relations, sexuality, love, fear, and insanity. They attack these disparate subjects by different methods: statistics, demography, economics, anthropology, social psychology, whatever seems more appropriate.[17] Although it is too early to assess their work, a preliminary reconnoitering – and the comparison of Cobb and the criminologists on the one hand and Ariès and Vovelle on the other – suggests one methodological imperative: Rather than relying on intuition in an attempt to conjure up some vague climate of opinion, one ought to seize on at least one firm discipline in the social sciences and use it to relate mental experience to social and economic realities.

That conclusion, however, sounds suspiciously like common sense. Few historians today would object to the notion of applying social science to their craft, but few would agree on how the application is to be done. Are we to rummage through the social sciences, trying on one discipline after another, until we find something that somehow seems to fit our needs? Methodological eclecticism provides no real solution to the problems of relating changes in attitudes to social and economic development.

Perhaps Vovelle's failure to explain the phenomena he describes so successfully may indicate a weakness in the way *mentalités* are usually conceived. According to a classic formulation by Pierre Chaunu – one that seems to command the assent of scholars of every stripe in France – *mentalités* exist on a "third level" of history. They belong to a superstructure, which rises above the more fundamental structures of the society and the economy, and therefore they develop in response to seismic shifts in the social and economic orders.[18] This three-tiered view of change suits a historiographical tradition that has been deeply influenced by Marxism. It also lends itself to functionalist social science; and it is congenial to quantification, because the statistical reconstruction of patterns of attitudes seems capable of revealing reality at the third level. But Vovelle, a Marxist-functionalist-quantifier, discovered that the curves of his graphs did not follow a pattern that made attitudes appear as a function of social and economic variables.

Perhaps the contributions to cultural history of Burckhardt, Huizinga, and even Lucien Febvre have been misconstrued by their successors; for those early masters attributed a considerable degree of autonomy to cultural forces. They did not treat culture as an epiphenomenon of society. They understood it as some current anthropologists do. The anthropological view of man as an animal who hungers for meaning, and of world view as a tenacious, ordering principle of social existence,[19] may ultimately go further than third-degree quantification to make sense of the material that the French are mining in such bewildering profusion from the riches of their past. Whether that prophecy proves true, it seems evident that the history of *mentalités* has developed into an important genre; it has already forced historians to see the human condition in a strange, new light.

ACKNOWLEDGMENT

Parts of this essay are reprinted with the permission of the *New York Review of Books*.

NOTES

1 Principal writings discussed in this essay include the following. By Richard Cobb: *Reactions to the French Revolution* (London: Oxford University Press, 1972); *The Police and the People: French Popular Protest 1789–1820* (London: Oxford University Press, 1970); *A Second Identity: Essays on France and French History* (London: Oxford University Press, 1969). By A. Abbiateci et al., *Crimes et criminalité en France sous l'Ancien Régime, 17e–18e siècles* (Paris: Armand Colin, 1971). By Philippe Ariés, *Western Attitudes toward Death: From the Middle Ages to the Present,* trans. Patricia M. Ranum (Baltimore: Johns Hopkins University Press, 1974). By Michel Vovelle, *Piété baroque et déchristianisation en Provence au XVIIIe siècle: Les Attitudes devant la mort d'après les clauses des testaments* (Paris: Plon, 1973).

2 *Contrepoint* 5 (1971):105–115; *L'Humanité,* February 18, 1972, p. 8; *La Nouvelle Critique* (1972); and Guy Lemarchand, "Sur la société française en 1789," *Revue d'histoire moderne et contemporaine* (1972):73–91.

3 The best in this tradition is represented by Albert Mathiez, *La Vie chère et le mouvement social sous la Terreur* (Paris, 1927); Georges Lefebvre, *Les Paysans du Nord pendant la Révolution française* (Paris, 1924); and Albert Soboul, *Les Sans-Culottes parisiens en l'an II* (Paris, 1958). For recent examples, see Régine Robin, *La Société française en 1789: Semur-en-Auxois* (Paris, 1970), and Claude Mazauric, *Sur la Révolution française* (Paris, 1970).

4 See the essays by Lucien Febvre reprinted in *Combats pour l'histoire* (Paris: Armand Colin, 1965), pp. 207–39; Georges Duby, "Histoire des mentalités" in *L'Histoire et ses méthodes (Encyclopédie de la Pléiade,* Paris, 1961), pp. 937–66; Robert Mandrou, "Histoire sociale et histoire des mentalités, *La Nouvelle Critique* (1972):41–4; Alphonse Dupront, "Problèmes et méthodes d'une histoire de la psychologie collective," *Annales: Economies, sociétés, civilisations* (1961):3–11; Louis Trénard, "Histoire des mentalités collectives: Les Livres, bilans et perspectives," *Revue d'histoire moderne et contemporaine*

(1968):691–703; and Jacques Le Goff, "Les mentalités: une histoire ambiguë," *Faire de l'histoire*, ed. Jacques Le Goff and Pierre Nora (Paris, 1974), 3:76–94.

5 André Davidovitch, "Criminalité et répression en France depuis un siècle (1851–1952)," *Revue française de sociologie* (1961):30–49; and Pierre Deyon, "Délinquance et répression dans le nord de la France au XVIIIᵉ siècle," *Bulletin de la Société d'Histoire Moderne*, 20 (1972):10–5.

6 For example, Leon Radizinowicz and Marvin E. Wolfgang, eds., *Crime and Justice*, vol. 1, *The Criminal in Society* (New York: Basic Books, 1971); and Hermann Manheim, *Comparative Criminology* (Boston: Houghton-Mifflin, 1965).

7 A. M. Guerry, *Essai sur la statistique morale de la France* (Paris, 1833); and Adolphe Quételet, *Sur l'homme et le développement de ses facultés, ou Essai de physique sociale* (Paris, 1836).

8 Enrico Ferri, *La Sociologie criminelle*, 3rd ed. (Paris, 1893), Chapter 2.

9 In 1960, Colombia reportedly had 34.0 murders per 100,000 population; the United States had 4.5; and France had 1.7: Marvin E. Wolfgang and Franco Ferracuti, *The Subculture of Violence* (London: Tavistock, 1967).

10 *Crimes et criminalité en France*, pp. 187–261; and Deyon, "Delinquance et répression."

11 Jessica Mitford, *The American Way of Death* (New York: Simon & Schuster, 1963); and Geoffrey Gorer, *Death, Grief, and Mourning in Contemporary Britain* (London: The Cresset Press, 1965).

12 Philippe Ariès, *Centuries of Childhood: A Social History of Family Life* (New York: Random House, 1965) and *Western Attitudes toward Death: From the Middle Ages to the Present* (Baltimore: Johns Hopkins University Press, 1974).

13 This literature is so enormous as to be symptomatic of the current crisis in the treatment of death. It may be sampled in three anthologies: Herman Feifel, ed., *The Meaning of Death* (New York: McGraw-Hill, 1959); Robert Fulton, ed., *Death and Identity* (New York: John Wiley & Sons, 1965); and Hendrik Ruitenbeek, ed., *Death: Interpretations* (New York: Delacorte, 1969).

14 It seems odd that Ariès ignores this crucial point, which has long been central in anthropological literature. See G. P. Murdock, *Social Structure* (New York, 1949, reprinted 1965, The Free Press).

15 For an excellent synthesis of work in these fields, which treats the mid-eighteenth century as a turning point in the history of the Old Regime, see Pierre Goubert, *L'Ancien Régime* (Paris: Armand Colin, 1969 and 1973), 2 vols.

16 Vovelle has associated himself with this tendency, which seems to be increasingly important in Marxist writing on the eighteenth century: See *L'Humanité*, February 18, 1972, p. 8.

17 To cite some examples of work now in progress, Pierre Chaunu is preparing a study of the evolution of attitudes toward death over several centuries in Paris; Jean Delumeau is completing research on forms of fear in the West;

J.-L. Flandrin on affectivity and sexuality among peasants of the Old Regime; E.-M. Benabou on *libertinage* and prostitution in eighteenth-century Paris; and J. M. Gouesse on attitudes toward marriage in early modern France. As an example of a book that successfully relates demography to attitudes toward death, see François Lebrun, *Les Hommes et la mort en Anjou aux 17ᵉ et 18ᵉ siècles* (Paris, 1971), which was discussed in a version of this essay that appeared in *The New York Review of Books* (June 13, 1974).

18 Pierre Chaunu, "Un Nouveau Champ pour l'histoire sérielle: le quantitatif au troisième niveau," *Mélanges en l'honneur de Fernand Braudel* (Toulouse, 1973) 2:105–25. This conceptual framework seems to have determined the organization of many recent works in French history. Thus Lebrun, *Les hommes et la mort,* Part I: *Structures économiques et socio-geographiques,* Part II: *Structure démographique,* Part III: *Mentalités;* F. G. Dreyfus, *Sociétés et mentalités à Mayence dans la seconde moitié du dix-huitième siècle* (Paris, 1968): Part I: *Economie,* Part II: *Structure sociale,* Part III: *Mentalités et culture;* Maurice Garden, *Lyon et les lyonnais au XVIIIᵉ siècle* Part I: *Démographie,* Part II: *Société,* Part III: *Structures mentales et comportements collectifs* (Paris, 1970).

19 For a cogent expression of this strain in anthropology, see Clifford Geertz, *The Interpretation of Cultures* (New York: Basic Books, 1973).

Part II
Structure, self, and evil

5

Architectonic man:
On the structuring of lived experience

ROM HARRÉ

Editors' introduction

Many contemporary thinkers have sought to recover the Renaissance notion that the human world is constituted of structures created and maintained by acts of human intelligence, imagination, and will - that social reality is an expression of *virtù* as well as *fortuna*. It is only recently, however, that scholars have begun to decode the exact nature of this structuring process. As such, their work gives empirical substance to the philosophical theses of symbolic realism and at the same time suggests a radical reformulation of organistic and mechanistic approaches in the human studies. Rom Harré's discussion of the *Umwelt* is a unique contribution to this project.

After commenting generally on the assumptions he brings to his essay, Harré describes a wide range of representative structuring, from broad macrostructures of space and time to the microstructures of everyday life. Then, in a concluding section, Harré traces some relations between *Umwelt* structures and social theory: Both may be representations of a cosmology and both implicate each other ontologically. In addition, Harré argues that a primary task of the social sciences must be to reconstruct the historical development of *Umwelten* and other structures of meanings.

In some respects Harré's essay recalls the nearly century-old debate between the functionalists and the evolutionists discussed in the earlier essay by Lyman. Just as the evolutionists were so concerned with the processual aspects of change that they could not stop to examine the content of the thing changing, so students of social and historical processes in our own day seem too hasty in asserting the never-ending flux to examine the composition of the thing in motion. The functionalists - contrary to much mistaken opinion in the history of anthropology - did not put an end to historical questions nor did they even call a halt to the evolutionist project. Rather, they reset the parameters of anthropological study just enough to ask for a description of sociocultural entities. These descriptions constituted the still frames depicting the passage of what was a moving picture of societies. Harré, interested ultimately in the processual development of forms of human experience, tells us to halt for a moment and capture the essence of that which is undergoing transformation. In the *Umwelt* he locates his strategic research site. In humans as architects of their experience he locates the action. Analysis of the nature and sources of the *Umwelt* constitutes the precondition for study of its past and the projection of its future.

Harré's essay thus has a special conjunction with those of Lyman and Darnton in the previous section. Lyman emphasizes the critique by neopositivists of the evolutionists' and functionalists' enterprise. Seeking to establish a truly scientific approach to the study of history and social change, the neopositivists failed to establish a grounded unit as a topic for their own proposed project. A phenomenologically informed science might recast the neopositivist position, placing the *Umwelt* at its center. The *Umwelt,* properly understood, might constitute the building block for a comparative historical sociology. Robert Darnton shows how an existentially informed history can still benefit from the work of those researchers known as moral statisticians. In terms of Harré's project, a collection of mundane facts, when illuminated by an approach that seeks to get at the prevailing structures of consciousness, could produce a new historical understanding, a social archaeology of consciousness past to match the social architecture of consciousness present.

Introduction

All our actions are carried out against a structured background, which makes various contributions to the action, by broadcasting, as from an endless tape, messages of reassurance and threat. Until recently this background was treated as part of the shared and taken-for-granted common sense world and, as such, assumed by sociologists to be unproblematic. The structure of this "background" world and the manner of its working on human social feelings was much discussed in the Renaissance, but it is only very recently that sociologists and (even more recently) social psychologists have turned their attention to it. In this paper I shall concur with these thinkers that the unrestricted or undeformed activity proper to human beings is to conceive and realize an almost unlimited variety of structural forms. I also share their view that some of these realized forms will be elevated to the status of microcosms. A contemporary version of this theory is part of the philosophical orientation called symbolic realism, a general view of men and women as agents, living according to rules, interacting through shared meanings, and forever structuring the material around them. This general orientation in the social and behavioral sciences is reflected in ethnomethodology, phenomenological and existential sociology, cognitive anthropology, and the sociology of the absurd. Drawing on findings from these subdisciplines, I shall touch lightly on various activities of architectonic man, in the hope of stirring further interest in this vital area of human action and understanding.[1]

The environment of action as meaningful to the actors, what Burke called the "scene," has several components.[2] A first division enables us to mark off the physically oriented component from the theoretical one. The physical scene can be considered either as to its spatiotemporal structure or as to the meaning of its components, like smells, colors, or the state of the weather. In this paper I shall be concerned only with the former, and shall speak of it, with a small measure of license, as the *Umwelt*.

Two preliminary questions need to be answered before analysis can begin. We must first take a stand on the central matter of the nature of the environment of social action, choosing whether we would line up with Skinner or with Kant, with those who regard the environment as external to action or with those who regard at least some of the properties of the environment of action as human products. I shall be working, in this paper, with a generally Kantian assumption, which seems to me so utterly indisputable that I can find little to debate about with the other side. That a traffic light is what it is as part of the environment of social action by a social endowment of red, green, and yellow with meanings, and that those meanings are embedded and maintained within a system of rules, seems to me so obvious that the idea that it is red as a physical stimulus that brings me to brake my car can scarcely be taken seriously. Furthermore it is also clear that the Skinnerian view must be wrong if applied to the institutional environment since that is a product of knowledge and understanding. I hope that as my analysis of the *Umwelt* unfolds we shall see that much the same is true of the physical environment as well.

The second question concerns not the nature of the social environment, but its origin. Why is the human *Umwelt* so highly structured? To this I wish to give the rather flat but theoretically important answer that structure-creating activity is natural to man, that men are architectonic, that is, makers of structure above all other things. The question, I believe, is not why does he create structures, but why does he create just these?

My main theme can be expressed most sharply by contrast with a recent statement by Bernstein.[3] He assumes that "symbolic systems are both realizations and regulators of the structure of social relationships." I hold, on the contrary, that social relationships are themselves a symbolic system,

a representation in a form of life of structures, the conceptions of which
are prior to their realization. Of course, learning the social system is learning a symbolic system, both in the sense that the social system is auto-
referential, in and of itself symbolic, and also in the sense that it may be
a kind of iconic representation of that society's theory of the nature of
people and their world, a theory in terms of which they can explain to
themselves and to each other the situation in which they find themselves.

Whence comes such a thesis and what is its justification? At the heart
of any theory of science and society is an image of man, a conception of
him as a creature defined by his powers and abilities, his failings and
liabilities. I want to redevelop, against some of the "self-images of the age,"
the Renaissance image of architectonic man, whose final elaboration and
to some extent perversion, appeared in the philosophy of Kant. This image
– that we are architectonic by nature, structure producers above all – was
seriously investigated by Ficino, Albertus Magnus, Bruno, Kepler, and
many others.[4] The atomism of the seventeenth century, which separated
men from each other and from their environment, and the strong Protestant opposition to the Hermetic and neo-Platonic cast of thought of the
social psychologists of the fifteenth and sixteenth centuries, led to a decline
in interest in these matters. Yet from Machiavelli to Kepler human life was
seen as the attempt to impose form, but whereas for Machiavelli this was
the mastery of *fortuna* by *virtù*, for Kepler the conceiving of form was an
endeavour to match structured thought to a preformed world. For the
purposes of social analysis I wish to take a Machiavellian view of the origin
of social form, and a Keplerian view of the forms of nature, modified by
the perception of Kant, that for the most general kind of structure, the
world behind the phenomena, we can deal only with the form we conceive
it to have. Architectonic man sets about the cooperative realization of
forms. In one category we try to realize our thought forms in concrete
objects, buildings, technologies, and productive devices, models in science
and works of art. In another category we try to realize our conceived
structures in abstract objects, scientific theories, and social institutions.
In this view societies and their institutions are representations, and it is no
wonder, then, that their structures are often isomorphic with the forms of
thought in other fields of realization. As Durkheim perceived, it is their
being shared that endows societal icons with a measure of intersubjectivity,
and not objectivity. I am far from wishing to follow Durkheim in supposing
that such shared icons and their products are in any sense the causal agents
of other such products or thought forms. Rather, I would accept the per-

ceived isomorphism of thoughts and products to be found in Durkheim and in Marxist thought, but I would reverse the order of causality.

Such reversed causality is not idealism in a new and hidden form, since I wish to stress even more strongly the existent character of social forms but also to emphasize that those forms only "fluoresce in the light of a rhetoric," as Coleridge once put it. This allows the student of the sociology of knowledge to turn his attention to the principles of the transformational processes by which icons in thought are realized as structures in the *Umwelt* and to examine the forms of the latter in terms of shifting rhetorics. How different a mental hospital looks when its structure is made luminous by the official rhetoric (a place of cure) and when its structure stands out in another light, say that of Goffman's dramaturgical rhetoric, in which the hospital is seen as a stage for dramas of social control and moral careers. But the source of both these structures is that they are representations by transformation of the shared societal icons among those who create and maintain the institution.

Our focus here, however, is on the rich, physical environment. There are the colors of things, their smells and tastes. There are the ever-changing seasons. Any or all of these features can have social significance thrust upon them. In some parts of the world the color of a person's skin can be treated as having social significance. In countries with very variable weather the moods of the inhabitants can be much influenced by these changes. The significance of such moods may be great and read back into nature as a kind of social meteorology.[5] I shall not be concerned with these features of the environment in this paper, but with the interrelated structures we impose on space and time and the structures we build with things and events within space and time.

The socially meaningful physical environment within which we live seems to have two degrees of structure, two levels of granularity, if you will. The coarse-grained structure consists of distinct and separated areas in space and periods in time, distinguished by markedly distinct social activities. For instance the social activities of the street and sidewalk are quite distinct from those inside a bank adjoining that street and opening off the sidewalk. This is one of those obvious truths that should yet surprise us and force us to ask how it can be so. How do I know socially speaking that I am in the counting hall of a bank and no longer in the street? And how do I know that this is a social distinction and not just a practical or pragmatic one? How do I know that I should behave reverently in a banking hall, and not just crudely and rudely grab my money and go? Part of the answers to these questions are to be found by looking at the decor of the banking hall. Our first task will be to examine some of the ways in which socially distinct areas and volumes of space and periods of time are demarcated and maintained. In this way the coarse-grained structure of the *Umwelt* will be revealed.

But each area and volume, and each period of time, and each thing within an area, and each pattern of action within a time has a structure that differentiates it from other things and makes it thereby a potential vehicle of significance or meaning. These are the fine-grained structures of the *Umwelt*. How are these structures socially significant? I shall try to establish, with a wide range of examples, that we create and maintain such structures and endow them with meaning as a kind of permanent or semi-permanent billboard or hoarding upon which certain socially important messages can be "written." The very fact of order, when recognized by human beings, is, in itself, the source of a message that all is well. Orderliness of the physical environment broadcasts a kind of continuous social Musak whose message is reassurance. But as we shall see, the fine structuring of the *Umwelt* allows us to give and receive much more specific messages, public statements of how we wish to be taken as social beings. I will try to show, in broad outline, how these more specific messages are achieved.

The macro-structure of space and time

As we pass through space and time we are continually adjusting ourselves to a complex social topography. Some regions are closed to us, some open, and for some various keys or magic passwords are required, such as "Oh yes, I'm a member here." Looking at this ethogenically we must ask how these barriers are established and promulgated, how they are maintained, how legitimately crossed, how their accidental violation is remedied, and what the social structure of the topography thus established might be.

As an introductory illustration consider the time barrier that separates the period before a school lesson from the lesson itself. It may be created by a bell ringing, but it separates two socially distinct regions. In the period before the lesson the social structure of the class is a complex network of micro-social groupings, one of which may include the teacher – and that is usually the tone-setting or highest social status group – and the whole interaction pattern is organized as "chat." After the lesson starts the social order simplifies into a one-many hierarchy, with the children oriented to the teacher, and with an almost complete disappearance of the chatting that characterized the previous period.

Spatial boundaries like fences or white lines on the ground demarcate socially distinct areas, according to such social topographies as the polarity between the safe and the dangerous area. Urban Americans are all too familiar with the feeling of relief and relaxation as one passes beyond Such and Such Street into a "safe" area.

In both space and time the structures created by boundaries and their associated barriers, the physical markers of boundaries – like fences in space and silences in time – can be differently related to deliberate human effort. The English Channel is *there,* as is the moment of death, and both have to be coped with. But a line scratched on the sand and defined, "That's your team's home base" or a beginning initiated by "O.K., let's get started" are creations, more or less free, and as such challengeable and subject to negotiation. Other human constructions have the permanence of geographical features, such as architectural or agricultural arrangements, whereas time is structured permanently by such artefacts as clocks and calendars. Our only social response to such entities as the English Channel or spring is semantic, one of negotiating meaning, expressed in such famous aphorisms as "Wogs start at Calais" or "Oh, to be in England now that spring is here." For our own intransigent artefacts, we negotiate the meaning of an hour or, for that matter, of the Great Pyramid. Finally, in complete contrast to these kinds of structuring are the wholly ephemeral ones, such as the lane changes in tidal flow traffic schemes, or the agreement of the order of speakers at a testimonial dinner. Most of the boundaries and barriers we will be examining in detail are neither so unresponsive to human renegotiation as the solar year or the Atlantic Ocean – though even these objects are not wholly so – nor as ephemeral as the chalked grid for street hopscotch.

A time period, whether natural or conventional, has a beginning and an end. The ritual or symbolic devices by which beginnings and ends are marked socially I shall call "openings" and "closings." Some openings and closings coincide with natural boundaries such as birth and death; others are imposed upon an otherwise empirically undifferentiated time.

An obvious place to look for openings and closings is the kindergarten. And indeed close observation of the way beginnings and ends of activities are managed yields a striking discovery.[6] The initial and final moves in the sequence of an activity are separated from the rest of the activity by being performed in a particularly flamboyant and exaggerated way. Their natural role as beginnings and endings is stylistically enhanced. The drama lesson, for example, was opened by a specially exaggerated moving forward of a portable proscenium, which had been moved several times previously in a routine manner without being read as an opening, since on those occasions the children did not, as they did in the stylistically empha- sized case, make haste to sit ready for the show and evince every sign of anticipation. In a similar manner the closing of a painting session was symbolically managed by a conspicuous and flamboyant "putting up of a brush," after which, without any words being said germane to the issue of closure, a ragged procession of stylistically flamboyant "puttings up" occurred. That closed painting for the day. However, in the same kinder- garten, meal time, a strictly marked and socially distinct period, with groups of four children eating together, each group supervised by a teacher or helper, was opened and closed with verbal formulae, "Alright, it's time for eating," after which hands were washed without further com- mand as a proper part of opening. "Now go and get a book" ritually completed the meal time, though the book was read, then, for fifteen minutes in the interests of digestion.

As a general rule things do not just start, they are opened, by the recital of a ritual formula or the performance of a symbolic action: "Oyez, Oyez, Oyez, as it pleases the Queen, Her Gracious Majesty," or cutting the ribbon to open the road, and so on. The variety and sources of such formulae would no doubt repay close sociological study. I propose to attend only to one such case, which illuminates an aspect of the problem of the origin of opening and closing rituals, those which are not simply stylistically emphasized beginnings and endings. In a recent study of the openings and closings in schools, a participant noticed that one of her teachers always opened the lesson with "Sorry I'm late" whether she was so in fact. So much had this become a ritual formula for opening that its bizarre quality had escaped almost everyone's attention. Lévi-Strauss[7] has offered an explanation of the way a particular form of ritual appears first as the form of a specially striking occasion that is then simply repeated, at first in remembrance of the special character of the original occasion and then as a ritual in its own right. The origin of the particular form and content of ritualized family quarrels can probably be explained in part in this way as well. Thus, in the case of the teacher, a specially striking tardiness, or perhaps a run of mishaps, most probably led to just enough repetition to ritualize the remark. Other participants in the study reported to the general effect that each teacher had a ritualized, inevitable opening phrase, but of course they were all different. Some had the quality of kindergarten openers, initial steps raised to symbolic quality, such as the reported "Right, turn your books over," uttered regardless of whether the books were in fact face up or face down.

Closure requires special attention and is highly ritualized. A student teacher of German reports that a class simply would not disperse quickly and in an orderly way when he said, "All right, that's all for today." His problem was solved by the teacher in charge, after an observation lesson, telling him that German lessons always ended with *Bitte ihr dürft gehen,* on the utterance of which the class dispersed instantly. But, having violated the traditional closing ritual with that class, it took the student teacher some time to reestablish it.

But the rituals of opening and closing are in fact often more complicated. Studies by Schegloff and Sacks have revealed a fine structure behind simple openings and closings.[8] They investigated the ritual forms commonly used to close conversations as distinct social times. At first glance a conversation, say on the telephone, seems to be closed by the ritual exchange

    A: 'Bye.
    B: 'Bye.

Schegloff and Sacks noticed that this "terminal exchange" was part of another more complex form, the "terminal section" of the conversation, in which the speakers cooperatively prepared the ground for breaking off their interaction.

Their studies have revealed two kinds of "terminal section." Sometimes when a topic of conversation has faded out one of the speakers may say something like "Well . . . ," marking a point where, unless a new topic is opened up by the other, a ritual of preclosing can take place. Here is a simple example:

Preclosing	A: {	Well . . . I'm afraid I must be getting along.
	B: {	O.K. See you then.
Closing	A: {	'Bye.
	B: {	'Bye.

The other form of "terminal section" involves a reference to some further, off-stage activities, whose natural progression allows the conversation to be properly closed without offense. For example, a caller may offer an opportunity for initiating a closing section to the person he has called by beginning the conversation with "I hope I'm not disturbing you" to which the other may reply "That's alright, I've just put the dinner on." The natural progression of the cooking process allows a person to break off with a terminal section beginning "I'm afraid I've got to go now, the timer went off," thus legitimizing the consequent "Bye then."

Closing then is achieved by ritual, warrantably placed, which creates a boundary between a talk time and some other social time. I have not addressed myself at all to the question of the accomplishment and reading off by members of the social quality of the periods thus bounded, only to the methodic maintenance and achievement of the boundary. How we know it was or is to be, of all possible social periods, a talk time, and of all possible talk times a gossip session, is another matter – one involving not only such questions as topic choice, "I say, have you heard about So and So?" but also the achievement of the knowing conspiratorial style.

The schema adopted by Schegloff and Sacks, that is a terminal section completed by a terminal exchange, is adequate to the understanding of other time boundary markings. The kindergarten day-closing procedure begins a terminal section with the arrival of a parent. This event alerts everyone to the possibility of closing. The arriving parent is greeted by the staff with a standard opening, *Dau,* the first member of an adjacency pair, calling forth *Dau.* The parent then pauses for a word. This period, a kind of preclosing, is extendable. It was timed from five seconds to fourteen minutes. The appropriate child "hangs around" the parent during the proceedings, opening up the possibility of generating a "with," a socially marked pair as belonging together, but not accomplishing it. The parent, after some Sacksian preclosings, finally does generate a "with" by pushing the child toward the cloakroom, whence both proceed, the child being notionally propelled by the parent, who by so doing makes a nice social point, proclaiming the necessity of urging a reluctant child to complete the terminal section, when it was she herself who initiated and prolonged the chat, while her child, emitting a whole range of signs of "anxious to go," just hung around. The pair emerge from the cloakroom as a differently marked "with," the parent holding the child's hand. Closing proceeds smoothly from then on, according to distinct patterns. If the child is with its mother the staff and mother do a terminal exchange, A: "Farvel," B: ". . . . vel," the child being ignored as a separate social entity. If the child is with its father or elder sibling, both members of the "with" are farewelled with a terminal exchange, one helper going to the trouble of calling the child's name to attract its attention for the terminal exchange. As there were no exceptions to this pattern at the kindergarten being studied, it illustrates dramatically an important point stressed in Richards,[9] namely that the mother-child dyad forms, for many purposes, a single social entity, the mother performing many practical or linguistic tasks, not on behalf of the child, but as the child's hands and tongue. Clearly even when the child is at the age of three or four years the mother still performs that function. In these closings – and the very same phenomenon was evident in day openings at the kindergarten – she is the social head and voice of the undissolved dyad and is so treated by the staff.

The problem of natural openings and closings arises as a separate issue. We have already noticed the technique by which natural initial and terminal parts of a sequence can be stylistically elevated to become openings and closings. But some natural events could find no other place in the sequence than as beginnings and endings. Such for example are spring and autumn, birth and death. They are not, therefore, available for stylistic heightening *as* openings and closings, they *are* openings and closings. But their importance is too great for them to merely pass by, unattended and unstressed. They become surrounded by ceremony, by which we accomplish birth and death, marriage and divorce, spring and autumn, sailings and landfalls. In general this network of natural openings and closings forms a closed system of metaphors, each binary opposition serving as a metaphor for the others. Close students of the ethnography of our tribe tell us that most of our surviving ceremonials by which these natural events are surrounded are derivative from performances supposed literally to accomplish or achieve the event, not as ceremonial but as natural. The problem of our current understanding of these events, and our current procedures for their ritual accomplishment *as* events, has recently been illuminatingly opened by Bocock.[10]

The boundaries of spaces may be marked by relatively insurmountable barriers, such as high, sheer walls or wide waterways. Such barriers enter social reality only when, with respect to some conception of the social arenas thus demarcated, they are given a meaning by a participant. Does the prison wall keep you in or the raging, unpredictable, and threatening forces of society out? Is a prison a cage or a refuge? Does its wall show its sheer face inwards or outwards? Clearly the sense of the wall, in its mathematical, vectorial significance, is a function of the way the areas within and without are socially conceived. But whatever the boundary means its maintenance can safely be left to the laws of physics and the devoted efforts of the Public Works Department.

All other barriers are marked by physically surmountable barriers, visible like low walls and white lines, invisible like the high and low status areas of a schoolroom, or the volume of private space around a person. Most boundaries tend to close up on themselves, enclosing areas, so that, in general, ingress round the back is not possible. Social areas have portals,

visible or invisible. These portals are generally valvelike, in that passage
out is generally easier than passage in, so that while not all who aspire
are admitted, all who have been admitted eventually come out. In public
buildings there is usually a ceremonial performance involved in achieving
entry, but a mere valedictory nod marks acceptable leaving of the enclosed volume or area. Even someone who has parked his car in the man-
aging director's own space, having failed to notice the invisible valve and
portals, has no great difficulty in removing his automobile from the private
space it had occupied.

Invisible boundaries, having no symbolic objects on display, must be
maintained through shared knowledge. Indeed learning a social environment involves much acquisition of knowledge of invisible boundaries. (This
is yet another way in which initiation into really being a member may be
achieved and the stranger marked out.) Invisible boundaries are usually
generated by some potent or sanctified object at their center. Goffman
and others have noticed the area around a "with," a group of persons going
together, and letting it be seen that they are so, an area that moves with
the "with," and around which contrary walkers skirt. Similarly a person
may leave a potent trace, such as a pair of sunglasses and a towel upon a
crowded beach, around which an unencroachable boundary is invisibly
drawn. Most striking of all, perhaps, a participant has reported that
around the door of the staff room in a school there is an arc of inviolability,
beyond which the pupils will not go, and if forced to do so, exhibit signs
of considerable uneasiness and distress.

The existence of boundaries creates the possibility of their violation, and
violations require remedies. The general form of remedial exchanges has
been analyzed by Goffman, and I shall follow his analysis.[11] The first point
to notice is that for a remedial interchange, say an apology to occur, there
must be someone whose space or time it is. It must in some sense be *their*
space or *their* time. For instance a lesson is a teacher's time, and a party
is the time of the hostess, just as my office is my space, and the kitchen,
the cook's. If the time or space is "owned" by no one, there can be no
occasion for remedy. For example, if I miss the train and thus exclude
myself from that period of time, that is, train journey time, I cannot
apologize for my lateness, for there is nobody whose time it is, except of
course mine. It is the guard's train but not his journey time.

Goffman's analysis depends upon an underlying distinction between
virtual and actual offense. To arrive late is to commit an actual offense,
and the person whose time it is must be apologized to, in the proper ritual

form. But the generality of Goffman's analysis is made possible by extend-
ing the notion of offense to virtual violations, which are remedied in
advance, so to speak. To get the water jug I must violate your table territory, which I remedy in advance by asking politely, that is, in proper
ritual form: "Would you mind passing the water jug please?" Which
allows, but never admits, the response "Yes, I would mind."

The general form then of remedial exchange is as follows:

A: Remedy: I'm terribly sorry I'm late.
B: Relief: That's O.K.

There are two further elaborations of this basic form, only one of which
is noticed by Goffman. He points out that quite frequently the remedy-
relief interchange, whose referent is the actual or virtual violation of
someone's space or time, is supplemented by a second interchange, whose
referent is the first interchange. Thus

A1:   Remedy: I'm sorry I'm late.
B1:   Relief: That's O.K.
A2:   Appreciation: Gee, I'm glad I didn't upset things too much.
B2:   Minimization: No, no, it was O.K.

A2 in the second bracket expresses appreciation for B's granting of relief,
and B2 minimizes the extent of his condescension, thus restoring to A his
status as a person in equal moral standing with B.

But particularly where time is concerned there is another form of remedial interchange, the counterapology. So far as I can see, the final product,
that is, maintenance of the boundary and equilibration of the moral standing of the people involved, is just the same as in the Goffman ritual. Consider the following:

A1:   Remedy: I'm awfully sorry I'm late.
B1:   Relief: That's O.K.
B2:   Counterapology: I'm afraid we had to start without you.
A2:   Counterrelief: Gosh, I should hope so.

To breach a boundary is to be where you are not supposed to be (rule
violation), or not expected to be (norm violation), and as we have seen
this may occur in time quite as well as in space. Goffman's remedial
exchanges allow for the management of the defilement of sacred or
proper territory, and for the violation of spatial and temporal boundaries. But how is being late or early a violation of a time boundary? If

early, you are present in a socially distinct period, which, for example, may be a preparatory period for the action to come. A great deal of backstage equipment may still litter the scene. The cooking utensils or the baby's toys may not yet have been put away. The style of the action may be inappropriate to the presence of a stranger. He is supposed to behave as guest, a style of action appropriate to a later period. Under these conditions a remedial interchange is required to maintain the social order, and the equilibration of civility may even require the early arrival to join the home team and pay the penalty by tidying up the sitting room.

To be late is equally the breaching of a boundary, since you were not there for some temporal sections of the action, though expected. Again, and now much more commonly, a remedial interchange is required. We need no special theory to account for the fact that late arrivals are very much more common than early ones. Of course late arrival may be part of a presentational sequence, susceptible of dramaturgical analysis, as when someone conspicuously arrives late to be noticed. Then the remedial interchange takes on a peculiarly ambiguous tone. To challenge the sincerity of the late arrival's apologies is to place oneself in the position of one who acknowledges the presentational character of the tardiness. And even to notice the late arriver, single him or her out, if only for reprobation, is of course to allow the device to succeed. Thus even in a conspicuously dramaturgical occasion, the late arrival's apologies tend to be taken at least for ritualistic purposes, at face value, and the remedial interchange is completed in the normal form.

Lastly there is the problem of warrantable intrusion. How does a child acceptably send a message across the boundary around the staff room door? This is a quite different sort of case from that which I shall call "pseudo-intrusion," when the hospital superintendent, for example, to whom the whole hospital "belongs" as his space, makes a show of apology on entering the Junior Residents' Common Room. To solve the staff room problem the following ritual seems widespread, at least in English schools. From some casual observation it seems to extend to office space boundaries as well, and doubtless to others. The invisible boundary is a half-circle around the staff room door, more or less encompassing the area from which one could see into the staff room through the half-open door, as people go in and out. The children with business in the staff room stand around outside this area waiting for the appearance of a moving teacher. They do not stop the teacher, for that would abort the process, but come up tangentially along side, and moving with the teacher ask for a message to be carried inside. The teacher continues to move throughout the exchange, and the child casts off at the boundary, leaving the moving teacher free to continue with momentum unaffected, right through into the staff room where the message can now be delivered inside the sacred territory.

The microstructures of spaces and times

How structured spaces and times have meaning
The procedures and rituals we have examined so far serve to divide or bound socially distinct spaces and times. Within those areas and periods there are spatial and temporal structures, the arrangement of furniture in a room or the complex orderliness of a meal. These structures have a social meaning, and before examining some examples in detail we must look at how meaningfulness is achieved. There are two questions involved: How is it that a physical entity can have meaning? And how do the people who give it that meaning and come to learn that meaning do so? In this paper I shall not be concerned with the second of these questions, though this should not be taken to suggest that I do not regard it as anything less than of the greatest importance, but I think very little is known about such processes.

The general form of the answer to the first question is implicit in my analysis so far. It is primarily by their structural properties that physical entities have social meaning. Social meanings are also given to and read off qualitative properties, such as colors – for example, red flags, brown shirts, black skins, and so on. These occur in the *Umwelt* but as separable items, so I shall not pursue the question of their semantics here. We are left then with entities differentiated by their structural properties.

The first distinction we must address derives from the commonplace observation that a semantic unit *is* a structure and *is embedded* within a structure or structures. Its internal structure presents no particular problems provided we recognize that the structure of the unit may be extended in space, in which case we shall look for its synchronic form, or extended in time, in which case we shall look for its diachronic layout. Provided entities are structurally differentiated they can bear distinctive meanings. In the traffic code a triangle has one meaning and a circle another, whereas in dog handling the melodic differences between one whistle and another, structurally differentiated in time, are distinct signals. In general the semantic field of an item includes relations of exclusion, such as that between a circle and a triangle, whose meanings exclude each other; and inclusive relations such as that between a triangle and its red color, relations that range from synonymy through metaphor to metonymy. To express a meaning, then, we must lay out as much of the semantic field as is required to distinguish this entity as meaningful from other items within their possible common contexts.

In studying social semantics it also is necessary to clearly distinguish the aetiology of the vehicle from the etymology of the semantic unit. Work in nonverbal communication studies often hovers on, if not actually falls over, the boundary between the two. The confusion is very clear in two recent studies of human facial expressions. Both pieces of work are characterized by first-rate observation and analysis, but marred by naïve interpretations. Eibl-Eibesfeldt noticed that in every culture from which information was available, the "eye-brow flash" was a fixed element in greeting.[12] It is clear in his exposition of this discovery that he takes it for granted that it must have a semantic identity. A little participant observation shows that this is just not so. The eyebrow flash, like any other structural unit, is capable of expressing a variety of meanings, and has culture-based semantic fields like any other lexeme. A very similar case is to be found in the superb studies of the aetiology of the human smile by Van't Hooff.[13] He shows that a plausible transition can be made from two basic "monkey faces," well differentiated in apes, to the laugh on the one hand and the smile on the other. But in discussing the semantics of the human smile and laugh he assumes that the meanings of these expressions derive by a parallel smooth transition from the ethological elements of the apes' behavior to which the musculature and neural circuitry of human beings is related by common origin. In a commentary upon Van't Hooff's analysis, Leach[14] demonstrates the difference between the description of the origin of these facial possibilities in respect of their adaptive value and the discussion of the semantics of the contemporary human smile, which can express anything from joy to vicious hatred. The smile is a structured entity, but it is capable of both internal differentiation and embedding in many contexts. How many smiles do we inherit and how many do we learn as part of our "language"?

To use the linguistic analogy to analyze the mode of working of structures and other features of the *Umwelt* is of course to invoke a metaphor to generate analytical concepts. And that metaphor carries with it assumptions about the connections that obtain between the meaningful entity and its understanding and subsequent action by those people who come across it. Nonverbal communication seems to involve a spectrum of ways of influence. At one end of the spectrum are influences that are purely causal, effects that are wrought upon the nervous system changing its state, and affecting our ways of acting, but never at any time coming into the awareness of the actor. A bad smell may make us feel sick without the relationship between smell and nausea ever coming under our scrutiny, and it seems that in prekinesic innocence the use of gaze, looking at one another for different times to integrate talk in a conversation, was just another such influence. And, like strong smells, only startling gazes, such as prolonged staring or complete refusal to meet the eyes of another, were actually noticed and explicitly interpreted. At the other end of the spectrum are influences that are to all intents and purposes mere words. One has to learn the meaning of flags to be a patriot, and to understand the "language" of flowers as socially mediating symbols to participate as a lover or a bohemian, just as one has to learn the significance of the forty or so smiles with which we decorate and reinforce our interactions to participate most effectively in any interaction.

Microstructures in space

Static ordered structures in bounded spaces. If we examine a permanent arrangement of furniture in an office we are studying a structure that is physical, laid out in space, and, as we shall see, is as such assigned a social meaning. Studies have shown that the way furniture is arranged in an office is not just a matter of convenience but rather is a symbolic representation of the standing of the person whose office it is. In general the principles seem to be the following:

1 The desk parallel to a wall is of lower status than that at an angle to a wall.
2 The desk against a wall is of lower status than that which is freestanding.
3 Sitting on the side exposed to the door is of lower status than sitting on the side away from the door.

Applying these rules together we find that the person whose desk is freestanding, at an angle to the wall, and who sits behind the desk facing the door occupies the highest category admitted by that organization, a fact expressed in his furniture for all to see, whereas he whose desk is up against the wall, with his back to the door on the exposed side, occupies the lowest status. Whatever airs he may give himself, his furniture shows his position for all to see. How far this code is general among bureaucratic man is uncertain, but the study reported covers both English civil servants and Swedish executives, so it has some measure of generality as a sign system. An explanation of the etymology of this semantics is readily forthcoming from Goffman's theory of front and backstage divisions of personal territory. The person of low status is totally exposed; he or she has hardly any backstage area. His whole official life is enacted on the front stage. He is under perpetual threat of supervision. But a simple visualizing of the plan of the office of the highest grade shows that tucked away behind his angled desk, he has the greatest amount of private space, of backstage area not capable of being overlooked, of any of the possible arrangements. Equally, and probably complementarily, the topology would admit of a Durkheimian account in terms of the protection of and at the same time the exhibition of the sanctity or inviolability of the highest status person, whose body is surrounded by a large protective area, freeing him from the possibility of profanation. There must surely be an element of truth in both accounts, and further study could probably elicit their balance in the way the furniture arrangement is read by the various individuals who act with it as their *Umwelt*.

A second and very illuminating example of micro-structured space can be found in the world of children. Children seem to have an immensely strong sense of order, but of their own devising. So far as I know the principles of this sense of order have not been closely studied, perhaps because there is still a predominance of the idea that children are incompetent adults, developing toward that apotheosis, a view that leads investigators to ignore the autonomous worlds of children in which they *are* competent. But, the reader might remark, parents often complain that their children are untidy, that is, disorderly. This, however, is not evidence for a lack of innate orderliness, since the concept of untidy is related to adult forms of order. Close observation shows that children create private worlds of intense orderliness. For example a tin box, a recently fashionable object among English school children around nine or ten years of age, may become just such a private world, inside which a carefully devised and strongly sustained structural arrangement of objects may obtain, according to *some* endowment with meaning. Accounts of the structure of tin boxes may be well worth eliciting. As a child gets older this and other private worlds grow and subdue the disorderly world around. The exasperated architectonic response of parents may be taken to show how far their forms of order are based upon a rationale that is obscure to the child and thus has a meaning opaque to him.

So far we have taken the physical topography as a datum and seen how it may be endowed with meaning. But the micro-structure of the *Umwelt*

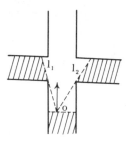

Figure 1. Lurk lines.

may be found in a different topography, in which the components of the socially conceived space may be thought of as organized by a social topography, where such a concept as "social distance" may express rather the rarity and difficulty of a transition from one socially marked space to another, rather than the time it takes to make the journey on foot, so to speak.

Goffman's analysis of the texture of threat in an urban *Umwelt* illustrates a space organized along one dimension of social meaning.[15] In a dangerous section of a city the grid pattern of streets is replaced by a modulating structure of clear and dubious areas, areas in which someone might be lurking, the possibility constituting the threat. The boundary between the space that can be seen to be empty and the space that is obscured Goffman calls a "lurk line." The threat texture of a grid pattern of streets, from a momentary vantage point in the passage of O, our man on Michigan Avenue, through the street corner, is seen in Figure 1. L1 and L2 are lurk lines and the shaded and unshaded areas represent the structure of the texture of threat. As O moves forward the structural properties of the space change.

A pleasanter illustration of social topography can be found in the social map of a kindergarten. The map is plotted in two dimensions, staff sanctity versus child sanctity and comfort versus threat. The geographical map of the kindergarten (including play area) is shown in Figure 2.

Plotting these areas on the social map we get the topography illustrated in Figure 3. On this map, (5) and (4), though geographically adjacent, and from a spatial point of view therefore easy of mutual access, are socially very distant, and passage from one to the other is very difficult for a child. Entry to (4) has the character of a special occasion and happens only under close supervision, occurring only for those whose job it is to wash the cups, or for a cooking group who prepare something for

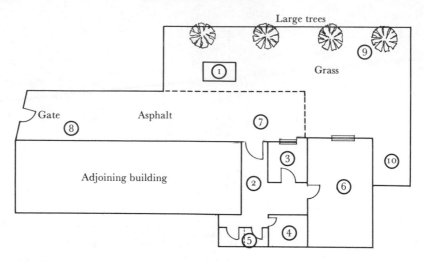

Figure 2. Layout of kindergarten. *Key:* (1) Wendy house, (2) Lobby, (3) Staff room, (4) Kitchen, (5) Lavatories, (6) Play room, (7) Near play area, (8) Far play area, (9) Distant grass, and (10) Unobserved areas. Observation of their movements shows that children do not play in the areas marked (9) and (10).

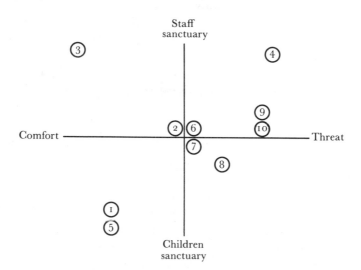

Figure 3. Social topography.

a playmate's birthday. (2), (6), and (7) are completely mutually open, and the children and staff pass freely from one to the other, without social portals, that is, rituals of passage like knocking, asking, or anything of that sort. There are such portals involved in the passage from (2), (6), and (7) into (3), the teachers' room, whose door is ordinarily closed. But if entered it is a place of great comfort, since it is where one is taken for mothering when lonely or hurt. It is equally a staff sanctuary protected by ritual. The staff assert that the toilets are a child sanctuary that they do not enter, but observation shows that this sanctity is notional.

Mobile objects with permanent or semipermanent spatial structure. Cars and people are prominent structured and mobile objects in the *Umwelt* and are to be considered as part of it. Their forms broadcast all sorts of messages. In this paper I shall concentrate only on people as structured objects and look at two examples of their structural properties: hair lengths and clothes as organized objects.

Hair length has once again, in recent times, come into use as a social and political symbol. Historically it has not been the length as such, but the long-short contrast that has had political significance; that is, the semantic unit "long hair" is embedded in the structure "long-short." This explains how "short hair" could be radical in 1640 and 1780 and reactionary in 1965. This example illustrates the way something that may appear at first sight to be a semantic unit in itself, is, on more careful analysis, seen to be significant only as a member of a pair. Long hair was recently used as part of a heraldic display symbolizing a radical political orientation. This went with round-lensed, steel-rimmed spectacles, flowing clothes, and so forth. The semantic unit comprised by the hair length is, for this total object, a diachronic entity – that is, it exists in opposition over time. Long hair is worn not just in opposition to the short hair of the "squares," but as opposed in time to short – that is, "long, formerly short." And of course either length can be a realization of either formula of opposition, the synchronic or the diachronic. The same explanation is available for the apparent contradiction between the role of a brassière as a radical garment in the late nineteenth century and its discarding by certain radical women in the late twentieth century. It is both in synchronic relation to those who continue to wear it and in diachronic relation to the previous state of radical women. And in some lexicons it has a meaning in itself, as a way of emphasizing basic femaleness or of inhibiting

physical actions supposedly appropriate to males, such as running or
chopping wood.

However as a general principle the basic form "x as opposed to y" has
no particular temporal order built into it. One could choose an instantia-
tion of the relation now, in anticipation of the appearance of its contrary
later. Though peculiarly appropriate to radical heraldry, the basic form
"x opposed to y" has been a very common form for the conveying of social
meaning. Women have used the up–down contrast in hair style for expressing sociosexual status; for example, at one time to put up the hair
showed that childhood had ended and that the woman was marriageable.
In a somewhat similar way the contrast clean-shaven–bearded expressed
social distinctions among the Romans. In early days slaves were clean-
shaven and their masters bearded, but in the reign of Hadrian a revolution
in shaving techniques brought Sicilian barbers to Rome and made shaving
much less disagreeable, with the consequence that Hadrian decreed that
slaves be bearded now that their masters were not.

However as Cooper has pointed out, both long hair and beards have
had a persistent standard meaning despite their frequent appearance as
members of contrasting pairs.[16] Long hair has generally been associated
with romanticism, femininity, and the like, whereas beards usually have
been associated with intellectual and moral status as opposed to political
status, with political status, then with conservatism and the authoritarian
father.

The design of people then forms a very striking feature of the *Umwelt*.
It is clear that such heraldic matters as hair length and type of eye decoration are parts of a more complex structure, the whole ensemble including clothes and shoes, ways of walking and of holding the arms, and so
forth. In the American West presenting oneself as a cowboy is done by
some cowhands even in their Sunday suits. It is predominantly marked by
their way of walking.

But far the most important structural element in the design of people
is clothes. To my knowledge relatively little has been done in the sociology
and social psychology of this field. There have been one or two inconclusive
studies relating skirt lengths to economic factors, but they have paid little
attention to the expressive features even of such correlations, if they could
be established. In this paper I can only draw attention to two features of
the clothes in personal and social design, basing my remarks on little more
than impressionistic evidence.

The first point to remark about clothes as structured entities concerns
their role in socially marking sexual differences, so that one can tell at

a glance whether one is going to meet a member of the opposite sex or of the same sex. Traditionally these have been marked by differentiating markers in all three possible modes: primary, secondary, or tertiary differentia. By primary I mean anatomical differentia based upon genitalia and mammary glands; by secondary I mean anatomical differentia such as relative hairiness, bone formation, general outline of the limbs, face and so on; and by tertiary differentia I mean markings by different forms of clothes, or by differential regalia, such as different forms of decoration as among the Australian aborigines, or by such matters as the length of hair. In societies where unisex fashions in the basic structure of clothing are predominant, such as among Western university students, or in the Muslim world, recourse may be made to secondary or primary differentia. Muslim men and women are differentiated by subtle stylistic differences in their *shalwa* and *kemis,* and by the use by woman of various forms of face concealment, elaborations on a tertiary theme. Occidental students generally have recourse to both secondary and primary differentia, in that the current fashion of long hair in both sexes has been accompanied by the growth of beards among men, marking them off at a glance. There are of course certain surviving subtle modifications of the unisex style so that some tertiary differentia do remain. But in general social marking is by secondary or primary characteristics. The survival of these markers through the transition to different forms of clothing discloses what may be a social universal, or equilibrating principle requiring that certain differentia be preserved through whatever transformation of the form taken by the *Umwelt.* The way such principles are recognized, learned, and promulgated is a much neglected branch of sociology.

But there are some structural differences in clothing that are manifestly but mysteriously related to the expression of social matters. So far as I can tell so little is known about these phenomena that I can do little but describe them. Both men's and women's clothing are modified diachronically along a number of dimensions, long–short, loose–tight, what I can only call "apex up–apex down," elaborated–nonelaborated, and there are no doubt others. To illustrate, the zoot suit of the 1940s had a very long jacket as its prime differentium, whereas the predominant jacket length in the 1950s and early 1960s was short. Trousers, which were tight in the Edwardian period, were styled in a loose manner up until the late 1950s. In the 1940s and 1950s men's clothes were designed as a triangle with the apex down, wide shoulders and narrow hips, but since then the introduction of flared jackets and trousers has created a silhouette with apex up. And of course elaboration with more buttons, waist coats with lapels, turnups, and so on has come and gone. I would like to put these changes to the social scientist as problematic, through and through, both as to their genesis and their spread through the population, not forgetting the attempts from time to time to introduce modifications that were selected out, such as the calf-length skirts in the late 1960s. I believe that in the iconography of clothing there is a ready-made model for all forms of social change and recommend it for the closest possible study.

Microstructures in time

Body rhythms, the Umwelt within. The idea that human life is carried on against a structural background is very old, but it has only recently returned to favor and, indeed, to explicit consciousness. As well as the structure of space and time, out-there, beyond our bodily envelope, there is a very complex temporal structure within: the biological rhythms. To a very large extent these are beyond our direct or even indirect control. They are the *Umwelt* within. Our mastery of them consists in our living in accordance with them, designing our timetables around their beat, and at the same time realizing that their ebb and flow has already entered consciousness and been given meaning. Sometimes this meaning is integrated into a cosmology, as for instance when sleep and waking are matched with life and death, and when, as in many cultures, the moon-linked female cycles acquire mystical significance. Some cyclic changes are read in a less spectacular dialect as the ebb and flow of moods.

The rhythmic cycles of human biology seem to be organized around three main "tides."[17] Central to much of life are the circadian rhythms, cycles of activity such as heartbeat, temperature, calcium excretion, adrenal discharges, and so on that are based on a periodicity of about one day and that in the absence of an external pacemaker like clock-based timetables or the diurnal day and night sequence run between twenty-three and twenty-five hours. There is mounting evidence that the source of the periodicity is genetic. Feeling great is quite definitely associated with a certain interlocking pattern of integration of these cycles, and the slipping out of phase of anyone of them may lead to a state that is read off as depression, persecution, threat of cosmic disaster, and even the "winter madness" among Eskimos. When their calcium secretion cycle gets out of phase with the other circadian rhythms they imagine all kinds of dreadful threats. What reading is given will depend upon the available lexicon. The maintenance of the usual twenty-four hour periodicity seems to be dependent on such factors of the external *Umwelt* as light and darkness, and possibly diurnal changes in the magnetic field.

Of equal importance for the maintenance of the tone of life is the "biological hour," the periodicity of bursts of adrenalin and other endocrine secretions that profoundly affect activity and general metabolic level. The biological hour in a normal healthy person usually lasts about 90 to 100 minutes. This periodicity becomes very prominent in sleep, when the overlaying effects of clock-based timetables is removed. REM sleep, periods of intense neural activity, apparently essential to mental health, are associated with, if not indeed caused by the periodic adrenal discharges that occur at 90 to 100 minute intervals. This rhythmic heightening and relaxing of activity apparently continues throughout the day, but is heavily overlaid by clock-based periodicities, which, based upon the 60 minute period, may not be entirely to our good.

Finally there are the many longer term cycles, whose existence is often very difficult to detect. The female monthly cycle is clearly a powerful and underlying determinant of many aspects of social life, and it may be that there are other long-term cycles, whose effects are less obvious, but that are nevertheless potent enough. There are certainly periodicities in some forms of mental disturbance, some of which are correlated with the lunar month, and there may be others. Such cycles structure time whether we like it or not, and all we can do in the face of their inevitability is to make sense of them within some interpretative scheme. But there are other microstructures in time which are through and through human products.

The structure of meals. A meal is a sequential eating of dishes that has a diachronic structure, while each dish, consisting of a variety of objects, is differentiated as a synchronic structure. Dishes will be differentiated according to the salt–sweet dichotomy, as well as more finely by their ingredients. Along the diachronic dimension we shall ask whether one dish is served before or after the other. For reasons that will emerge we will be using a generally syntactical model for the analysis, though its applicability to the analysis of meals derives from their formal properties rather than their function as the vehicles of social meaning, though they do indeed have that function. As a part of the *Umwelt* a meal may be orderly or disorderly, and as orderly it of course contributes a general air of stability and rightness to the day.

There are two sets of distinctions to elucidate: those between cuisines and those between meals within a cuisine. Both the rules of cuisine and the rules for meals generate menus, plans for meals, which are concretely realized as actual structures in time, the elements, dishes, having spatial and gustatory structures, with the general role of deipneme. The rules ensure that despite the great variety of specific food items there occurs a

repetition day after day, week after week, of structurally isomorphic
sequences, at a fairly high level of perception, which are designated as
proper meals. Since structure is, by itself, a source of intelligibility, the
Umwelt is stabilized at that point and needs no further referent. Standard
meals are nonthreatening meals; witness the intriguing sight of British
families going abroad with cars loaded with cornflakes and baked beans,
because "the children won't even try French (German, Greek . . .) food,"
exemplifying that otherwise dark saying "I haven't tried it so I don't
like it."

Mary Douglas offers an analytical scheme based upon the main dish
principle, with stressed-unstressed elements as the principal dichotomy.[18]
For English home cooking the application of this principle yields the
following general formula:

   Proper meal, $M = A + 2B$

where A is stressed and B is unstressed. For example such a meal might
be concretely realized in A = meat and two vegetables, $B1$ = soup, and
$B2$ = sweet. Douglas offers no structural principle that would explain
why soup comes before meat and vegetables, and never afterwards,
while the sweet always follows the meat course. However she does show
convincingly that each dish is a model of the meal, having the general
structure:

   Proper dish $= a + 2b$

again based upon the stressed-unstressed principle as in meat and two
vegetables or melon with sugar and ginger.

Other cuisines can be structurally differentiated using Douglas's principles. The Danish cuisine seems to have the structure:

   $A + B + 2C$

where both A and B are stressed and C is unstressed. Each item of
smørrebrød is prepared on a neutral base of ryebread. One meat or fish
element and one vegetable element are equally prominent, and there are
usually two unstressed elements, such as a dab of sauce and a sprig of
parsley. There are variations on this theme, as for instance if both
stressed elements are vegetable, one of the unstressed is a shred of meat
of some sort. And just as in English cuisine the unstressed elements may
be omitted without destroying the dish, or meal, so among the complete
forms one does find among the offerings of the smørrebrød some items
that are merely

$$A + B$$

where both elements are stressed. One never finds, so far as I can ascertain, either A simpliciter, or A + B + C, three stressed elements.

The high degree of structural differentiation of meals not only serves to stabilize the *Umwelt* for a while, but allows social meaning to be given to meals and dishes, as the differentiated elements in a simple symbolic system. A meal or meallike social event, such as drinks, can convey a message, or express a structural feature of the relations among the people attending it. The elements may have a more nearly semantic etymology. Perhaps this is part of the explanation of the alleged but quite mythological aphrodisiac properties of certain foods, such as oysters and champagne. They may have come to be sexually meaningful objects (the open sea shell and the bottle with spurting foam as female and male symbols), so that though they have no special biochemical properties and are not causal agents in the ordinary sense, they may nevertheless be effective agents of sexuality as the bearers of a message.

Mary Douglas has also offered a convincing example of a structural differentiation as the basis for differentiable social meaning in her analysis of the contrast between meals and drinks. She has shown that each of these events has meaning as a member of a pair. Each represents or marks paired structural social properties and so enables someone to perceive or express certain social differentia. Her distinction between meals and drinks is drawn as follows:

"Drinks" are not structured internally. One is offered either tea or coffee, or if they are alcoholic drinks there is no formal transition from one kind to another. Indeed one is enjoined to stick with whatever one started to drink. I am told this rule has no biochemical foundation as a specific prevention against a hangover, so following Douglas we might more plausibly treat it as a social injunction to secure the unstructured form of drinks. And there is rarely, in Western society, any fixed number of drinks one may take, though the rule of three, one drink to begin with and two replenishments, which may of course be merely token toppings of the first, is widespread. There may sometimes be a notional limitation on number, as witness the English expression, derived from naval custom, "Have the other half?" for the offer of the nth drink in a series, no matter how large the value of n may be.

Food (canapés) accompanying the drinks is unstressed, and it may be eaten in any order and unceremoniously with the fingers.

Such food has no salt–sweet structure; all the substances consumed may be sweet, for example, as in coffee with sugar and sweet biscuits, or all salt, as with a Gibson and salted peanuts. But the rule of consistency – either salt or sweet – tends to prevail.

Basically the unstructuredness of drinks makes them less serious, less socially potent, though they may actually occupy more time than a meal. The distinction between meals and drinks serves, then, to mark a social differentium between more serious and more ephemeral or superficial social relations. As Douglas remarks

Drinks are for strangers, acquaintances, workmen, and family. Meals are for family, close friends, honoured guests. The grand operator of the system is the line between intimacy and distance. Those we know at meals we also know at drinks. The meal expresses close friendship. Those we only know at drinks we know less intimately. So long as the boundary matters to us (and there is no reason to suppose that it will always matter) the boundary between drinks and meals has a meaning.

She also remarks on the meaning of some intermediate cases, such as the cold, fork supper, by which fine gradation of the gradual admission into and rejection from intimacy may be mediated.

Our conclusion must be that the structures whose repetition we find in the temporal *Umwelt* have, in themselves as structures, no obvious, specific, social significance, though a close study of their etymology may yield something of the sort. But, being structurally differentiated they can acquire symbolic significance as the vehicles of meaning. In general, however, this aspect of the structured *Umwelt* serves rather to deprive it of threat, and thus to allow the action to continue unimpeded by the distractions of maintaining vigilance.

Interaction between Umwelt structure and social theory

The representation of a cosmology

The *Umwelt* structure may be an icon of a particular people's theory of their own society; that is, the physical structure of the *Umwelt* may function as a meaning-bearing entity, an icon of the content of certain propositions within the cosmology of a people. A detailed and well-documented example is Pierre Bourdieu's analysis of the microcosmic organization and meaning of the Berber house.[19] One might also cite Lévi-Strauss's analysis of the meaning of the siting of an Amerindian village.[20] I will not discuss those individual items that have a social or cosmological significance in themselves, but only the way messages are conveyed by various structural properties of the house, which match and hence express (according to Bourdieu) some central structural properties of the Berber cosmology, that is, of the content of certain of their important beliefs, as expressed in certain sayings and other explicitly ideational expressions.

Once again we find the two dimensions of *Umwelt* analysis: the structure of the entity, in this case the house, and the structure of the larger entity into which the house fits. And, of course, certain elements within the house are themselves structurally differentiated, and some qualitatively differentiated, as for example light and dark, or fresh and preserved. The appearance of both structurally differentiated elements, for example, forked and straight, and qualitatively differentiated ones, at the same level of analysis, shows that we are dealing with basic semantic units, the higher order structure having the character of syntax.

Our problem is how does the house as a structure, as a social or cosmological microcosm, express the macrocosm. There seem to be two distinct ways: In one the representation is established by *isomorphism* of structure; in the other by *conventional* assignment of meaning to generate a symbol. An etymology for the symbol can be reconstructed from the folksayings, in terms of which the particular assignment of meaning makes sense. It is as a symbol, not as structured isomorph, that the fire is conceived by the Berber as the representation of the female principle in the house.

For the purposes of this paper I shall pay attention only to the spatial organization as microcosm. It seems from Bourdieu's account that structural properties of the house represent at two levels of sophistication. The ridge pole rests in the fork of the central wooden pillar, and this is read as an icon of the male–female relationship. Here the structural isomorphism is exceedingly simple. A considerable amount of social meaning is taken to be vested in this conjunction, and a good many of the rituals associated with procreation are related to it. Furthermore the ridge pole and supporting pillar are the central metaphors in a large number of sayings and expressions by which the Berber social organization of the male–female dichotomy is described (and no doubt promulgated as rules and norms).

But Bourdieu has shown that the structure of the house is a microcosm in much more subtle ways. The division of the house into a light part and a dark part matches the division of social time into night and day, and the openness of the light part is in contrast to the closedness of the dark part, matching the division between public (male) life and private (female) life. But these simple homologies are only the basis for more elaborate structures. "The opposition between the world of female life and the world of the city of man is based upon the same principles as the two systems of opposition that it opposes." In short, private life is not female life, but is symbolized as the procreative part of life, that is, as female-male. So the fact that the light part is in some sense the preserve of the women, where cooking and weaving are done, leads to the inner homology that the light part is to the dark part as public is to private as male is to female as Female-female is to female-male. Thus in general

a : b as b1 : b2

Finally the house can be considered in its geographical isomorphisms. These arise from the relation of the door, as a place for going in and coming out to the cardinal points as social objects. Going out one faces the geographical East, the direction of worship, with the warm South on one's right. Coming in one faces the wall of the loom, which being illuminated by the door is treated as bright, honorable, and so on – in short as the "East" of the inner space. On one's right on entry is the wall with the fire, the "South" of the interior. Thus the door is the point of logical inversion through which one passes from macrocosm to microcosm and back, always in the same relation to the social and cosmological significance of these structured spaces.

The ontological status of the Umwelt

Among the many questions that remain to be considered I should like to address two: the problem of the ontological status or mode of being of the structures out of which we build the *Umwelt*; and the problem of the diachrony or historical origins and principles of change of these structures.

The *Umwelt*, I have argued, is a physical structure endowed with social meaning. But since the physical world is potentially infinitely complex and susceptible of all kinds of structural analyses and deliberate reconstructions, might we not be tempted to think that the structures I have been talking about are projections upon the world, mere shadows cast by ideas? To draw this conclusion would be to overlook two essential features of the *Umwelt*. The first point to notice is that the *Umwelt* is, at least in part, built or constructed out of materials some of which are themselves constructed out of other materials, the so-called raw materials, by deliberate human action. This aspect of *Umwelt* construction could be considered within that part of social activity Marxists call praxis. From the point of view of this essay though I want to draw attention only to the nonideational character of the constraints upon construction. The limits of human power to modify material, and the limits of modifiability of material, constrain human action at any given epoch. Frank Lloyd Wright could envisage an *Umwelt* of mile-high apartment blocks but, thank goodness, he could not at that time realize them materially.

The second point is closely connected with this. Any symbolic system must be embodied in physical structures. While the existence of a semantics, a set of readings organized as a meaning field, is a necessary condition for there being a symbolic system, it is certainly not a sufficient condition. A symbolic system is only a system of symbols if there exists an embodiment of the conceptual structure in a physical structure available intersubjectively. Indeed, it is my view, but I cannot substantiate it here, that a symbolic system is essentially intersubjective, and that private, individual-centered manipulations of that system, "in the mind" so to speak, are derivative activities, depending upon imperfect but indispensable isomorphisms between the nervous system of the thinkers and the physically embodied symbolic system. Of course the existence of a structurally differentiated set of physical objects is not a sufficient condition for a symbolic system either, since these structurally differentiated objects must be read as semantically differentiated symbols. A structurally or otherwise differentiated set of objects and a shared semantic interpretation are both necessary conditions for the existence of a symbolic system, even of so generalized a kind as the *Umwelt*. The structures are then in the world, but they are revealed only by human activities. But unless matter were susceptible of certain forms of organization and these forms could be perceived to be differentiated by people, thought patterns, themselves structures in the nervous system, would be sterile and void.

The historical sources of meaningful structures
The problems of diachrony, the principles of historical processes, turn around the fundamental distinction between Lamarckian and Darwinian theories of historical change. Toulmin has gone so far as to argue that the dichotomy differentiates not just forms of historical explanation, but serves to define the very notion of an historical explanation, which he takes to be Darwinian.[21] Thus for him only Darwinian explanations are historical explanations. This view is a very strong one and has to be modified in certain respects. Toulmin himself introduces the useful distinction between coupled and uncoupled historical processes, that is, between those where the mutant forms are related to the environment in which they will have to survive and those where they are not. Characteristically in human products there is some attempt to design the product to fit anticipated environments, so that the human product, be it a new production technique or a new theory, is adjusted in advance to a possible or even probable environment. Following Toulmin, I should like to take a modified Darwinian view, that is, a view that is fundamentally that of mutation and selection by the appropriate environment, modified by the perception that in

the case of human products the mutants may show various degrees of close coupling.

The source of these mutants, as indicated at the outset of this essay, appears to be the enormous redundancy of the human nervous system – the unrestricted conceiving and realizing of an almost unlimited variety of structural forms. We proliferate structures in thought, according to principles we do not yet fully understand, and only partly in imitation of the forms we find around us. These forms are extremely various and include at the least the forms behind language, such as semantic fields and syntactic structures, as well as icons of structures outside ourselves, but of which we ourselves might form components. These peculiarly human qualities have meant that much free creative use of the imagination is possible. By "free" I mean independent of the existing environment of the organism. Some of the imaginings are of new and different forms of life, of new and different productive processes whose adoption would modify forms of life, new styles of decoration, melody and song, new cosmological speculations, words and tools, and so on almost indefinitely. The possibilities of conception and practice are continually being enriched by a process relatively independent of the environment. The trials of new conceptions as efforts to bring understanding, and of new practices to bring mastery, act as a Darwinian filter, exterminating those that are too inefficient, confusing, or painful. Those conceptions and practices that survive these tests become the customary ways.

But this is to describe an idealized version of the process. In fact the Darwinian filters of social and technical trials are less efficient than those of the biological environment, since it is regrettably true that favored ideas can be *made* to work and their failures consciously or unconsciously suppressed, while old ideas embodied in outdated techniques can be maintained by oppressive institutional devices long after their relative unsatisfactoriness could have been discovered.

The history of the *Umwelt*, its forms of construction, and the systems of meaning that endow its structures with their semantic load are evolving like any other human product, and under the constraints of a Darwinian relation to their environment, which is human thought and practice. To fill out the diachronic dimension we need to collect and analyze the successive forms taken by the many structures and rituals I have noted and supplement that by a natural history of those rituals themselves. Ethnography can be some sort of guide, but it would be deeply fallacious to suppose that the practices and theories of a near-contemporary tribe, however remote and however simple their technology, were images of the practices and theories of the ancestors of our civilization. A thorough penetration of the historical dimension of our *Umwelt* remains to be achieved, but that material is in the files, so to speak, since our literary heritage includes among much else, representations of most of the ritual and symbolic structures whose embodiment in the structure of the environment creates the *Umwelt*.

Conclusion

Tentative though these remarks on the *Umwelt* have largely been, they do point the way both to new directions of research and to a new conception of the way human beings achieve sociability. Human beings manage their lives by following rules and readings and endowing the world and other people and their actions with meanings. Yet the achievement of meaning is not just by referential convention, but by the making and understanding of structure. People can be regarded as naturally structuring; that is, we seek the explanation of the general tendency to create structures not in the particular circumstances of structural work, but in the genetic endowment of man. However unlike other architectonic creatures, such as bees and coral insects, human beings are capable of free creation of structures, though probably within some limits set by yet unknown universal constraints. Common observation suggests that any correctly produced structures do not satisfy people for very long and that the attempt to modulate or modify structures already existent is a very strong human tendency, again one whose origins may have to be looked for in the physics and chemistry of the nervous system. Thus we must add *Homo architectonicus* to the many other characterizations of man, such as *Homo sapiens, Homo ludens,* and the like.

NOTES

1 See Mary Douglas, "Deciphering a Meal," *Daedalus* (1972); and Erving Goffman, *Relations in Public* (London: Penguin, 1972). Also see Kurt Lewin, *Principles of Topographical Psychology,* trans. F. Heider and G. M. Heider (New York: McGraw-Hill, 1936).

2 Kenneth Burke, *A Grammar of Motives* (Berkeley and Los Angeles: University of California Press, 1969).

3 Basil Bernstein, "Social Class, Language, and Socialization," in *Language and Social Context,* ed. P. P. Giglioli (Harmondsworth: Penguin, 1972).

4 See Francis Yates, *The Art of Memory* (London: Routledge & Kegan Paul, 1966).

5 Davy, *Consolations in Travel* (London, 1830).

6 These observations were made in the Halvdags børnehave Skovvang, Århus, Denmark, and I am grateful to the staff, K. Eskerod, L. Lund, and J. Hansen, for their cooperation.

7 Claude Lévi-Strauss, *The Savage Mind* (London: Weidenfeld & Nicholsen, 1966), pp. 30-3.

8 Emmanuel A. Schegloff and Harvey Sacks, "Opening up Closings," in *Ethnomethodology*, ed. R. Turner (London: Penguin, 1974), pp. 233-64.

9 M. P. M. Richards, *The Integration of a Child into the Social World* (Cambridge: Cambridge University Press, 1974).

10 Robert Bocock, *Ritual in an Industrial Society* (London: Allen & Unwin, 1974).

11 Goffman, *Relations*, 1972.

12 I. Eibl-Eibesfeldt, "Similarities and Differences between Culture in Expressive Movements," in *Non-Verbal Communication*, ed. R. A. Hinde (Cambridge: Cambridge University Press, 1972).

13 J. A. R. M. Van't Hooff, "A Comparative Approach to the Phylogeny of Laughter and Smiling," in ibid., pp. 209-38.

14 Edmund Leach, "The Influence of Cultural Context on Non-Verbal Communication in Man," in ibid., pp. 315-44.

15 Goffman, *Relations*, 1972.

16 W. Cooper, *Hair* (London: Alden Books, 1971), pp. 134-48.

17 See G. G. Luce, *Body Time* (New York: Pantheon Books, 1971).

18 Douglas, "Deciphering a Meal."

19 Pierre Bourdieu, "The Berber House or the World Reversed," *Echanges et communications: Mélange offert à Claude Lévi-Strauss à l'occasion de son 60ᵉ anniversaire* (The Hague: Mouton, 1971).

20 Claude Lévi-Strauss, *Tristes Tropiques*, trans. J. Weightman and D. Weightman (London: Jonathan Cape, 1974), pp. 220-1, 234.

21 Stephen E. Toulmin, *Human Understanding*, vol. 2 (Oxford: The Clarendon Press, 1973). [Compare the Darwinian versus Lamarkian distinction to that between functionalist and positivist theories of social change, as outlined by Lyman in this volume. (Eds.)]

6

Social theory as confession:
Parsonsian sociology and the symbolism of evil

PAUL G. CREELAN

Editors' introduction

American functionalists such as Talcott Parsons locate the sources of order in certain functional prerequisites of society as a whole. In contrast, many French structuralists follow Claude Lévi-Strauss in seeing order as immanent in the structure of the human mind itself. Thus these schools respectively seek to lay bare either the universal supraconscious or the universal unconscious principles that structure the human world. These principles are seen as lying above or beneath various objectifications in myth, kinship, and other contents or concrete meanings of particular societies. Yet, while the starting point of both these schools is phenomenological – that is, given in the immediate experience of the actor – both schools reject this level of analysis in favor of an austere or positivistic approach.

Perhaps, however, by subjecting Parsons's sociology to a semiotic analysis, the more existential, praxiological roots of American structural functionalism may become visible. To the extent that Paul G. Creelan's paper is successful in this, it suggests the possibility of linking the bifurcated tendencies of the social sciences since Weber: the search for the essence of structure (of the mind, of society, of kinship, of language) and the search for the concrete meanings generated or given in everyday life.

The assumption that paradigmatic language can reveal human identity in the context of an historical participation in the sacred has been elaborated by Paul Ricoeur and Mircea Eliade. Drawing on their hermeneutic phenomenological method, Creelan reinterprets Parsonsian sociology by focusing on the actual texts of the founder. In this analysis are revealed the structures of symbol and myth that echo within Parsonsian discourse as potential modes of existence for modern persons. The person is language, and language in its essence appears as sacred myth. The structural positivism of Parsonsian sociology is thus dissolved in an exegesis of the very language and discourse in which systems become articulated as realities, even while the phenomenology of the sacred steers clear of the alternative positivism of Lévi-Strauss. Creelan's essay thus illuminates both French and American structuralisms and suggests a way in which sociology can be connected to public histories and personal enactments. Moreover, in discussing sociology's relation to the questions of good and evil, as of the person, the community, and the polity, Creelan's essay leads us to Manfred Stanley's discussion of the prerequisites for a humanistic polity and civic discourse.

[We] can express [our] aim . . . in *one* phrase: A self-understanding (critical philosophy) of the age concerning its struggles and wishes. This is a task for the world and for us . . . It is a *confession*, nothing else. To have its sins forgiven, mankind has only to declare them for what they are.

> Karl Marx, letter to Ruge, September 1943,
> in *Writings of the Young Marx on*
> *Philosophy and Society* (Garden City, N.Y.:
> Doubleday, 1967), p. 215.

In recent years students of contemporary social theory have suggested that texts of modern social science, normally put forth as objectively verifiable factual accounts of social reality, actually embody normative intentions manifest in expressive structures of symbol. For example, in their essay "Some Puzzling Aspects of Social Interaction," Moore and Anderson raise the issue of whether the texts of contemporary social science do not serve as the vessels of myth by means of which modern man provides himself models for his experiences and action:

As we see matters, one of the principal activities of social scientists will be, or should be, to continue the work begun (for our civilization) by Homer and Hesiod: i.e., to continue the job of constructing folk-models for the instruction and diversion of our fellow creatures. We have no reason to believe that a more scientific, and less haphazard, approach to the problem will insure success or even survival.[1]

Moore and Anderson do not speculate as to why modern social scientists would disavow this function of providing normative models, nor do they analyze how the "myths" that reside in sociological texts are constructed; instead, they merely suggest that these texts embody mythic forms.

Perhaps this should not surprise us, in that literary stylistic devices have not been a typical concern of readers of modern social and psychological works. Yet students of ancient and medieval thought have long assumed that a central part of their scholarly task is to be sensitive to meanings hidden between the lines – in symbolic configurations, double meanings, and contextual associations – and they have even suggested the possibility of a writer's engaging in extensive camouflage of the true meaning of his text. More recently Peter Gay's *Style in History,* Stanley Edgar Hyman's *The Tangled Bank,* and Richard Harvey Brown's *A Poetic for Sociology* have begun to open this mode of analysis again.[2] Focusing on social scientific writings, they have inspected imagery, syntax, and semantics – the rhetorical and aesthetic character of the written text – seeing it merely as a central focus of a wider context of meaning. Their assumption is that content is resident in all the linguistic forms of the text and, moreover, that deeper meanings may be expressed in language that is ordinarily dismissed as irrelevant to a univocally conceived theory, as for example, in much of what is ordinarily taken as rhetorical language in Marx.

Such an increased perspicuity vis-à-vis the meanings of scientific texts coincides with a mitigation of scientific realism – the assumption that a final and ultimate comprehension of reality is possible. Instead, by seeing scientific writings from the perspective of symbolic realism, the claim of such texts to transparent facticity falls apart, allowing new questions about the nature, origins, and meanings of scientific truth to emerge. Likewise, such a perspective encourages a corresponding appreciation of the embeddedness of science in the broad streams of cultural and social life. It is toward the end of furthering such discourse between social science and wider dimensions of culture, particularly social ethics and religion, that the present chapter is offered.

In this essay I shall attempt to explain the nature and construction of the mythic structures in the writings of Talcott Parsons, a leading contemporary social theorist. First, I shall seek to establish the existence of a duality of myths in Parsons's texts, arising out of a conflict as to the recommended course that modern social life should follow. This situation of conflict demands not only a duality of myths, but also that the actual experience of conflict itself be the final expressive signification of the texts. After discussing the stylistic devices by which Parsons represents the general situation of conflict, I shall elaborate the first of the conflicting myths and its intention. I then shall suggest the manner in which the recognition of the failure of this myth to express a comprehensive image of man impels a movement toward an alternative myth to guide human intentions. But this alternative also will be revealed to have its limitations, thus fixing the overall movement in a conflict between the two structures of myth and their respective intentions.

Utterances of conflict

The point of departure in our analysis is the style of writing manifest in the Parsonsian texts. No student who has lingered over Talcott Parsons's work can have failed to notice a unique style of expression that, despite its abstract impersonality, has become deeply associated with the man. Among graduate students, Parsons's writings have stood in some respects like a temple into whose holy recesses even the most able would only gradually be introduced. From other perspectives, of course, the Parsonian texts sound only as tinkling cymbals, notable solely for the profuse obscurantism manifest therein. But whichever view one takes of the value of Parsons's work, our initial, immediate impressions of both the man and his thought are formed around the inimitable style encountered in his texts. Reflection upon the intrinsic nature and significance of this style thus may provide an important clue to the meaning of Parsonian sociology as a whole.

One recent, but brief comment upon the nature and significance of Parsons's style is that of Alvin Gouldner, who remarks that Parsons's prose is "more Delphically obscure, more Germanically opaque, more confused and confusing by far, than that of any other sociologist of whom I know"; indeed "from its beginnings" it was "a byword for obscurity among American sociologists."[3] Gouldner unhesitatingly interprets this obscurity to be an elitist maneuver designed to surround the system and also its author with an aura of mystery and profundity so as to gain both status and students:

> To publish in a very difficult style is almost equivalent to *not* publishing. In reading an extremely obscure work, those first drawn to it are dealing with a not yet truly public object, but with something that is more nearly akin to a "cult object." It is much like reading an unpublished and privately circulated manuscript, which has in effect, the aura of a "secret teaching." Because of its difficulty the work must be given an "interpretation." Its interpretation and understanding are, in part, dependent upon a personal acquaintance with the author, and knowledge of it often implies a special relation to him.[4]

Gouldner thus assumes that obscurity may have a positive significance, creating something hidden and thus valuable, something that only an initiate may be given. This interpretation of Parsonian obscurity as an elitist ploy is further associated in Gouldner's critique with another more wide-ranging conclusion, that the Parsonian system is also a disarming, soothing apology for an exploitative capitalist order, that indeed behind the seeming verbal muddle there is a rapacious single-mindedness interested solely in the maintenance of the modern situation of egoistic capitalism. Gouldner's suggestion is that Parsons magically lays an aura of systemic harmony around a social reality, that is, capitalism, which in truth holds profound antagonisms and basic conflicts within it:

It is not the cleavages in the social world that are real to Parsons, however, but its unbroken oneness; the fact that it all grows out of one elemental stuff, social action, into increasingly differentiated structures. At any rate, this is one of the ways in which Parsons constitutes the oneness of the social world. The most important expression of Parsons' vision of the social world, however, is his conception of it as a *system*. Parsons thus actually has two different metaphors in terms of which unity is expressed: the social world as organic differentiation from a common substance, and the social world as a single system. The metaphor of organic differentiation is less focal and controlled; the metaphor of system is labeled and deliberately employed.[5]

In my view, Gouldner's understanding of Parsons is too much impelled by his own project of mounting a Marxist critique of contemporary sociology and society, for which he uses Parsons as an exemplary foil. It is my suggestion that such a project is unwarranted, that Gouldner overlooks the degree of actual ambivalence in Parsons's attitude toward the individualistic capitalist order of modernity, that he fails to see how deeply Parsons's theorizing is actually informed by a definite alternative model of community that radically contrasts with individualistic capitalism. While Parsons's alternative to modernity conflicts with the ideal of utilitarian individualism, I suggest that Parsons puts forth this alternative ideal with the same ambivalence as he puts forth the individualistic ideal. By denying Parsons's ambivalent inclination toward the communal alternative, Gouldner fails to inquire why Parsons also withdraws from this alternative as well, thus neglecting an instruction of considerable importance for Gouldner's own Marxist, communal theorizing.

In contrast to Gouldner's assumption that the Parsonsian texts are hopelessly obscure, I would emphasize instead the qualities of affective neutrality and relentless prolixity, traits that bespeak their character as utterances of a psyche whose intentions for his own history and that of his community are faltering in a personal "Slough of Despond." Parsons's coldly abstract style reflects profound conflict regarding certain alternative ways of life he finds available for himself and his society, alternatives whose forms are only obliquely and dimly presented as normative models precisely because of the conflict of commitment and the guilt involved in that conflict. In his confrontation with the dilemma over individualism versus communalism, which he admits impels his own life work, Parsons finds the salient alternative involved on each side to be unacceptable, indeed sinful; but he can find no way out, for himself or for others, no exit from a condition that is basically one of culpability and self-accusation.[6] Thus the distanced, highly intellectualized objectivist attitude in which Parsons situates himself toward modern man and his society, by means of which he expresses his own position, bespeaks the personal state of a guilty soul, unwilling to take one path rather than another because all available roads lead to perdition. The Parsonsian texts are mixed messages that rightly cause anxiety to those who encounter them, and yet perhaps the only alternative to complete despair for a conflicted man is to utter his indecision. It is not clear, however, that Parsons really acknowledges the degree of indecision in his work. Rather he may experience the conflict of meaning more in the tacit struggle to articulate, the struggle to lay hold of firm meaning that often underlies his incredible prolixity, as if quantity of words will put down the demons of ambiguity that hover around his verbalizations about social life.

Parsons's abstract removal from his work, his avoidance of the passion that abundant imagery, metaphor, and personal allusion would express, as well as his scrupulous avoidance of commitment to any particular concrete system of personal values for social life, all are interesting to compare to B. F. Skinner, whose unwillingness to give a precise name, or meaning, to his subjects' behavior may also be less a neutral stance of an objective observer than the position of a man who dramatically portrays real struggles of modern history in his experiments, who knows that his subjects' behavior represents conflicting ways of life, but whose representative ambivalence about these alternatives even prevents their being given their proper name, their true meaning. Skinner ultimately did not join the real prototype of his fictional utopia, *Walden II,* just as Parsons similarly retreats from active advocacy in modern life by remaining on the cloistered paths of Harvard Yard. Both Skinner and Parsons thus represent what may be the typical stance of modern man, edging obliquely toward life, mired in profound doubts about how precisely they are to live their allotted time.

What then are the paradigms of life that are attended by a guilt that increases the distance with which they are apprehended? To decode the alternative modes of life whose conflict is imbedded in the tangle of Parsons's texts, we must first understand that the abstract and formal language of Parsonsian speech, as well, for that matter, as that of the Skinnerian texts with their experimental reports has actual reference to a rich set of very concrete images at the most primitive level of thought, images in whose outlines the true issues of the Parsonsian dilemma emerge.

The machine and the animal

The two images most characteristically associated with the general system concept in Parsons's synthesis are the machine and the animal. These images appear in Parsons's *The Structure of Social Action* as the foremost examples of systems that he presents. Explaining the nature of the units of scientific theoretical systems, Parsons notes:

On the physical and biological levels it is easy to see what is meant by them. A steam engine consists of cylinders, pistons, driving rods, boilers, valves, etc. Similarly an organism is composed of cells, tissues, organs. A part in this sense is a unit, the concrete existence of which aside from its relation to other parts of the same whole, is meaningful, "makes sense." A machine can actually be taken apart. An organism cannot be taken apart in the same sense, at least without permanently destroying its function, but a dead organism may be dissected and its parts thus identified.[7]

Elsewhere, Parsons states:

At one pole or extreme is the mechanist core, is where all the important "properties" of the concretely functioning parts can be defined independently of their relations to the other parts or to the whole . . . Above all, it is the case where the parts can, in fact, be concretely separated from their relations and still remain the same. Thus we can take a steam engine apart and actually examine its pistons, record their size, shape, tensile strength, etc. . . .

Now precisely in so far as a whole is organic this becomes impossible. The very definition of an organic whole is as one within which the relations determine the properties of its parts. The properties of the whole are not simply a resultant of the latter. This is true whether it be an organism or some other unit, such as a "mind," a "society," or what not. And in so far as this is true, the concept "part" takes on an abstract, indeed a "fictional" character. For the part of an organic whole is no longer the same, once it is separated factually or conceptually from the whole. Perhaps the classical statement of this point is that of Aristotle, that a hand separated from the living body is no longer a hand except in an equivocal sense, as we would speak of a stone hand.[8]

Thus the machine and the animal provide the fundamental images that lie beneath Parsons's notion of system. Gouldner also notices this and suggests a dynamic of mutual identity between these images: "Proto-plasmic organic differentiation is the genetics of oneness; system mechanics are the synchronics of oneness. There is a kind of a Rousseaueanism here: Social systems are born as living organisms, but everywhere they are becoming machines."[9] My own perception of these two images derives from prior work with the texts of B. F. Skinner in whose experiments the drama of animals turning into machines and vice versa emerges far more transparently than in the Parsonsian synthesis. Nonetheless, this fundamental transformative magic is practiced by both these theorists.

Yet the tension between these two images had unsettled another Harvard-educated mind before Parsons or Skinner were born. In his famous autobiography *The Education of Henry Adams,* this American exemplar

wrote a chapter entitled "The Dynamo and the Virgin," about his experience in the Paris of the Great Exposition of 1900. The images relate to
the juxtaposition of the machines Adams encountered at the exposition
with the cathedrals inspired by the Virgin that he also encountered
throughout France. While the Virgin is not the animal that occurs in the
Parsonsian system, nevertheless the organic quality of the woman and her
body is closely related to the organicity of the animal. Moreover when
Parsons later turned to psychoanalysis it was indeed the great Oedipal
mother whose sexual attractions were conceived to move the elements of
"the social system." Thus Adams's considerations on this duality of images
and the ideals embodied in it are instructive.

At the Great Exposition, Langley taught Adams

The astonishing complexities of the new Daimler motor, and of the automobile
which, since 1893, had become a nightmare at a hundred kilometres an hour,
almost as destructive as the electric train which was only ten years older; and
threatening to become as terrible as the locomotive steam-engine itself which was
about exactly Adams's own age.[10]

The foremost symbols of the new age were displayed in the Great Hall of
Dynamos and began to be felt as a "moral force, much as the early Christians felt the Cross."[11] Adams could not explain precisely how he came to
regard the dynamo as a silent but infinite religious force. He was, however, deeply troubled by Langley's sentiments that "the new forces were
anarchical, and especially that he was not responsible for the new rays
that were little short of patricidal in their wicked spirit toward science."[12]

In opposition to the chaotic anarchism associated with the machine
and by implication with men and societies who used the machines, Adams
placed the generative organicity of the Virgin, whose unifying presence
and power had also overwhelmed him on his visits to Lourdes and to Notre
Dame. The cathedrals had drawn men together in work and worship for
centuries; rather than anarchical and individualistic, the cathedrals were
integrative and communal symbols. The alternative symbols of the dynamo and the Virgin thus opened up a tension Adams described as "the
knife-edge along which he must crawl."[13]

In Europe "the woman had once been supreme" and indeed "still seemed
potent, not merely as a sentiment but as a force."[14] The harmonious
warmth, generativity, organicity, and beauty of the Virgin held a creative
power that drew beings together in harmonious union both mystic and
sexual.

Why was she unknown in America? Evidently America was ashamed of her, and
she was ashamed of herself, otherwise they would not have strewn fig leaves so

profusely all over her. When she was a true force, she was ignorant of fig leaves, but the monthly magazine-made American female had not a feature that would have been recognized by Adam. The trait was notorious and often humorous but anyone brought up among Puritans knew that sex was a sin.[15]

Adams observed that "in any previous age, sex was strength; the goddess was worshipped because of her force . . . she was the animated dynamo; she was reproduction, the greatest and most mysterious of all energies; all she needed was to be fecund."[16] But in this country she was unknown, the profound individualism of competitive capitalism and its machines having drained the organic life and communality from America.

However, if Henry Adams perceived an impossible gap between the anarchic individualism of the dynamo and the sympathetic organicity of the Virgin, Talcott Parsons's simultaneous inclusion of both of them as images associated with system signifies an attempt to bridge that gap, to forge a new unity where Adams felt most conflict. The question, however, is whether these two images really find harmonious integration. If, as two contradictory modes of social life, they cannot be joined, then Parsons is in fact denying their conflict and creating an illusory reality to be worshipped as a resolution of the current historical predicament.

In fact such an illegitimate claim for valuation has historically been understood in the Western biblical tradition as an instance of the sin of idolatry, the setting up of an object whose value as an ultimate reality is only illusory, a trick of the eye or the imagination. In fact, I contend that Parsons, though hesitantly and with profound guilt, nevertheless, in his conjunction of the images of the animal and the machine, does actually allow himself to create an idolatrous metal animal of iron or brass or gold, the substance of tools, or coin, or homage. A central image of the Old Testament is that of the golden animal of Sinai, the idol created out of coins and jewelry, its creators' wealth taken as a divine substance. I suggest that the mechanical animal – the fundamental symbol of the Parsonsian social system – is similarly gilded and stands before us in the Parsonsian texts as a cultural symbol of modern life, a symbol of the forms of the idolatry of modern man.

The perfidy of idolatry lay in its elevation of human acts or products to a sacred status. Moses smashed the Tablets of the Law on the head of the idol in his anger at his people's lifting up their own creation as divine. Even in its status as a counsel to certain works, the Mosaic Law in Israel presupposed the magnificent promise of divine life and protection given to Abraham by the world-transcendent God. The people of Israel were thus understood to be supported from their beginnings by divine life in all their efforts to formulate and live by the Law. In no sense then was

constitution or performance of the Commandments assumed to be like the
idol, solely a human creation, a vain expression of prideful self-sufficiency.
In its truest moments the striving of Moses' people to formulate and fulfill
the Law was to be the moving of the Spirit of Yahweh among themselves,
and thus the glory of such fulfillment of their brotherhood was God's
alone.

The evil of idolatry, however, lay in elevating merely human works and
faculties to the status of an ultimate reality so that the idolater really
worships only himself and his own agency as he adores the idol he has
fashioned. Gold and metals that glitter have traditionally been associated
with the fashioning of such objects. In "Paradise Lost," a poem known well
by Parsons's father, Edward S. Parsons, who was both a Milton scholar
and a Congregational clergyman, we find the precise conjunction of a
demonic labor, the creation and gilding of false gods and temples. The
first act of the devils upon falling into hell was to set to work ransacking
a hill that "Shon with a glossie scurff, undoubted sign/ That in his womb
was hid metallic ore." The devils were led on by Mammon, "the least
erected spirit that fell/ From Heaven, for ev'n in Heav'n his looks and
thoughts/ were always downward bent, admiring more/ The riches of
Heav'ns pavement, trad'n Gold/ Then aught dwine on holy else enjoy'd/
In vision beatific." After this crew had "dig'd out ribs of Gold" from "the
bowels of their mother Earth," they in an hour "with incessant toyl and
hands innumerable" fashioned a splendid Hall for their consultation as
a society in hell, says Milton: "let none admire/ that riches grow in Hell;
that sayl may best deserve the precious bone."[17]

It is my suggestion that, in Parsons's imaging forth of the social system
under the figure of a giant metal animal, he simultaneously creates but
also condemns an idol, a product of the works or, in Parsonsian terms, the
acts of sinful men. While it is thus understandable why Parsons takes
great pains to dissociate himself from such a creation, yet this idol may
be the only reality about which he can speak, the only alternative to silence
being an act of confession of the existence of the evil of idolatry in himself
and in his society.

It is ironic that a deification of human agency would appear as the
product of a man whose father began his career as a minister of the God-
centered Calvinist faith of Congregationalism; not "faith," however, but
rather human works are the cornerstone of Parsonsian voluntarism. For
Parsons the act of voluntaristic freedom is not so much the act of discovering value or having value revealed to oneself; instead it is an act in which
man actually confers value upon specific social acts out of his own autonomous will: "In the Beginning was the Deed." The very engagement in a

particular form of social action is tantamount to conferring value upon it. Parsonsian man does not really hear the call of which the Calvinist theologian had so much to say; instead he utters it to himself in performing his tasks. In essence ultimate ends and ultimate values are the voluntary products of human agency, just indeed as the Golden Calf was erected by Aaron and worshipped by the Israelites at the foot of Mount Sinai. The freedom to enact whatever works they choose, expressed in the Parsonian principle of voluntaristic freedom, holds a presumption that the Bible condemns as idolatrous and that the Puritan religion especially condemns.

It is important to be clear about the exact status of voluntarism within Puritan culture, out of which Parsons himself emerged. The Congregational Church Covenant in fact has been said to express a principle of voluntarism. This description contains an important element of truth, but outside the total context of ideas in which the Puritan idea of the Church Covenant arose it alone is likely to be seriously misleading. Its truth lies in the fact that Separatists and Congregationalists insisted that the power of Christ, embodied in the church, works in mysterious conjunction with the will of man. The visible church, William Ames says

differs from the mystical Church, the gathering of which together into one is not prescribed unto men, but performed immediately by divine operation, but the gathering together into an instituted Church is so performed by God that his command and man's duty and labour do come between.

However, Ames immediately adds, the church is formed by the power of God,

is ordained by God and Christ only, because men have neither power of themselves to institute, or frame a church unto Christ, neither have they by the revealed will of God any such power commited to them; their greatest honor is that they are servants in the House of God.[18]

Ames does not say that the churches men establish by voluntary association must meet certain requirements of some revealed constitution whose content men may know; rather he says solely and simply that men have no power *of themselves* to form churches. He says nothing about the marks of the true church or the qualities of an ecclesiastical polity. Ames finds it completely sufficient to say that a church is formed when believers are joined together by a special bond of grace among themselves, a pregiven communal bond that is the body of Christ. Only a society to which Christ has given his life is truly a church, as in the Pauline text. Ames distinguishes the body of Christ from a voluntary civil society:

This joining together by convenant doth only so far forth make a Church as it respects the exercising the communion of Saints: for the same believing men may

join themselves in covenant to make a city or some civil society, as they do immediately respect a common civil good, but they do not make a Church but as
in their constitution they respect holy communion with God among themselves.

Hence the same men may make a City of civil society and not a church; or a
Church, and not a City; or both a Church and a City.

Neither doth some sudden joining together and exercise of holy communion
suffice to make a Church, unless there be also that constancy, at least in intention,
which brings the state of a body, and members in a certain spiritual policy . . .

But unto everyone of us is given grace according to the measure of the gift of Christ.
Wherefore he saith, when he ascended up on high, he led captivity captive, and
gave gifts unto men . . . And he gave some, apostles, and some, prophets and
some, evangelists; and some, pastors and teachers. For the perfecting of the Saints,
for the work of the ministry, for the edifying of the body of Christ (Eph. 4:7-8,
11-12).

In fact, if a single phrase had to be chosen to summarize everything that
Separatists and Congregationalists abhorred, it might in fact be "voluntary
religion." No act "grounded only upon the will of man, and not upon the
word of God . . . can be an act of Religion," says William Bradshaw;[19] to
ascribe religious value to any such merely "voluntary" act is to make it an
act, as Bradshaw puts it, "of superstition" or, in my terms, of idolatry.
Thus the covenant that the Puritan believer joined is not seen as something
he has chosen out of his own sovereign will, deciding between good and
evil. Puritan voluntarism rather implied that human wills were thoroughly
disposed by divine grace and revelation toward that which is God's higher
purpose for them, which is to join with others who manifest the Spirit for
mutual edification. By insisting that the act of consent whereby believers
form a church is voluntary, Separatists did not mean that the church was
created by the concurrence of sovereign wills; they meant rather that a
living temple can only be built of living stones. Indeed to confuse the civil
order, formed from the former sort of covenants, with the order of a true
visible church is to "spread a veil of darkness upon the people . . . and
keep from their eyes the kingdom of Christ."[20]

Thus if Talcott Parsons's earliest work, *The Structure of Social Action*,
views society as a voluntaristic community in which men proudly con-
gratulate the righteousness of their sovereign decision to choose one normative order rather than another, they stand accused by the deepest spirit
of Parsons's cultural heritage, which assails such a vaulting freedom, such
an idolatrous assigning of divinity to merely human works. To the true
Calvinist, man does not choose God or reject him; rather it is God who
lifts up man. Thus for Parsons voluntaristic freedom is spoken but is not

fully owned; its character as a delusion of the Devil that results in man's lifting up some merely human acts and creations to a holy place causes Parsons to recede from voluntaristic freedom into the distance from which he gives his abstract speech about it.

If it is true, however, that the Parsonsian principle of voluntarism celebrates certain forms of human agency to an inordinate extent, precisely which forms of human agency are these that end in idolatry? It is my suggestion that the idolatrous forms of human agency are associated with the dual images of the machine and the animal that Parsons fuses to create the idol. My hypothesis is that the two images in which the concept of system is manifested – the machine and the animal – represent dual forms of presumptive human works associated in the case of the machine with the cultural complex of modern capitalism studied by Max Weber and, in the case of the animal, with archaic communistic societies living under the symbol of the totem animal that Durkheim found to express the social order of the tribe.

Asceticism: Idolatry according to Weber

The full significance of the machine image associated with modern capitalism cannot be understood apart from the symbols derived from ascetic Protestantism that permeate Parsons's work. More specifically, the idolatrous voluntaristic "acts" associated with the machine may be seen to be the motions of ascetic work analyzed by Max Weber in his essays on Protestantism, rationalization, and capitalism. Weber shows how, in the Puritan communities whose history informs Parsons's cultural heritage, specific acts eventually came to supplant a more experiential sense of grace and to serve as the signs of predestination for the believer. A much greater emphasis came to be placed upon spiritual discipline with its mutual attention to members' performance of specific actions, fulfillments or omissions of the conditions of the Covenent, "the Law." In the Puritan community members bound themselves more stringently to each other's promises and threatenings to uphold the commonly agreed upon conditions of the Covenant. As Weber suggests, the motions of work became these conditions, came to signify salvation, to keep off the threatenings of both God and man in the Puritan communities, and to allow the reception of divine promises. However, Weber does not analyze the specific tensions that arose in Puritanism around the fear that these works were being taken as idolatrous substitutes for the deeper life of grace.

The primary symbol of the Puritan community is given in the Parsonsian texts by the most familiar image associated with the social system, the famous box that signifies the A-G-I-L schema. It is interesting to note that the two foremost proponents of American social science theory, Parsons and Skinner, both hold up a box-shaped structure as the central framework that gives form to individual and social existence. I believe that for both theorists this box in fact represents that box that for the Old Testament Israelites symbolized the Covenant with Yahweh, the receptacle of the Tablets of the Law to which the believer was bound by a dynamic of promise and threatening, the very Ark of the Covenant. If one in fact revises the A-G-I-L sequence of letters – and reads them from right to left as in the ancient Hebrew – one is left with the Latin word L-I-G-A, meaning "bond" or "tie." The actors in the Parsonsian world thus are united in a bond that is symbolized by a box, bound to a common law, as were the Old Testament Israelites to whom Congregationalists looked for the forms that would guide their own communities. However, the centrality of the symbol of the Ark of the Covenant for the Parsonsian social system expresses its emphasis upon the voluntaristic act, upon the works or conditions of the Mosaic Covenant. The earlier Abrahamic dimension of the Covenant, that in which Yahweh promised divine life and power to fulfill whatever works were necessary, is neglected. Instead Parsons emphasizes a voluntary religion as the nature of the social system, a way of life that tends to substitute specific human works or acts for a receptivity to and expression of divine revelation and the Holy Spirit.

What then is the nature of the law of this community? Weber's study in fact chronicles the transformation of Calvinistic religions like Puritanism from experientially rooted religions of faith and regeneration to works-oriented moralistic religions that emphasized a certain form of human striving as against a searching receptivity toward grace and its totalistic transformation of the soul. Such works emerge as fundamentally ascetic and negative, based in a radical dualism between the soul and the body, between heaven and spirit and the world and the flesh from which emerges the ethical imperative of rejecting or at least controlling the latter. Man was understood as the same as his soul and other than his body. Indeed man is so radically individualized that all other men and all nature become radically other, seen with wariness and suspicion from a negative, rejecting attitude. The individual soul's basic project became to escape its confinement in the body and the world of bodies and at all events to master the influence of these bodies over itself.

Many of the Calvinistic themes of this asceticism are taken from Plato, who gives the body an eschatological force, as in his reference to the Orphic origins of the term *soma* for the body:

It was the Orphics in particular, I think, who imposed that name, in the belief that the soul atones for the faults to which it is punished, and that for its safekeeping it has, round about it, the body in the likeness of a prison: hence, that it is, as its name implies, the *soma* [the jail] of the soul, until the soul has paid its debt, and there is no need to change a single letter.[21]

In the Orphic interpretation the body was not the origin of evil, but rather a penal institution in which the soul expiates a former guilt, the body thus signifying the inimical transcendence of the judge and his sentence. As well, however, the body, like all jails, was itself a place of temptation and corruption so that the soul's confinement in the body was both expiation for past evil and occasion for an on-going need for such expiation. Existence for the Orphics was an eternal relapse.

This interpretation of the body as an instrument of reiterated punishment is articulated by Plato in his own new interpretation of the soul, which may be called puritanical: The soul is not from here; it comes from elsewhere; it is divine; in its present body it leads an occult existence; the existence of an exiled being that longs for its liberation and strives to master the temptations and contaminations of its imprisoned environment. The dividing line is not so much between the gods who have kept immortality for themselves and men, who have only vain hope for their share; it runs right through man, separating his godlike immortality from the corruption of the body. When this anthropological dualism emerges within Protestantism, largely through the vehicles of Platonism and Gnosticism, the Calvinist vision of man's entire being as depraved fades and we find him split into a godlike part and a demonic part. Man is the same as his elevated soul, but radically other than his stigmatized body and the other bodies and the natural world that surround it.

While the ascetic interpretation of religion is founded only upon a negative impulse it is readily emergent when men have lost any sense of a positive experience of divine life, when they turn to rely upon their own power, comprised largely of acts of negation, to transport them out of the finite realm. Such a development occurred in the Puritan tradition toward the middle of the seventeenth century in the emergence of what Perry Miller has called a rationalistic "Puritan scholasticism." Mind and soul were set against emotion and the body in the development that is often

taken to be the essence of Puritanism, but which is in fact only an emergent
development within the overall movement.

As such asceticism developed within American Puritanism, the ethic
of the manipulation and mastery of an evil nature and body expressed the
antipathy of the Covenanters, as this tradition of Puritans came to be
called, toward the world and the flesh. The ascetic impulse was transformed into a striving to stand above and to control a world that seemed
to be the embodiment of evil. Such a project of rejecting the world and the
flesh in an impulse of mastery is, however, only a negative thrust against
creation, and not a movement toward God, as the Puritan theologian of
the Great Awakening, Jonathan Edwards, pointed out in his critique of
ascetic Puritanism. Asceticism is purely an act of human will and its status
as virtue is thus a worship of mere human agency thrusting itself toward
nothing except itself. Within the framework of the ethic of work, the major
symbol and agent of this negative thrust became the machine, the instrument of distance from and domination over the sinful world and the sinful
flesh of its operator. The ascetic work ethic is thus the Law of the Covenant
that is symbolized by the Parsonsian box.

The Parsonsian social system thus manifests the Puritan development
of the ultimacy of work as the sign of its highest expectation. Not only
does Parsons set certain acts at the center of his analysis of the dynamics of
promise and threatening, but Parsons's principle of complementarity provides an analog to the Congregational church discipline, in the conception
that equilibrium in the social system is maintained by ego's fulfilling the
expectations of alter, thus gratifying alter so that alter behaves in a way
that gratifies a fulfillment of ego's expectations. Thus when one behaves
in conformity of another's expectations, he elicits a favorable response
from the other that leads one to continue so behaving without any change.
Without the favorable response or with the provision of an unfavorable
response, the action would be likely to change. By such a mutual dynamic
of providing promises and sometimes threatenings to each other, the social
system maintains equilibrium; says Parsons, "the complementarity of
role-expectations, once established is not problematical . . . No special
mechanisms are required for the explanation of the maintenance of complementary interaction-orientation."[22] Such a principle is, however, no
more than a secular version of the bond of promise and threatening of the
famous Covenant that united American Congregationalist communities,
whose members relied upon each other for support and sanction in their
common life as members of a spiritual body. Parsons's use of the symbol
of the Covenant bond is analogous to a similar usage of the dynamic of

promise and threatening by the other major American descendant of Puritan culture, B. F. Skinner.

And yet it may be questioned whether there is not more suspicion and distrust in the Parsonsian social system than communal harmony. To the extent that ascetic individual works came to be emphasized as the ground of salvation to the exclusion of the experience of the common in-dwelling of the Holy Spirit in the community, the Puritan communities became profoundly individualistic and antagonistic, engendering pressures to which the revivals of the Great Awakening gave satisfaction. In the Parsonsian-Weberian world of modern capitalism, suspicious, competitive individualism ultimately prevails. The puritanical suspicion of the world of others as potentially evil leaves the Parsonsian ego alone and antagonistic to such others who must be rejected or mastered or both. One side of Parsons's pattern variable duality expresses the extreme egoistic position quite well: the self-oriented, affectively neutral, universalistic, specific side. At this extreme one discovers the anarchic, competitive modern world of universal others, bent only upon their own self-preservation and enhancement achieved in a movement of rejection and domination of others. Parsons's assumptions about influence within the system in fact leaves egoistic exploitation as a distinct possibility; for example, in his discussion of the interdependence of system units, Parsons grants far more freedom to individual actors in affecting the outcome of the system than is ordinarily supposed: "in a system of interdependent variables . . . the value of all the others are known."[23] The system in fact becomes, as Gouldner puts it, a "surprise machine" in which effective influences and their true outcomes are always masked from view. A Hobbesian ego's mastery of his world, social as well as natural, remains a distinct possibility in the Parsonsian system, the remainder of the system becoming merely a tool for its purposes, a machine with enormous leverage for selfish purposes.

Gouldner legitimately questions whether Parsons's conclusion that the society whose members are each imbued with the spirit of gain still shares a common bond precisely by their normative allegiance to the Protestant Ethic, is but a Satanic illusion. It is as if communality would be created for all the devils in hell if they lived in closer conformity to the norms of the place. Are we to believe that the company of devils would then be any less self-centered, alienated, and treacherous than before? The supposition that this is so is merely a trick of words, a delusion that can justly be called Satanic in its quality of attaching an appeal to something that is inherently treacherous.

It may be suggested that the postulation of this Law of the Ark of the

Covenant simultaneously defines both the goal of ascetic escape, but also the condition of bodily imprisonment of the soul. As a law defines both the realm of interdiction and the realm of purity, so the box as itself a material structure signifies both the material world as a jail but also the imperative to flee its confines. Besides being a vehicle of the ascetic interdiction the box also signifies the world and the flesh from which the soul or the Parsonsian ego must strive to escape. Such dualistic meaning also attaches to other associations to the Parsonsian box. To escape from the world and the flesh modern man must actually use parts of nature in his efforts to control and dominate nature. He must, for example, turn his body, a part of nature, back upon nature in his effort to master and dominate it. This he does through incessant work, acts of mastery that become writ large in the machine and the bureaucracy. However, Weber found these mechanical instruments to be iron cages whose existence he lamented. Ironically, the ego's attempt to escape from the world and the flesh becomes the very occasion for the construction of a new jail comprised of natural elements in which man does not even realize he is imprisoned. The ego, working with a machine or in a bureaucracy symbolized in Parsons's box, very much resembles the rat in Skinner's box, frantically operating the level of a machine that he believes grants him domination over and distance from a world he views as profoundly evil, while all the time the rat and the Parsonsian ego remain in the prison of the box. The emergence of this wholly new prison casts a specter of hopelessness over the whole project.

Finally Parsons, like Weber, seems to realize that the ascetic project of escaping from the world and the flesh is hopeless, futile, and frustrating. Man inevitably remains trapped within nature, bound to machines in bureaucracies, the iron cages by means of which he had hoped to escape nature. Indeed, as long as he remains under the ascetic version of the Law, man stands accused as hopelessly evil; despite all the efforts of the Parsonsian ego or the Skinnerian rat to escape from the material world he remains condemned as deeply sinful under the ascetic Law. However, the very hopelessness of the ascetic project impels Parsons to a perspective beyond the Protestant ethic. A futile law holds the seeds of its own destruction; indeed its impossibility of fulfillment raises questions about why it was enacted in the first place. Perhaps the real crime is that man could assume his potency to escape from the world and the flesh in the first place, to assume a godlike, infinite soul as his essential nature.

Ritualism: Idolatry according to Durkheim

The discovery of the futility of the ascetic law, that the ascetic negative thrust is only a bondage to nothingness, occasions a profound nostalgia for the rejected structure of human existence within the world and within the flesh. This nostalgia for a return to embodied existence in the framework of nature is given form by the other symbol that Parsons associates with the system concept, that of the animal. Parsons's elaborations of the symbol of the animal come in his presentation of Emile Durkheim's sociological works, particularly *The Elementary Forms of Religious Life*, first presented in *The Structure of Social Action*.[24] Herein the animal is set forth as the totem symbol, the bond of unity between man and a divinized society, and also between man and a divinized nature. In the tribal brotherhood man and nature and society in fact form an undifferentiated divine whole, a perfectly integrated, indeed ritualized harmony whose forms manifest themselves as the primordial archetypal moments in which an ancestor god walked the earth.

In such a world everything is related to as part of everything else; sacred mana flows through the body of the world; all life manifests the splendor of divine, enchanted archetypes; suffering is as unreal as the unique historical human individual who would have to emerge to experience it or give it meaning for himself. In the communalism of the tribe, individual identity or responsibility are unknown and unsupported by the view of life as an eternal return of that primordial moment of creation, *in illo tempore,* when nature and society and man rested in the divine bosom. The communalism of tribal existence, mirrored in the regularities and harmonies of natural patterns, thus appears in Parsons's system (in juxtaposition to the individualistic dynamo), under the symbol of the totem animal. In this image is expressed the ascetic modern Protestant's nostalgia for a social framework that is not a lonely crowd of universal others, for a natural existence that does not have to be denied and mastered as if contact with it would mean defilement. Under the image of the totem animal, Parsons symbolizes archaic social order with its collectively oriented, affective, particularistic, and diffusive dimensions from the pattern variable scheme. Parsons's simultaneous and sudden removal to the archaic Durkheimian world quiets the tragic unease that plagues the modern Weberian realm. As Mircea Eliade and Paul Ricoeur suggest, the world of archaic man is conceived as a perpetual victory of the gods of order against the primordial forces of chaos; the ceaseless enactment of the ritual of order-giving creation is soothing balm for the individualistic ascetic man who would propel himself clear out of the finite world.[25] As opposed to the ascetic negativism of the Protestant Ethic, Parsons juxtaposes the animal's surrender to the rituals of nature – the native dancer's total immersion in the entrancing movements of a ritualized art of the cosmos.

The typical creation ritual of archaic religion, as characterized by Durkheim, and by Eliade and Ricoeur, is of considerable interest here insofar as the Parsonsian texts may be seen to hold the symbols of its structure. Moreover, it is precisely these ritual actions that Parsons also finds to be the idolatrous forms of human agency. The rituals of the Australian aborigines as well as of other archaic cultures provide a renewal of the drama of creation, in which the god who establishes order and being emerges victorious from a battle with the god of primordial chaos. The magnitude of this ritual in the New Year's festival at Babylon is well known. A whole people, in the presence of the gods assembled in effigy, reenacts the original battle in which the world order was won, reliving together the fundamental emotions of the songs that are sung during festivities – the cosmic anguish, the exaltation of battle, the jubilation in triumph. At first the god is lost, held prisoner in a mountain or a cave; the people, thrown into confusion, weep for him as for a suffering and dying god; it is at once the death of a god and the return of creation to chaos. Then, however, the imprisoned god revives with the aid of the ritual, takes up his weapons, enters into an encounter with the hostile forces of chaos, from which he emerges victorious. Finally the sacred marriage revives all the life-giving forces in nature: The king enacts a rite of fertility with the Terra Genitrix after which there is communal feasting and dancing. Society and nature are revived together; in the fertility rite of the totem religions, the divine animal lives again.

In reading the sociologist to whom he is most indebted for the emphasis on order and harmony in the social system, Parsons found not only Durkheim's deep fascination with the totem animal but also elaborate descriptions of such primitive rituals. From Durkheim's book *The Elementary Forms of Religious Life,* Parsons learned of the importance of Australian ritual instruments, "the eminently sacred things"; "there are none which surpass them in religious dignity."[26] These instruments are the churinga, the nurtunja, and the waninga. The first, the churinga, is a kind of bull roarer, to use the English phrase, which is used in rites of fertility and reproduction. The nurtunja and the waninga are long, vertical supports, "either a single lance or several lances unite into a bundle, or a simple pole."[27] As is indicated by their sometime constitution out of lances, these latter are associated with battle, with the mythic battles of the gods and ancestors of the past against gods of chaos and disorder, but also with current battles against hostile tribes in which these instruments serve as rallying points against an enemy. They also, like the churinga, possess a somewhat sexual character when they stand at the central point of tribal ceremonies. Says Durkheim:

Fixed in the earth, or carried by an official, they mark the central point of the ceremony: it is about them that the dances take place and the rites are performed. In the course of the ceremony the novice is led to the foot of a nurtunja erected for the occasion. Someone says to him, "There is the nurtunja of your father; many young men have already been made by it." After that the initiate must kiss the nurtunja. By this kiss, he entered into union with the religious principle which resides there; it is a veritable communion which should give the young man the force required to support the terrible operation of sub-incision.[28]

In their use in rites of battle against forces of chaos, in the phallic rites of sacred marriage, or in celebrative dances, all the instruments represent the communal identity of the tribe united in the eternal organicity of the animal species. The associated symbol of tribal unity is the sacred place or sanctuary in which these instruments are stored when not in use – the ertnatalunga. As the collective treasury of sacred symbols, the ertnatalunga, the earthen house in which they dwell, represents even more profoundly than the individual instruments the tribal harmony with the cosmos. Durkheim himself presents an analogy between the ertnatalunga and the Ark of the Covenant:

And the churinga are not left at the free disposition of everybody: the ertnatalunga where they are kept is placed under the control of the chief of the group. It is true that each individual has specific rights to some of them; yet though he is their proprietor in a sense, he cannot make use of them except with the consent and under the direction of the chief. It is a collective treasury; it is the sacred ark of the clan.[29]

I believe that in the Parsonsian system's oscillation of meaning from the Protestant L-I-G-A to the world of the tribal cosmos, the A-G-I-L box represents the communal symbol of the pagan tribes, the ertnatalunga, the source from which spring the ritual dances of archaic man. The iron cage of the A-G-I-L box, which holds modern man in ascetically taut bonds, is simultaneously the storehouse of the more labile energies of the archaic ritual dance. Indeed, left in the order in which Parsons actually presented the letters that form the box – A-G-I-L – we have a word that almost forms the adjective "agile," the character of the dancer, the warrior, or the lover, the ritual actors of the ceremonies of the tribe. Insofar as Parsons eventually came to suggest that it was an erotic attraction to the great Oedipal mother that provides the energy that impels the social system, the actors within it do in fact become lovers instead of workers, lovers indeed of an omnipotent woman, a divine woman. The Parsonsian box may be not merely the source but also the receptacle of the passion of the ritual dancer, whose rite signifies fertility and culminates in copulation with the womb of the Terra Genitrix. The Skinner box, too, responds with the natural fruits of the fertility rite after the rat has shaken the bar, or symbolically, copulated into the womb of the earth mother.

Thus on the A-G-I-L side of the Parsonsian box we perceive the ritualized world of tribal man, a perpetual dance that celebrates the emergence and victory of life, order, harmony, and being in an enchanted world whose archetypal regularities confer the status of divinity upon them. Within Parsons's system it is this totemic ritualized communal world that is juxtaposed to the ascetic individualistic world of modern industrial capitalism.

Yet Parsons also seems to condemn existence in the ritualized world of the Creation myth as well. Man is a prisoner in this world as well, for, while there exists no ascetic dualism in the creation myth, there exists the tension between ritual and history, between earthly existence conceived as divine and thus eternally static as against finite existence conceived as a realm of history and change, the emblem of finitude. If the ascetic myth divinizes a part of man separate from his body and the finite world, the creation myth divinizes that body and all the world that it inhabits and, as divine, requires it to be eternally unchanged. However, Parsons's Judaeo-Christian heritage also condemns the acts of the ritual dance as idolatrous in that its recovery of the world and the flesh does not proceed to a recognition of its finitude and its residence in history. In Parsons's Puritan heritage the Redemption gave salvific life to history but did not deny history. The Puritan's path was never circular, but was a pilgrimage through an eminently historical route. Ritualism, however, divinizes a particular form of communal identity against all others. Such a way of life is not only fruitless, but it is pridefully evil in its divinization of a finite condition. Thus Parsons steps away from the pagan dance as well.

Conclusion

We return now to the question posed at the beginning of the discussion; having suggested that the images of the machine and the animal reflect two entirely different paradigms of life in society, we may question what Parsons creates when he puts the images together to create the metallic animal. First we may ask how he does this, to which it may be answered that while the worlds of the universal other and the tribal brother are radically antithetical to each other, Parsons's texts from *The Structure of Social Action* to the pattern variables of *The Social System* actually serve to set this thesis and antithesis oscillating in the reader's mind in a rapid alternation of meaning that befalls a man when he is confused. Neither one deep structure nor the other of the contradictory alternatives emerges with clear-cut emphasis and yet both are suggested. The oscillation suggests a synthesis, yet if one arrests such a verbal wavering, one discovers the alternatives to be fundamentally opposed to one another. It may be suggested, however, that Parsons's fusion of the opposites is representative of the existence of modern men who constantly define and redefine in their lives these radically divergent ways to compensate for the inadequacies of either definition; that at one moment for example a modern bureaucracy is viewed as a jungle of greedy, competitive, exploiting individualists, while at another it becomes a tribal unity whose members feel a profound bond of belongingness. By rapidly oscillating between these two perspectives man is allowed to deny the conflicts and strains of each as an autonomous mode of life; the ascetic individualist indulges his nostalgia for embodied communalism, whereas the communalist escapes the ritual sameness of life by assuming the ascetic identity. Such existence is admittedly schizoid, but by such means modern men may endure.

In the final analysis, however, the contradiction remains. The sense of the wholeness of the social system conveyed in the Parsonian texts is a mere conjuring, an illusory product of tremendous will and velocity in its rapid alternation of images, but still a man-made work that creates something purporting to be what it is not – in short, an idol. It is, however, the very project of assuming the truth of either of these myths from which Parsons finally withdraws as an evil commitment. The dualistic assumption that a part of man, his soul, is thoroughly divine is in fact very similar to the assumption that human life as ritualized into archetypal forms is also divine. Both hold a presumptuous denial of human finitude. By divinizing works of man both myths have an idolatrous tendency. In the end Parsons embraces neither myth, even while uttering both with profound hesitation, not in prayer, but in a confession of the dynamics of modern evil.

NOTES

1 Omar Moore and Alan R. Anderson, "Some Puzzling Aspects of Social Interaction," *Review of Metaphysics* (1963):471.

2 Peter Gay, *Style in History* (New York: Basic Books, 1974); Stanley Edgar
   Hyman, *The Tangled Bank: Darwin, Marx, Frazer and Freud as Imaginative
   Writers* (New York: Atheneum, 1962); Richard Harvey Brown, *A Poetic for
   Sociology: Toward a Logic of Discovery for the Human Sciences* (Cambridge:
   Cambridge University Press, 1977).
3 Alvin Gouldner, *The Coming Crisis of Western Sociology* (New York: Avon
   Books, 1970), p. 200.
4 Ibid., p. 202.
5 Ibid., p. 210.
6 Talcott Parsons, "Building Social Systems Theory," *Daedulus* 98 (1970):826-75.
7 Parsons, *The Structure of Social Action* (Glencoe, Ill.: The Free Press, 1968),
   p. 30.
8 Ibid., p. 31.
9 Gouldner, *The Coming Crisis,* p. 210.
10 Henry Adams, *The Education of Henry Adams* (New York: Book Club of
   America, 1928), p. 379.
11 Ibid., p. 381.
12 Ibid., p. 383.
13 Ibid., p. 386.
14 Ibid., p. 387.
15 Ibid., p. 389.
16 Ibid., p. 390.
17 John Milton, "Paradise Lost," *The Complete Poetical Works of John Milton,*
   ed. Douglas Bush (Boston: Houghton Mifflin, 1965), pp. 228-9.
18 William Ames, *The Marrow of Sacred Divinity* (London), pp. 141-2.
19 William Bradshaw, *The Use of Things Indifferent* (1601), p. 23.
20 Ibid., p. 142.
21 *Cratylus,* 400c.
22 Talcott Parsons, *The Social System* (Glencoe, Ill.: The Free Press, 1951), p. 494.
23 Parsons, *Social Action,* p. 45.
24 Emile Durkheim, *The Elementary Forms of Religious Life* (New York: The
   Free Press, 1965), p. 141.
25 Mircea Eliade, *The Myth of the Eternal Return* (New York: Pantheon, 1954);
   and Paul Ricoeur, *The Symbolism of Evil* (Boston: Beacon Press, 1967).
26 Durkheim, *Religious Life,* p. 145.
27 Ibid., p. 146.
28 Ibid., p. 143.
29 Ibid.

7
Dignity versus survival?
Reflections on the moral philosophy
of social order

MANFRED STANLEY

Editors' introduction

Today we appear to be faced with apocalyptic potentials such as those implicit in Malthusian food scarcities, n^{th} country nuclear dilemmas, and "ecocide" brought about by global environmental pollution. In the face of these dangers, many thinkers have advocated (or warned against) a cybernetic social order. In this imagery the social machine, rather than being an instrument to serve humane values, becomes an end in itself. More importantly, under the regnancy of technicism - the ideology of the cybernetic order - the very vocabulary by which social purposes could be discussed is either absorbed by the state or reduced to the sphere of personal opinion. Objectivity and reason come to be defined in terms of efficiency for systems maintenance, whereas feelings and values are relegated to the private realm. In such a circumstance the ideas of citizenship and polity atrophy, and it becomes impossible to express values institutionally or, indeed, to act socially as a moral agent.

This situation (whether already here or only possible), appears to confront us with a cruel choice: that between dignity and survival. For if survival requires a totalizing application of instrumental reason to all public areas of life, the human status of the person, as a socially valued end in himself, is diminished or made obsolete.

Those who wish to defend dignity against technicism, however, lack an adequate conceptual vocabulary through which to articulate their cause. Of central importance, then, is an analysis of the conceptual and preconceptual foundations of dignity. Manfred Stanley's essay offers such an analysis and, in so doing, it also suggests ways in which humanistic values may be defended intellectually and made to inform political discourse and action.

Introduction

Our planet is clearly being pushed toward a technological unification that
cannot be integrated by a market-oriented individualism. The emerging
technological power over nature is so immense as to induce in many people the awe once associated with the assumed primeval powers of magic
itself. Further, many social problems can no longer be contained within
the parochial boundaries of nations. For these and other reasons, agnosti-
cism concerning public values and privatism concerning morals are coming to be considered by many thinkers as sociologically dangerous to the
species survival of human beings.[1]

Yet unlike some earlier historical periods of transition to new moral
constitutions, modern thinkers (not to mention the general educated
populace) seem not to comprise a public addressing each other about the
general moral implications of shared and new ideas. Rather they tend now
to be experts – at home in small domains of specialized information and
techniques – and laymen in all else. The increasing intellectual impene-
trability of modern science and much of modern philosophy to vast numbers of people underscores the sociological importance of rhetoric for the
moral mobilization of mass populations.

A vital element of rhetoric is metaphor. Old and new elites are struggling not just for power, but also for legitimacy to name the nature of
modern problems and the means to solve them. The designation of the
world as a composite of definable problems amenable to solutions by techniques of various sorts is itself a venture into the rhetoric of social order.

A fundamental intellectual problem posed by pessimistic critics of
modern civilization is the manner in which social order is to be legitimated
in our conflictful era. "Order" is meant here in the most inclusive sense:
the evolution of a society's symbolic representations of the links between
nature, society, and self. Where there is not adequate and shared symbolization of order in this sense, people are bereft of a vocabulary with
which to articulate a legitimate account of what and how they wish to
preserve, to control, to solve, and to change. The vocabulary of community
becomes degraded into propaganda; the social (as against chronological)
meanings of time itself become problematical; and there is confusion
regarding by whom and on what bases it is decided how new tools are to
be assimilated into the life of society. In this context the most significant
form of cultural pessimism is that based on the expectation that the logic
of utility for mere physical survival will provide the basis for new symbolic
structures of order in place of earlier but failing paradigms.

The accumulation of social problems to the point of a potential crisis of species survival is generating a rhetorical conflict that will affect all existing ideologies and induce acute ambivalence in all moral reflections. That conflict is the contest between two justifications for social order. One is the principle of human dignity, the other that of human survival. The first is embodied (for modern Western societies) in the vocabulary of abstract humanism and in the civil practices of liberal democratic societies. The principle of survival, on the other hand, is what primarily legitimates a new moral vocabulary (and several associated social practices), stressing the symbolic reconstitution of the world as a problem-solving system. Such a new moral totalization must ultimately stabilize around a technological metaphor. The reconstitution of a world metaphor is a supremely religious, as well as social, phenomenon, affecting and affected by events in all secular social domains.

This essay examines the conflict between the rhetoric of survival and the rhetoric of dignity as a conflict between two ways of justifying social order. It is not that survival and dignity are irreconcilable. They must be reconciled if we are to survive both as a biological species and as something more than that. The intent of this essay is to address critically the proponents of three intellectual positions:

1 those who recognize no potential conflict between survival and dignity
2 those who recognize the conflict merely by recourse to the rhetoric of abstract humanism, on the apparent assumption that the meaning of human dignity is sufficiently self-evident that most people will act effectively in its name when challenged by social phenomena that portend human indignity
3 those who recognize the conflict on so pessimistic a level as to conclude that, in the name of dignity, all steps toward reconstituting the world as a problem-solving system must be opposed

The moral ends of survival and dignity can indeed conflict, but not necessarily so. If they are not to conflict, certain steps must be taken. One of these is the conceptual clarification of what the ends of survival and dignity imply for models of social order. Because the connections between survival and social order have been far more extensively explored in the general literature than have the connections between dignity and social order, this essay will stress the latter. Indeed, our primary purpose is to salvage the concept of human dignity from the dangerously abstract humanistic rhetoric to which it has been entrusted.

To stimulate an appreciation of the issues that control the standards for adequate speech about dignity, we begin in Section I with some pessimistic and optimistic interpretations of a social order based primarily upon survival: the cybernetic vision of society as a problem-solving system. Then, our main task, the conceptual clarification of the term "dignity," is taken up. Among other things, we criticize in Section II the motivational and instrumental notions of dignity that are implicit in technicist thinking. Then, in Sections III and IV we outline the requirements for an acceptable minimal definition of dignity. Finally, in Section V, a set of standards for political and social action implied by our perspective is briefly spelled out, whose implementation may help to create a social order that can reconcile human survival and human dignity.

I

Cybernetic order: Toward a vision of survival

The effective symbolic reorganization of the world according to a technological metaphor is the final stage of a process that can be called technicism.[2] There is a difference between the meaning of technique in the universal sense of instrumentality and technique in the context of a technicist culture. A simple instrumental orientation pictures human agents utilizing techniques to manipulate some aspects of the world in the service of humanly defined intentions that are not themselves techniques (love, domination, salvation, beauty, etc.). "Technicism" is a term that represents a world symbolization in which the notion of purposeful agents has been displaced by a world picture of self-regulating, ultimately biophysical processes that evolve as natural systems whose ends are the effective adaptation and expansion of the human species in physical nature. According to this view, the older vocabulary of consciousness, purpose, and volition is destined for obsolescence along with other premodern vocabularies like those of magic, supplicatory religion, and witchcraft.

In pessimistic terms, critics of technicism argue that modern societies are converging toward a social order dominated wholly by techniques. What this means is that modern societies are becoming ensembles of social organizations that persist only because most persons are coming to experience their interests, energy, and hopes as irrevocably tied to their functionary status in the service of some physical or social technique. The pessimistic assumption is that the asserted goals of techniques are themselves adaptive techniques of rhetoric; that is, talk about "goals" is seen as an instrument of persuasion. All that finally counts is the self-perpetuation of bureaucracies, methods, and functionaries whose original stated purpose was solving particular problems or providing specified services. In this pessimistic diagnosis, technicism is considered to be an ideology in which society is viewed as a structure of means: an assemblage of activities whose outcomes are not really controlled by human agents able to institute authoritative purposes in whose name physical and social techniques are definable as means. Techniques, rather, become the outcome of natural selection processes, with species enhancement their ultimate (metaphorical) purpose.[3]

The most subtle form of pessimism about technology is based on the thesis that full technicism is not just a secular condition. "Nothing belongs any longer to the realm of the gods or the supernatural," writes Jacques Ellul. "The individual who lives in the technical milieu knows very well that there is nothing spiritual anywhere. But man cannot live without the sacred. He therefore transfers his sense of the sacred to the very thing that has destroyed its former object; to technique itself."[4] Implied here is a view of technicism as nothing less than a form of eschatology, but it is not the eschatology of *Homo faber*. In the technicist eschaton, the ends of technology are no longer the nontechnological purposes of separately identifiable human agents. Techniques cease to be mere tools in the hands of human artificers of a uniquely human destiny. Rather, they are clues to a destiny (*eschatos*) in which men will endlessly produce and consume products in a setting of engineered security free of the conflict-ridden politics of cross-purposes.

Cybernetic technicism is an eschatology of a world beyond politics. In the place of politics and its dangerous illusions is a stable order based on the calibration of human activities in terms of natural self-regulative processes. This is not a trivial vision, nor has it been articulated simply by pessimistic detractors. It has its optimistic partisans who see in it an aesthetic grandeur of Platonic proportions. The original Platonic vision of society was organized around the assumption that nature was divided into that which was real and that which was mere appearance. The real was hierarchically arranged according to ascending levels of purity of form, or Good. Apprehension of these levels was not simply an act of intellectual cognition but an experience of inner illumination as well. The Platonic Republic was stratified according to people's diverse capacities for relating to these truths, and justice was defined as the degree to which persons were functionally ordered and treated according to these capacities. It was a society designed for stability, and because its focus was timeless truth, the vision was static.

The modern mind does not believe in Platonic truths anymore. But it still generates Platonic visions of social order. The stable point of moral reference for the most influential of these is not Plato's hierarchy of forms, but rather the objective requirements of a society organized for the un-limited production and consumption of goods and services. In this sense, the great tradition of Saint-Simonist technocratic sociology and its off-shoots can be loosely thought of as a modern version of societal Platonism. According to this perspective, sociotechnical logic is itself the criterion of stability according to which society should be organized. Production is the moral reference point. Without production as the ultimate goal, men are condemned to scarcity and moral chaos, but if enough can be produced, eventually all reasonable wants can be satisfied and conflict transcended by the self-evident virtues of cooperation. It is a moral vision because technology is here viewed as the domination of an indifferent nature that can only be molded to human desires by collective social discipline and mass moral enlightenment about the meaning of real, as against only subjectively apparent, interests.

As in the Platonic Republic, people are defined in terms of their capa-cities to relate to a stable point of moral reference. The modern schools are regarded, like the Platonic dormitories, as institutions that exist to reorient persons from their parochial loyalties and provincial illusions to the societal functions it is deemed necessary for them to perform. (This, in essence, is what the concept of technologically rational manpower allocation is about.) Like the original, the technicist Republic has its elite; at its apex sits, as philosopher king, the cybernetic systems engineer.

This vision, inherent in the work of Saint-Simon, was elaborated by August Comte, the man who coined the term "sociology." Although Comte considered himself a fully secular theorist of development, he believed that Positivism (as a mode of consciousness as well as a methodology capable of harnessing natural laws) was the final stage of history. For Comte, as for Saint-Simon, salvation for ungrounded individualism was a function in a productive sociotechnic engine that benefited everyone. There was nothing indirect about the religious significance of all this for Comte. The sociologists were originally meant to be the new priests of his Church of Humanity.[5]

This technicist vision has received powerful impetus from the con-temporary promise of automation and electronics. As these technologies take the place of human labor, they open the way for more free time and hence subjective freedom on the part of large masses of people. In Zbig-niew Brzezinski's notion of the technetronic order, a split-level society is envisioned: a knowledge-possessing technocratic elite working full time to maintain the system and a mass population freed from labor functions by technetronics for the leisured pursuit of all gratifications consistent with societal stability.[6] Like the Platonic elite, the modern elite is in principle open to penetration by those with the requisite aspirations and skills; the modern version of the myth of the metals is Brzezinski's meritocratic democracy.

In his own picture of such a society, Donald Michael reveals the mystic element of this modern Platonic elitehood. Discussing the man-machine relationship experienced by his "cyberneticians," he says that they

> will be a small, almost separate, society of people in rapport with the advanced computers. These cyberneticians will have established a relationship with their machines that cannot be shared with the average man any more than the average man today can understand the problems of molecular biology, nuclear physics, or neuro-psychiatry. Indeed, many scholars will not have the capacity to share their knowledge or feeling about this new man-machine relationship. Those with the talent for the work will probably have to develop it from childhood and will be trained as intensively as the classical ballerina.[7]

For many thinkers, especially those with technocratic inclinations, the cybernetic model seems to provide a totalistic vision of order that effectively balances personal usefulness and freedom with collective organization for survival. It also seems eminently practical in the sense that it promises to be the most empirically likely surprise-free projection of present developmental trends. The cybernetic model appears to assure, without recourse to violent revolution, the millenium of stable public organization for productivity combined with some valued privatistic freedoms. However, it does all this at a price.

One element of that price is the apparent Platonic permanence of the gap between a powerful elite and a powerless mass. The cybernetic conception of freedom seems to promise personal control over one's private life but at the expense of conforming to the sociostatic norms of the systems engineers in public activities.[8]

Furthermore, the functionary as a generalized social type is not compatible with the classical notion of the citizen. The essence of the functionary is that he is no longer responsible as a whole person for his actions in relation to the polity of which he is a member. The role of functionary thus implies a quite different conception of political obligation than does that of citizen.

Applied to whole societies, the cybernetic vision is today still more imagery than theory, more rhetoric than substance. But, like all great visions of order, it contains elements of prophecy. Some thinkers force the cybernetic imagery into the procrustean bed of current sentiments. Thus, like organism and mechanism in earlier times, cybernetics is interpreted as ideologically compatible with human voluntarism in those societies in which both efficiency and freedom are important values.[9] However, imagery often carries the seeds of new sentiments. Some thinkers would argue that the cybernetic vision implies a humanity with no unique place in nature, a society without personal deeds, a population without citizens, and a civilization in pursuit of no destiny.

There are, too, the seeds of an aesthetic in cybernetics, an aesthetic that Arthur Koestler has captured so well that his words are worth quoting at length:

Close your eyes. Imagine Europe up to the Urals as an empty space on the map. There are only fields of energy: hydro-power, magnetic ores, coal-seams under the earth, oil-wells, forests, vineyards, fertile and barren lands. Connect these sources of energy with blue, red, yellow lines and you get the distributive network. Blue: the joint electric power-grid stretching from the Norwegian fjords to the Dnieper Dam; red: the controlled traffic-stream of raw materials; yellow: the regulated exchange of manufactured goods. Draw circles of varying radius around the points of intersection and you get the centres of industrial agglomeration; work out the human labor required to feed the net at any point and you get the adequate density of population for any district, province and nation; divide this figure by the quantity of horsepower it produces and you get the standard of living allotted to it. Wipe out those ridiculous winding boundaries, the Chinese walls which cut across our fields of energy, scrap or transfer industries which were heedlessly built in the wrong places, liquidate the surplus population in areas where they are not required, shift the population of certain districts, if necessary of entire nations, to the spaces where they are wanted and to the type of production for which they are . . . best fitted; wipe out any disturbing lines of force which might superimpose themselves on your net; that is, the influence of the churches, or overseas capital, of any philosophy, religion, ethical, or aesthetical system of the past.[10]

Perhaps not surprisingly, these words are put into the mouth of a Fascist preaching order.

It is important, however, that the pessimistic interpretation of the cybernetic rhetoric of order not serve as the basis for a new form of Luddism. After all, the market paradigm is in some trouble, and there is a valid search going on for a new model of social order. We do live in the context of a fundamental crisis of legitimacy and authority. That is, the contradictions and inefficiencies of market rhetoric are increasingly recognized, and yet no new symbolic order has emerged to replace it. The mystique of revolution is no substitute. Hobbesian state-of-nature struggles for power, gnostic countercultural rejections of the whole empirical world, and solipsistic exhortations to "do your own thing" characterize the social (and symbolic) landscape. Meanwhile we move inexorably toward problems of species-survival such as population explosions, ecological catastrophes, and superweaponry, that all require decisions enforceable on massive collective levels. Short of totalitarianism, these decisions cannot be taken in the absence of a legitimate social order adequate to these challenges. To gain the loyalty and acquiescence (as against the cynical resignation) of modern populations, that order must not contradict the humanistic aspiration for personal dignity, participation, and self-development that is the sole unquestioned legacy of Western civilization. The cybernetic metaphor has potentialities that are open to optimistic as well as pessimistic prognostications.

Even a brief listing of the optimistic claims made for cybernetics by its proponents suggests its importance as a new rhetoric of order. First, the cybernetic model subsumes the advantages and traditions of the two master (and competing) metaphors of Western civilization: mechanism and organism. Second, the cybernetic notion is connected with a major intellectual movement, general systems theory, that constitutes a new intellectual generalism capable of organizing and interrelating the various contemporary departments of the intellectual division of labor. For those who think in these terms, of course, cybernetics is no metaphor; it is a theory of reality. Third, the cybernetic model appears capable of subsuming (rather than displacing) the master legitimating paradigm of liberal societies, the market principle. Fourth, the cybernetic model is the intellectual foundation of a new humanism that resolves some of the tensions between current definitions of public and private interests. Finally, the cybernetic paradigm is the intellectual rationale for an aspiring social-engineering elite (i.e., policy scientists), who seek to revive on a nonideological basis the nineteenth-century goal of a problem-solving social science.

It is not difficult to demonstrate that many of these claims, resting as they do on philosophically questionable bases, invite new forms of reification (e.g., society as a servomechanism) and reductionism (e.g., the multiplicity of social meanings all labeled as information). Whatever the criticisms, the cybernetic metaphor cannot simply be dismissed. It is too socially useful for that. An adequate analysis of cybernetics as theory, metaphor, and social control heuristic is a project that will take many years and the best efforts of dedicated minds. One requirement of such a project, for those who worry about technicism as a phenomenology of indignity, is a reexamination of the conceptual status of human dignity itself. Such a reexamination, to be of any practical significance, must be on a level commensurate with the details of the great debate on social order we have just sketched. It is time, now, to address some foundations of this task.

II

Introduction

Are there any effective limits to what can be done to people in the name of their collective good? If there are not, then there are no barriers to the technological manipulation of persons, so long as this is carried out in the name of social welfare. If there be such limits, however, whence comes their power? And can one be sure that defending such limits is not to act against the public interest in the name of some romantic defense of parochial privilege?

To pose such questions is already to assert that there is more than one way of being human. There would be no problem if one thought without question that the human was essentially a biological fact and that sociology had as its sole object the study of the formal complexities displayed by large population aggregates of highly intelligent organisms.

The most basic way of saying that being human is something more than membership in a socially organized population of intelligent organisms is to insist on the importance of the idea of a uniquely human dignity. If the dignity of the human means anything, it must refer to something so morally intrinsic to what one means by being human that its claims can be asserted against any momentary definition of social welfare, perhaps even species survival itself. Talk about dignity – or dignity talk as we shall call it – is speech about standards in light of which all models of social order can be judged. To deny the importance of dignity talk, then, is to say that there is no moral meaning to being human except social forms and that any social order can be evaluated only in terms of its own survival or the efficient execution of its own stated goals. Dignity talk presupposes that the human takes many forms, only one of which is the social. The social is something that we share with animals and insects. It is the collective form taken by biological creatures when we look upon them as organized populations. Humanity can manifest itself also in political, religious, artistic, and other forms, some of which we are driven to think of as more uniquely human, despite difficulties we experience in defining exactly what we mean by this. (We just know that chickens may have pecking orders, but not gods.) Humanity can manifest itself in highly organized forms, leaving little room for personal demonstrations of human agency, or the opposite. But in whatever forms we find humanity organized, systematic speech about social order always occurs in metaphors (organic, mechanical, theatrical, familial, etc.). Yet we sense that dignity talk is about something that lies beyond the bounds of metaphors.

If dignity talk, then, is speech about standards for evaluating the claims of social order, it is important to ask when and why such speech is or is not socially effective. Speech, after all, is more often than not socially ineffective. And its ineffectiveness is not necessarily rooted in the intellectual invalidity of one or another proposition. Validity is not necessarily power. Indeed, as we shall argue with respect to dignity talk, the very need to speak polemically in the form of propositions may itself reflect a crisis of faith in the reality of that which is the object of discourse. It is this crisis that we must examine if we are interested in the pessimism that is so prominent a feature in many Western reactions to the advent of the modern technologically organized social order. It follows then that the mere existence of dignity talk as such does not in itself constitute a barrier to indignity. Nor does the intellectual validity of dignity talk, however important this be, guarantee its social effectiveness.

If we are interested in dignity talk as a mode of action (i.e., holding society to account and setting limits to the technological manipulation of persons), we must attend to the relevant aspects of this task. There are two in particular that inform our treatment of dignity talk in this essay. One is the relation between the theoretical (intellectual) and the pretheoretical (experiential) dimensions of that which we speak. Another is the distinction between those features of dignity talk that are of purely intellectual interest and those that are of sociological significance. We wish to inquire into the degree to which modern culture (official categories of reality talk) and society (structure and organization of social practices) can be thought of as permitting the exercise of dignity talk as a contribution to effective moral action. Just as society can sentence people to death by physical extinction, it can sentence ideas to death by abstraction and irrelevance to social practice. Has this happened to the notion of dignity in any irrevocable way? How would we know? What kind of dignity talk is of greatest significance for judging a technicist social order and for helping to set limits to its legitimation?

To proceed effectively along these lines it is desirable to begin with a conceptual analysis of contemporary dignity talk. Only in this manner can one raise and pursue questions about the proper place of definitions, about

the relations between intellectual validity and social significance, about
the continuities between intellectual and experiential aspects of moral life,
and about the place of metaphysical problems in the worlds of social
practice.

The concept of human dignity. Dignity, according to the dictionaries,
means the quality of being worthy of merit, desert, honor, or respect. This
of course is not very helpful. We should then begin by asking what it is we
really want to know about the notion of dignity and its uses.

Dignity talk is not rooted in abstract intellectual curiosity about definitions. It is inspired by one or another experience of indignity. Like justice,
dignity is one of those terms that is not universally translatable, yet has a
universal resonance. There does not seem to be any society in which people
are normally and collectively treated with the casual disdain reserved for
the truly profane and inconsequential things of this world. Perhaps, then,
an approach to the problem by way of a direct search for plausible definitions is not the best way to begin. For one thing, the traditional definition
of dignity as worthy of respect has virtually no prescriptive implications
except perhaps the general precept that one should respect that which
is worthy. Further, a definition of such generality does not indicate what
precisely is the object of respect. More specifically, when we speak of
human dignity, it is not clear what the referent of human really is. Is it
the body? the mind? the ego? the soul? the personality? some special
capacity? some collective social formation? More important still, the general definition of dignity does not tell us why something is worthy of
respect. It tells us nothing. It does not even tell us how to find out what
it is about the object that is worthy of respect. In other words, there is no
total context in terms of which a claim that something is an object worthy
of respect becomes intelligible to a person who challenges the claim with
the question "why?"

Let us then examine three different ways in which the question of dignity
can be addressed: the phenomenological, the constitutive, and the definitional approaches. This classification should be regarded as a simple
heuristic device with which to organize a number of thoughts about a
complex topic.

By "phenomenological" I mean those approaches that begin by defining
events and acts that are recognizable as indignities and then proceed to
analyze the properties of such experiences to isolate deeper layered implications of what is meant by dignity.[11]

Such an exercise leads naturally into the second, the "constitutive" (or
"conceptual") approach. Here the intention is to identify presuppositions

and assumptions that make dignity talk intelligible. Such efforts are conceptual since it is not necessary, in such an approach, to impute ontological status to these assumptions. The intelligibility of dignity talk need presuppose only the acceptance (for whatever reason) of the constitutive rules from which the propositions of dignity talk can be logically derived. Because of its importance for our subsequent discussion, this approach requires some further attention here.

The concept of constitutive rules was developed by John Searle: "Regulative rules regulate a pre-existing activity, an activity whose existence is logically independent of the rules. Constitutive rules constitute (and also regulate) an activity the existence of which is logically dependent on the rules."[12] In Searle's usage, the notion of constitutive rule is logical. His most effective examples are drawn from games, and his subject matter is the philosophy of language. Thus his concern is with the logical presuppositions of certain kinds of speech, not the sociological, cultural or historical aspects of speech. Something like this method also appears in H. L. A. Hart's examination of the concept of natural rights.[13] Hart argues that talk about rights is intelligible only if there is acceptance of the one logically necessary presupposition to all such talk: the equal right of all men to be free. Charles Taylor has extended this line of reasoning to methodological questions in political science in a way more relevant to our own concerns. In Taylor's view these constitutive presuppositions are embodied in both a society's language and social practices, a distinction he regards as rather artificial. Thus people need not be intellectually aware of the constitutive assumptions of their society. They accept them every time they act out socially instituted practices.

The situation we have here is one in which the vocabulary of a given social dimension is grounded in the shape of social practice in this dimension; that is, the vocabulary wouldn't make sense, couldn't be applied sensibly, where this range of practices didn't prevail. And yet this range of practices couldn't exist without the prevalence of this or some related vocabulary. There is no simple one-way dependence here. We can speak of mutual dependence if we like, but really what this points up is the artificiality of the distinction between social reality and the language of description of that social reality. The language is constitutive of the reality, is essential to its being the kind of reality it is. To separate the two and distinguish them . . . is forever to miss the point.[14]

Put in this way, this is a very strong claim indeed and, perhaps, unacceptable on its face. But if one introduces a caveat, then the central importance of Taylor's point is preserved while the form of the claim is made more subtle. That caveat is that in many societies there is more than one language applied to social practices (the most immediately obvious example of this being the distinction between the language of participants and the language of scientific observers of a social practice). The full force of Taylor's argument becomes evident in his examples (the concepts of "voting" and "bargaining"). Later in the same essay, analyzing the concept of "legitimacy," Taylor calls these constitutive rules "intersubjective meanings." And he sharply distinguishes these from "subjective meanings" in the sense that the psychologist means by the term "attitude." Intersubjective meanings, for Taylor, are not the sum of individual subjective attitudes. Rather they are the assumptions implicit in the structures of social practice. In this sense, they are truly intersubjective, not multisubjective. One perhaps should add that to describe constitutive rules in Taylor's sense as noncognitive – as presuppositions of practice – does not mean they cannot be given intellectual form.[15] Indeed Taylor does exactly this in his examples of voting and bargaining. It is rather to say that the primary social significance of such rules is not their cognitive status in the minds of individuals, but their latent status as presuppositions of practice. They take on intellectual form only when people consciously seek the deeper intelligibilities of their actions, which does not happen often.[16]

One further step is required to adapt these considerations to our purposes, before moving on to the third approach: the effort to actually define the meaning of dignity.

The examples drawn from Searle, Hart, and even Taylor primarily focus on the logical relationship between constitutive rules, speech, and social practices. If, however, one is interested in social, cultural, and historical dynamics, more than logic becomes involved. The ontological status of constitutive rules becomes an issue, along with the sociocultural determinants of public opinion, motive, belief, and faith. What to the logician may be constitutive rules become, for the sociologist interested in the well springs of action, popular assumptions presupposing the intelligibility of existence itself. This must be kept in mind as we turn now to the problem of definition.

In approaching the problem of definition, it is well to recall that strong cases can be made by those who deny the dignity of humanity or who consider the whole question meaningless.[17] But the stakes are too high for us to become discouraged. Dignity talk, however indirectly, deals with the limits that can be set on the technological manipulation of humanity. In other words, dignity is a code word for whatever is considered to be intrinsically inviolable or "sacred" about the human status.

Dignity talk is talk about the limits of permissible profanation of the human. Hence, if dignity talk is considered unintelligible to the modern intellect, then it must follow that there are no theoretical limits to the social legitimation of technicism. These are the stakes. Now to the problem.

Let us begin by eliminating from serious consideration two kinds of definition that do not, in my view, sufficiently reflect the direction of our concerns. This will enable us to move with better foundation to the requirements of a definition that does attend to these concerns. These two approaches may be called the "motivational" and the "instrumental." They are best assessed by way of illustration.

The motivational approach to dignity can be detected in the arguments of Ervin Laszlo. His most direct attempt to define dignity is this:

Human dignity, I suggest, resides in the sum of the satisfactions of the human being: in the sum of the matchings of innate norms with the corresponding environmental states. Thus human dignity signifies the being (biological need - environmental matchings) as well as the well-being (cultural requirements - environmental matchings) of the person. An existence in which intrinsic requirements are matched with extrinsic conditions possesses excellence and is worthy of esteem.[18]

To understand what Laszlo is doing here, one must know what he means by "being" and "well-being."

Both being and well-being can be viewed as states brought about by the matching of intrinsic norms or codes of the organism in the environment. These are normative organism-environment transactional states, representing specific input-output patterns . . . My thesis is that both the biological being and the cultural well-being of the individual represent normative organism-environment transactional states, in which the individual's needs and demands are matched by the appropriate environmental states and events.[19]

This transactional cybernetic view of dignity rests on the concept of need motivation: "The preservation of such transactional norms may well provide the basic motivation of behavior - cognitive as well as non-cognitive - and define the basic 'need' of the individual."[20] Laszlo denies that this is biologically minded behavioristic reductionism on the ground that his notion of need includes cultural as well as biological needs.

Our objection to this motivational approach is twofold: its particular kind of abstractness and its arbitrariness. All important definitions of dignity are abstract, but this cybernetic approach abstracts the uniquely human condition out of existence by subsuming it under general systems analysis. Despite all talk of culture, in the end the human is considered an organismic phenomenon, and the concept of cultural need becomes a residual category for needs talk that does not quite fit into an organismic view of man.

More important, there is an arbitrariness in Laszlo's use of the need concept. Most significant efforts in Western moral philosophy have sought to avoid the kind of relativism implied in the idea that dignity (or for that matter happiness, love, and other such resonant notions) can be reduced to manipulated need satisfactions, to the contentment born of some homeostatic equilibrium between the human condition and its environments. It is not that men do not have needs. It is rather that dignity has usually been imputed to some aspect of the human-as-such, some unique characteristic beyond the arbitrariness of need and the possibility of satisfaction: something that cannot be reduced to motives but rather informs all motives.

Another approach congenial to the modern mind is the instrumental definition. Abraham Edel has apparently taken this tack:

Dignity is now regarded as an ideal, like justice or well-being, and it is evaluated by the type of life it makes possible, the human purposes it helps achieve, and the human problems to whose solution it contributes. These purposes and problems constitute its psychological and social base; its function is the articulation of principles and the mobilization of multiple human energies and feelings, furnishing a direction for the achievement of purposes and the solution of problems both perennial and contemporary . . . As a dynamic ideal it is united in a powerful way with the ideals of well-being, justice, liberty, equality, and in the efforts to remove the major discriminations and exploitations that have beset mankind. If the appeal to human dignity can play a large part in such enterprises it earns its keep quite easily.[21]

The major difficulty with this view, in my judgment, is that of the instrumentalist approach to experience generally: the danger of trivialization through the reduction of ends to means. If dignity is really nothing but a construct that serves as a means for the mobilization of effort to attain particular ideals, then – no matter how noble these ideals may be – dignity is reduced to their handmaiden. Further, one's sense of human dignity becomes perhaps irrevocably tied to one's faith in the attainability of these ideals. Yet there are cases in history, both well known and unsung, when persons have reacted with great dignity precisely when in deepest despair about the attainability of any other ideals. There are times when dignity, far from being a means toward any other end, becomes the only end there is. Why? Because there is an unarticulated connection for many people between their assertion of or appeal to dignity, and their inchoate sense of truth concerning something about the human status itself. The instrumental approach seems not to allow for any crisis of dignity per se, apart from the particular ideals to which it may be instrumental. To see why this is so, we should perhaps reflect a moment on how the instrumentalist might respond to these objections.

The instrumentalist might reply that only his approach makes possible the avoidance of clashes between ultimate values. Suppose, for instance, liberty and equality are both considered sacred values. Is not an instrumentalist approach toward dignity helpful in distinguishing between such values, enabling us to stress one at one time, another at another time, depending upon what seems morally appropriate (i.e., conducive to our sense of dignity)? In this usage, dignity functions as a kind of indicator of our moral sense about the appropriate connections between our general moral traditions and the concrete situations in which we find ourselves. The trouble with this approach, again, is its triviality. When dignity talk serves merely as a kind of psychic moral thermometer, it becomes little more than a cry of pain or a slogan for battle.

This connection between psychological reductionism, instrumentalism, and trivialization is also illustrated in the discussion of dignity by the utilitarian philosopher Jan Narveson. Dignity, he writes, "is not something opposed to utility, but simply the sense that one's utilities are to count – which is just what utilitarianism is all about. That is, dignity is not separate from one's other desires, but simply is the sense, or desire that one's other desires are to be counted." In Narveson's view, dignity reduces either to the "equal claim of all persons' desires to be satisfied" or merely to one more desire among others, worthy of no special weight in itself. The psychologistic reductionism inherent in such instrumentalism is revealed in Narveson's interpretation of his own argument:

Indeed, it seems clear that our account of utility implies that a person's dignity, in the irreducible sense, should count for roughly as much as the person having it wants it to count for, relative to his other desires. That a person's dignity would be offended is *prima facie* a reason for not doing what would offend it; but which of his other desires is to count as outweighing his sense of dignity is up to him.[22]

What, in our view, is left entirely out of account here is the relation between theoretical and pretheoretical (i.e., taken-for-granted life world) levels of discourse. Put another way, the connection is ignored between people's moral responses and what they assume to be fundamentally true about the world and humankind's place in it. In the instrumentalist approach, dignity talk is a means and, hence, can be multifunctional. This precludes the possibility of a fundamental crisis of dignity itself; dignity talk cannot reflect upon its own possible obsolescence.

Yet the challenge of indignity inherent in technicism requires this possibility for a reflexive discourse about dignity. Technicism entails the
possible misuse of technological metaphors in the service of ontological
claims about what humankind and the world actually are. Ontological
arguments are truth claims. If dignity talk is to be a mode of action, it
must be prepared to engage in speech about what is true or not true about
the world, however partially it is given us to know such things. Truth talk
about the world can sometimes legitimate indignity, not by changing our
emotional sense of indignity, but by persuading us that our emotional
sense is irrational – out of tune with reality. This situation constitutes a
fateful civil war of conscience. Before it a purely instrumental approach
is helpless, since those who prize philosophical integrity often regard themselves, in such a war, as invited to sacrifice precisely their utilitarian
instincts in favor of the higher virtue of fidelity to truth. Such a conflict
is a tragedy and should be avoided whenever possible. A purely instrumental approach does not contribute to the goal of establishing a reflexive
dignity talk.

III

Some requirements for a definition of dignity
We should begin by acknowledging that dignity talk as such is a Western
phenomenon. Any definition whatever will be an observer definition,
heavily influenced by the categories of Western discourse. There is no hope
of scouring the languages of the world for terms that translate into dignity
on some minimum level of universal equivalence. So perhaps we should ask
why it is that one would even want to engage in dignity talk on any level
more universal than the avowedly culture-bound preoccupations of Western metaphysics.

The answer is best given by way of an analogous situation. Consider
the concept of religion. Many, if not most languages of the world do not
have terms that translate into "religion." It appears that the historical
emergence of religion as a specialized term is a response to a process of
institutional differentiation and specialization that is associated with increased cognitive self-consciousness. Institutional specialization generates
multiple mental worlds, multiple accounts of reality, multiple standards
of legitimation, and so on. A specialized term for religion emerges when it
begins to occur to people that religious categories are but some among a
number of possible modes of discourse about the world. Specialized re-

ligion talk, one could well say, emerges in an inverse relationship to the taken-for-grantedness of religious accounts of the world.

Yet, scholars and thinkers of all sorts have generally considered this insufficient reason for treating religion as a concept of less than universal relevance. Why? Because what we reflectively call religious categories arise out of types of questions and answers about experience that are of universal scope, in whatever form they may appear. We may say that these questions and answers revolve around a universal set of hermeneutic problems, the citation of two of which will immediately illustrate both the universality and the ultimately religious nature of such problems. These are the problems of origins (how did we come to be?) and theodicy (why is there suffering and evil?). Whatever the form of the queries or the answers, no known society would find these questions unintelligible. This is because they pose the problem of interpreting experiences that are of the essence of the human condition as such.

Can such an approach be validly applied to the concept of dignity too? What experiences of such primordial quality generate the universal hermeneutic ground for our specialized vocabulary of dignity talk? I believe that virtually all the answers that could be given to this question are ultimately subsumable under one concept: moral significance. Is there any record of a society in which the human status is regarded as essentially trivial? To be sure, there are some in which the data of human experience are regarded as illusory, and there is certainly no universal agreement on what the essentially human is, or in what sense it is significant. But it is, I think, safe to say that the destiny of the human is everywhere considered (and institutionally treated) as a serious, not a trivial or profane, question. There is controversy, of course, as to why this is so. Answers can range from parochial formulations (e.g., stories of how the gods created us) to universal observer interpretations (e.g., the social control functions of dignity myths). In an investigation such as ours, the requirements for a definition of dignity will necessarily fall closer to the latter than the former sort. However, there are differences among sociological observer definitions, even those broadly labeled functional. Some are more abstract, more crassly instrumental, more removed from the intuitive intelligibilities of universal experience than others. It is to avoid such pitfalls that we shall pursue in deeper detail three more specific requirements of effective dignity talk in relation to the significance of the human status as such.

Universality. Given the radical cultural variability in how the human status is defined, the first important requirement for effective dignity talk is a definition that is reasonably universal without being so abstract as to be useless for concrete purposes. Let us note but one of myriad examples of how cultural parochialism can contaminate the search for such universality. It may have been noticed by the reader that we have tried to refrain from referring to the human being. Instead, our vocabulary has stressed the notion of human status. The reason for this is a desire to avoid conflating such terms as "person," "ego," "self," "subject," and "agent" into a single concept, a conflation that is central to the modern Western phenomenology of the human. This conflation has facilitated a persistent tendency in the West to define the human both too atomistically and too holistically. The definition is too atomistic because all these notions became, in recent centuries, associated with the organically observable individual. Yet it was also too holistic because, once imprisoned within the individual, these varied concepts were fused into a single broad conception of the human-as-individual (atomistic egoism), and it became difficult to cite just what it was about the individual that was worthy of such dignity. This is one source of the cultic individualism (and social nominalism) of modern times.[23]

It is probably impossible, however, to achieve any universal definition of dignity that is not flawed to some extent by the cultural parochialism of the language (and its associated histories) in which the effort is being made. Therefore two related requirements of a good definition should be noted. Close attention need be paid to the distinction between a strong and a weak definition and to the problem of prescriptive content. These last two requirements merit further comment.

Strong versus weak definitions. A strong definition of dignity constitutes an almost automatic response to indignity. It provides an enclave of sanctity in a world of price, a prophetic staff in the court of power. A strong definition has almost automatic prescriptive significance; its roots are planted deep in the soil of institutions, its intelligibility is evident to intuition and intellect. Such a definition, however, is as little a product of intellectual fiat as of wishful thinking. Rather it is in itself an institution. It is produced not primarily by philosophers but by the organic processes of history and society. Such a definition of dignity is an aspect of fundamental order itself; extreme intellectualization of the issue is but a sign of faltering confidence.

We must content ourselves here with the search for a weak definition. A weak definition of dignity cannot be self-evident, fructified by the soil of daily custom. It is more in the nature of a barrier against dehumanization, erected by strenuous mental effort and designed specifically to address intellectual (and rhetorical) tendencies that appear to legitimate, condone, or disguise indignity. All this is not to say that a weak definition of dignity is therefore an instrumental definition, fashioned to function merely as humanist propaganda. Rather, a weak definition is weak because it is minimal: It is a necessary but not a sufficient condition for an efficacious response to indignity. A weak definition of dignity is the fruit of a search for the minimal, intellectually secure, foundations of dignity talk. Such minimal intellectual requirements are not pretheoretically self-evident. They are not safely rooted in the soil of custom. If they were, such a self-conscious search for purely intellectual foundations would not be necessary. If the contrast is unclear, consider the Greek notion of the human as part of a comprehensive logic of natural development or the Christian view of the human as sanctified by the image of God. Contrast these orientations (and the sense of human dignity that attended them) with the modern perspective in which the truly human world is scientifically regarded as a domain of mere symbols secreted by intelligent animals – a world of language but not of nature, a social world but one unratified by divine law, a historical world but one with no intelligible *telos*. In a world so devoid of pretheoretical faith in suprahuman supports, a conception of human dignity cannot be a ringing declaration of dogma. It can only be a statement of possibility: the possibility that the darkest indignities of one's time may yet prove to be irrational and that dignity may not be incompatible with reason. For a weak definition to play such an historical role, however, it must be fashioned with our third requirement in mind: some relevance to the problems of political action.

Prescriptive significance. The worlds in which "is" and "ought" were innocently fused have proven vulnerable to the acids of social complexity and critical intellect. Therefore, the requirement that a conception of dignity have some prescriptive significance does not mean one within which "ought" and "is" can dwell together without friction. What, then, does prescriptive significance imply in the modern context? It implies that the conception must not be so abstract that it can mean just anything in practice. To be sociologically relevant, a conception must be such as to allow for a reasonably operational standard for discriminating between practices that instantiate the conception and those that do not. With respect to our purposes in this study, three such politically strategic criteria especially are worth noting.

Human dignity should not merely be defined as whatever conduces to the survival of man as a species. This would be to confound human dignity with whatever is considered functionally requisite for species survival. I stress this because technicist reasoning and social practice are founded on species survival as the primary end. Our whole study is based on the recognition that there can be tension between survival and dignity as moral ends and is dedicated to finding ways of using technologies without becoming technicists. Therefore we need a perspective on human dignity that makes it possible to ascertain when dignity has been violated in the name of survival. To put it another way, we need to be able to distinguish between human man and posthuman (or technicist) man.

A second politically relevant criterion is that dignity must be conceptualized in a way that represents an adequate challenge to the prescriptive efficacy that technicist ideology and practice can achieve in the organization of public life. To take a single but crucial example, consider the rhetoric of authenticity and liberation as an antitechnicist strategy. If this counterculture rhetoric becomes the conceptual cornerstone of dignity talk, the road to a technicist resymbolization of man and society is virtually unencumbered. Liberation from many social norms in the name of a cult of authentic selfhood is quite compatible with a technicist social order. If one is willing to define one's moral destiny in privatistic terms, leaving the task of running the public order to systems engineers, then a nontotalitarian politics of trade off between private communities and state authority is conceivable. But if one's concern is with technicism as a threat to human dignity, the conceptualization of dignity must provide a basis for criticizing and redeeming social institutions beyond the antinomian criterion of simply getting them off one's back.

Rejecting a cult of the self is not the same thing as abandoning the notion that every self somehow partakes in the condition of being human. Therefore a conception of human dignity addressed to the challenge of technicism should encourage a philosophical perspective on social science theory itself that attends constantly to links between social structure, history, and the creative agency of all selves.

The conceptualization of human dignity should be usable for grounding in it a diagnosis and critique of technicist trends in all social institutions; revealing the ways in which persons can and do become defined as morally superfluous to the public order (the primordial indignity); helping to redesign zones of personal and collective agency to create conditions more appropriate to the requirements of human dignity.

Perhaps we are ready now to consider more directly what such a conceptual approach to dignity might entail.

IV

A definitional approach to dignity

It will be helpful to begin by distinguishing between some terms that are related in moral discourse and yet differ in ways that illuminate the special meaning of dignity that we wish to stress in this study. Two terms in particular come to mind that would be fruitful to distinguish from dignity: "honor" and "respect." For many purposes dignity, honorableness, and worthiness of respect are validly regarded as synonyms. How can they be usefully discriminated?

A distinction between honor and dignity was recently stressed by Berger, Berger, and Kellner. Honor is the reward of the efficacious performance of duties linked to status, whereas dignity "as against honor, always relates to the intrinsic humanity divested of all socially imposed rules or norms."[24] Honor is associated with a "hierarchical view of society . . . and . . . is a direct expression of status, a source of solidarity among social equals and a demarcation line against social inferiors."[25] Honor and dignity, therefore, are different in an important sense:

In a world of honor the individual *is* the social symbols emblazoned on his escutcheon . . . In a world of dignity, in the modern sense, the social symbolism governing the interaction of men is a disguise. The escutcheons *hide* the true self . . . In a world of honor, identity is firmly linked to the past through the reiterated performance of prototypical acts. In a world of dignity, history is the succession of mystifications from which the individual must free himself to attain "authenticity."[26]

The implication here is that dignity talk arises in a society in which the subjective self and the social order are no longer confidently intertwined. Dignity, per se, becomes an issue when the moral meaning of what it is to be essentially human is rendered ambiguous by social and cultural instabilities. Whether these instabilities are social (e.g., class wars, economic collapses, etc.) or cultural (e.g., conflicts between secular and sacred categories, radical pluralism of life-styles and values, etc.), they have in common the effect that people begin to suspect that their human interests may not be congruent with their social identities.

As regards the term respect, that which has dignity is, of course, in one sense by definition, worthy of respect. However not all forms of respect connote an identical meaning of dignity. Man can impute respect worthiness to himself in the same sense that he imputes it to any formidable species of animal. Yet the respect that he pays himself as king of the beasts

is not the same as the respect implied in the phrase human dignity. There
seems something special about the intrinsic worth that goes with the notion
of the human as something that is, though less than divine, yet more than
animal. Why is this so? We respect an animal in a rather metaphorical
sense, like we respect the power of a hurricane. Unless we ascribe some
sacred significance to an animal (in which case we do not really see it as an
animal), what we really mean by respecting it is that we acknowledge its
performance in the light of its limited potential. We respect a fleet-footed
horse, a majestic lion, or a graceful bird. The respect worthiness we impute to the human transcends this. The almost universally evident temptation to attribute divine qualities to extraordinary standards of human
performance implies an unwillingness to circumscribe the conception of
the human by purely secular (i.e., biological, physical, or other definitive)
limitations. There is, traditionally, a subjective sense of awe connected
with this very lack of definitive limitations to human potency. Human
voluntarism is awesome, in other words, because it seems to reflect powers
that overflow the finite properties of any specific human being defined as
a determinate object. This view was given probably its first philosophically
explicit formulation by Pico della Mirandola in 1487. Pico describes God
as having given man "a share in the particular endowment of every other
creature." That is, man is free of all lawful archetypes so he may trace
for himself the lineaments of his own nature according to his free will.
Thus, man is a creature "neither of heaven nor of earth, neither mortal
nor immortal."[27]

The dignity of the human status, then, resides in the extraordinary
human capacity for intentional creativity (and, of course, destruction).
Humankind participates in that potency capable of world creation and
destruction. Therein lies its mystery, its dignity, its awesomeness. This
power, if it be assumed to exist, transcends utilitarian definitions of personal interests. Respect for it rests not just in how it is used, nor even in
its recognition by any one individual person. Human dignity as respect
worthiness rests in the sheer factuality of human potency and in the
assumption that to be human is somehow to share in this power for agency,
regardless of one's personal desires or merit. To no other creature of
(profane) nature is imputed such potency for creative and destructive
agency. The eclipse of honor is a crisis of one or another society; the
possible eclipse of dignity would be an ontological crisis of the human
status itself. Without dignity, man would be man (as a biological object).
He would not be any longer human.

These remarks should help us to comprehend the nature of the pessimism that afflicts many modern intellectuals regarding their civilization's capacity to preserve human dignity. To make this connection one must not think of pessimism merely as a personality trait, as a pattern of temperament, nor even as socially oriented anxiety whose object is the fate of one or another society or institution. The appropriate orientation is best introduced by reflecting on a paradigm situation. The situation is that of a person who, despite appropriate motivation, reasonable education, and freedom from political tyranny, nonetheless comes to feel that what goes on in the world has no coherent relationship to his morally intended actions. (We must assume here a person whose intentions conform to the dominant values of his culture and who thus justifiably considers himself representative of the publicly professed traditions of his society.) If, for such a person, there is a sharp discontinuity between "self" and "world," between moral intentions, actions, and outcomes, then it is both the meaning of the world and of his own agency in it that are at stake. Pessimism, in this sense, is a crisis of confidence in the efficacy of human intentionality in relation to the world in which one resides (or, indeed, perhaps in the very knowability and coherence of one's surroundings as a world).

Such pessimism questions the moral intelligibility of experience as a whole and, in principle, is ultimately incompatible with all rational claims to human dignity. This, I submit, is so for the same reason presented in our earlier discussion of human versus nonhuman respect worthiness: dignity claims only make theoretical sense when the privileged ontological status of humankind is pretheoretically taken for granted. By reflecting a bit further on this connection between pessimism and the notion of ontological privilege, we may clarify further our sense of what human dignity is and then be ready to proceed to more explicit definitional considerations.

Despite its vagueness, the notion of privileged ontological status is important for comprehending any discussion of human action within an ethical frame of discourse. What the term connotes is the assumed potency (not dominance) of human agency as a creative phenomenon in nature. "Will" (and its variations), as a technical philosophical concept is, of course, a product of Western metaphysical discourse.[28] However there is a loose, minimal sense in which the concept has a more universal significance. It is unusual to find a society in which the purposiveness of a human agent, including the power both to help sustain harmonies and to engender chaos, is not accorded a special respect. This respect is sometimes

ascribed exclusively to Western technological *hubris*. But Western civilization is marked by extremes in this regard. Society, in a collective sense, is
often regarded by Westerners as capable of achieving anything through
the deliberate application of technology. On the other hand, Western
culture also produces numerous theories about how helpless the self is in
affecting the world (e.g., theories of inverse relationships between functional rationality and substantive rationality, theories of alienation, of
inauthenticity, etc.). In primitive societies with myth-oriented cultures,
one could almost say the reverse was true. In such societies there was far
less emphasis on the omnipotence of collective technologies, but a much
greater sense of the self as agent. Indeed, this power was considered of
cosmic and magical proportions. Hence, in such societies, witchcraft was
always an object of the most rigorous social control. Westerners sometimes
forget that witchcraft beliefs reflect a profound confidence in the powers
of individual human agency over natural forces. It is this respect for the
power of human agency that is signified here by the phrase "privileged
ontological status." (Naturally, the metaphysical explanations for this
power vary greatly between societies, as do the prescribed ways of controlling it.) The truly terminal crisis of human dignity would be a total loss of
pretheoretical confidence in the efficacy of human cognition for comprehending a world, and in human agency for acting upon it. Such a loss of
confidence is a loss of dignity because humankind would have to be re-
defined as primordially helpless, of interest only as one among the many
crystalline shapes of matter indifferently created and destroyed by the
morally blind processes of nature.

Human dignity, it seems then, requires a philosophical anthropology
appropriate to it: a life world in which certain things are regarded as true
on a pretheoretical level.[29] We previously said that the primordial experience that generates a felt need for dignity talk is the sense of some threat
to the moral significance of the human status and its place in nature. One
must also ask, what kind of philosophical anthropology implicit in the
culture of a people can support such a conviction of human significance?
Any general answer must necessarily be very abstract since cultures vary
so radically in content. But this much can be said.

First, there must be an implicit ontological assumption that the subjectively experienced self is grounded in some kind of "world" that (whatever
the requisite preparations) is ultimately intelligible, accessible to human
comprehension.

Second, there must be an implicit ontological assumption that the self
(whatever the requisite preparations) is potent in relation to its ground,

that the self can act in or on the world, in a manner informed by the world's intelligibility.

In short, we are saying that human dignity is based on the pretheoretical conviction that the self is grounded in a world from which it derives its significance, that the world is ultimately intelligible, and that the self partakes in potency to affect the world. All else is relative.

These general comments suggest the following definition of human dignity. Human dignity is the respect worthiness imputed to humankind by reason of its privileged ontological status as creator, maintainer, and destroyer of worlds. Each self shares in this essential dignity (i.e., is recognizable as a moral entity) insofar as it partakes (whether by conscious intention or not) in world-building or world-destroying actions. Thus, human dignity, in its collective and individual forms, does not rest on intention, moral merit, or subjective definitions of self-interests. It rests on the fact that we are, in this fundamental way that is beyond our intention, human. We are moral agents. Only suicide – the ultimate act of ontological self-rejection – can release us from that condition into which, to use Heidegger's term, we have been "thrown." The assertion of human dignity, then, is the constitutive act of moral consciousness. It is the entrance ticket to the community of formal moral discourse. To assert dignity is both to acknowledge the factuality of human creative agency and to accept responsibility for its use.

Given this definition, it now makes sense to ask under what conditions human dignity is likely to be taken for granted (possibly to the point where no special vocabulary for it exists). Four interrelated classes of conditions have been implied in our analysis thus far. These may be labeled phenomenological, psychological, theoretical, and sociological. Explicating them briefly provides an opportunity to summarize our reflections and direct them to this point.

Phenomenological conditions. Human dignity is experientially possible in any culture with a pretheoretical structure of consciousness that supports it.[30] This means a life world in which human agency is perceived as something that cannot be reduced exclusively to any deterministic account of humankind derived from observations of nonintentional phenomena. Different cultures have diverse ways of articulating such a basic phenomenology. In some, the human is considered partly divine. In others the human is the highest (e.g., the most perfectable, or most complex, or more self-conscious, etc.) stage in the evolutionary dynamics of nature itself. In still other cultures the human is that which is considered capable of self-determination and, therefore, can only be spoken of "objectively" in terms of metaphors (e.g., organism or machine).

Another feature of such a phenomenology is that human agency is perceived as of extraordinary, even unpredictable, potency. This potency is never trivial. It is significant, rather, on a world-creating or world-destroying scale. Therefore, human potency, in many such cultures, is considered to take on the quality of the numinous and become the stuff of myth and legend.[31]

Psychological conditions. The psychological correlate of the pretheoretical experience of dignity is a sense of awe in the presence of an intrinsically important, perhaps sacred, phenomenon. Thus, the respect imputed to human status is not merely an intellectual acknowledgement. It is a holistic experience involving awe and fear as well as other motives including, according to circumstance, identification, commitment, and obligation.

Theoretical conditions. Cultures vary widely in the degree to which pre-theoretical assumptions, attitudes, and experience are reflexively articulated in intellectual forms such as philosophy, theology, or science. Theory is regarded by its producers as an outcome of collective, elite, transgenerational intellectual effort. These characteristics, it is understandably supposed, produce the most refined corpus of truth claims possible in a given society to date. Since influential theories are generally reinterpreted until they are congenial (or irrelevant) to important social interests, certain types of theory eventually emerge as institutionally sanctioned reality talk.[32] When theory (in this general sense) becomes a major component of a culture, it takes on a kind of official status that lends certain ideas some independent historical influence in their own right. That is to say, theories begin to function as historical gatekeepers that help determine the intellectual respectability of pretheoretical assumptions and convictions.

In those cultures with a heavy theory component, therefore, human dignity requires both substantive theory and methods of theorizing that are compatible with it. If a society's dominant intellectual traditions downgrade the importance of human agency in their theories about the world, or if dominant intellectual methods persistently ignore the requirements of showing connections between human agency and the structure of the world, then these intellectual traditions will contribute to the atrophy of human dignity (though they may, of course, contribute to the prevalence of dignity talk!).[33]

Sociological conditions. Finally, there is the sociological component of human dignity. The social organization of a society can itself be such as to reveal or to conceal the facts of human agency (facts that include the generative consequences of personal action, the *loci* of opportunity for altering established structures, and the creative powers of language). Just as theory can encourage or impede human dignity by structuring the way people believe and think about the world, so a society can be organized in such a way as to permit or impede people's recognition of their powers to act upon their world in morally consequential ways.

We thus far have not spoken of the substance or scale of the "worlds" that are the presumed objects of human potency, just as we have not been specific about the notion of the "human." This obviously is because of the variability in how the "human" and its "worlds" have been concretely conceived in diverse cultures and epochs. What, then, have we achieved with this more abstract approach?

Our procedure affords us the basis for a view of human dignity as an ideal type applicable to many varied contexts. Further, it enables us to distinguish between strong and weak definitions of dignity according to the criterion of what is meant by the world in which the human presence is considered morally efficacious. Thus, for the strong definition of dignity, we must imagine a society (nowhere fully incarnated) in which the world that grounds the self is a seamless web incorporating all dimensions of human experience: physical, social, and temporal. In such a world, almost anything the self does or fails to do ramifies in a kind of sacred arc. That is, the pretheoretical interpretation of the world is such that all is interconnected. Everything – naming, technical activities, social interactions of all kinds – has potential ritual significance. Even the ubiquitous taboos surround the self with myriad reminders of human potency in the very structure of being.

As regards weaker definitions of dignity, here the worlds in which the human presence potently resides are much more restricted. In these worlds, experience is more or less fragmented and compartmentalized. The glorious claims of human potency have undergone major humiliations. Our modern world has been racked, for example, by at least four such humiliations. These are: the Copernican, in which the earth as human world is cast out of the centre of the cosmos; the Darwinian, in which the human is degraded to a stage in the evolution of the animal; the sociological, in which the human story loses its mythical dimensions and is degraded to a function of social order; and the Freudian humiliation, in which human intentionality itself becomes a secret agent of the hidden beast in human form.

Can those worlds appropriate to a strong definition of human dignity disappear, rendering a strong definition historically obsolete? The answer to this is clearly yes. But a further question remains: Is it possible for a world to emerge in which *any* definition of dignity, however weak, is irrelevant?

For those whose response to this question would be uncritically affirmative, human dignity is just another culturally relative concept like witchcraft, demons, or phlogiston. What would be required to support a contrary claim: the claim that the concept of human dignity has a timeless significance? It would be necessary to show that there is, in some irreducible and universal sense, a world that requires the active agency of all human selves to create, maintain, or destroy – a world that is both a truly human product and in which all humans dwell. If such a world exists, then human dignity (in however weak a form) legitimately retains its place in the moral vocabulary of humanity.

There is such a world. It is language itself, a world for which all persons, intentionally or not, share some degree of responsibility because they all possess some degree of potency over it. This generalization does not, of course, apply to language alone. Humans produce a number of specifically human environments not reducible to language such as iconic, mathematical, musical, and gestural environments. However, for our purpose, language possesses a privileged position. Aside from gestures, the linguistic mode of symbolization is the only one in which all members of a society (except those who literally cannot speak) are actively involved. Although we always know more than we can tell, it is nevertheless through language that we all predominantly communicate. Therefore it is the status of language as a form of human agency, and its relation to the possible meanings of person and action, that presents the critical issue for human dignity in an age of symbolic pluralism, doubt, and disunity. As speakers we are often united, for through words we help create new forms of symbolic life that eventually dominate our collective conscience. As listeners we reside in a fully humanly produced world. And as interpreters of the speech of others, we become (however involuntarily) responsible moral participants in a community – the community of language. *How* we do these things is, of course, a desperately important question for those concerned with the empirical foundations for a moral philosophy of dignity. *That* we do these things is beyond reasonable doubt. We may believe that language is the voice of gods or men; we may admire the democratic flexibility or the authoritative traditions of language; we may claim our interpretive rights over language or delegate them (knowingly or not) to experts. The fact remains that we each, through our partially but necessarily idiosyncratic understanding and use of language, help - in however small a way - to construct and alter the social world. And because of that fact, in this weak minimal sense at least, we all possess the dignity of potency in relation to a world for which we are collectively and individually responsible.

V

Toward a politics of competence

It must be granted that the tension between survival and dignity as moral ends is a potential cultural conflict of truly great historic proportions, unlikely to be resolved in practice during this century. The issue involves questions of the highest theoretical magnitude that cannot be addressed within the existing academic division of labor. Nor can these questions be resolved by the sentimental pieties and bureaucratic tinkering to which contemporary liberalism has been reduced. The fate of language, our common instrument for world creation, is surely one of these great questions.

Even if we optimistically assume that these questions will be taken up by contemporary thinkers with the requisite erudition and imagination, it is reasonable to ask (especially of a sociologist) what good this will do if unaccompanied by practical efforts to modify the organization of society in some way.

Space does not permit a systematic exposition and defense of the following arguments, but there is a theme that ties them all together. Perhaps the most adequate way of putting it is that we need a critical politics of competence. The point is that there are certain activities whose proper aim is to reverse the present tendencies toward linguistically, cognitively, and socially disarming the citizenry. (It is ironic that Americans should be so concerned with keeping their guns when in so many ways they are being more effectively disarmed of their cognitive, social, and political defenses.)

This program of efforts to maintain and increase the linguistic competence (and therefore the dignity) of the person as a political agent can be carried to considerable lengths under the auspices of the present social order of industrial democracies. This is because many of the ways in which giant social institutions are disarming the citizenry of their competences are questionable from the standpoint of the cultural and juridical traditions of these societies. Very briefly, there are three dimensions of a practical politics of competence implied by the conceptualization of dignity developed in Section IV.

We need an Orwellian attack upon the degradation of our language for purposes of commercial and political manipulation. The truth in advertising campaign is but a bare beginning. The entire relationship between persons and language must be reexamined in the light of the demonstrated power of language to manipulate fantasies, create pseudo-events, and control symbolic experiences of all sorts. A politics of competence begins with the question of whether we can any longer afford the luxury of allowing the agents of powerful institutions to do anything they want with man's most significant symbolic phenomenon: language.[34]

We need a logic of moral accounting integrated into our juridical theory of legitimate institutions. It is a striking social and cultural fact that Western civilization, having once had a logic of moral accounting, has totally abandoned the project instead of reforming and updating it. I refer to the Roman Catholic tradition of casuistry. The fact is that at least some acts committed by men of power once were subjected to a logic of justification wholly devoted to practical reasoning in the light of certain broad moral principles (and, of course, dogmas). Major examples were debates over the meaning of just price and just war. For various complex reasons, including misuse of the relevant casuistical techniques, this approach to moral accounting was abandoned. It has actually never been replaced, and today uninformed people virtually equate casuistry with sophistry. Yet there has been in American history at least one major episode of public debate on a level of the most creative casuistical standards: the debate over ratification of the Constitution, whose monument is *The Federalist Papers*. Today there are no standards of moral accounting. In their place we have mindless appeals to slogans like "national security," "the free world," "law and order," "liberation," "self-actualization," and the like. A politics of competence begins by recognizing these as the clichés they are and proceeds by experimenting with their translation into accounting procedures.

We need to reverse tendencies toward the irrational specialization of labor. The concept of citizen as a social role requires critical examination from an important sociological perspective: the structure of specialization. The social division of labor is not just one among a number of structural facts about society. In modern societies the social division of labor is one of the primary structural prisms through which language as symbolic experience and action is refracted. We now know some things about the division of labor in industrial societies that help explain how extreme specialization threatens the integral competence of the person as political agent.

For example, specialization can proceed to a degree that is demonstrably irrational in its effects. Social structural specialization is often replicated on the level of subjective consciousness. Carried to a certain point, specialization can induce in a population general incompetence and helplessness. This is a true destruction of human dignity and finds its roots in the debilitating idea that it is dangerous to act except in professionalized, role-defined, and credentialed settings. The sociological dimension of a politics of competence should therefore be a concerted pressure toward the definition and reversal of irrational specialization in all aspects of life. This is tantamount to a general critique of unlimited professionalism. With respect to language, such a critique encourages a never-ending examination of technical vocabularies and their uses for social control through mystification. Without such social attention to the proper limits of professionalism, most cultural advances in symbolic competence will prove sociologically fruitless.[35]

It is difficult to see how efforts like these can be mounted in society if they do not begin in the universities. Yet these now produce more specialists and technocrats than genuinely educated people, more experts than thinkers. As a civilization, we are in some danger of cultural amnesia, of forgetting things that our best educated ancestors understood well. Many of us float on the ocean of the present, clinging like shipwrecked sailors to the flotsam of great ideas systematically developed by thinkers of the past. It is a standard American truism that education has political consequences. One is sometimes led to wonder how many appreciate the sober depths of truth in this cliché.[36]

ACKNOWLEDGMENT

I would like to express my gratitude for very helpful comments on the first draft of this essay to Sara Stanley, Emily Haynes, and Richard Harvey Brown. Thanks are also due to the National Endowment for the Humanities, whose fellowship award for the year 1973–74 facilitated some of the research on which this essay is based.

NOTES

1 The "models of doom" literature is bibliographically summarized (and
critically assessed) in *Models of Doom*, ed. H. S. D. Cole et al. (New York:
Universe Books, 1973). A striking necrological inventory of twentieth century
casualties of present world social systems is Gil Elliot, *The 20th Century Book
of the Dead* (New York: Ballantine, 1972). A sobering treatment of world
survival chances is Robert L. Heilbroner, *An Inquiry into the Human Prospect*
(New York: W. W. Norton, 1974). A more prescriptive treatment of world
survival policy problems is Garrett Hardin, *Exploring New Ethics for Survival*
(New York: Viking, 1972).

2 In several works I have been treating the concept of technicism as one
important instance of transferring technologically pregnant metaphors from
science to social theory and policy analysis. Cf. my "Technicism, Liberalism
and Development" in *Social Development*, ed. Manfred Stanley (New York:
Basic Books, 1972), pp. 274-325; "Prometheus and the Policy Sciences" in
Alienation, ed. Frank Johnson (New York: Seminar Press, 1973), pp. 221-49;
"Literacy: The Crisis of a Conventional Wisdom," *School Review* 8, 3 (1972):
373-408. The purpose of these investigations is to show the pessimism of
humanistic intellectuals regarding technology is inspired not so much by the
physical effects of technology as by the linguistic effects of technological
metaphors applied to language and social institutions. My studies in this topic
culminate in my book *The Technological Conscience: Survival and Dignity in
an Age of Expertise* (New York: The Free Press, 1978).

3 The most comprehensive exemplification of the phenomenology and cultural
psychology appropriate to the pessimistic view of full technicism is probably
Hannah Arendt's depiction of the society of "labor" developed in her *The
Human Condition* (Garden City, N.Y.: Doubleday, 1958).

4 Jacques Ellul, *The Technological Society* (New York: Vintage, 1964), p. 143.
Presumably the sense of this passage is similar to Henry Adams's description
of his impulse in the Gallery of Machines at the Paris Exposition of 1900 to
pray to the dynamo as Christians had once prayed to the cross (cited in Leo
Marx, *The Machine in the Garden* [New York: Oxford University Press, 1964],
p. 347.)

5 That this engineering-priestly motive in sociology played an important role in
early-twentieth-century American collectivism is amply documented by James
Gilbert, *Designing the Industrial State* (Chicago: Quadrangle, 1972). To some
extent this orientation has been transferred from sociologists to those administrators who see themselves as an elite of social engineers. For instance, cf.
William Scott and David Hart, "Administrative Crisis: The Neglect of Metaphysical Speculation," *Public Administration Review* 33, 5 (1973):415-22.
Scott and Hart argue that because public administrators are an elite, they
should abandon their pretensions of technocratic neutrality and return to

serious metaphysical analysis of what man and society can be. Although they make no mention of it, this is, of course, exactly what cybernetics as an ideology is all about. For further thoughts on this, cf. Robert McClintock, "Machines and Vitalists: Reflections on the Ideology of Cybernetics," *American Scholar* (1966):249–57.

6 Cf. Zbigniew Brzezinski, "America in the Technetronic Age," *Encounter* 30, 1 (1968):16–25. Also his *Between Two Ages* (New York: Viking, 1970).

7 Donald Michael, "Cybernation: The Silent Conquest," *Automation*, ed. Morris Philipson (New York: Viking, 1962), pp. 123–4.

8 For the concept of sociostatic norms, cf. Allen Schick, "The Cybernetic State," *Trans-Action* 7, 4 (1970):15–26. Schick means by sociostatic norms, norms that are "the servomechanistic trigger of public action." As he points out, "A cybernetic state operates under sociostatic norms: employment rates, poverty levels, educational criteria." For norms to function in this manner they must be translated into the quantitative-operational terms appropriate to the cybernetic notion of meaning as "information." Thus it is clearly appropriate to regard the "social indicators" movement as a stage in the evolution of a cybernetic society. Schick's essay is one of the very few known to me that seeks to distinguish bureaucratic from cybernetic society. Its focus is primarily upon the legal sociology of this distinction. I have further developed this notion of the ultimate split between the private and public self into a formulation of a "libertarian-technicist" model in chapter 2 of my book, entitled *The Technological Conscience*. The burden of my effort was to show that counterculture libertarianism was not incompatible with cybernetic technicism.

9 Cf. for instance, Amitai Etzioni, *The Active Society* (New York: The Free Press, 1968).

10 Arthur Koestler, *Arrival and Departure* (Berkeley: Medallion, 1960; [orig. pub., 1943]), p. 130.

11 For dignity needs a way of expressing itself, of shining forth, of having a 'sphere of free influence.' Such an analysis of the concrete experience . . . of 'indignities' is merely an indirect approach to the full phenomenon of dignity. But before any more direct exploration it is of paramount importance to face the concrete situations out of which the present outcry for human dignity was born. This may not add up to a meaningful definition. But more important than a definition is the vivid experience of what it means to have the kind of intrinsic worth which is disregarded in dehumanizing treatment. (Herbert Spiegelberg, "Human Dignity: A Challenge to Contemporary Philosophy," *The Philosophical Forum* 9, 1, 2 [1971]:61).

A similar methodological approach is used with respect to the concept of justice by Edmond Cahn, *The Sense of Injustice* (Bloomington: Indiana University Press, 1949).

12 John Searle, *Speech Acts* (Cambridge: Cambridge University Press, 1969), p. 34.

13 H. L. A. Hart, "Are There Any Natural Rights?" *Philosophical Review* 64 (1955):175–91.

14 Charles Taylor, "Interpretation and the Sciences of Man," *Review of Metaphysics* XXV, 1 (1971):3–51 (quotation on p. 24).

15 Searle comments on this point too: "Can one follow a rule without knowing it? It bothers some people that I claim that there are rules of language which we *discover* even though, I claim, we have been following them all along." *Speech Acts,* pp. 41–2. For further explanation of Taylor's examples, see note 16.

16 The possibility should be explored that the methodology appropriate to analyzing constitutive rules is perhaps phenomenology. The parallels between what Searle does, for instance, with the concept of "promising" and what Husserl meant by eidetic reduction, while certainly not exact (e.g., one stresses conceptual, the other perceptual, reduction) are nonetheless intriguing and invite exploration. The same could be said of Taylor's method of explicating his examples. For instance, in his example of "bargaining" (pp. 23–4), he reduces the concept of bargaining, as a special form of negotiation, to constitutive assumptions that are really those of the market economy itself. These assumptions include "distinct *autonomous* parties in *willed* relationships," plus distinctions like "entering into and leaving negotiations" (emphasis added). Although Taylor does not carry out a conceptual reduction to any degree of the sort that Searle does with "promising," one could imagine, from what he says, how he might proceed. "Self autonomy," "will," and "instrumentality" of social relations are but three of the constitutive rules assumed to underlie the practice of bargaining as contrasted with other forms of negotiations. (It should be noted in passing that Marx's discussion of commodity consciousness in the first volume of *Capital* rests upon a similar methodology.)

17 For example, see the series of essays in the special numbers on human dignity in *The Philosophical Forum* 9, 1/2 and 3/4 (1971).

18 Ervin Laszlo, "Human Dignity and the Promise of Technology," ibid. 9, 3/4 (1971):165–99 (quotation p. 178). I am not concerned here with criticizing Laszlo's work as a whole. As regards this particular essay, I largely agree with the comments on Laszlo by Wilbur, Peterson, and Watson in their essays included in the collection cited in footnote 17.

19 Ibid., pp. 166, 167.

20 Ibid., p. 170.

21 Abraham Edel, "Humanist Ethics and the Meaning of Human Dignity," in *Moral Problems in Contemporary Society,* Paul Kurtz (Englewood Cliffs, N.J.: Prentice-Hall, 1969), pp. 227–40 (quotation p. 238).

22 Cf., Jan Narveson, *Morality and Utility* (Baltimore: Johns Hopkins University Press, 1967). The quotations are all from pp. 184–5. A parenthetical observation might be of interest before proceeding. These three orientations have been presented as they have because of the developmental suggestiveness of this order of precedence. If one inquires into the psychobiography or even the historiography of dignity talk, it may well turn out that the emergence of dignity as an intellectual problem begins with the phenomenology of indignity

and profanation, proceeds through efforts to explore the constitutive foundations of a more positive reaffirmation about the human status, and ends with systematic definitional preoccupations.

23 One of the best short discussions of the human as a problem in categorization is Marcel Mauss's essay "A Category of the Human Spirit," reprinted in *The Psychoanalytic Review* 55, 3 (1968):457–81. In an important commentary on this essay Lawrence Krader (ibid., pp. 482–90) approaches the same problem from what is in one sense the opposite direction from Mauss. As he himself says:

> Mauss has advanced the notion of the person in its phenomenality as a category of the existent human spirit whose emergence is a cultural universal. His essay has been interpreted here as the opposite, not in its universality, but in its particularity, and in this sense as a phenomenology of the particular: the cultural-historic events of Western Civilization are the field of application of the concept of the person, which is then applied to intercultural phenomena (p. 490).

So, for Mauss the emergence of the person was a generalization of universal scope. For Krader the person is a Western concept that migrated from Western moral, legal, religious, and intellectual experience into Western technical science and other institutions of (now) world significance. The issues raised in these pages constitute a profound hermeneutic problem for the whole notion of a social science.

24 Peter Berger, Brigitte Berger, and Hansfried Kellner, *The Homeless Mind* (New York: Vintage, 1973), p. 89.

25 Ibid., p. 86.

26 Ibid., pp. 90, 91.

27 Giovanni Pico della Mirandola, *Oration on the Dignity of Man,* trans. A. R. Caponigri (Chicago: Henry Regnery, 1956), pp. 6ff.

28 Cf., V. J. Bourke, *The Will in Western Thought* (New York: Sheed & Ward, 1964).

29 The notion of the "life world" is used here in the sense developed by Husserl, Schutz, Merleau-Ponty, and Berger and Luckmann. For a good short treatment of the life world notion that includes some of the problems which still require attention, see Ludwig Landgrebe, "The World as a Phenomenological Problem," *Philosophy and Phenomenological Research* 1 (1940/41):38–58.

30 The term "structures of consciousness" is not, of course, being used here as equivalent to subjective attitudes. Rather it refers to a facet of culture: a structure of shared categories of meaning that function as cues, or grooves for thought, on the subjective level. The term is characteristically used by Benjamin Nelson throughout his many publications on this topic. A good source for an introduction to his use of a vocabulary for the study of structures of consciousness is his "Actors, Directors, Roles, Cues, Meanings, Identities: Further Thoughts on 'Anomie'," *Psychoanalytic Review* 51, 1 (1964):135–60.

31 The term "numinous" is meant in Rudolf Otto's sense. See his *The Idea of the Holy* (New York: Oxford University Press, 1967).

32 This is perhaps obvious with respect to social and psychological theories. However it often appears to be the case also with physical theories. By way of example, one may recall the influence of Aristotelian physics on medieval Roman Catholic theology, of Newtonian physics on eighteenth-century social thought, or Darwinian biology on nineteenth-century social thought and so on.

33 An example of theory that downgrades human agency in this way is the more extreme deterministic forms of social science. An example of intellectual method that does the same thing is the habit of grounding theories about humankind in metaphors that uncritically reduce human action to objectified language not appropriate to it.

34 This proposal is not intended as a venture into censorship any more than are "truth in advertising" or "libel" legislation. It is rather in the spirit of Orwell's awareness of the sinister political implications of habitual carelessness in the uses of language. See also George Steiner's reflections on the relations between language and political inhumanity in his essay "The Hollow Miracle," in his collection of essays, *Language and Silence* (New York: Atheneum, 1970), pp. 25-109. Ultimately our new consciousness of the problem of language must reveal the technicist superficiality of our presently institutionalized conception of "literacy." Some giant steps toward the recovery of the traditional dignity of this concept have been taken by the Brazilian theorist and practitioner of adult literacy education, Paulo Freire. For an appreciative criticism of Freire's position on these matters, see chapter 8 of my book.

35 The division of labor was of central moral as well as scientific interest in sociology from Adam Smith through Karl Marx to Emile Durkheim. For a recent argument that occupational specialization is an independent variable in the sociology of knowledge, see Joseph Bensman and Robert Lilienfeld, *Craft and Consciousness* (New York: John Wiley & Sons, 1973). Some powerful essays on the problem of human scale in technological, institutional, and role specialization have been written by Ivan Illich. I think they are more important than his more popular, but to me overrated, essays on the specific issue of schools. See Ivan Illich, "Institutional Spectrum," *Deschooling Society* (New York: Harper & Row, 1970), pp. 51-64, and the essays in his *Tools for Conviviality* (New York: Harper & Row, 1974).

36 American discussions of education and the uses of the intellect have been devastated by irrelevant polemics on the democratization of student involvement in decision-making. Recently there has been a reaction and even, on occasion, a return to discourse about the nature of an educated man. It seems to me that the time has come for a most thoughtful perusal by academics of Julian Benda's *The Betrayal of the Intellectuals* (Boston: Beacon Press, 1955). The issues raised there, however controversial, are surely no less relevant today than they were in 1928. It is hard to imagine a more salutary event for American educators than a great debate about the contemporary implications of that book.

Part III
Praxis and utopia

8

Dramaturgical discourse and political enactments: Toward an artistic foundation for political space

TRACY B. STRONG

Editors' introduction

The routinization of political action requires that certain ground rules not be called into question. Just as discourse within a specialized scientific community is governed by that discipline's reigning paradigms, so public discourse is in some sense made possible by paradigms through which political thought and action may be expressed. America and other advanced industrial societies are experiencing crises of political rhetoric much as the human studies are experiencing crises of scientific discourse.

One reason for the political crises of rhetoric is that currently available forms of speech fail to provide a language of public moral agency by which the rightness – rather than merely the efficiency – of public policies might be measured. In contrast to the organicist-mechanist paradigms currently in use, a dramaturgical model of the polity would provide a more adequate and humane civic *lingua franca*.

But who is to create such a paradigm, and how might it be done? In addressing these questions, Tracy B. Strong argues that the task of political philosophy is to provide such paradigmatic ground rules and, thus, to create a space (*agora*) defined by such rules. The manner in which this may be done can best be understood through an analysis of the relation of an audience to a dramatic presentation. By exploring some of the differences and similarities between drama and politics (and especially contemporary American politics), it is possible to discover the conceptual tools by which political philosophers and sociologists can recover an artist's relation to the political process, a relationship that involves both nearness and farness, both theoretical engagement and dispassionate critique.

A question that is answered in a natural way and that is grounded in just
as natural a way is seriously no longer a question . . . We call natural what
is understood without further ado, and is self evident in the realm of everyday understanding . . . The natural is always historical.
                              Martin Heidegger, *What is a Thing?*, pp. 38–9.

This essay is a preliminary attempt at sketching out some ground rules
for the development of discourse that speaks both meaningfully and theoretically about politics today. I assume that many of our old forms of
political language have become increasingly vague and without sensuous
reference to the contemporary world. I do not, indeed, I could not pretend
to have developed a new discourse in this essay. Not only the limitations
of my ability and the brevity of this essay, but also the nature of such a task
render this impossible: One does not simply *invent* a new language. Hence,
the conclusions of this essay can be no more (and should be no less) than
descriptions of what the structure of such discourse might be. A little over
three hundred years ago, for example, Hobbes drew upon the experience
of his time to liberate men and women from the old pictures and prisons
in which he felt their language had held them. I cannot write a treatise;
in fact, I shall contend that the fact that a treatise cannot be written is of
central importance to the possibility of political discourse. I hope only to
draw upon some elements of our experience to suggest what a political
theoretical statement would have to take into account.

I

We have all had, as private individuals at least, the experience of finding
it impossible to explain to someone precisely what we mean. In such
situations, the speaker may come to despair of words themselves and
conclude that language is inadequate to the task. "If you don't understand
me, I simply can't explain it" is the rhetorical reaction of a person confronting a situation for which he or she no longer has words.

Similarly, we have all had the delight of agreement and the pleasure of
shared knowledge. We all know the feelings of relief and possibly even of
high satisfaction associated with a moment of insight: "I see what you
mean." That we turn easily to the language of vision gives a strange,
though natural, metaphor. "Seeing what you mean" indicates that we
have penetrated to the logic or grammar that makes intelligible what the
speaker is trying to get across. The metaphor is not accidental: the Greek
root for "to see" is *theorein,* from which we derive the word family for
"theory."

What then do we see in the politics around us? This essay has its point of departure in the fact that, from observation of contemporary political patterns in America, one must be struck by the degree to which various factions seem to be talking about different worlds in mutually impenetrable languages. It is not clear that there can be common discourse between the "Pig Nation Amerika" of some groups and the "American Dream" that informs others. I am not noting here that recent years have witnessed an increasing index of disagreement, even of violent disagreement. So much would in fact itself be heartening, for such quarrels have provided the very stuff of politics ever since men moved from the tribes to the cities. Disagreement and argument indicate, after all, that the interlocutors are asking the same questions: to be able to disagree with someone you have to know what he means. The case I note here occurs rather when the "sides" do not so much oppose each other on the same field, but seem to be playing different games by different rules. They pass each other by, unacknowledged and unacknowledging, self-confirmed in the confidence of their own clarity.

In such confrontations, dialog becomes impossible: The two parties remain mutually inpenetrable and soon discover that it does no good to repeat their arguments loudly and slowly. As Hannah Arendt has noted, in such a breakdown, politics moves toward violence, or the silence of anarchic terror or, perhaps most characteristically, toward withdrawal.[1]

Such political autism has not always been the norm, nor is it universally so now. More importantly, however, when such breakdowns have occurred in times past - I think here of the early Reformation or of the French Revolution - a new prose and definition for politics often became available such that political life returned once again as possible. Michael Walzer has written eloquently about the political and intellectual chaos in Europe at the beginning of the modern era. He argues that the Faustian ambivalence that Marlowe, among others, so vividly portrayed, was resolved for many by the Revolution of the Saints. Calvinism gave a new life to politics, and the forms it initiated remain characteristic of much political activity to this day.[2] One might trace similar dynamics in the period of the French Revolution and in the work of Lenin and the Bolsheviks in 1917. The efforts of Mao Tse Tung, whether successful or not, to build a new man through a Great Proletarian Cultural Revolution are but the most recent and interesting examples of a kind of political activity that seeks to reground man's perception of the political world.

It is my contention, then, that revolutions such as these function to give to their participants, and eventually to others, a new way of thinking about or conceptualizing the political world. Calvin, for instance, demonstrates to men that the starting point for any meaningful conception of the world has to be the common and universal alienation of men from a hidden God. This paradoxically democratic starting point – that, before anything else, all men suffer the same affliction – becomes the basis for the reflections of Hobbes and Locke and much of the foundation of our contemporary conceptualization of politics. (That the two Englishmen severely changed Calvin's understanding of the nature of original equality is less important than that they thought in the same form.) Again, the possibility that one human being could separately be both a human being and a king – a notion on which our conception of office depends – is first elaborated by Hobbes in his distinction between natural and artificial beings in the *Leviathan.*[3] Without this notion of person, much of our contemporary political notions are impossible.

This is not a paper about the substance of such developments, but rather about what they represent. For whatever reason, once a new way of looking at politics is introduced successfully, it tends to become difficult, if not impossible, to look at the political world except in terms of those categories. The distinction between natural and artificial men is not something that stands out like a person having both legs and arms. It is a manner of conceiving of a human being that we now tend to accept as natural and, certainly, as an enduring and permanent characteristic of the political world. The lack of this distinction colors the world of, for example, the *polis* in a very different fashion and so removes that time from our common knowledge.

On this basis, one might then speak of such transformations as changes in the grammar of our political understanding, comprehending by that term those structures, not necessarily apparent, on which the rest of our discourse is erected and by which it becomes intelligible. Such transformations have been the subject of a good deal of recent debate in the philosophy of science; a brief discussion of some of the issues there may suggest some of what is at stake in the present one.

The seminal work here (though hardly the first to advance such notions) is Thomas S. Kuhn's *The Structure of Scientific Revolutions.* Kuhn identifies a set of "paradigm changes" or, as he later calls them more accurately, if less felicitously, "recontextualizations." He sees these as those points in the development of Western science at which, in circumstances and ways not totally explained, men and physicists moved from one understanding of the world to another, from Ptolemaic to Copernican astronomy, or from Newtonian to Einsteinian physics.

Kuhn's work has provoked a storm. He was (and is) accused of many major scientific sins: irrationalism, historicism, relativism. I have examined this debate elsewhere and have no intent of replaying the many and often silly ramifications of the controversy.[4] I do think, however, that Kuhn's language is often unclear, occasionally even confused, partly because his manner of discussing the revolutions with which he is concerned suffers (especially in his earlier work) from an inadequate vocabulary. It is useful for my purposes here to try to trace out the source of such inadequacies, not in the spirit of setting Kuhn's straight, but rather to show precisely how powerful his analysis can be. He often refers, for instance, to "paradigm shifts" as "gestalt switches." Here he borrows from the vocabulary of N. R. Hanson (especially in *Patterns of Discovery*) and has in mind for transformations in the history of science an analogy that draws upon the experience of anyone who has struggled to see Jastrow's duck-rabbit as, say, a duck. One experiences a feeling of relief and completeness when, finally, one is able to see it like that. This sort of language, however, is misleading. We can see the duck-rabbit as either a duck or a rabbit. With a little practice, we can move back and forth at will, and though we can never see both at the same time, the two pictures are of the same epistemological level. Such parity is not, however, true of changes from Newtonian to Einsteinian physics, nor of switches from one context of political perceptions to another. In these cases, there is no going back: The new supercedes the old, and the old persists only as a worn-out and partially useful anachronism. The new effectively eliminates the possibility of the old.

Kuhn's language does get him into trouble, for it blurs an important distinction. It is one thing for a picture to simply replace another, as does a duck the rabbit the first time one sees it like that. It is another, even though related, problem to see the world so new that there is no going back. After Hobbes, for instance, the old idea of order, which W. H. Greenleaf argues informed the medieval and early modern world, is simply no longer available for important political thought.[5] This is not to say that Hobbes wrought such a change single-handedly: The importance of Kuhn's work is precisely that it focuses us on the process of the shift. After reading Kuhn, we realize that there is a problem in accounting for the dynamics of the change that occurs when men go from one way of conceptualizing the world to another. In his terms, men do move from one period of normal science to another. The problem is how, and on this Kuhn's book has little to say.[6]

Here, then, is the problem that exercises me. I am not so much concerned with why men came to accept one political world view rather than another. The "why" focus is at the center of most of the critiques of Kuhn. In my understanding, however, we must first account not for why such shifts were accepted, but rather must acknowledge the fact that they were and try to understand how. Once the structure of such revolutionary transformations is sketched out, it may then be possible to suggest some forms of writing and discourse that might (though certainly not necessarily) produce similar transformations in our time. Our problem is that we seem to be at a moment in history when attempts at theoretical writing usually find no friction in the world they address. Men talk, but nothing moves.

One might speak, then, of "normal politics," and refer by this borrowing to the politics of a country or group that, when confronted with a political problem or choice, generally speaking knows what to do. In politics and in physics, in fact in any facet of life, things are normal when one knows one's way about, when the streets of the town are familiar. For instance, until quite recently in American politics, it was generally acceptable to suggest that the problems that arose with the introduction of black Americans into a fuller political life would be taken care of by the same processes that had served other immigrant groups. The franchise, education, and time: All of these were thought sufficient to guarantee the gradual introduction of blacks into the mainstream of American life. Well-meaning white Americans no longer have such confidence, it seems to me, and often simply do not know where to turn. A whole territory that we had thought to be safely settled and mapped out is suddenly revealed as mysterious, hard to forecast, and potentially hostile.[7]

Indeed, if events get sufficiently out of hand, normal politics is no longer possible, and if no new form of politics is forthcoming, men and women may turn to other forms of activity. They will cope with the problems of their lives in violence, religion, millenarianism, private enterprise, withdrawal, in the grail quest of the "search for community," or in "doing your own thing," "getting your head [or, more threateningly, your shit] together."[8] In such times, political roads appear closed or nonexistent; we might say that we do not know our way about politically. Though politics may never be as clear cut as, say, etiquette, it is still appropriate to speak, as does Burkart Holzner, of "common knowledge." This term refers not only to those matters that the typical person in a society knows, but also those deemed "hardly worth further investigation," where "the authority upon which this knowledge is asserted needs no further explication."[9]

For there to be the common knowledge that makes normal politics possible a certain regularity and rationality has to be assumed. We have here a preliminary clue to the problem of "not knowing your way about." "Not knowing your way about" is, however, for Wittgenstein, the paradigm of a philosophical problem. It occurs most frequently when the context that makes a proposition sure or gives a statement meaning is obscured or altered, such that the judgments one makes no longer correspond to the world for which they are supposed to be appropriate. Perhaps the most familiar example here is the puzzlement that Westerners evidenced over the apparent Japanese "habit" of "smiling" upon the receipt of bad news.

In *On Certainty,* Wittgenstein extends the problem of change in context from casuistical cases to an apparently more general formulation. "It might be imagined," he writes, "that some propositions of the form of empirical propositions were hardened and functioned as channels for such empirical propositions as were not hardened, but fluid."[10] He goes on to indicate that the relation between "channels" and "fluid," or between "context" and "facts" will alter with the passing of time. This is very close to the notion of paradigm shifts in Kuhn, even if the latter's revolutionary rhetoric suggests a more ironic fatalism. In any case, if this relationship can alter, then as Richard Bernstein notes in his analysis of the "displacement hypothesis," as he calls such changes, the "conceptual framework in which we now think of ourselves and others as agents can be displaced by a radically different scientific framework."[11] And, by extension, there may be periods in which we do not have a world of common knowledge about politics at all, much in the way that we seem to be losing our familiarity with the religious mode.[12]

II

Before entering into a discussion of the structure of transfigurations from one conceptual framework to another, it is necessary to investigate what exactly is involved in having a given conceptual framework for politics. To paraphrase a famous question of Kant: How is (any) particular form of normal politics possible?

I might make here a distinction between a realm of unquestioned propositions and a realm of unquestionable ones.[13] If a statement is unquestionable, men (some men, some of the time) refrain from questioning it, either from lack of time, or dimness of insight, or from strength of moral compulsion. Any society depends on a number of unquestionable assertions; indeed, they determine its nature and character. In the Declaration of Independence: "We hold these truths to be self-evident." In other words, for there to be the "we" that is properly American, *these* truths must be *held* to be self-evident. By implication, such truths are not naturally self-evident; otherwise, there would not be all the fuss. Men can apparently however hold them to be so, that is, agree that these truths should form the code by which other actions will be governed. (Incidentally, this should give some clue as to the particular insecurity Americans have about their identity and to the necessity of various institutions designed to eliminate "un-American" behavior.) An unquestionable proposition is one that can be referred back to a realm that legitimates it; in the case of the Declaration of Independence, it is the act of commonly holding. If it were one of the Ten Commandments, it would be that "God so ordered." In both cases, the legitimating source is deemed sufficient.

The ebb and flow of quarrels about such a class of propositions (i.e., does the Constitution guarantee the inviolability of private property? Can Communists be forced to register? etc.) are the very fabric of politics. These issues are, however, made possible – that is, one can quarrel about them – only because a more basic structure of political life has been accepted. This structure constitutes the realm of the unquestioned. An example drawn from the world of physics may perhaps serve to elucidate the difference. In 1881, Michelson and Morley undertook a famous experiment to determine the effect on the speed of light of the ether drag. They set up an elaborate apparatus that should have given them a definite figure of the influence of the speed of the movement of the earth upon the speed of light. After painstaking experimentation, they found no such difference and concluded that something must have gone wrong with their experiment. We know now, of course, that their experiment showed what was in fact the case, that the speed of light is not relative to the speed of the source of its origin. One might be tempted to conclude here that the Michelson-Morley experiment proves what Einstein discovered some years later. This, however, is a mistake. Michelson-Morley proves Einstein only if we are operating with a concept of length and velocity characteristic of relativistic theorists. I want to claim here with Paul Feyerabend that Michelson and Morley were using conceptions of length appropriate to a Newtonian context, and that given this context there was no way that they could have concluded anything about their experiment except that it was a failure.[14] The class of presuppositions delineating what one means by length (in a given context) forms an unquestioned group of absolute presuppositions about the structure of the particular world that we are investigating. They are, in fact, definitive of that structure: One would not know how to ask a meaningful question about relativistic length and, at the same time, be doing relativistic physics. If we are going to do physics now, we have in fact accepted this understanding.[15]

The sort of change that occurs between different periods of common knowledge will then be of a radical sort. If Kuhn, and Marx, and Quine, and others have anything to tell us, it is certainly that the dimensions by which one (historical) perspective is informed may be very different from those by which another is informed.[16] The sort of change that takes place between two political and scientific epochs is not simply a matter of the conclusions about the proper form of the state, but rather such a change is central to the whole of what might count as politics, of what counts as evidence and what as fact, and of what is contentious and what might appear secure. For instance, most facts we associate today with childhood simply were not available to people living in the seventeenth century. It is only in modern times that we have thought a child something other than a small adult. It is not until Rousseau and Pestalozzi that the modern notion of children as a separate sort of being fully emerges.[17] A whole realm of statements and claims presently entertained about children and even made the subject for scientific information would simply have been unintelligible 250 years ago. It is not that knowledge was incomplete then (was our knowledge of physics incomplete without Einstein?), but rather that the (whole) world in which men lived did not include beings such as we now see as children.

We know, however, that people and societies have made the move from one context of understanding to another. Indeed, we know from anthropological and social-psychological studies that rites of passage perform this function on an individual level every generation. We also know that in politics, as in physics, we associate these shifts with the writings and theories of one or a number of individuals. Copernicus, Newton, Einstein, Machiavelli, Hobbes, Rousseau: I do not think that our identification of changes with men is merely a matter of shorthand. These men have formulated an understanding of the world in a manner so powerful that subsequent generations approached the world in their manner.

III

Thus far I have characterized periods of normal life as those in which a certain conceptualization of the world holds sway, such that when confronted with a problem one knows (or could know) what to do. Each such period, then, has a rough rationality and common sense appropriate to

it.[18] I noted also that shifts in the realm of the unquestioned do take place.
I am not interested here in what causes such changes to happen (such is
the problem that exercises both Marx and Kant in their own ways), but
in the structure of the process in which such changes are in fact made.
We know that men and women went from living in a realm where politics
was conceived in a feudal manner to one in which it was thought of in a
bourgeois manner. How does a person go from seeing the world in one way
to seeing it in another?

Analyzing this question is particularly difficult. Most of the cases I shall
deal with below are drawn from individual experience: The group experience is only suggested by extension from that of the person. Nonetheless,
they seem to me to suggest a way to begin to look at this problem: What
transpires when men move from one context to another? What are the
states through which they pass? What is their relationship to those who
prepare the new context for them? We have some knowledge from anthropological studies of rites of passage about the physical and psychological
dynamics of the movement from childhood to adulthood. We know, to use
Victor Turner's phrase, that the individual goes through a "liminal" period, generally outside of the village, where he is neither what he has been,
nor yet what he is going to be, and that such a loss of identity appears to
be a necessary stage in the transition.[19] But can such a process be further
unpacked? And how can one describe the nature of writings so convincing
that their understanding becomes internalized to the point of becoming
natural and unquestioned?

An immediately accessible example of this experience seems to me to
occur in the act of being a member of an audience at a dramatic representation. During such times, one accepts principles of behavior characteristic of being-an-audience, which are different than those of everyday
life. We have all heard the story of the racist running up onto the stage
at the end of *Othello*. Why does his behavior seem wrong? In fact, why *is*
it wrong? The answer here must be determined by the particular quality
of a spectator's relation to and understanding *as a member of the audience*
of what is happening on stage. I would suggest that the would-be rescuer
of Desdemona is out of place and time because he has not come to accept,
for the time at least, the fact that what transpires on stage has an existence
appropriate unto itself; he has failed to acknowledge that he is a member
of an audience.

Some writing is best analyzed, as Stanley Fish has persuasively argued,
not in terms of what it means, but rather in terms of what it does to those
who are its audience. Indeed, the search for the meaning of a drama, or

of a piece of political theory, may be a misguided enterprise. Perhaps, Fish remarks, "the word 'meaning' should be discarded, since it carries with it the notion of message or point. The meaning of an utterance . . . is its experience – all of it – and that experience is immediately compromised the moment you try to say anything about it."[20] So, also, here I seek in drama (and in political theoretical writing) not the meaning,[21] but rather the manner in which the drama works. To understand how drama works, we must see what it does.

To be an audience is to be moved, not simply to sit passively and take in. The audience for *The Eumenides* was transformed; that for *End-game* may be forced to confront both themselves and the meaning of art.[22] As audience we cannot deny that something did take place: So much must be acknowledged. I shall attempt here to give an extended analysis of this compulsion and try to make some sense of the relation between stage and audience in a play. The theater provides a good entry into our problem because as a member of an audience one may acknowledge the force and feel the effect of what is going on on stage without having to worry about the reality or truth of the events.[23]

Nietzsche's analysis of these matters remains, I think, among the most incisive. I do not intend here to deal with all the problematic aspects of the historical validity of his opinions on *Euripides* or the origin of the chorus. What matters is his analysis of how tragedy produced its effect, an analysis that he sought for some time to transplant into Germany through the music drama of Richard Wagner. Characteristically, Nietzsche places great emphasis on the physical relation of the audience and the stage in Greek theater. The setting and perspective are preliminary necessities for the transformation that is sought. In the eighth chapter of the *Birth of Tragedy* he writes:

A public of spectators as we know it was unknown to the Greeks: in their theatres, the terraced structure of the concentric arcs of the spectator place made it possible for everyone actually to overlook the whole world of culture around him and to imagine, in stated contemplation, that he was a chorist (my translation).[24]

The German word for "overlook" is *übersehen*. Both languages permit the double meaning, intended by Nietzsche, of "survey" and "fail to see." I interpret this passage to mean that the audience, "in sated contemplation," has before it during the time that it was in the particular location of the "spectator place" only that which was on stage. The intensity of the focus was such that the rest of the world could at the same time be taken into account, ignored, and subsumed onto the stage (which is that particular German concept, not explicitly used here by Nietzsche, of *Aufhebung*).

As spectators, the audience knows that there is nothing that it can do about anything that occurs on stage. Indeed, this is what makes one an audience member, as opposed to a well-meaning redneck. Everything that occurs on stage has an awful necessity to it (particularly, in Greek drama where, as Nietzsche emphasizes, the plot is known) and thus there is nothing that anyone can do about the drama unrolling before his eyes, even though he knows the outcome. The spectator then will not, Nietzsche continues, "run up on stage and free the god from his torments."

On stage, in addition to the various protagonists, there is the chorus, "natural beings," as Nietzsche continues, "who live ineradicably, as it were, behind all civilization and remain eternally the same, despite the change in generations and the history of nations." The chorus only witnesses the action; in this it is much like the spectators who also do not act, but only behold "in rapt contemplation" the action on stage. To know the truth about a situation so profoundly that one can do nothing about it, is, according to Nietzsche, the basic characteristic of the "Dionysian." Thus both the spectators and the chorus are in a "Dionysian state."[25]

Relations between the events taking place and their spectators are, however, not reciprocal. The actors on the stage are in the presence of the audience – they are seen. The reverse is not true. The audience is not in acknowledged presence of the actors. (A familiar phenomenon: The play is broken if an actor talks with a spectator.) The players do not recognize the audience, and there is no way in which the audience, as audience, can compel the action on stage to acknowledge it.

This analysis allows Nietzsche to make sense of exactly how an audience might be transformed and educated to new cultural and social demands. The *Oresteia,* after all, is on one level a trilogy about competing principles of social organization, which it presents as equals, along with an outline of their possible resolution.[26] (Such resolution and rebirth was the intended effect of Wagner's work.) According to Nietzsche's reading of the audience-stage relationship, the audience (who do not relate to the stage in a reciprocated manner) is, by virtue of its Dionysian state, emotionally swept up onto the stage through the equally Dionysian medium of the chorus. In the same section of the *Birth of Tragedy,* Nietzsche writes: "The proceeding of the tragic chorus is the dramatic protophenomenon: to see oneself [as embodied in the chorus] transformed before one's very eyes [as spectator] and to begin to act as if one had actually entered into another body, another character . . . And this phenomenon is encountered epidemically: a whole throng experiences this magic transformation."

Such a transformation, or at least the seeds of it, lasts beyond the moment of the theater. For Nietzsche, this is the important social and cultural aspect of the play; the illusion created in the theater and accepted by the audience must be so powerful that it makes a potentially permanent and on-going difference in the audience much in the way that a congregation might be moved by one of Donne's sermons or a Puritan community might discuss the theological issues of that day's sermon as a matter of immediate theoretical significance.

It is important to understand here that Nietzsche does not find the message in Aeschylus particularly important. The dramatist is not arguing for one side over another; he writes neither plays of propaganda, nor dramas of resignation. Indeed, the didacticism implicit in the former is only appropriate to a world in which common knowledge is basically secure and in which a writer may thus concentrate on matters of practical, as opposed to theoretical, importance. Rather, Aeschylus is trying to provide a context for making sense of the various competing and diverse aspects of the confused moral and political landscape of the time. It is thus not inaccurate to speak of him as attempting to ground, through artistic means, a new moral community in a sort of new unquestioned absolutes, a renewed state from a new foundation.[27] Merleau-Ponty writes eloquently of this process. Speaking of Husserl, he notes that this philosopher uses

the fine word *Stiftung* – foundation, establishment – . . . to designate those operations of culture which open a tradition, continue to have value after their historical appearance, and require beyond themselves acts [*opérations*] both other and the same, in which they perpetually come to life again and again . . . [This tradition is], as Husserl remarks, the power to forget origins, to give to the past not a survival, which is the hypocritical form of, but the efficacy of repetition or life, which is the noble form of memory.[28]

In such a *Stiftung,* the past is annihilated: It no longer persists as a possibility. Merleau-Ponty is here referring to the grounding of a new artistic style or vision, but his remarks would seem to apply to the development of any new metaphorical or symbolic system of representing the world. It is convincing as any successful metaphor must be not because it describes the world better, but because it represents it more satisfactorily. As Clifford Geertz has remarked:

The power of a metaphor derives precisely from the interplay between the discordant meaning it symbolically coerces into a unitary conceptual framework and from the degree to which that coercion is successful in overcoming psychic resistances such semantic tension inevitably generates in anyone in the position to perceive it.[29]

Such regrounding is the possible result of many, if not all, kinds of dramatic writing. (One might argue here about Brecht and the Living Theater, but I think they serve only to raise precisely these questions.) Such situations seem to me to strongly resemble what Aristides Zolberg has called "moments of madness," which occur during the early stages of a revolutionary situation. Such moments when "all is possible," are precisely times when all concerned integrate their life into a new form, indelibly marked by that immediate experience. Anyone who participated in the various important political movements in the United States since 1960, such as the early civil rights movement, the various student revolts, or the draft resistance, knows what communities were founded and remain resonant from those times. *Stiftung* is an ever-recurrent possibility in times of chaos, when "imagination takes power."[30]

Drama, however, is written, not just enacted and experienced; as this also is true of political theory, we must investigate the dynamics of that sort of writing best structured to produce the change of conceptualization. To paraphrase Abbie Hoffmann, there is a manner in which one may legitimately say that the role of the political theorist is to shout theater in a crowded fire. It is true that such transformations of perception are rare and revolutionary. But it will not do to conclude as Althusser, for instance, seems to have, that a writer only has effect when what he writes coincides with, catalyzes, and overdetermines a particular situation.[31] The inertia or dynamism of history is not the only kinetic force: We must reckon also with the production of conviction and action on the part of those who come in contact with the new word.

IV

Wittgenstein has probed, perhaps deeper than anyone else, into the traps that language can lay and the convictions that it can elicit. He is concerned to liberate men and women from the illusions from which they do not know they suffer;[32] his analysis of how these traps operate provides a good entry into the manner in which language may create conviction. I propose to examine here in a very brief fashion Wittgenstein's understanding of discourse, in the hope that it may provide some solutions to our problem.

It is generally known that the later writings of Wittgenstein adopt neither the essay form characteristic of most recent Anglo-American thought, nor the numbered paragraphs associated with his earlier thought and much writing about logic, nor yet the treatise favored by Continental

writers. Instead, the *Philosophical Investigations* are a series of sequen-
tially numbered paragraphs, which he characterizes as remarks. Sometimes these form a fairly long chain; often there seem to be abrupt switches
in subject matter. The most important linking feature, Wittgenstein
claims, is that the "thoughts should proceed from one subject to another
in a natural and unbroken order." Wittgenstein recalls that he had made
several unsuccessful attempts to fashion a whole out of his writings, but
had realized that he

should never succeed. The best that I could write would never be more than
philosophical remarks; my thoughts were soon crippled if I tried to force them on
in any single direction against their natural inclination – and this way, of course,
was connected with the very nature of the investigation. For this compels us to
travel over a wide field of thought criss-crossed in every direction. – The philosophical remarks in this book are, as it were, a number of sketches of landscapes
which were made in the course of these long and involved journeyings.[33]

These remarks are prefatory to the body of the *Philosophical Investigations* and are, I think, deserving of close attention. As far as I know, with
the exception of a few essays, the form and intention of the *Investigations*
has received little attention.[34] Key perhaps is Wittgenstein's contention
that the course and presentation of his thought make necessary the peculiar
format that he selects. An intention of the book may be expressed in the
following collage of citations. Wittgenstein wishes to "assemble reminders
for the particular purpose" (#127) of "treating an illness" (#225), which
will allow one to be capable of "stopping doing philosophy" when one
wants to. (#133) Such an aim can have many targets. For one, it would
seem that Wittgenstein seeks a solution to the "problem of metaphysics,"
which Kant identifies at the beginning of the second preface to the *Critique
of Pure Reason.* For another, he seems to argue that most traditional
philosophy reflects somehow a diseased intellect or soul. Most important
here is, however, the sort of conviction that Wittgenstein wishes to elicit
in the audience of his philosophy. Stanley Cavell has written eloquently
about this matter and I cite him here at length.

[T]here is virtually nothing in the *Investigations* which we should ordinarily call
reasoning; Wittgenstein asserts nothing which could be proved, for what he asserts
is either obvious (#126) – whether true or false – or else concerned with what condition, whether by proof, evidence or authority, reasoning would consist in. Otherwise there are questions, jokes, parables, and propositions so striking (the way lines
are in poetry) that they stun near belief. (Are we asked to believe that "if a lion
could talk we could not understand him"? [II, p. 233].) Belief is not enough. Either
the suggestion penetrates past the assessment and becomes part of the sensibility
from which assessment proceeds, or else it is philosophically useless.[35]

The last lines are the most important. Wittgenstein is not aiming at convincing a person or an audience of the validity of a particular position. Instead, he is trying to make that position seem natural, very much in the sense that I described. Such an unquestioned natural *Stiftung* was also achieved for the spectators in the audience-stage relationship in Aeschylean drama. Much as Wagner for Nietzsche was to make "art become natural," so Wittgenstein wishes to (re-) make the world around us natural, to present it to us in such a manner that no possible doubt whatever might remain.

If this analysis of the strategy of drama and the investigations of Wittgenstein be correct, they confront us with a common central concern. For human beings to change their lives and for that change to be permanent and significant, no doubt at all must remain about the truthfulness of the new conditions under which one comes to act. To have no doubt at all is to live in a realm of the unquestioned. It is to have words and a grammar by which one can make some sense to oneself and to others of the world around. It is a change in the consciousness of who one is and of the world in which one lives. "Presume not that I am the thing I was," the newly crowned Henry V proclaims to Falstaff, in a great moment of self-consciousness. "For God doth know, so shall the world perceive, that I have turned away from my former self." To have the words and actions to formulate such a change is to have effectuated the transformation: So one might understand the dramatic activity of political theorists.

V

The question may now be posed as to the techniques that stand available to a political theorist in our day and age. I have suggested elsewhere the proposition that the relation of words to the world is significantly different in our age than in previous ages.[36] Indeed such fears for the growing ineffectiveness of political language are at least as old as Thucydides's analysis of the rhetoric of Athens caught up in the throes of the end of the Peloponnesian War and as recent as George Orwell's elaboration of Newspeak. Such concerns reflect a fear that we are increasingly in a political situation in which no words will be of any use. This was the predicament I noted at the very beginning of this paper. In such a situation, how may a political theorist write or construct an argument so as to symbolize and elaborate a particular way of seeing the world? When all past political metaphors seem to have failed, does there remain a grammar for political theory? The relationship of language and political life in the *polis* dissolved and left, as J. P. Vernant's analysis seems to show, nothing in its place. It took the notion of community, as elaborated by early Christian religious thought, to bring politics back into a meaningful relationship with human beings.[37] However, since no contemporary political theorists, at least none of whom I know, may pretend to play the role of Christ, are there any more modest devices that might be serviceable? In the writings of Nietzsche and Wittgenstein, I find a number of signs that seem to point to an answer.

First among these is silence. I mean: not saying anything. This will perhaps prove to be the most controversial, or at least the most unsatisfactory, for writers about politics are perhaps as naturally garrulous as politicians. Yet, if the changes in our political world are of the magnitude and scope that they appear to be, there are many situations about which we not only do not know precisely what to say, but where anything we say would necessarily be wrong. The forcefulness of the plays of Beckett is their ability to evoke precisely this awareness of our condition, that now in politics, as in the past in religion (and, as Nietzsche argued, in the future in morality), men wait in an endgame, unable to stop, yet unsure of why they keep on going. We have all encountered such situations in our personal life, and we know the difficulty we have in simply shutting up. It is, I contend, the first step toward the acknowledgment of our humanity to recognize that sometimes there may simply be nothing to say. ("Why" Beckett was asked, "with your despair about language and the human condition, do you keep on writing? – That's what I am trying to find out.") Cordelia knew this, even if Lear never learned.

Perhaps this is not much of a contribution. However, the first prerequisite for the dramatic transformation that I noted as characteristic of the audience relationship established in Greek drama was precisely this Dionysian element of self-knowledge and helplessness. Silence is certainly not the last word in such matters; it is not even the first word. But it may be a necessary preliminary step to realize that at a given point there is nothing one may say about, for instance, the trial of the Chicago Seven, which is not somehow distorting. Whatever one may say will inevitably become ideological – a choice that one may perhaps not want to refuse, but that should not be mistaken for theory. In fact, in times of social chaos, direct argumentative discourse must often be ideological. If there be no generally accepted epistemic community in politics, then to argue for a point of view will seem hopelessly one sided. Government itself, as Hegel notes in the chapter on "Absolute Freedom and Terror" in *The Phenomenology of Mind* can only "exhibit itself . . . as a faction."[38]

In such times, silence is probably a necessary preliminary step. If possible, theorists associated with a transformation of language such as those I have noted must abandon the essay or treatise for a more dramatic form of writing. Wittgenstein knew this about philosophy: Writing must now by its own existence create and select an audience.

A few forms of discourse do seem to accomplish this. We have looked at the play; indeed historically the periods immediately preceding epic political theory have been ones of great drama, as in Greece and Elizabethan England. A full analysis of modern drama would be necessary to completely develop this notion;[39] however, some techniques characteristic of modern philosophy and literature do appear to develop the sorts of relations between text and reader that made the sort of dramatic development I have discussed possible.

In Nietzsche and Wittgenstein, especially, one finds extensive use of the aphorism. The most important rhetorical fact about an aphorism is the built-in dramatic activity of the reader. At first encounter, an aphorism may appear meaningful to a reader, or superficial, or trivially true, or simply nonsense. The writing itself thus provokes an automatic selectivity of interest; only those who feel touched and moved will continue to listen. Those who do not react, will not react: In an important sense, the aphorism is not meant for them. Hence, if the aphorism read seems truistic, or patently false, or nonsensical, it will be forgotten, and jog perhaps only thoughts as to the foolishness of men who might consider such statements meaningful. If, on the other hand, one is touched and responds, then something has been stirred. Only at this point can exegesis begin and can the aphorism start its work. In a sense, the aphorism is the pure fool of discourse; the attempt to find it out, to discover its nature and name, will stir up the fermentation that rests within it, much in the way that Oedipus brings himself to light. An aphorism then presents itself as an answer for which we do not know the question. The reader in discovering the question finds the world that makes the aphorism common-sensically true.

The activity of building the question for the answer we might feel available admits of formal categorical thought only with great difficulty. Since one is trying to reconstruct and recover the landscape that makes the aphorism the case, contextualization and conceptualization are necessary. The aphorism is not out there, waiting to be assimilated to preexistent categories: The breakdown of preexisting categories is the problem, and it is new categories that make the aphorism show sense that we must uncover. If an aphorism breaks in, like the Furies it must be dealt with. A serious reader of an aphorism is forced to participate in the creation of a world, for without such creation, the aphorism will not exist at all; if, however, sufficiently ruminated, it may penetrate below the point of simple acquiescence until it seems perfectly and transparently true. The situation of something being obviously true corresponds to the establishment of a set of unquestioned presuppositions that, we argued, were the aim of political theory. To have found an aphorism is to have created a world.

A second style of discourse that produces a possible recontextualization in its readers is the riddle. This seems to be, in fact, an appropriate form of philosophical discourse when nothing other than perfect clarity will do. In a riddle, the reader is given a set of seemingly unrelated elements ("black and white and red all over"). Here he or she is asked to come up with a constitutive logic for this landscape ("what is . . . ?"). When the seeker has arrived at an answer, the problem itself disappears; such, of course, was the traditional fate of the Sphinx. It is literally impossible for a riddle to pose a problem twice, so much so that we tend even to avoid putting ourselves in the position of asking a riddle to someone already informed. ("Stop me if you know this one.")

Riddles are then possible forms of inquiry and discourse appropriate to situations in which one does not know one's way about with the material at hand, when, in other words, the problems are of a philosophical and theoretical nature. The apparently innocent beginning of Rousseau's *Social Contract* – "Man is born free and is everywhere in chains. How did he arrive in this state? I don't know. What can render it legitimate? That is the intention of this work" – expresses Rousseau's intention to bind morally together those elements of the social world of which he had previously shown the anthropological constitutive logic and division in the *Discourse on Inequality*.[40] There he demonstrated the derivation of the gulf separating man and citizen; in the *Social Contract,* he attempts to make sense of those facts of contemporary society that appear to him as a riddle. "How is it that man is born free and is everywhere in chains?"

The riddle is, however, a problematic form of discourse: It must be posed. The words "born free and everywhere in chains" are always paradoxical; they are not a riddle until someone and some events make them such. The riddle is a formulation of events, the form of discourse where all the data are given. The problem is not to uncover some new element, which will bring all of the other ones into some coherence, but rather to figure out a way to see the already existent data in such a way that they make sense together.[41] All that we need is there to know; the answer will make clear what is going on, so much so that one may feel mildly upset at

having missed one riddle like the one before it. Lévi-Strauss has analyzed
the structure of riddles and (unwittingly) brings out its potential political
theoretical use. The riddle brings "together elements doomed to remain
separate . . . (T)he answer (to a riddle) succeeds, against all expectations
in getting back to its question."[42] One may then think of a riddle as a
metaphor in the making. To quote Clifford Geertz again: "When a meta
phor works, it transforms a false identification . . . into an apt one [and
can become an] extrinsic source of information in terms of which human
life can be patterned."[43] Once a metaphor is accepted, social action is
possible.[44]

VI

All this may be scant consolation to those who wish a formulation of the
political world of sufficient grace and power to prevent the autism of
violence. We are, however, without speech for a political community. Such
a lack of a controlling vision is perhaps what Nietzsche had in mind when
he lamented the disappearance of philosopher statesmen in our times and
predicted thereupon the advent of "wars for possession of the earth," such
as men have "never seen." Discourse such as considered above will not
provide a handbook of "do's" and "don't's": Machiavellianism knows only
of the past.

Such discourse will be inherently political in form and may enable us to
again understand the world in a political manner. It reminds us of the
necessary and permanent disjuncture between the claim of the individual,
outrageous though it seem in riddle or aphorism, and the particular social
arrangement toward which such a claim is directed, though that world be
as empty as the present community of discourse. Additionally, and perhaps
more importantly, although work done in such a vein may appear foolish
and foolery, if done well it can only attest to what remains an ultimate
hope, that men and women be serious and responsible enough to themselves and each other to choose that their work be witness to their words.[45]

The selection of dramatic metaphors for my discussion is not simply a
matter of convenience or intrigue. Art cannot name that which besets the
contemporary polity, any more than it might provide a remedy. It can
however force upon a writer and his or her audience a responsibility for
such discourse that, done seriously, can provide us with a world that,
whether we accept or reject it, we must nonetheless acknowledge. After
all, we may not be persuaded by a play, but if it be a good play, we have

no choice but to recognize that it is there. And drama may then become
the first step toward prose.

ACKNOWLEDGMENT

A much earlier version of this was given at the APSA meetings December of 1971.
I am grateful to the comments of the panelists, especially Aristides Zolberg.
Thanks also to Robert Eden and Helene Keyssar Franke.

NOTES

1 See Hannah Arendt, "Reflections on Violence," *New York Review of Books,*
   February 27, 1970; and her comments on Melville's Billy Budd in *On Revolution* (New York: Viking, 1963), pp. 73ff; I have explored this topic more fully
   in a forthcoming essay entitled "Civil Disobedience and Legitimacy."

2 See Michael Walzer, *The Revolution of the Saints* (Cambridge, Mass.: Harvard
   University Press, 1965) and his "On the Role of Symbolism in Political
   Thought," *Political Science Quarterly* (1967).

3 Thomas Hobbes, *Leviathan,* Chapter 16; he is not the first of course. Ramifications and problems with this new and modern notion of the individual are
   to be found in Machiavelli and Shakespeare (*Henry VI,* 3; *Richard III*; Henry
   IV, 2).

4 Thomas S. Kuhn, *The Structure of Scientific Revolutions* (Chicago: University
   of Chicago Press, 1962). See my "The Activity of Political Science as Science"
   APSA 1973 mimeo. See also Derek Phillips, "Paradigms and Incommensura-
   bility," *Theory and Society* 2, 1 (1975):37-61; and Norwood R. Hanson, *Patterns of Discovery: An Inquiry into the Conceptual Foundations of Science*
   (Cambridge University Press, 1970).

5 See W. H. Greenleaf, *Order, Empiricism and Politics* (London: 1964).

6 See, though, Thomas S. Kuhn, "Reflections on my Critics," *Criticism and the
   Growth of Knowledge,* ed. I. Lakatos and A. Musgrave (London and New
   York: Cambridge University Press, 1970), pp. 231-78.

7 The literature here is immense, but see: Stanford M. Lyman and Marvin B.
   Scott, *A Sociology of the Absurd* (New York: Appleton-Century-Crofts, 1970),
   pp. 89-111 and 71-7; Erving Goffman details the mechanisms by which such
   disorientation can be achieved in *Asylums,* pp. 14-66. Such considerations
   also lie at the bottom of Hannah Arendt's argument in "Truth and Politics"
   in *Between Past and Future* (New York: Viking, 1968), pp. 227-64.

8 If one can get through the kooky language and the fact that he does not mind
   the change, the whole process is well described in Norman O. Brown, *Love's
   Body* (New York, 1966). See the bemused response by Herbert Marcuse,
   "Review" in *Negations* (Boston: Beacon Press, 1968).

9 Burkart Holzner, *Reality Construction in Society* (Cambridge, Mass.: Alfred Schenkman, 1972), pp. 183ff. (This book came out the same time as Peter L. Berger and Thomas V. Luckmann's better known *The Social Construction of Reality* (Garden City, N.Y.: Doubleday, 1967) and is, I think, clearer and occasionally more sound.)

10 Ludwig Wittgenstein, *On Certainty* (Oxford: Basil Blackwell, 1969), p. 15, #96.

11 Richard Bernstein, *Praxis and Action* (Philadelphia: University of Pennsylvania Press, 1971), p. 282.

12 This, after all, is the meaning of Nietzsche's observation that "God is dead," as it is that of Weber's *Entzauberung der Welt.*

13 This distinction has a close cousin in R. G. Collingwood's "absolute" and "relative" presuppositions in his *An Essay on Metaphysics* (Chicago: University of Chicago Press, 1972). A link between Kuhn and Collingwood is drawn in Stephen Toulmin, "Conceptual Revolutions in Science," in *Boston Studies in the Philosophy of Science,* vol. 4, ed. R. Cohen and M. Wartofsky (Dordrecht: Reidel, 1969), pp. 331–37.

14 See P. K. Feyerabend "Consolations for the Specialist," in *Criticism and the Growth of Knowledge,* p. 221. See also his "Against Method," *Minnesota Studies in the Philosophy of Science,* vol. 5, ed. M. Radner and S. Winokur (Minneapolis: University of Minnesota Press, 1970). See W. Sellars, *Science, Perception and Reality* (New York: Humanities Press, 1963), pp. 124 and 328.

15 See my "The Activity of Political Science as Science," pp. 22–5 and the references cited there.

16 I am not sure how far W. V. O. Quine would accept the adjective "historical," but see his "Two Dogmas of Empiricism," *From a Logical Point of View* (Cambridge, Mass.: Harvard University Press, 1964); "Meaning and Translation" in *On Translation,* ed. R. Brouwer (Cambridge, Mass., 1959) and "The Scope and Language of Science," *British Journal in the Philosophy of Science* (1957):1–17.

17 See Philippe Ariès, *Centuries of Childhood* (New York: Random House, 1965).

18 The notion of "Common Sense as a Cultural System" has been developed in a manner importantly relevant to my considerations here in an unpublished paper by Clifford Geertz, "Common Sense as a Cultural System" (Princeton, IAS, 1973). I am grateful to Dr. Geertz for making this paper available to me.

19 Victor Turner, *The Ritual Process* (Ithaca: Cornell University Press, 1967), pp. 94ff., esp. p. 106.

20 Stanley E. Fish, *Self-Consuming Artifacts* (Berkeley: University of California Press, 1972), p. 425. See also Helene Keyssar-Franke, "The Play's the Thing," *Educational Theatre Journal* (1974).

21 I must reiterate here, and as much as I can, that I am concerned with how political theory works, how it becomes convincing. I repeat that while the question of the content of political theory is a related question, it is not the only way of approaching such matters. I suspect that the concentration solely

on content leads to the judgment that "political theory is all subjective" or that "political theory is all ideology in disguise" (whatever these epithets mean).

22 See Stanley Cavell, *Must We Mean What We Say?* (New York: Charles Scribner's Sons, 1969), pp. 115–62. I owe a general debt to Cavell's work, which it is a pleasure to acknowledge.

23 I suspect the country of Kierkegaard's "teleological suspension of the ethical" to be similar territory.

24 The most developed analysis of the physical characteristics of Greek theaters and temples bears out Nietzsche's analysis. See Vincent Scully, *The Earth, The Temple and The Gods: Greek Sacred Architecture* (New York, 1969) for a breath-taking investigation. Translations by the author in the text are from Nietzsche's *Gesammelte Werke, Musarionausgabe*, 23 vols. (Munich, 1920–29).

25 I have developed this notion of Dionysian extensively in my *Friedrich Nietzsche and the Politics of Transfiguration* (Berkeley and Los Angeles: University of California Press, 1975).

26 See inter alia, H. D. F. Kitto, *Form and Meaning in Drama* (New York: Barnes & Noble, 1957).

27 The best example of such a conscious concern in American history that I know of is Abraham Lincoln, "Address Before the Young Men's Lyceum," *Collected Works*, 1, ed. Roy P. Basler (New Brunswick, N.J.: Rutgers University Press, 1953), pp. 108–15. For commentary, see material in Harry Jaffa, *Crisis of the House Divided* (Seattle: University of Washington Press, 1973); and Edmund Wilson, *Patriotic Gore* (New York: Oxford University Press, 1966).

28 Maurice Merleau-Ponty, *La Prose du monde* (Paris, 1968), p. 197 (my translation). A full translation by John O'Neill appeared as *The Prose of the World* (Evanston, Ill.: Northwestern University Press, 1973).

29 Clifford Geertz, "Ideology as a Cultural System," in *Contemporary Analytical Theory*, ed. D. Apter and C. Andrain (Englewood Cliffs, N.J.: Prentice-Hall, 1972), p. 195.

30 Aristides Zolberg, "Moments of Madness," *Politics and Society* (1972).

31 L. Althusser, *Pour Marx* (Paris: Maspero, 1965).

32 The best analyses I know of here are Cavell, *Must We Say What We Mean?*, Chapter 3 and H. Pitkin, *Wittgenstein and Justice* (Berkeley: University of California Press, 1972).

33 Wittgenstein, *On Certainty*, Preface.

34 Aside from the material mentioned in n. 32, see R. Goff, "Aphorism as Lebensform," in *New Essays in Phenomenology*, ed. James Edie (New York: Quadrangle); and E. Heller, "Nietzsche and Wittgenstein," in *The Artist's Journey into the Interior*.

35 Cavell, *Must We Say What We Mean?*, p. 71.

36 Tracey Strong, "Hold on to Your Brains: An Essay in Meta-Theory," in *Power and Community*, ed. P. Green and S. Levinson (New York: Pantheon, 1971).

37 See J. P. Vernant, *Mythe et pensée chez les grecs*, 2 vols. (Paris: Maspero); and S. S. Wolin, *Politics and Vision* (Boston: Little, Brown, 1960), Chapter 3.

38 G. W. F. Hegel, *The Phenomenology of Mind* (New York: Harper & Row, 1967), p. 605.

39 J. L. Styan, *The Elements of Drama* is a good but very preliminary step in this direction.

40 Jean-Jacques Rousseau, *Oeuvres complètes de J. J. Rousseau*, 13 vols. (Paris, 1865–70).

41 I have addressed the narrowness of the notion that science progresses by acquiring "new facts" in my "Activity of Political Science as Science."

42 Claude Lévi-Strauss, *The Scope of Anthropology* (London: Jonathan Cape, 1967), p. 38–9. See also the opening pages of his *La Pensée sauvage* (Paris: Plon, 1962) on games and rituals.

43 Geertz, "Ideology as a Cultural System," pp. 195 and 199.

44 Turner, *Ritual Process*, p. 36.

45 See Cavell, *Must We Say What We Mean?*, pp. 347–8 and Paul Ricoeur, *History and Truth* (Evanston, Ill.: Northwestern University Press, 1965), pp. 197–222.

9

Toward a semiotic of utopia:
Political and fictional discourse in
Thomas More's *Utopia*

LOUIS MARIN

Editors' introduction

The paradigm crises facing the human studies manifest themselves on three levels: moral philosophers' concern for what ought to be the case, social theorists' interest in what is the case, and activists' focus on how to move from the "is" to the "ought." Each of the three domains is articulated through its own form of discourse. Hence, the question arises as to the relationships between their respective grammars.

Thomas More's *Utopia* offers an occasion for the critical illumination of this problematic situation. As Louis Marin explains, in More's book there are two principal levels of discourse, the "ought" and the "is": the fictional or utopian discourse outside of time and the historical-political-economic analysis within contemporary time. Hence, the central question of Marin's essay is how these two forms of discourse can be linked.

Thomas More attempts this himself through two devices. First, all the discourses are presented as dialogs and so there is a stylistic continuity between them. Second, between the text's conversations about contemporary events and about the Isle of Utopia, there is yet a third dialog on how to advise a prince. The prince is the principal actor in the theater of practical politics. His adviser must give him not only tactical advice as to means, but also utopian advice as to ends, and his framework for that advice implicitly must be some model of what society ought to be like. Thus the role of the adviser is a strategic site at which the fictional and political forms of discourse converge.

To be useful, the prince's adviser must not be merely a philosopher; he also must be pragmatic – his advice has to work in this world. But this means that the adviser must be incremental and reformist in the specific content of what he has to say. In so doing, however, he reduces his utopia to a kind of heuristic image that may inform current policy but that normal political action can never create.

Ironically, this also is the dilemma of the contemporary political intellectual. There is no way by which current action within the established frame can reach utopia, while the utopia may exist in the mind of the philosopher adviser, so long as he is confined to the existential political discourse dictated by his current condition he can not transcend it and achieve a radical reformulation of social relations.

Yet Marin suggests a resolution of this paradox: He urges intellectuals to burst the bonds of both political and fictional discourse and to combine them in a new dialectical discourse that, while pushing off from the practical politics of the day, also begins the voyage to Utopia. Through such a dialectical method, Marin argues, literary textual analysis can become a kind of political analysis, and sociologists' analyses of society can become, self-reflectively, a kind of political advocacy.

> Time past and time future
> Allow but a little consciousness.
> To be conscious is not to be in time
> But only in time can the moment in the rose-garden
> The moment in the arbour where the rain beat,
> The moment in the draughty church at smokefall
> Be remembered; involved with past and future.
> Only through time time is conquered.
>
> T. S. Eliot

My intent in the following pages is to study and compare the political and the utopian forms of discourse in Thomas More's *Utopia*. This topic could seem somewhat literary for a collection of essays on political theory and social philosophy. Nevertheless, I have chosen it for this reason: More's *Utopia* is a rather rare, almost unique example of both forms of discourse – political analysis and a utopian vision of society – put together in one book and combined in the same literary structure.

The comparison of these two forms of discourse is already made for us, so to speak, and we have only to pay careful attention to the way in which they are connected. The very title of the work seems to reflect by a single expression the two sides of our problem: "The best state of a commonwealth" – this, the political side – "and the new island of Utopia" – this, the utopian one (More, 1964:1). Thus *Utopia* offers the exceptional opportunity to directly apply a structural literary analysis to deal with the subject matter and with the ideological and philosophical meanings involved in it. We find a ready-made textual experiment, in which we have only to separate the parts and make their relationship obvious.

But this essay would remain merely a structural analysis of More's book, a piece of literary criticism, if, in our treatment of the text, we did not show the very contemporary problem that is at stake in it: the functions and relationships of utopian and sociopolitical discourse. Today the social sciences not only study society but also intend to transform it. Implicit in such a purposive use of social-scientific knowledge is some vision of a good or at least better society. Yet can such utopian visions in fact be translated into practical social-scientific proposals? By analyzing its style and methods, we can make of More's *Utopia* an analog of the processes and relationships that might exist between discourse that defines effective means of improving the society existing here and now, and utopian discourse that displays an image or reified model of a possible society out of our grasp but having nevertheless something to do with the society in which we live. In other words, this essay is not only an attempt to reveal the static structure of a text and tentatively to relate this structure to a historical context (England at the beginning of the sixteenth century), but also, and principally, to advocate a dynamic or dialectical type of reasoning for the social sciences: a reasoning that is at once theoretical and practical – a theoretical practice that can yield practical theory – a reasoning that is both a political and a scientific discourse. Beginning as a structural analysis of a text and of a literary genre, the essay ends as a political manifesto for a certain kind of knowledge.

What is involved in More's book is the relationship of political analyses with utopian description; what is involved in the content of my discussion of it is the relationship between literary structures and social processes, actual and idealized; what is involved in the formal development of this paper is the dialectic between theoretical knowledge and political practice.

What then are the basic assumptions of my essay? We can define them on four levels: On a first level, the *conceptual* level, utopian discourse fills up a site historically and theoretically unoccupied at the time when it was expressed, the site of the dialectical resolution of an historical contradiction. Utopian discourse can be considered as the "zero degree" of the dialectical synthesis of contraries in knowledge as well as in history: It is elaborated in the gap between opposites; it expresses neither one opposite nor the other. To give an example, More's Utopia is neither a town nor a country, but it is in-between. It exists in the middle of the historical, sociological, and ideological changes that occurred at the beginning of the sixteenth century and concerns the opposition between town and country. On a second level, the level of *imagination*, utopian discourse works as an imaginary scheme of figurative text. It displays an imaginary solution, a fiction that reconciles contradictory terms; it is a simulation or simulacrum of a synthesis. That explains the specific mixture of the narrative and the descriptive modes in utopian discourse and its relation to myth as well as to theatrical stage. On a third level, the level of *representation*, a utopian scheme operates as a matrix that generates space. It organizes a fictitious place as an ordering of space. It builds a society by making places for various activities (social, religious, political, and economic), which are connected through harmoniously architected space (Marin, 1973:10–11).

If these are the basic assumptions about utopia, it appears that the structural analysis of utopian texts can be considered as the reproduction of utopian processes, but critically and at yet another level of discourse. This fourth, *methodological* level, uses a dialectical-structural analysis to reconstruct the meaning of an object, for example a text, by extracting from it sets of relations based on a logic of binary oppositions and by defining at the various levels of the analysis, through models and diagrams, generative and transformational rules of the semantic contents that were initially antithetic, to solve their opposition. We find in this rather extensive definition of structural analysis the very components of the utopian discourse as I attempted to describe it briefly above: first, a construction of a rational model by a logic of oppositions and contradictions; second, a projection of this model in a metaphorical space to visualize it; third, a regulation of the functioning of the model to integrate the oppositions and the contradictions in a nonconflicting whole. In other words, structural analysis could be considered as an example, among many others, of a utopian process in the field of social sciences today. But structuralism is utopian in this sense only when we use it critically, without reifying the model in a representation of reality, without imprisoning its explanatory and transformational power in ontological assumptions about human mind or a social unconscious, much as More's friends sought to do when they asked him: "Where is Utopia, the blessed island?"[1] The critical use of structural analysis requires an awareness of its utopian function and an effort to conceptualize its own critical consciousness as a method. But this formalization is not only an epistemological reflection on the method itself – a theory corresponding to a methodological practice within the so-called objective sphere of science – but also an attempt to display the practical (ideological and political) content implied in the very use of the method regarding its object, which is, generally speaking, society. The critical consciousness of the utopian fiction of structural analysis gives way to a dialectical use of reason in the social sciences.

In this spirit, when this essay ends with an exposition of Marxist theses about political and utopian discourses, this does not mean that the categories of Marxism are, in the mid-twentieth century, the final word of a social-scientific analysis but that, regarding the historical and ideological content of More's *Utopia*, regarding this kind of utopia, such categories are its truth. My paper by its own development, by the method it uses, shows in itself that Marxist theses on Feuerbach are not the end of historical and social sciences; rather, the very processes these categories made obvious as applied to More's *Utopia* are at work in my essay and need to be conceptualized along the lines just indicated.

Thus I shall begin with a detailed analysis of the composition of More's *Utopia* to point out the connection between a political discourse and a utopian one and to show the significations resulting from this connection. Then I shall give an example of these meaning effects by selecting the famous discussion about criminality and enclosures and its illustration by the "utopia" of the Polylerites. I shall end this essay in a more theoretical way with some general propositions in ideology, political discourse, and utopia. More precisely, in this last part of the essay, I intend to show how the dialectically structured relationships between theory and practice in More's *Utopia* affect an integration of the utopian way of thinking and of the pragmatic way of dealing with social reality. This integration seems to be the only possibility of facing and escaping two dangerous reefs social scientists encounter when, deliberately or not, they are involved in political action: dreams on the one hand – romantic revolutionism or fanciful projections – or, on the other hand, mechanistic social engineering – an attempt to reform society by merely applying to it reductivistic explanations.

I. Political discourse and utopian discourse in More's *Utopia*

As it is well known, More's *Utopia* is made of two books: the one more directly related to the contemporary state of affairs in England at the beginning of the sixteenth century; the other devoted to a description of "the newly discovered island," Utopia. A key problem facing us here is the relationships of the two books.

Book 1 begins as a historical narrative of commercial negotiations between Henry VIII, king of England, and Charles, the future Charles V, king of Spain. The date of the diplomatic talks is indirectly given by reference to an historical event in England and also by their taking place at Bruges in Flanders. During a temporary break in the negotiations, More goes to Antwerp to visit his good friend, Peter Giles, and one Sunday after the mass, on the parvis of the finest church of Antwerp, he meets Raphael Hythloday, a sailor coming back from travels in the New World. Peter

Giles tells briefly the story of Raphael, and a second meeting with Raphael occurs in the garden of More's house. During his visit, Raphael relates his travels and for the first time alludes to Utopia. Raphael refuses to fascinate his friends with tales of exotic monsters, but intends to examine laws and customs of foreign countries "living together in a civilized way" and particularly the manners and the life of Utopians (More, 1964:15).

But More defers his account of Raphael's description to report a long dialog with Peter Giles and Raphael about the counseling of a prince. Why and how to be the chief advisor of a prince? The first level narrative then reappears at the end of Book 1 after a short introductory dialog. There thus arises an essential question that leads to the heart of our problem: why this deferment of the description of Utopia? Why does More's *Utopia* have two books, one concerning mainly political and social problems, the other a description of Utopia itself? A provisory answer can be given: The fundamental law of Utopia is the common property of goods. But if communism is the right remedy to mankind's misfortunes and poverty, it is not More's solution, for More has no representation at all of a communist state. Communism cannot be argued or demonstrated. It has to be presented as a picture, which, as such, possesses its own evidence.[2] Now the difficulty concerns the connection of such a picture to discourse in general and especially to political discourse dealing with reality, with making plans and actualizing them. In deferring the description of Utopia and the exhibition of the picture of a communist state, More answers indirectly our question: There is no way of approaching Utopia. Utopia is not realizable and does not have to be realizable to have its efficacy. This is the difference between political discourse and the representation of Utopia. Why and how to give advice to kings? ask More, Giles, and Raphael. The political answer is reformism, provisional remedies, and half-way measures. But the indirect answer given by the two books and by the fact the first was written *after* the second is that political activity is useless. The only thing useful in solving the problems raised by political plans and projects is communism, and this cannot be dealt with by political discourse.[3]

We can draw a first general scheme of More's first book of *Utopia*. It is a historical-fictional narrative framing all the book; as well as a travel story told by Raphael framing the picture of Utopia; and, between the two frames, a dialog that separates the picture of Utopia from its narrative frame and that gives the picture an independent existence. The social, economic, and political content of the dialog textually isolates the utopian content from any realistic setting. It severs its links with all historical reality.

But the structure of this third, dissociating part is itself complex. We can summarize it in this way: The interlocutors come up to three real problems with three possible, partial remedies: the problem of the increasing criminality in England with its social cause, unemployment, and the causes of unemployment: enclosures and monopolies; the problem of the imperialist wars with an analysis of the international situation and of the balance of powers in Europe; and the problem of social welfare with the description of the exploitation of their subjects by monarchs and the exposition of various remedies such as restrictions on private property and money, on the power and income of kings, or on the canvassing and the purchase of public offices.

A radical and permanent solution is Utopian communism, but it is preceded by a short dialog between the statesman and the utopian traveler. More advocates the possibility of changing things little by little, by good advice and progressive reforms. Raphael thinks it is useless: "By this approach, I should accomplish nothing else than to share the madness of others as I tried to cure their lunacy" (1964:50). Utopian communism is out of the sphere of political achievements. Nevertheless it is not an unrealistic solution. Why? Because it is already realized. Where? In Utopia; that is, no-where. This rather paradoxical answer, which poses the general problem of Utopia as such and through it the question of the nature of a social "possible," is explicitly given by the author. "The kind of things which Plato creates in his Republic, the Utopians actually put in practice in theirs" (1964:50).

The issue I raise is neither a false problem nor only a stylistic one: The same device recurs three times in the political discourse itself; the same structure relating Book 1 to Book 2 is repeated in Book 1. After every political analysis and project, the political argumentation suddenly breaks and a micro-utopia is described: the Polylerites, the Achorians, the Macarians, every one of them being a step toward Utopia. These utopias are completely different from the historical examples Raphael also uses. These historical materials are to be worked up by the political discourse to test and to verify its own statements. They give material to induce the general inferences of the discourse. The utopias, in contrast, are essences inserted in the political discourse and constitute blueprints of Utopia. They designate utopian paradigms: labor and internal exchange; war and external relationships; money and means of internal and external exchanges. What are the functions of the utopian kernels in Book 1? To answer this question would be to solve the problem of the role and the meaning of utopias in history. I shall now indicate only the hypothetical principle of a solution.

Utopias are not images. They are not illustrations exemplifying the elements of the political analysis. They displace such analysis. That is, the differences between the political or historical level and the utopian one designate in effect what I call "utopian practice," the matrix producing and shaping the utopian representations that makes it visible but also blocks its power.[4]

Now as we come to the composition of Book 2, we note that its structure is the reverse of the first. The reversal will give us new lights to solve our problem. There is no dialog in Book 2. The description of Utopia is a long reply to a question asked by Raphael's friends, but it is also a terminal answer: When at the end of the book More speaks again he speaks only as a reporter of Raphael's words but not as a protagonist in the dialog. There is no narrative either. But as before, the description is part of a narrative that begins when Raphael decides to relate his travels, and it is worth noticing that Raphael does not tell the story of his return from Utopia to Portugal and England. There is no return from Utopia in the textual form either. The narrative shifts at the end of the book directly from the description to the first level narrative on which were located the meeting in Antwerp, the break of the commercial talks, and the like. So a connection is lacking between the description and the plane of the historical narration. In other words, Utopia is not only an island geographically; its description also is structurally isolated from the rest of the book. It possesses its own independence among the various stylistic and compositional devices that pattern the book as a whole. The picture is outside its frame.

But if there is neither a dialogical nor a narrative framing of Utopia, little stories are inserted within the description. They occupy the same structural position in Book 2 as the little descriptions of Book 1; the former are historical-fictional stories. Then what are their functions not only in the textual economy but as connecting elements between the political and the utopian discourses? Here too, we can only summarize these various stories. They can be grouped in three sets: At first, two foundation stories, the one at the beginning, the other at the end of the book, both focused on the eponym hero of the island, Utopus. In the first, Utopus turns a part of the continent into an island by excavating a channel "on the side where the land was connected with the continent." This violent partition is at the same time an act of naming. Abraxa becomes Utopia. It is also the transition from nature to culture: "Utopus brought the rude and rustic people to a perfection of culture and humanity" (1964:60). At last, it is the time when the division of labor is also a communion of labor: the first act of communism.

Utopus appears again, near the end of the book, when he establishes tolerance as the religious credo of the Utopians: "He made the whole matter of religion an open question" (1964:134). In his ultimate appearance, the founder of Utopia opens the closed land he built to all beliefs, to all ways of worshipping God, to the dead themselves. So we find, inserted in the descriptive frame, three structural relations between the two foundation stories:

1 from an open universe (the continent) to a closed world (the island)
2 from a closed world (religious sectarianism) to an open universe (tolerance)
3 from a mundane plane (on which the first relation takes place) to a religious plane (on which the second relation takes place)

This schematic summary induces us to consider the stories inserted in description not as independent stories destined to illustrate narratively some parts of the representation, but as episodes of a single narration that is not really a "story," but the model of the real history in which are clearly shown some features of the historical events More is involved in. At the same time, however, the model conceals the actual meaning of this history. It is an ideological representation in Marx's sense; to find the real historical structure, we have to turn upside down the representation of the relations between the structure of productive forces and the structure of social relations of production.

We also find two other types of stories: the first ones concern the relationships between Utopia and other "utopian" countries surrounding it. All deal with money, trade, commercial competition, and imperialist wars and are expressly said to illustrate utopian conceptions of economic exchanges and their results, wealth or war. In other words, these stories are negative, pejorative ones: They recall utopian expansion, its imperialism corrupting other peoples by its money, punishing heavily any bad deed in commercial matters. But we have to remember these political events occur only in the world of no-where, in representation and not in reality. By them, unexpected new events happen in utopian time: It is not a timeless duration. History is inserted in the description but in such a way as to reduce history to a mere component of the utopian representation. The picture, being fictitious, irrealizes history, but conversely, Utopia acquires some actuality by the historical time these narratives introduce to the island. And this is not a mere aesthetic device; given the contents that are at stake – war and aggressive expansion in all its forms, money and its corruptive power – it is also political.

The second type of story concerns the relationships between the real historical world – the Western World from which Raphael and his companions are coming – and the world of Utopia. "In place of wares to sell," Westerners give Utopians ancient Greek books, the art of making paper and printing (1964:103–4, 106). They also communicate some notions of the Christian religion to them. The stories of the contacts of Utopia and the Western World are all positive: They narrate the cultural assimilation of Utopia in both profane and religious domains – a quick, achieved and deep acculturation. As previously, we can summarize the analysis in stating three structural relations, giving a firm pattern to all these stories scattered in the description:

1 a relation of opposition between the fictitious world and the historical world
2 a relation of expansion from inside (the island) to outside (the other "utopian" countries) by money and war, a relation that is valorized negatively
3 a relation of assimilation from outside (Western World) to inside (Utopia) by culture and religion, a relation that is valorized positively

Our analysis has discerned again in the description of Utopia a model emerging from a description strewn with short, apparently unrelated stories. What is its meaning? It would show us the structure of actual history if and only if we reverse the relations in the model and especially if we permute the locations of history and of fiction in it. The positive and fictitious assimilation of Western culture and religion by the new world is a story that conceals the negative and real expansion of the old world by war and economic exploitation. All these stories would have been an achieved example of an ideological construction if they had not been told in their inverted images a half-century before the actual history of the exploitation of America by Europe really happened.

Thanks to these two transformations, two facts are made obvious: First, the stories enclosed in the description outline a projective model of history. (Historical time is projected into a geographical space and the contemporary period into a duration out-of-time.) By inverting these two projections, we obtain historical time and contemporary period, but in the terms of a model of history and not of history itself. Second, the model that is built in the description of Utopia is not a mimetic model homologous to reality itself. We have to invert its structures to find the true model. In other terms, it is a model pervaded by the conflicting ideologies of social classes in struggle for power. Directed against feudal aristocracy and borrowing many features from the medieval way of living, More's discourse reveals the ideology of the ascending class, the bourgeoisie in the first step of its development. But it reveals it by an ideological critique of this ideology. At the very time when Utopia maintains a flourishing trade with other countries and launches colonial and imperialist wars against some of them, the blessed island is a communist state from which money is rejected and which refuses private property.

We have to remember that this analysis concerns only the perfusion of the historical and political discourse within the description of Utopia. Description is the characteristic mode of discourse in most utopias. I am not trying, in this essay, to make a stylistic and semiotic analysis of this mode and to show how by only reading a text we construct a mental image characterized as a synoptic, total, and harmonious one. I am only pointing out the fact that More's Utopia, as many other utopias, is a poetic fiction.

What is a fiction? Here we must differentiate fiction from related notions like image, picture, even representation. Fiction operates to neutralize differences, to deny opposites, to negate contraries, and to open a free poetic space disengaged from oppositions. These are stated, but in a negative mode; they are neither suppressed nor reconciled in a superior unity. To take two examples in More's *Utopia*, Utopian fiction begins by neutralizing a geographical and political opposition that provides a content to the political discourse of the time. If America and Europe, the New World and the Old World are basic contraries, Utopia is neither Europe nor America, neither the New World nor the Old World. Its name itself reveals the poetic process that gives birth to the new island: U-topia, neither America nor Europe, no-where. If money and poverty are basic contraries in the political, social, and economic discourse assumed by More himself, Utopia, as a communist state, is neither poor nor wealthy: This is the fiction of its communist organization.

After the first operation of neutralization, there the process of composition of the contrary poles that have been negated begins. But this process of conjunction of the opposites does not express the truth of an historical or political situation, a truth that could be objected to or argued for. It lies outside the scope of a judgment of falsehood or truth. Utopia is America and Europe, but not as their reconciliation that can or could be the truth of the relationships of Europe and America. It is a new object that jolts together the differences between Europe and America and gives them a location, a shape, and a form. Likewise, Utopia knows money and poverty, not as a reconciliation of money and poverty, but as a new object totalizing the oppositions between money and poverty.

In conclusion, by utopia I mean: first, a utopian practice that neutralizes the historical, political, and real oppositions in a given society. From this point of view the utopian practice is a critical process, but one that remains incomplete as we shall see in a moment. I further mean by this term a utopian representation that totalizes the negated differences or oppositions in a textual construction and that restates them on another plane, in a new object that is no longer historical, political, and real, but poetic. It does not refer to the past, but alludes to the new, to the "possible" already at work in the present.

II. An example of the connections between
political discourse and utopian discourse

Usually it is taken for granted that the Book 1 of *Utopia* has a historical and political content: It is a lucid analysis of the political and economic situation of England at the beginning of the sixteenth century, often quoted by historians today. I shall select in this book a part of the dialog about counseling a prince, which in itself is a dialog at a dinner in John Morton's house. Morton, the archbishop of Canterbury and the chancellor of England, was known as a rather Machiavellian politician. The theme of the discussion is the increasing criminality in England and the various ways of reinforcing repression, principally by death punishment for thieves. Opposing himself to an English lawyer supporting repression, Raphael vindicates two basic assumptions; the first is religious: "Theft alone is not a grave offense that ought to be punished with death" (1964:20). The punishment is disproportionate to the offense. God has said, "Thou shall not Kill" (1964:22). The second assumption is pragmatic: "No penalty that can be devised is sufficient to restrain from acts of robbery those who have no other means of getting a livelihood" (1964:20). Raphael investigates the objective causes of criminality in England, but his inquiry is disconnected from the theological assumption according to which "Human life cannot be equivalent to money," private property cannot balance human life (1964:29). This disjunction of the causes and their legitimation, the gap between two different types of statements, is the place in which the utopian practice is at work, producing a utopian representation in the middle of the political argumentation.

In other words, the political discourse is not consistent with its legitimation; it is an unfounded discourse. There is a break between the factual, historical analysis and its critical truth, its epistemological basis: It cannot base itself scientifically. Hence the juxtaposition of the two basic statements vindicated by Raphael. But this break is significant for our critical reading. There is an objective truth that is signified by the missing link between the theological thesis and the social and economic analysis. An equivalence is established by real English law between human life and money, since a thief is convicted to death for stealing money; moreover this equation has something to do with the extension of the enclosures of sheep pastures. Yet this relationship between specific legal provisions and a specific way of exploiting land cannot be thought and determined in a critical and scientific way. So the relationship between an empirical assumption, historical or political, and its epistemological basis is exhibited by utopian representations. These representations are substituted for a conceptual framework that is missing because it was not available at the time when More was writing. Thus the only basis Raphael can provide for his political analysis is theological. God has said, "Thou shall not kill" (1964:22). Human life is not equivalent to a certain amount of money. Of the reduction of human life to a quantitative unit – which is at once ideally denounced by Raphael and actually stated by the English law – we have to find the objective truth. The latter is neither negative as in Raphael's religious assumption nor positive as in the lawyer's discourse. It lies, so to speak, on the reverse side of social reality. The utopian representation shows it, but not as a scientific or theoretical relationship, only as a representation.

Now we have to test this textual hypothesis by a close investigation of Raphael's reasoning. He states two main causes of the increasing criminality in England: the dissolution of the manorial feudal structure and the constitution of a protocapitalist economy. These two causes are the two stages of a single process entailing two results: the creation of a "lumpen proletariat" of unemployed farm workers and their exodus to towns where they become thieves.

What is Raphael's social and political solution? To reintroduce the feudal structure, but corrected, rectified by social and economic initiatives. How? By converting the noblemen's varlets, attendants, and fellows into wool craftsmen and by connecting them with farmworkers having cloth-working as complementary resources. The political reformist discourse seems socially, politically, and economically realistic. Yet, in fact, it is contradictory. Its solutions are at once archaic and modern. Its features are to be developed on the same level as the objective analysis of economic and social causes. This consists in inserting human initiatives into the text of objective historical causes and effects, initiatives that are imagined to play the same role as the objective, deterministic causes. In other words, the political discourse does not actually criticize the situation. It displays its possible solutions at the surface of the real situation as it is viewed by the politician.

Raphael's project expresses the contradiction between the feudal structure of relations of production and the development of productive forces that, in fact, demand new relations of production. The lesson we can draw from Raphael's discourse is that a real contradiction cannot work as a political project. It is not possible to join together contradictory terms as in Raphael's project of developing a wool craftmanship complementary to a polyvalent agriculture in the social structure of the manor. This project was in fact the historical policy of the kings of England at the beginning of the sixteenth century and it failed for objective reasons.

Returning to the problem of increasing criminality, Raphael explains that the thief steals money and violates the law of private property because he is led to robbery by misery and distress. In solving the problem of misery, the reformist politician will solve the problem of criminality and he will protect social order and private property. We can sketch the chain of causes and effects on which Raphael's political reasoning lies:

Peasants → unemployed people → misery → thieves → death punishment

The English lawyer keeps only the last two terms of the chain. Raphael by a more extensive analysis displays the first three steps of the process. But he does not transcend the surface of the social situation; instead, the explanation he gives, which is also a legitimation, conjoins the moral relation of idleness to misery and the social relation of misery to larceny. Yet the moral reform can only justify the economic reform; it does not explain it.

Unemployment generates idleness; idleness, misery; and misery, criminality. Hence curing idleness and misery consists in suppressing unemployment. Thus the only justified punishment is labor. But this very punishment is contradictory to the question it has to solve, since establishing this punishment (labor) comes to suppress objectively the offense for which it is intended. In other words, the legal system of punishment proposed by Raphael after his objective analysis negates the very legal system of punishment by negating its object. A deep enough reform of the social relations of production makes the reform of penal law irrelevant, but the reform itself sketched by Raphael is the projection of the contradiction that causes it.

Now it is at this moment that a utopia is invoked as a neutralization or projection, a displacement or rearticulation of the reality once portrayed. Thus the Polylerite society is described (1964:15) as a closed and hidden country, a satellite of Persia in which all needs are satisfied; its soil is fruitful and the Polylerites ignore exterior trade and war.

This micro-utopia seems an example completely irrelevant to the problem of legal punishment of larceny in Raphael's analysis: No misery means no larceny. But, in fact, there are thieves in this utopia. How is this possible since that country knows neither misery nor unemployment? There is only one explanation: The legal system of punishment in this utopia is not in fact what it seems - a penal law - but a representation of the best organization of the real society, an organization Raphael could not theorize in his actual political discourse.

The Polylerite legal punishment consists in working continuously: Convicts, who wear uniforms, are no longer individuals but interchangeable parts of the productive whole. However they receive wages (in food or in money to buy food), which are aimed only to make up their labor power. The utopian description provides a legal system of punishment for offenses that cannot occur in the terms of the utopian representation. What does this complex process mean? Only one thing. In the relationships between the whole Polylerite society and its convicts, the story makes obvious a fundamental part of its system that can be shown only regarding convicted thieves: the selling of the labor power for a salary purposely to make up this labor power. Neither the political reformist discourse developing the linear chain of causes and effects in the historical contemporary society, nor the fully utopian description of a society ignoring scarcity and consequently without private property, could show this element.

So it is necessary to sketch a model that, at one and the same time, is distanced from the historical and political reality and that is structured by its specific contradiction: a model able to show fictively the neutral possibility of its transformation. It represents a society with two classes between which only one type of exchange can exist: labor power for salary, a quantitative exchange of human power and money. And we find among the Polylerites a just equivalence of money and human life, an equivalence discarded and refused before by Raphael for theological motives.

The critical strength of utopian thought is made obvious in the model it creates. A utopia is not the inverted images of reality - not, for example,

a place where there is no thief because an ideal country ignores scarcity.
Utopia is not an inert model that mechanically inverts the negative relations of reality into positive ones. It is a critique of reality, albeit a figurative rather than a theoretical one. For the modern reader obviously, the
theoretical concept corresponding to the discrepancy between the political
analysis of reality and the utopian model is the concept of commodity
applied to labor.

Now what are the relationships between theory and practice corresponding to those between utopian representation and historical reality? One
process for decoding these relationships is the mere syntactical inversion
that signifies a real overturn of the social surface. The robbed are the
robbers and the robbers, the robbed. Proletarian workers anticipated by
Polylerites' convicted thieves are in fact the robbed class, and the bourgeois
exploiters, represented by the robbed Polylerite free citizens, are in fact
the thieves. Such a syntactic inversion of passive and active modes points
out a theoretical and practical overturn of the social surface: a theoretical
one by which its structure or its intelligibility is made obvious; a practical
one that is the revolutionizing process.

But this inversion is not achieved by the utopian discourse, which remains on the level of representation. The theoretical concepts corresponding to it by a theoretical and practical counterdisplacement and inversion
are the social and economic phenomenon of exploitation theoretically
expressed by the concept of surplus value.

A diagram can summarize our critical analysis:

Political discourse . . .	Unemployed people =	Workers	Owners = Robbed people	Sixteenth- century England
Utopian discourse . . .		Convicted thieves	Free citizens	Persia, Polylerites

III. Political discourse and utopia

Now I can draw, in a more general way, some consequences from my
analysis of Thomas More's *Utopia* about the relationships between
political and utopian forms of discourse. These consequences can be
summarized by two theses in which I use the term "ideology" in the

Marxist sense to express the basic structures of discourse. In the first thesis, I state that utopia is an ideological critique of ideology. In the second, I assume that a distinction between utopia as representation and utopian practice allows my own critique to theorize utopia, this theorizing being a critical introduction to a theory of practice.

Utopia is a critique of the dominant ideology in as much as its fictive discourse projects and displaces the historical reality into a model, a fiction that works on a different level from that on which political discourse is engaged. The critical power has two sources. On the one hand it derives from the projection of a given reality in a different place and time not located in historical time or geographical space; on the other hand, from a displacement of that reality. That is to say, the analog model resulting from the utopian projection is structured differently from the reality expressed by political discourse. Political discourse expresses reality by justifying and valorizing it positively or negatively even though it formulates plans and projects about the future. It captures reality and its dynamic processes in a closed system of ideas, the function of which is to legitimize reality according to the interests of a group class against other groups or classes. Utopia on the contrary is a representation inserted in a fable that, by the process it implies, calls in question the ideological content of political discourse. Utopias imply a questioning and estrangement that suspend the presupposed self-evidentness of political discourse to reveal its ideological basis.

The utopian critique also belongs in the same way to the ideological basis it criticizes. This is because the two operations that produce the utopian representation (projection and transvaluation or displacement) are not themselves taken into account and theorized. Thus utopian thought is ideological insofar as it remains unaware of its own methodological and epistemological basis. The utopian critique is ideological because it does not possess the theory of its critical power, the theory through which utopian discourse could become self-reflective on its own social location and interests. Utopia as such is a transvaluation of the real society, but its "negativity" remains imaginative. Utopia is created within real history, within the dominant ideology and within its self-contradictions. Yet at the same time utopia as a representation is without, fantastically outside this society, this history, this ideology. This point is important and may be illustrated by a brief analysis of Marx's fourth thesis on Feuerbach (Marx and Engels, 1959:244). Feuerbach analyzes the duplication of the world into a religious projection that is both imaginary and real. His critique makes obvious the dissolution of the religious world into its secular basis. The image men take for a real world is only an image, but they are unaware of the fact it is a duplicated image of the real world in a mirror. They take it for an actual, transcendent world. But Feuerbach's critique remains insufficient. The truly critical question is: How is it possible that such an image could have been created? To answer such a question, it is necessary to point out the way in which the self-contradiction of the secular basis itself parallels the cleavage between the base and its religious duplication. Feuerbach's analysis is a reductive critique, not a really critical critique. He merely inverts the ideological representation. To understand the critical process, we have to discern its two phases. First, Marx calls into question the duplicative process itself and not only one of its poles, the religious duplicate. Second, Marx argues that the duplicative process is an effect of a duplication within the real world itself. The religious imaginary world is the manifest product of a concealed process in the secular real world. To take the example used by Marx himself, the duplication of the earthly family into an imaginary holy family has to be understood as a self-contradiction of the secular family. This is a critical theory of the human family. And the removal of the contradiction of the human family is a practical strategy about the human family. This is a revolutionary process. Thus the theory of the heavenly utopia leads to a practice that is in fact a practical theory, in as much as the theory was already a theoretical practice.

These comments concern our first thesis that utopia is an ideological critique of ideology. In what follows we will treat our second thesis, that our theorizing of utopia can lead us to a critical theory of practice. Utopia is a representation, a poetical device through which the reverse side of the social actuality expressed by political discourse is imaginatively portrayed. Reality is the missing term of utopian representation; however the representation refers to this term, not as a present reality, but as a missing referent. The very word "U-topia" expresses this difficult notion. Utopia is not an imaginary and unreal place; it is no-where: This means a place without determinations other than negative ones. Utopia is structured by a "neither . . . nor" pattern. It refers to a reality that is not displayed in the picture, a reality that may be the implicit or ultimate term of comparison, but that is not a referent, even an allegorical one.

What then is utopian practice? We conceive it as a power of production that is at once shown and concealed by the product it builds up. This concealment explains why, from the perspective of the dominant ideology, utopias are viewed only as representations, as dreamlike paradigms or imaginary dreams, to be judged by the positivist criteria of being real or unreal; instead, however, as we have tried to show, the social and political self-contradictions are not so much hidden in utopias as they are in political discourse and in the dominant ideologies implicit in it. In contrast, utopian practice builds up the utopian representation in the middle of the contradictions, but it does not span the contradictory poles as does reformist political discourse. The utopian practice creates a picture that conceals and reveals the self-cleavage of social reality. But the utopian practice does not negate this self-contradictory reality by transforming it practically: It only indicates reality as self-contradictory through poetic devices that draw the image of its negation.

To take the example we already have used, moral or utopian Marxist analysis gives way to Marxist theoretical discourse. That is to say, Marx shows us how to theorize his own critique of bourgeois ideology by calling in question the very possibility of an existing religious ideology. This is a transcendental question in a Kantian sense, but Marx applies it to social entities. Thus he finds a theoretical basis for a practical transformation of social reality that will overcome its self-contradictions. In comparison to the critical Marxist analysis, utopian practice operates morally and poetically; it works out the transcendental questioning as a process of fiction (neutralizing the opposite poles of the real self-contradiction and totalizing them by displacing and transvaluating them). It does not overturn the social reality but exhibits the negative image of this reality in an harmonic totality.

We are attempting here, by a critical theory of utopian discourse, to develop the concept of utopian practice. Perhaps this may be achieved basically by integrating into a consistent structure the inconsistencies we find in the utopian text. In other words, by critically reading the utopian text and structuring its dissonances into a coherent pattern, utopian practice joins together the various kinds of differences we find in the utopian representation. As such, moreover, the concept of utopian practice suggests the possibility of a theoretical-practical concept made up to know and to transform social reality – to know social reality by transforming it, to transform it through knowledge. Utopias are the figurative anticipations of a praxis, but they neither achieve nor complete the theoretical-practical process. In utopias, practice is fiction and theory is no more than representation. We must, so to speak, turn the utopian scheme upside down and displace it from right to left to obtain the dialectical relationship

between a theory of social system and a strategy of political action. This
can be summarized as follows:

Fictional Utopia	Utopian fiction as neutralization	Utopian representation as fantastic totality
Unalienated praxis	Theory (system)	Practice (strategy)

This means two transformations: first, to put fiction in the place of
representation and vice versa and, second, to change representation into
theoretical questioning and fiction into revolutionary practice. These two
operations transform utopia into a strategic system that is revolution. By
system, I mean the reframing of social and political reality in a practical
theory that makes intelligible the pattern of its inner relationships. The
given reality is structured into an intelligible object by methods and processes that are constituent parts of this object. By strategy, I mean the
operations aiming at the transformation of reality, a revolutionary project that finds its purposes, its intelligibility, its rationality in the system,
but conversely, that gives the system its operative field, its proofs, its
truth as well as its practical verification.

Utopia does not rebuild reality in its concept through its critical questioning. It represents the negative image of this reality through a poetical
fiction (or a fictive neutralization). Utopia is a blind representation because the utopian practice that makes it a picture has no access to a critical
awareness of its own productive operations. But utopia does indicate –
through a fictive and uncriticized manner – the theoretical instruments
that would make it possible to know these antagonisms, that is, the theoretical concepts corresponding superstructurally to a definite phase of the
social and historical processes. In other words, utopian discourse is ideological, but it also has the value of anticipating theory. This value, however, can be realized only when the theory is itself worked out, when new
historical conditions occur, and when their actual possibilities are joined
together, that is, when critical theory becomes a bridge between the possible and the real. Taken in a restricted sense, utopian discourse has had
this critical value from the end of the sixteenth century to the middle of
the nineteenth. Today, however, utopian fiction is to be found in social
theory; and only by becoming critically self-aware of this can we make such
theory become a mode of praxiological consciousness. The representations

that utopian fiction generates are no longer blessed islands and fantastic other worlds. These fantasies must be uncovered in the social sciences themselves, not to dismiss social theory as an unreliable discourse for social and political analysis and guidance but, on the contrary, to give way, when criticized from within, to a theoretical practice and a practical theory. Critical consciousness of sociological utopias is not an act of dismissal but of self-transformation. It is a means by which the social sciences can move from scientism and social engineering to a dialectical use of reason, both in, and between, the social sciences and political action.

REFERENCES

More, Thomas, *Utopia,* ed. E. Surtz (New Haven and London: Yale University Press, 1964).
Marin, Louis, *Utopiques, jeux d'espaces* (Paris: Minuit, 1973).
Marx, Karl and Frederick Engels, *Basic Writings on Politics and Philosophy,* ed. Lewis S. Feuer (New York: Doubleday, Anchor Books, 1959).

NOTES

1 For the analysis of More's friends' responses to his book on a particular point – the question of private property – see Jack H. Hexter, *More's Utopia: The Biography of an Idea* (Princeton, N.J.: Princeton University Press, 1952), p. 43–8.

2 In the present essay, I could not discuss fully the question of community of property in More's *Utopia* as I did in my book on the subject. Basically, I agree with the way in which Hexter poses the problem in his book when he criticizes both the Marxian interpretation by Karl Kautsky and the Christian ones by Campbell and Ames. I precisely agree with him when he shows that the key solution lies upon the analysis of the structure of *Utopia* (p. 34). However, granted these very grounds of the textual study, we differ about the interpretation to give on political, ideological, and philosophical levels to its results, since Hexter seems to me to dissolve the specifity of Utopian representation in the historical and ideological picture of More's ideas of the good society.

3 To be more precise, it is not the whole Book 1 that has been written after the Book 2, but only the major part of it and particularly the Dialog of Counsel. This point has been clearly demonstrated by Hexter in his book I already cited. (See Part 1: The Anatomy of a Printed Book, p. 11–30). If the historical and stylistic evidences given by Hexter reinforce in a way my own analysis of the relationships between utopian (Book 2) and political discourse (roughly Book 1), they are insufficient as such to account for the textual effects of More's book as

a whole on the reader. A semiotic and semantic analysis may give new insights on the specificity of such utopian discourse.

4 As far as I understand the profound and exhaustive study of the Dialog of Counsel made by Hexter, his analysis does not take into account the relationships between what I called the micro-utopias and the various stages of the political and philosophical discourse in which these "utopias" are embedded. As I attempted to demonstrate in my own book, a careful study of the text shows that the utopias of Polylerites, Acharians and Macarians are not mere illustrations of Raphael's political and philosophical arguments. They displace these arguments and project them on another level. These two processes – a displacement or roughly metonymic process and a projection or a metaphorical one – have to be analyzed as such in order to understand how utopian representations are functioning in relation to political discourse.

CONTRIBUTORS TO THE BOOK

RICHARD HARVEY BROWN, formerly a senior social policy consultant, has lectured at such universities as the New School for Social Research and the University of California. Currently he is Associate Professor in Sociology at the University of Maryland. Dr. Brown is the author of *A Poetic for Sociology: Toward a Logic of Discovery for the Human Sciences.*

STANFORD M. LYMAN is Professor and Chairman of Sociology in the Graduate Faculty, New School for Social Research. He is the author of *The Asian in the West, Chinese Americans,* and *The Black American in Sociological Thought*; with Marvin B. Scott he has written *The Revolt of the Students, A Sociology of the Absurd,* and *The Drama of Social Reality.*

PAUL G. CREELAN is Assistant Professor at Rutgers University and also has taught at the New School for Social Research. His primary research interest is the semiotics of sociological theory.

ROBERT DARNTON, formerly a journalist with *The New York Times,* is Professor of History at Princeton University. Dr. Darnton's publications include numerous essays in historical and literary journals, as well as *Mesmerism and the End of the Enlightenment in France.*

ROM HARRÉ is Fellow in Philosophy at Linacre College, Oxford, and the University Lecturer in Philosophy of Science. Harré's recent books include *The Philosophies of Science, The Principles of Scientific Thinking, The Explanation of Social Behavior* (with P. F. Secord), and *Causal Powers* (with E. H. Madden).

L O U I S   M A R I N is Professor of Romance Languages at Johns Hopkins University. He also has taught at the University of California, San Diego, and the University of Paris. Dr. Marin has written on the relations between art, critical theory, and social action, and is the author of *The Semiotics of Utopia*.

M A N F R E D   S T A N L E Y, Professor of Sociology at Syracuse University, edited *Social Development: Critical Perspectives* and is the author of *The Technological Conscience*.

T R A C Y   B .   S T R O N G, currently Associate Professor of Political Science at Amherst College, is the author of *Friedrich Nietzsche and the Politics of Transfiguration,* as well as articles on politics, art, and social theory.